The Cambridge Companion to the
Spanish Inquisition

Founded in 1478 and not permanently abolished until 1834, the Spanish Inquisition has always been a notorious institution in history as an engine of religious and racial persecution. Yet Spaniards themselves did not create its legal processes or its theoretical mission, which was to reconcile heretics to the Catholic Church. In this volume, leading international scholars assess the origins, legal practices, victims, reach, and failures of Spanish inquisitors across centuries and geographies. Grounded in recent scholarship and archival research, the chapters explore the Inquisition's medieval precedents as well as its turbulent foundation and eradication. The volume examines how inquisitors changed their targets over time, and how literal physical settings could affect their investigations and prosecutions. Contributors also demonstrate how deeply Spanish inquisitors cared about social status and legal privilege, and explore the scandals that could envelop inquisitors and their employees. In doing so, this volume offers a nuanced, contextual understanding of the Spanish Inquisition as a historical phenomenon.

LU ANN HOMZA is a Professor of History at William & Mary. Her research focuses on the religious, legal, and cultural history of Europe, especially Spain and Italy, between 1300 and 1650. Previous publications include *The Child Witches of Olague* (2024), *Village Infernos and Witches' Advocates: Witch Hunting in Navarre, 1608-1614* (2022) and *The Spanish Inquisition, 1478–1614: An Anthology of Sources* (2006), the first collection of translated sources from the Spanish Inquisition.

Cambridge Companions to History

Cambridge Companions to History provide accessible and thought-provoking introductions to key topics, eras, places and figures, invaluable to both the student and scholar. Edited by leading academics, each volume contains specially-commissioned essays by a team of expert contributors from around the world, presenting cutting-edge research and suggesting new paths of inquiry for the reader. Companions are designed not only to offer a comprehensive overview of their chosen topic, but also to provoke debate and discussion. Like the highly successful Cambridge Companions to Literature and Cambridge Companions to Philosophy series, these volumes are ideal for use by students, and will be of interest also to the curious general reader.

A full list of recent titles in the series can be found at the following address: www.cambridge.org/history-companions.

The Cambridge Companion to the
Spanish Inquisition

Edited by
LU ANN HOMZA
William & Mary

Shaftesbury Road, Cambridge CB2 8EA, United Kingdom

One Liberty Plaza, 20th Floor, New York, NY 10006, USA

477 Williamstown Road, Port Melbourne, VIC 3207, Australia

314–321, 3rd Floor, Plot 3, Splendor Forum, Jasola District Centre, New Delhi – 110025, India

103 Penang Road, #05–06/07, Visioncrest Commercial, Singapore 238467

Cambridge University Press is part of Cambridge University Press & Assessment, a department of the University of Cambridge.

We share the University's mission to contribute to society through the pursuit of education, learning and research at the highest international levels of excellence.

www.cambridge.org
Information on this title: www.cambridge.org/9781009456791

DOI: 10.1017/9781009456807

© Cambridge University Press & Assessment 2026

This publication is in copyright. Subject to statutory exception and to the provisions of relevant collective licensing agreements, no reproduction of any part may take place without the written permission of Cambridge University Press & Assessment.

When citing this work, please include a reference to the DOI 10.1017/9781009456807

First published 2026

Cover image: 1804–24. "For having moved his tongue differently." *Por mober la lengua de otro modo*. Sepia gouache. Author: Francisco de Goya. Location: Museo Del Prado-Dibujos, Madrid, Spain. Source: Album/Alamy Stock Photo

A catalogue record for this publication is available from the British Library

A Cataloging-in-Publication data record for this book is available from the Library of Congress

ISBN 978-1-009-45679-1 Hardback
ISBN 978-1-009-45682-1 Paperback

Cambridge University Press & Assessment has no responsibility for the persistence or accuracy of URLs for external or third-party internet websites referred to in this publication and does not guarantee that any content on such websites is, or will remain, accurate or appropriate.

For EU product safety concerns, contact us at Calle de José Abascal, 56, 1°, 28003 Madrid, Spain, or email eugpsr@cambridge.org

Contents

List of Figures page vii
List of Contributors viii

Introduction: Beginnings, Endings, Myths 1
LU ANN HOMZA

Part I The Institution

1 Procedures and Goals 23
LU ANN HOMZA

2 Inquisitorial Careers 45
KIMBERLY LYNN

3 Pursuing Life Stories: Inquisitors and Suspects 72
JOSÉ LUIS LORIENTE TORRES

4 Scandals 95
LU ANN HOMZA AND AMANDA L. SCOTT

Part II Targets

5 Conversos 117
GRETCHEN D. STARR-LEBEAU

6　Moriscos　142
STEPHANIE M. CAVANAUGH

7　*Alumbrados*　164
JESSICA J. FOWLER

8　Protestants　185
DORIS MORENO-MARTÍNEZ

9　Old Christians　209
CRISTIAN BERCO

10　Texts　231
PATRICIA W. MANNING

Part III　Geographical Reach

11　Sicily　257
MARINA TORRES ARCE

12　Mexico　278
MARÍA JESÚS ZAMORA CALVO

13　Peru　301
ANA E. SCHAPOSCHNIK

14　Cartagena de Indias　321
ANA MARÍA DÍAZ BURGOS

Index　345

Figures

3.1   Bernard Picart. "The Inquisition Room."   *page*   76
5.1   Tunisian al-buraq.   122
11.1   Calendar of the court of Sicily between 1623 and 1698.   261
14.1   Plan of Cartagena de las Indias.   323

Contributors

CRISTIAN BERCO is Professor in the Department of History at Bishop's University. His most recent book, *From Body to Community: Venereal Disease and Society in Baroque Spain* (Toronto, 2016), has won multiple prizes. His most recent articles and book chapters include "Fashioning Disease: Narrative and the Sick Body in the Spanish Inquisition" in *A Companion to the Spanish Renaissance* (2019), "Determining Insanity in the Inquisition: Sensory Perception and Legal Culture in Seventeenth-Century Lima" in *eHumanista: Journal of Iberian Studies* (2017), and "Perception and the Mulatto Body in Inquisitorial Spain: A Neurohistory" in *Past & Present* (2016).

STEPHANIE M. CAVANAUGH is Associate Professor of History at the University of New Brunswick. Her recent book chapters include "In Defense of Community: Morisca Women in Sixteenth-Century Valladolid" in *Women and Community in Medieval and Early Modern Iberia* (2020) and "Serán Siempre Moros? Assessing Conversion During the Expulsion of the Moriscos" in *The Conversos and Moriscos in Late Medieval Spain and Beyond. Vol. 4: Resistance and Reform* (2020).

ANA MARÍA DÍAZ BURGOS is the Eric and Jane Nord Associate Professor of Hispanic Studies at Oberlin College. Her book *Tráfico de saberes: Agencia feminina, hechicería e inquisición en Cartagena de Indias, 1610–1614* appeared in 2020. Her recent book chapters and articles include "Inquisitorial Mission or Colonial Protocol: Rethinking the Spanish Black Legend in the Long Eighteenth-Century

Cartagena de Indias" in *The Black Legend of Spain and Its Empire in the Eighteenth Century: Constructing National Identities* (2024), "Transgresión y envejecimiento: El caso de Doña María Ortiz Nieto (1683–1702)" in *Edad de Oro* (2023), and "Marital Pains, Heterodox Cures: Alternative Economies of Sorcery and Witchcraft in the Inquisition of Cartagena de Indias" in *Women, Witchcraft, and the Inquisition in Spain and the New World* (2021).

JESSICA J. FOWLER is Associate Professor of Latin America and the Atlantic World at University of Montana Western. Her recent book chapters and articles include "Definition and Exclusion: Containing Alumbradismo" in *Inquisición y lenguaje, siglos XVI–XIX* (2024), "Process and Punishment: Alleged Alumbrados before the Mexican Holy Office, 1593–1603" in *Colonial Latin American Review* (2020) and "Questioning the 1623 Edict of Grace: Differentiating Between Orthodox and Heterodox Interiority" in *Culture & History: A Digital Journal* (2017).

LU ANN HOMZA is Professor of History at William & Mary. Her most recent books include *The Child Witches of Olague* (2024) and *Village Infernos and Witches' Advocates: Witch-Hunting in Navarre, 1608–1614* (2022). In 2006, she published the first English-language collection of documents from the Spanish Inquisition.

JOSÉ LUIS LORIENTE TORRES is an independent scholar working in Spain. His first book, *Los discursos de la vida: autobiografía e Inquisición en la Edad Moderna*, was published in 2025. His most recent articles include "Las autobiografías como fuentes para el estudio del artesanado en época moderna: El caso de Juan Borgoñon" in *Historia social* (2024), "Voices in the Courtroom: the Role of Notaries in the 'Inquisitorial Autobiography'" in *Culture & History: A Digital Journal* (2024), and "The Discursos de la Vida in Inquisitorial Documentation: Autobiography Between Orality and Memory" in *Journal of Early Modern Studies* (2024).

KIMBERLY LYNN is Dean of the Honors College, Professor of Humanities in the Department of Global Humanities and Religions, and Affiliate Professor of History at Western Washington University. With Erin K. Rowe, she edited *The Early Modern Hispanic World: Transnational and Interdisciplinary Approaches* (2017). Lynn published *Between Court and Confessional: The Politics of Spanish Inquisitors* in 2013.

PATRICIA W. MANNING is Professor in the Department of Spanish and Portuguese at the University of Kansas. Her books include *An Overview of the Pre-Suppression Society of Jesus in Spain* (2021) and *Voicing Dissent in Seventeenth-Century Spain: Inquisition, Social Criticism, and Theology in the Case of El Criticón* (2009).

DORIS MORENO-MARTÍNEZ is Professor of Modern History at the Universidad Autónoma in Barcelona. Her most recent book and articles are *Casiodoro de Reina: Libertad y tolerancia en la Europa del siglo XVI* (2017) and "Los autos de fe de Valladolid de 1559, un espectáculo emocional y politico," in *Investigaciones históricas: Épocas moderna y contemporánea* (2024), "Creure i viure a la Barcelona moderna a través de les fonts inquisitorials," in *Pedralbes* (2019), and "Aproximación al nicodemismo del protestantismo español del siglo XVI: Lenguaje y prácticas sociales" in *Studia historica/Historia moderna* (2018).

ANA E. SCHAPOSCHNIK is Associate Professor of History at DePaul University. Her book *The Lima Inquisition: The Plight of Crypto-Jews in Seventeenth-Century Peru* appeared in 2015. Her most recent article is "The Dungeons of the Lima Inquisition: Corruption, Survival, and Secret Codes in Colonial Peru" in *Colonial Latin American Review* (2020).

AMANDA L. SCOTT is Associate Professor of History and Women's, Gender, and Sexuality Studies at Pennsylvania State University. Her book *The Basque Seroras: Local Religion, Gender, and Power in Northern Iberia* appeared in 2020. Her most recent articles are "Death in the Indies: Basque Immigration and Memory in the Sixteenth and Seventeenth Centuries" in *Bulletin of Spanish and Portuguese Historical Studies* (2023), "Hot on the Trail: Pilgrimage and Crime in

Early Modern Spain" in *The Journal of Social History* (2023), "Sisters and Seroras: Basque Women and the Early Jesuits" in *The Journal of Jesuit Studies* (2022), and "Bullfighting, the Basque Clergy, and Tridentine Reform" in *Renaissance Quarterly* (2020).

GRETCHEN D. STARR-LEBEAU is the Jeanne and George Todd Professor of Religious Studies at Principia College. Her most recent books are *Seven Myths of the Spanish Inquisition* (2023) and, with Charles H. Parker, *Judging Faith, Punishing Sin: Inquisitions and Consistories in the Early Modern World* (2017).

MARINA TORRES ARCE is Professor in the Modern and Contemporaneous History Department at the Universidad de Cantabria. Her most recent book chapters and articles include "Political Conflict and Pacification in the War of the Spanish Succession: the Palermo Revolt of 1708," in *Pacification and Reconciliation in the Spanish Habsburg Worlds* (2025); "Cities and Urban Life in Early Modern Spain," in *The Routledge Handbook of Spanish History* (2024); "El tribunal de la Inquisición de Navarra: la unidad religiosa en una zona de frontera," in *Historia imperial del Santo Oficio (siglos XV–XIX)* (2022), and "De comisarios, confesores y vecinos: la proyección de la Inquisición al finales del Antiguo Régimen" in *Principe de Viana* (2021).

MARÍA JESÚS ZAMORA CALVO is Professor of Spanish Philology at the Universidad Autónoma de Madrid. Her book *Women, Witchcraft, and the Inquisition in Spain and the New World* appeared in 2021.

LU ANN HOMZA

Introduction: Beginnings, Endings, Myths

The creation of the Spanish Inquisition belies easy explanations. Monarchs Ferdinand II of Aragon and Isabella I of Castile inherited a highly complex social, political, and religious environment when they married in 1472 and thereby joined their two kingdoms, though their "unification" of Spain was far from total. Castile preserved its own legal code, while each of Aragon's three territories – Aragon proper, along with Valencia and Catalonia – had its own legal systems and privileges vis-à-vis the Aragonese monarchy. Grasping why Ferdinand and Isabella decided to ask Pope Sixtus IV in 1478 for permission to establish an inquisition that eventually would encompass nearly all their territories requires a quick survey of nearly 100 years of earlier history.

Modern scholars agree that one of the most important precipitating factors behind the Spanish Inquisition was the tremendous religious violence of 1391. Up to that date, Spain had Europe's largest population of Jews. But in June of that year, a local ecclesiastic in Seville incited fellow Catholic Christians to attack the city's Jewish quarter, whose residents were forced to choose between Christian baptism or death. News of the assault spread; similarly violent riots traveled along the Mediterranean coast, reaching Valencia, Barcelona, and the island of Mallorca, as well as Castile, touching Cuenca, Madrid, Toledo, Soria, and Logroño.[1] The respective monarchs of Aragon and Castile tried to protect their Jewish subjects without success.[2] The aggressors in the attacks appear to have come from all socioeconomic levels. The violence did not ebb until the autumn of 1391.

We know very little about how the Jewish communities in Spain reacted to the attacks, but the outcome was clear. Surviving Jewish enclaves were in ruins, and Spain now had a population of involuntary converts to Christianity. The fact that baptisms had been carried out by force did not nullify them, since the Christian sacraments were effective simply by being performed. The scale of the conversions was unprecedented; there were no measures in place to facilitate the converts' integration into the new religion. Families throughout Aragon and Castile found themselves "mixed," with some members continuing to be Jewish, and others newly identified as Christian.[3] Moreover, the waves of conversion in 1391 seemed to augur an impending apocalypse, and renowned preachers such as Vincent Ferrer took advantage of the moment to intensify their missionary efforts.

Historians of Spanish Judaism agree that after 1391, any remaining Jews were subjected to some twenty years of additional pressure to convert. One pivotal moment occurred in January 1412, when the Castilian crown issued the Laws of Valladolid: Those mandates called for the complete segregation of Jews and Muslims from Christians in towns throughout the kingdom and allowed only eight days for the relocations to occur. The same Laws also severed all economic contacts between Christians and infidels, and prohibited emigration. The ultimate goal of these powerful mandates was to force conversion to Christianity.[4] The king of Aragon, Ferdinand I, who was also co-regent in Castile, blocked the implementation of the Laws of Valladolid three weeks after they were issued. He also prohibited officially the application of those Laws in Aragon in July 1412.[5]

Meanwhile, a disputation, with papal approval, was arranged for the city of Tortosa in Aragon, beginning in 1413 and extending through 1414. The disputants were Christian theologians – some of whom had converted from Judaism – as well as rabbis. The discussion was hardly open-ended: Its point was to prove that the truths of Christianity were apparent in the Talmud. Jews were forced to attend. The pressure to convert was extraordinary; many families did so en masse.[6] A year later, in 1415, Pope Benedict XIII, who was residing in Aragon during the papal schism, issued a papal bull that endorsed a weakened version of the Laws of Valladolid. That bull also spurred conversions.

Thus the 25-year period between 1391 and 1415 produced an entirely new stratum of people within Castile and Aragon: individuals who had converted from Judaism to Christianity, and who became known as conversos. With conversion, professional opportunities opened up significantly; furthermore, there was no ban on noble status for the converts. Conversos became bishops, tutors to the royal family, and highly-placed administrators.[7] As they rose, they inspired resentment from both their former co-religionists and especially so-called "Old" Christians who had no historical connection to Judaism.[8] Concerns with genealogy surged.[9] In June 1449, rebels in Toledo promulgated a controversial ordinance that was approved by the city council: It prohibited any "converso of Jewish descent" from holding a political office or ecclesiastical benefice in the city or its surrounding territory.[10] Known as the "Sentencia-Estatuto," the Toledo order also prohibited the legal testimony of conversos against old Christians. Despite an adamant papal bull and a chorus of theological writings that rejected such distinctions among Christians, kings of Castile endorsed the racialist principle of the Sentencia-Estatuto in 1451 and 1468. Social tensions did not abate; there was more conflict between conversos and old Christians in Toledo in 1467, Sepúlveda in 1468, and Seville and Jaén in 1473.[11]

Old Christians justified their hatred of conversos by claiming the converts were secret Jews who continued to practice Mosaic Law, even if the conversos in question were great-grandchildren of individuals who had been forced into Christianity in 1391. The alleged link between conversos and Judaism was dangerous because baptized Christians – including those baptized involuntarily – risked being labeled heretics if they followed the beliefs or rituals of a non-Christian religion. Heresy was deliberate, persistent, and public religious error against the Catholic faith. What conversos were accused of doing was called "judaizing": if they practiced circumcision, adhered to Jewish dietary laws, or appeared to be observing Saturday as a holy day by not working or cooking, they were liable to accusations of heresy. Modern scholars have spent decades debating whether the converso population of Spain was "truly" Jewish or Christian: If the former, then the eventual persecution of them appears justifiable from a standpoint of Christian orthodoxy; if the latter, then the Spanish Inquisition becomes a racial rather than religious project. The best studies today allow for a broad range of cultural preferences and religious convictions among Spain's converso population and insist that it cannot be interpreted in terms of uniformity to a single religious outlook.

How, then, did the Spanish Inquisition come into being? Even while distracted by a war of succession to the Castilian throne, in the 1470s Isabella and Ferdinand had to have been aware of the social and religious tensions between conversos and Old Christians.[12] The two rulers called a council in the winter of 1477 for Castile's leading ecclesiastics: Their intent was to improve the education and performance of the clergy; their group met in Seville. The council passed measures on Latin learning (now required); a basic level of literacy, as well as legal and theological training (now required); a minimum number of yearly Masses at the parish level; a prohibition on carrying arms or having concubines; and an obligation of clerical residence for parish priests.[13]

Yet as Isabella and Ferdinand oversaw their council, they heard multiple anecdotes from a Dominican friar, Alonso de Hojeda, about the judaizing that allegedly was rampant among Seville's conversos. The monarchs took Hojeda's comments seriously; they consequently wrote to Pope Sixtus IV, requesting a bull that would allow them to name two or three bishops or priests to act as inquisitors in their kingdoms. Sixtus IV replied with the bull on November 1, 1478: The document gave Ferdinand and Isabella permission to name two or three inquisitors over the age of forty who had theological or law degrees. Remarkably, the monarchs' right to name inquisitors was granted in perpetuity, and no other mandate was allowed to block the papal bull. Sixtus soon realized his error in giving the king and queen too much autonomy; he tried, but failed, to reverse his trajectory and place inquisitors under episcopal control.[14]

The Spanish monarchs did not act instantly upon receiving Sixtus's document; instead, Seville's archbishop, Cardinal Pedro González de Mendoza, launched a campaign to instruct the city's conversos in Christianity, on the grounds that religious instruction had been lacking.[15] In the end, in September 1480, in the northern Castilian city of Medina del Campo, Isabella and Ferdinand named two Dominican friars as inquisitors. Those inquisitors arrived in Seville in November 1480; they carried out their first public sentencing of judaizing heretics, in which six individuals were burned at the stake, in 1481. Unfortunately, all the trial evidence for the earliest inquisition trials in Seville has disappeared.

It is an open question as to whether the Spanish monarchs envisioned their new Inquisition as simply a temporary strategy or a permanent institution, but there is no doubt that the converso population was its original target. The fact that conversos in Seville fled when the first inquisitors arrived justified expanding the Inquisition's reach, not least because bishops in Castile, who had traditionally monitored the presence of heresy, were bound geographically to their dioceses. Although the first Spanish inquisitors were supposed to travel, it quickly became apparent that they would be more effective if they were based in tribunals in particular cities. The location of the tribunals sometimes changed over the first several decades of the Inquisition's existence; they also could be merged. Ultimately, the Kingdom of Castile ended up with twelve permanent tribunals, while the Kingdom of Aragon had three on the mainland, with an additional three for the islands of Mallorca, Sicily, and Sardinia, and then eventually yet three more for the American outposts of Mexico City, Lima, and Cartagena de Indias.

Simply counting the number of tribunals might lead us to think that the establishment of the Spanish Inquisition was seamless, but it certainly was not. Castile had no history of medieval papal inquisitors, which meant there was no historical precedent to block Isabella's innovation, but Castilian cities could still resist. The inquisition tribunal in Valladolid, for example, was approved in 1485 but not begin work until 1488 because the city's royal court of appeals suspected inquisitors would interfere with its cases and jurisdiction. It took a royal visit from the monarchs before Valladolid would allow inquisitors to enter.[16]

The Kingdom of Aragon presented far more difficulties. There, medieval papal inquisitors had existed, but historical precedent dictated that they could only be named by popes or masters-general of the Dominican order, not by Aragonese kings. Furthermore, the *fueros* or privileges of Aragon, Valencia, and Catalonia prohibited non-Aragonese officials from serving in their territories. When Pope Sixtus IV named Castilian Tomás de Torquemada as inquisitor-general in October 1483, with Isabella and Ferdinand's explicit support, the appointment violated

Aragon's constitutional norms. Torquemada and his royal patrons did not back down. In April 1484, Torquemada held a meeting in the Aragonese town of Tarazona, where the Aragonese parliament or Cortes was in session: There, he announced the impending appointment of inquisitors to various places within Aragon itself. In May 1484, Torquemada followed up by naming two Dominican friars as inquisitors for Aragon's capital, Zaragoza. One of those inquisitors, Pedro Arbués de Epila, was subsequently murdered in the Zaragoza cathedral on September 15, 1485, in a plot concocted by some of the city's conversos.[17] The legal and political response to the Arbués assassination was ferocious, but that did not stop residents in Barcelona and Valencia from resisting, either.

The most famous example of defiance toward the Spanish Inquisition occurred in the town of Teruel, in southern Aragon. In April 1484, Inquisitor-General Torquemada named a Basque Dominican, Fray Juan de Çolivera, as Teruel's inquisitor; on May 24, Çolivera entered the city. While Teruel's citizens were quick to admit the right of an inquisition to exist, they asserted that they already possessed the legal mechanisms to monitor heresy. The city's lawyers and notaries also immediately cited legal barriers to Çolivera's presence. He was only twenty-four and thus too young to act as an inquisitor, since the position had a minimum age of forty. He was uneducated. There were grave doubts about the authenticity of his powers, because he did not present original documents with the required seals. Finally, he was not from Aragon.

By June 14, Çolivera had left Teruel for the nearby town of Cella: There, he attempted to start heresy investigations into Teruel's converso community, opened a case against Teruel's counselors for sedition, and placed an ecclesiastical interdict on Teruel itself.[18] In August 1484, Teruel's citizens appealed to Pope Sixtus IV, not knowing he had just died. Sixtus IV's successor, Pope Innocent VIII, tried to allow Spaniards to appeal to Rome for relief against the Spanish Inquisition, but in 1484 Ferdinand decreed the death penalty and confiscation of goods for anyone making such an appeal without royal permission and then repeated this prohibition in 1509.[19] In February 1485, Ferdinand issued a call to arms against Teruel's rebels. In March 1485, inquisitors formally entered the town with the help of an army. In 1485–7, Inquisitor

Çolivera and his inquisitor-colleague, Martín Navarro, held thirteen public sentencings, called *autos de fe*, in Teruel. Out of some eighty defendants, 82 percent received the death penalty. At this moment in time, Teruel had between 1,550 and 1,750 inhabitants.[20] As had been the case in Seville in 1480–1, many converso residents of Teruel ran away.

If the Spanish Inquisition's overwhelming target in its first years of existence was judaizing conversos, its apparent failure to stamp out that heresy had horrific effects upon Spain's remaining Jews. The reasoning of both Spanish inquisitors and Spanish monarchs was that close living quarters and friendly relationships between conversos and Jews corrupted the former into Jewish rituals and beliefs. The solution ultimately was expulsion of Spain's Jewish population.[21] The first ejections of Jews were either mandated by royal decrees, or carried out by popular demand, with royal approval thereafter. At the end of 1482, Jews were forced to leave Jerez de la Frontera; they were expelled from the rest of Andalucia in 1483. Jews were forced out of Zaragoza, Albarracín, and Teruel in 1486; when Granada was officially conquered in January 1492, the small community of Jews there was given one month to leave the city.[22]

By the end of 1491, it appears that Ferdinand and Isabella were convinced that unbaptized Jews must convert to Christianity or leave.[23] They issued the Alhambra Decree on March 31, 1492, which mandated that Jews in Castile and Aragon had to convert to Christianity by July 31 of that year or depart. Important rabbis who held government positions begged Ferdinand to change his mind: He did not, though he ultimately gave Spain's expelled Jews until 1499 to convert and return. The Expulsion created a new generation of conversos; the Jews who left Spain – in total, perhaps 150,000 to 165,000 – went primarily to Portugal, where they would again be forced to convert or leave in 1497.[24]

It can be exceedingly difficult for modern readers to grasp what the Spanish monarchs thought they were gaining with a state-administered inquisition and the eventual ejection of a not insignificant proportion of their population. There is no evidence that these events were due to political or financial strategies on the part of Ferdinand and Isabella. Ferdinand did not benefit politically from agreeing that the first inquisitors should go to Seville; he was not king in Andalucia. He and Isabella had plenty of problems with the relatively independent Castilian aristocracy, but they pacified rebellious impulses with patents of nobility and gifts of land. There is no proof that they sought to stir up hatred toward a converso elite to give the nobility a new enemy and deflect attention from themselves. There are no signs that Ferdinand wanted Jewish assets.[25] Instead, these monarchs inherited a long tradition of religious values that prioritized Christian orthodoxy, dismissed tolerance, and expected secular rulers to care about and take steps to ensure the salvation of their subjects. Unlike earlier monarchs in Spain, Ferdinand and Isabella were in a sufficiently secure political position to put religious measures into effect.

Whether or not the monarchs imagined the Spanish Inquisition from the start as part of their institutional church and state, what they created lasted a very long time, from 1478 to 1834. How then did the Inquisition end, and what myths did it accrue?

There is hardly any controversy among scholars as to how the Spanish Inquisition finally disappeared, though it was a dialectical process that took far more time than its founding. After the war of the Spanish Succession (1701–14), Spain's monarchy became Bourbon rather than Hapsburg. The new king, Philip V, was the grandson of French king Louis XIV; he abolished the fueros of Aragon, Valencia, and Catalonia between 1707 and 1716, after which the kings of Spain ruled their territory for the first time as a coherent political unit. Philip V's heirs had absolutist pretensions. A unified Cortes for both Castile and Aragon met only three times in the eighteenth century, and two of those meetings were to recognize royal heirs. In 1737, the Spanish crown made church properties subject to taxation. In the second half of the eighteenth century, Spain's Bourbon monarchs funneled money into the navy, created a standing army via conscription, and regularized taxes.

Still, one of the largest problems for Spain's Bourbon kings was what to do about the French Revolution and its aftermath. By the opening of that tumultuous event in 1789, Spanish political loyalties had become traditionally French, but the question was whether the country would seek to protect the French king, Louis XVI, or accept the revolutionaries' demands. After Louis XVI was executed for treason on January 21, 1793, and France's revolution swerved into ever more radical territory, Spain declared war, which lasted until 1795. In August 1796, Spain signed an offensive and defensive pact with France. As evidence of its condition as a French satellite state, Spain went to war against Britain in October 1796.

Circumstances for Spain worsened with the crowning of Napoleon Bonaparte as emperor in 1804. In October 1805, a French-Spanish naval coalition was defeated by Admiral Lord Nelson in the Battle of Trafalgar. In 1807, Spanish king Charles IV and his royal favorite, Manuel Godoy, allowed Napoleon's troops to cross Spain in order to invade Portugal. A year later, in January 1808, French imperial troops again entered Spain under the pretext of supporting the army in Portugal; this time, however, they arrived with Napoleon's orders to seize important Spanish fortresses.

These events scandalized contemporary Spaniards, who viewed the French incursions as humiliating invasions. In 1807, the mightily discontented heir to the Spanish throne, Prince Ferdinand, planned a coup against his father, Charles IV: the plot was discovered, and Ferdinand forgiven. On March 17, 1808, however, a popular uprising against the royal favorite, Godoy, occurred in the town of Aranjuez, where the royal family was staying in anticipation of the French military's southward march. A band composed of soldiers as well as ordinary residents and peasants forced Charles IV to dismiss Godoy; on March 19, the king abdicated, and his son became King Ferdinand VII. In April 1808, Napoleon invited Charles and Ferdinand to the French border city of Bayonne, ostensibly to help them sort out the Spanish monarchy. On May 2 and 3, 1808, citizens in Madrid revolted when French troops there appeared to be trying to transport the royal princesses to French territory. On May 10, Napoleon forced Charles IV and Ferdinand VII to resign their Spanish kingdom to his brother, Joseph.

The new French–Spanish king Joseph I entered Madrid on July 20, 1808, but quickly had to retreat because Spaniards loyal to Ferdinand launched the Peninsular War, often known in Spanish history as the War of Independence. This conflict lasted from 1808 to 1814. It featured British assistance for the Spanish insurgents, as well as the first documented instances of European guerrilla warfare. The French ultimately were defeated in 1813 in the northern Spanish city of Vitoria-Gasteiz, which is the capital of the Spanish Basque country in the province of Álava.

At first, war with France looked as if it would destroy the Spanish Inquisition. Napoleon abolished it in July 1808; on December 4, 1808, via the decrees of Chamartín, he formally ended the Old Regime in Spain and absorbed all the possessions of the Spanish Inquisition into the national patrimony. Yet Napoleon's executive actions produced a patriotic backlash. Individuals who conceived of themselves as loyal Spaniards *supported* the Inquisition as a reaction to the French invasion and a way to demonstrate their fidelity to the Catholic religion.[26] Furthermore, Spanish rebels against France and Napoleon *wanted the restoration of the Spanish monarchy.* In no way were Spanish forces questing after a secular, liberal republic. The basic theory behind Spanish resistance was that the sovereign will of the nation had not been consulted about the royal abdications. Ultimately, the notion of national sovereignty justified convening the Spanish Cortes, which met in the Mediterranean port of Cádiz, beginning September 24, 1810.

In May 1811, the Cádiz deputies voted to create a special commission to consider the inquisition question; eleven months later, deputy José Riesco asked the Cortes to clarify whether the Inquisition would be re-established. The special commission was forced into a decision: four of its members wanted the Inquisition to be refounded, with one opposed. Over the rest of 1812, however, opposition to restoring the Inquisition grew, to the point that the question was ultimately moved to the Commission for the Constitution, which had to determine whether the Inquisition conformed to that new charter. When the Commission announced its opinion on November 13, 1812, it made two points: first, Catholicism would be protected by laws in conformity with the Constitution; second, the Inquisition did not conform to the Constitution. The second point was approved by only six to five, with four commission members refusing to vote because the question was too delicate.

From January 4 to January 22, 1813, the Cádiz deputies debated the inquisition question as a full body. They gathered and perused inquisition documentation; they argued historically. Individuals in favor of the Inquisition contended that without it, the monarchy could not take sufficient steps to protect the nation's religion. Individuals against the inquisition's re-establishment insisted that it actually impeded the growth of Catholicism because of the fear it engendered: Heretics did not end up truly converted by the inquisitorial process but were merely frightened into appearing so.[27] Opponents also noted that the constitutional principle of the separation of powers meant that religious legal cases pertained to bishops, with secular courts having the ability to apply temporal penalties according to the law.[28] One recent historian thinks it remarkable that *any* of the deputies at the Cortes of Cádiz dared to critique the Inquisition's existence, since negative attitudes toward it could so easily be interpreted as anti-patriotism.[29]

Significantly, none of the deputies at Cádiz attempted to diminish the importance of Catholicism within the Spanish state; instead, their arguments were linked to a more general debate about the power of the Church. The two groups belonged to competing Catholic cultures.[30] On the one hand, some elevated the values of obedience and faith: They envisioned a Catholicism firmly and absolutely tied to the papacy and Rome; they wanted a national church, and the Spanish Inquisition was an essential mechanism for that outcome. On the other, some preferred to decentralize ecclesiastical power and reinforce the authority of bishops: They might have taken the authority of the papacy for granted, but they were less interested in hierarchy. It's worth noting that figures who would have affected the Cádiz discussions about the Inquisition were missing. Both Pope Pius VII and Ferdinand VII were being held captive by Napoleon; the inquisitor-general, Ramon José de Arce, had integrated himself into the court of Napoleon's brother, Joseph I. Without these "extraordinary circumstances," the debate and vote over the Inquisition "would have been impossible."[31] In the end, in January 1813 the deputies at Cádiz decided that the Spanish Inquisition was incompatible with the 1812 Constitution they had created, but the vote was hardly overwhelming, just ninety to sixty.

The measures passed by the Cádiz Cortes, including the 1812 Constitution, were doomed to fail because the king restored after the Peninsular War – Ferdinand VII – would never accept them. He was released by the French in March 1814; he arrived in Valencia on April 16 of the same year. He was greeted with a document signed by sixty-nine deputies from the Cádiz Cortes that encouraged him to dissolve the Cortes and annul the Constitution. General Francisco Javier Elío, General in Chief of the Army, swore to preserve the monarchy with all its rights and offered military support. On May 4, 1814, Ferdinand VII signed the "Valencian Decree" and revoked the constitutional regime. On May 5, he proceeded toward Madrid: members of the Cortes put up no resistance and on May 10, Ferdinand dissolved that parliamentary body.

Ferdinand VII formally restored the Spanish Inquisition on July 21, 1814: In his announcement, he bemoaned the audacity of Spanish life during his absence and proposed redirecting the Inquisition's activities toward censorship.[32] In April 1815, Francisco Javier Mier y Campillo, bishop of Almería, was named inquisitor-general. He quickly published an edict that spelled out his wish to restore peace to Spanish consciences after the turmoil of war. He offered a period of grace for potential heretics until the end of 1816, during which time everyone would be admitted to reconciliation to the Catholic Church without fear of dishonor, confiscation of goods, or significant penalty.[33]

The restoration of Ferdinand VII lasted six years, and it was not successful. The average tenure for his ministers was a mere six months. His royal finances were a catastrophe. The only economic solution Ferdinand would entertain involved recovering Spain's American empire, whose members had started to set up independent, albeit supportive juntas in 1808, and which began to enjoy free trade with Britain and the United States during the Peninsular War. Spanish American Creoles in particular had a history of bitterness over the Spanish crown's preference for *peninsulares*, that is, Spaniards born in the peninsula, and Latin Americans in general resented their second-class treatment in the Cortes of Cádiz. By the time Ferdinand returned to the throne in 1814, Latin American independence movements were well underway, though he was determined to reassert Spanish authority over them. Yet his reasoning was circular. Although silver from America might solve his bankruptcy, only a solvent state could reconquer America.

In 1815, Ferdinand sent 10,000 troops to the Americas under the command of General Pablo Morillo y Morillo: the invaders successfully recovered the city of Cartegena and overthrew insurrectionary forces in the Viceroyalty of New Granada. Four years later, the balance of war had shifted, and Spain's army in the Americas had shrunk to 2,500 men. Ferdinand could neither pay his small army overseas nor promote the military men at home whom he had inherited from the war against France. When the king's government began to amass an expeditionary army in Andalucia to send across the Atlantic, two junior officers "pronounced" for the Constitution of 1812.

A "pronouncement" (*pronunciamiento*) was an officer revolt.[34] From January to February 1820, this one remained a purely military sedition. But then military forces in other parts of the country refused to act against the rebels – a "negative" pronouncement – and forces in Barcelona, Zaragoza, Pamplona, and La Coruña rose in support. From 1820 to 1823, moderates in Spain attempted to resurrect and revise the Cádiz Constitution, which appeased neither Ferdinand VII nor the progressives who wanted the constitution implemented in its original form. During this three-year period, the Spanish Inquisition ceased to act. When Ferdinand was restored in all his monarchical rights in April 1823, thanks to an invading French army of 100,000, he found himself obligated to European powers that pressured him to liberalize his state.[35] Though he once more annulled the 1812 Constitution, he did not formally re-establish the Spanish Inquisition. The Inquisition was only finally and forever revoked in July 1834 by Ferdinand's widow, Queen Maria Cristina, who was acting as regent for their daughter Isabella after the king's death in September 1833.

The Spanish Inquisition lasted 356 years: Critics and supporters existed from its earliest history to its very end and beyond. In the nineteenth century, American historian William H. Prescott (1796–1859) asserted that the Inquisition condemned Spain to backwardness, while Spanish academic Marcelino Menéndez y Pelayo (1856–1912) credited it with preserving the orthodoxy of Spanish Catholicism.[36] More importantly, however, over time the Spanish Inquisition has played a crucial role in the development of myths about the so-called Spanish "character" as well as Spanish history. In the sixteenth century, Charles V and his heir Philip II fought endless religious wars against followers of Martin Luther and John Calvin. Protestant dissidents in the Holy Roman Empire, the Netherlands, France, England, and Scotland accordingly crafted a portrait of Spaniards that highlighted their greed, deceit, cruelty, and incompetence. They were helped along by native Spaniards such as Bartolomé de las Casas, who had witnessed Spanish atrocities in the Americas and who spoke publicly about what they had seen. Such voices – which were transmitted widely in print and translated into various languages – were consolidated into a "Black Legend" of Spain by the end of the sixteenth century. That "Legend" described Spain as an absolutist, pitiless, unethical state that thrived on surveillance, repression, and viciousness.[37]

The Spanish Inquisition was an integral part of this portrait, and Spanish Protestant refugees also helped spur the notion of early modern

Spain as relentlessly, fiercely oppressive in terms of religion.[38] For example, in 1567 a pseudonymous author – Reginaldus Gonsalvius Montanus – published a Latin treatise entitled *A Discovery and Plaine Declaration of Sundry Subtill Practices of the Holy Inquisition of Spain*. The true author was Antonio del Corro, who had managed to escape from the San Isidoro monastery in Seville in 1557 when that monastery's residents were targeted for Protestant sympathies by inquisitors. Corro eventually landed in the Netherlands; his polemic was translated into English, French, Dutch, and German within a year of its original publication. In it, Corro assumed the worst practices of the Spanish Inquisition were routine; he excoriated the Inquisition's legal processes, dishonest personnel, acceptance of flawed witnesses, and use of torture.[39]

In the latter half of the eighteenth century, when numerous Europeans were contemplating the merits of religious toleration, Portugal as well as Spain were critiqued as fundamentally backward and incapable of intellectual, social, political, and economic progress. The presence of the Spanish Inquisition was purportedly responsible for Spain's allegedly regressive nature. By the time American historian Henry Charles Lea (1825–1909) published his four-volume *A History of the Inquisition in Spain* in 1906–7, he felt confident highlighting Spain's degenerative state and pinning the blame for it on a clericalism that ultimately benumbed the intellectual talents of multiple generations.[40]

Literature and art contributed to this negative portrait as well. There was a wide readership for captivity narratives penned by individuals who had fallen into the hands of Spanish inquisitors.[41] The creation of the "Gothic" novel – full of sentimental romance, binary categories of good versus evil, and terrifying situations – also deployed the Inquisition as a villainous trope. In Matthew Lewis's *The Monk* from 1796, Anne Radcliffe's *The Italian* from 1797, and William Henry Ireland's *The Abbess* from 1799, inquisitors tortured defendants, accused them of crimes they had not committed, "eye[d] prisoners with curiosity but not pity ... [and] seem[ed] stamped with the character of demons." They operated out of dark rooms dominated by large crucifixes. They declined to acknowledge the truth uttered by witnesses. They were emaciated, hollow-eyed, and fanatical. They had a limitless capacity for wickedness.[42] Significantly, no matter where the story was located, all the inquisitions and their inquisitors conformed to a type, which was modeled on popular understandings – or myths – of the Spanish Inquisition.[43]

As readers will see in the following essays, the Spanish Inquisition was a far more complex religious, legal, and historical institution than such myths allow. Its official governing body never could dominate institutional practices in the periphery, thanks to the tyranny of distance as well as the ways in which inquisitors and their staff were embedded in local circumstances. Inquisitors and the men who worked for them could be more or less competent. They could have greater or lesser senses of discretion and privilege. They could decide to follow or to bend the rules. Their targets could change over time and across geographies, but their theoretical goals always were supposed to remain the same: namely, to investigate potential heresy and restore those in religious error to the Catholic Church.

As readers explore the essays in this volume, they will notice common themes as well as interpretative differences about the Spanish Inquisition's motives and impact. Modern scholars have figured out which victims were prosecuted, and when, in the history of the Spanish Inquisition. But we continue to probe the legal, pastoral, and political motives that incentivized men to become inquisitors or work for inquisition tribunals. We conflict on the degree to which inquisitors in general were capable. We do not agree on whether we should characterize the Spanish Inquisition as a machine, yet we also admit that inquisition prisons and their administrators were hardly foolproof in terms of secrecy or even flight when it came to the incarcerated. As editor, my hope is that these chapters will deepen readers' understanding of a legendary institution in Western history and amplify their awareness of how historians build their arguments from the surviving evidence.

Notes

1. Jonathan Ray, *Jewish Life in Medieval Spain: A New History* (University of Pennsylvania Press, 2023), 195–204.
2. Ray, *Jewish Life*, 200–3, notes that local lords sometimes pressured Jews to accept conversion as a way to calm things down.
3. Families could still be in a hybrid religious state decades after 1391: Ray, *Jewish Life*, 205.

4. Philip Daileader, *Saint Vincent Ferrer, His World and Life: Religion and Society in Late Medieval Europe* (Palgrave Macmillan, 2016), 113–16.
5. Daileader, *Saint Vincent Ferrer*, 121–23.
6. Ray, *Jewish Life*, 214–16; Daileader, *Saint Vincent Ferrer*, 118–20.
7. Henry Kamen, *The Spanish Inquisition: A Historical Revision* (Yale University Press, 2014), 37–9.
8. Ray, *Jewish Life*, 213, 220, 251.
9. David Nirenberg, "Mass Conversion and Genealogical Mentalities: Jews and Christians in Fifteenth-Century Spain," *Past and Present* 174 (2002): 3–41.
10. Kamen, *The Spanish Inquisition*, 42.
11. Ray, *Jewish Life*, 254; John Edwards, *Ferdinand and Isabella* (Routledge, 2013), 70.
12. José Meseguer Fernández, "El period fundacional (1478–1517)," in Joaquín Pérez Villanueva and Bartolomé Escandall Bonet, eds., *Historia de la Inquisición en España y América* Vol. 1 (Biblioteca de Autores Cristianos/Centro de Estudios Inquisitoriales, 1984), 290–1.
13. Helen Rawlings, *Church, Religion and Society in Early Modern Spain* (Palgrave Macmillan, 2002), 50–3.
14. Meseguer Fernández, "El período fundacional," 300–6.
15. Edwards, *Ferdinand and Isabella*, 72.
16. Ángel de Prado Moura, *El tribunal de la inquisición en España (1478–1834)* (Actas Editorial, 2003), 23–5.
17. Edwards, *Ferdinand and Isabella*, 77. Kamen, *The Spanish Inquisition*, 61–3.
18. Manuel Sánchez Moya and Miguel Ángel Motis Dolader, "Autos de fe celebrados por el tribunal del Santo Oficio en Teruel (1485–1487)," *Sefarad* 77 (2017): 315–51.
19. Kamen, *The Spanish Inquisition*, 157.
20. Sánchez Moya and Moris Dolader, "Autos de fe," 321. Manuel Sánchez Moya, *La Inquisición contra la ciudad de Teruel (1484–1485)* (Instituto de Estudios Turolenses, 2020).
21. Ray, *Jewish Life*, 108–18. Ferdinand and Isabella's willingness to expel their Jewish population contrasts with the priorities of medieval monarchs in Spain who generally attempted to protect the same minority.
22. Ray, *Jewish Life*, 260–1.
23. Edwards, *Ferdinand and Isabella*, 82, believes the point of the general expulsion order was to encourage or force conversion.
24. For the effects of the 1492 Expulsion, see Jonathan Ray, *After Expulsion: 1492 and the Making of Sephardic Jewry* (New York University Press, 2013).
25. Kamen, *The Spanish Inquisition*, 54.
26. Ferdinand Peña Rambla, *La inquisición en las Cortes de Cádiz: un debate para la história* (Universitat Jaume I, 2016), 12.
27. Peña Rambla, *La inquisición en las Cortes*, 209–11.
28. Peña Rambla, *La inquisición en las Cortes*, 217.

29. Peña Rambla, *La inquisición en las Cortes*, 11.
30. Carlos Rodríguez López-Brea, "El final de la Inquisición," *Historia Constitucional* 15 (2014): 573–9.
31. Peña Rambla, *La inquisición en las Cortes*, 12–13.
32. Miguel Jiménez Montserín, "La abolición del Tribunal (1808–1834)," in Villanueva and Bonet, eds., *Historia de la Inquisición*, 1480.
33. Jiménez Montserín, "La abolición del Tribunal (1808–1834)," 1481.
34. The *pronunciamiento* would become the most potent weapon of liberal reform in the Spanish nineteenth century. See Pamela Beth Radcliff, *Modern Spain, 1808 to the Present* (Wiley-Blackwell, 2017).
35. Emilio La Parra and María Ángeles Casado, *La Inquisición en España: Agonía y Abolición* (Catarata, 2013), chapter 6.
36. For important critics of inquisition who lived in late fifteenth- and sixteenth-century Spain, see Stefania Pastore, *Il vangelo e la spada: L'inquisizione di Castiglia e i suoi critici (1460–1598)* (Storia e Letteratura, 2003). Menéndez y Pelayo's views can be surveyed through his three-volume *Historia de los heterodoxos españoles*, published in 1880. For Prescott, Richard L. Kagan, "Prescott's Paradigm: American Historical Scholarship and the Decline of Spain," *The American Historical Review* 101 (1996): 423–46.
37. The specific term "Black Legend" was created by Spanish journalist Julián Juderías, who first deployed it in a sequence of essays in 1913: "La Leyenda negra y le verdad histórica," *La Ilustración Española y Americana* (January 8, 15, 22, 30; February 8, 1913), and in augmented form as a book, *La Leyenda negra y la verdad histórica* (Tip. de la Rev. de Arch., Bib., y Museos, 1914). See Margaret Greer, Walter D. Mignolo, and Maureen Quilligan, eds., *Rereading the Black Legend* (The University of Chicago Press, 2008), chapter 1, as well as all the essays therein.
38. A. Gordon Kinder, "Creation of the Black Legend: Literary Contributions of Spanish Protestant Exiles," *Mediterranean Studies* 6 (1996): 67–78.
39. Edward Peters, *Inquisition* (The Free Press, 1988), 133–4.
40. Kagan, "Prescott's Paradigm," 433–4.
41. Peters, *Inquisition*, 190–2.
42. Peters, *Inquisition*, 207–11.
43. Peters, *Inquisition*, 213.

Suggestions for Further Reading

Edwards, John. *Ferdinand and Isabella*. Routledge, 2013.

Homza, Lu Ann, ed. and trans. *The Spanish Inquisition, 1478–1614: An Anthology of Sources*. Hackett, 2006.

Jiménez Montserín, Miguel. "La abolición del Tribunal (1808–1814)." In Joaquín Pérez Villanueva and Bartolomé Escandell Bonet, eds., *Historia de la*

Inquisición en España y América Vol. 1. Biblioteca de Autores Cristianos/ Centro de Estudios Inquisitoriales, 1984.
Kagan, Richard L. "Prescott's Paradigm: American Historical Scholarship and the Decline of Spain." *American Historical Review* 101 (1996): 423–46.
Kamen, Henry. *The Spanish Inquisition: A Historical Revision.* 4th edition. Yale University Press, 2014.
Kinder, A. Gordon. "Creation of the Black Legend: Literary Contributions of Spanish Protestant Exiles." *Mediterranean Studies* 6 (1996): 67–78.
Nirenberg, David. "Mass Conversion and Genealogical Mentalities: Jews and Christians in Fifteenth-Century Spain." *Past and Present* 174 (2002): 3–41.
Peña Rambla, Fernando. *La inquisición en las Cortes de Cádiz: un debate para la historia.* Universitat Jaume I, 2016.
Peters, Edward. *Inquisition.* The Free Press, 1988.
Ray, Jonathan. *Jewish Life in Medieval Spain: A New History.* University of Pennsylvania Press, 2023.

Bibliography

Daileader, Philip. *Saint Vincent Ferrer, His World and Life: Religion and Society in Late Medieval Europe.* Palgrave Macmillan, 2016.
Edwards, John. *Ferdinand and Isabella.* Routledge, 2013.
Greer, Margaret, Walter D. Mignolo, and Maureen Quilligan, eds. *Rereading the Black Legend.* The University of Chicago Press, 2008.
Jiménez Montserin, Miguel. "La abolición del Tribunal (1808–1834)." In Joaquín Pérez Villanueva and Bartolomé Escandell Bonet, eds., *Historia de la Inquisición en España y América* Vol. 1, 1424–86. Biblioteca de Autores Cristianos/Centro de Estudios Inquisitoriales, 1984.
Juderías, Julián. *La Leyenda negra y la verdad histórica.* Tip. de la Rev. de Arch., Bib., y Museos, 1914.
Kagan, Richard L. "Prescott's Paradigm: American Historical Scholarship and the Decline of Spain." *The American Historical Review* 101 (1996): 423–46.
Kamen, Henry. *The Spanish Inquisition: A Historical Revision.* 4th edition. Yale University Press, 2014.
Kinder, A. Gordon. "Creation of the Black Legend: Literary Contributions of Spanish Protestant Exiles." *Mediterranean Studies* 6 (1996): 67–78.
La Parra, Emilio, and María Ángeles Casado. *La Inquisición en España: Agonía y Abolición.* Catarata, 2013.
Meseguer Fernández, José. "El period fundacional (1478–1517)." In Joaquín Pérez Villanueva and Bartolomé Escandall Bonet, eds.,*Historia de la Inquisición en España y América,* Vol. 1, 281–370. Biblioteca de Autores Cristianos/Centro de Estudios Inquisitoriales, 1984.

Pastore, Stefania. *Il vangelo e la spada: L'inquisizione di Castiglia e i suoi critici (1460–1598)*. Storia e Letteratura, 2003.
Rodríguez López-Brea, Carlos. "El final de la Inquisición." *Historia Constitucional* 15 (2014): 573–9.
Nirenberg, David. "Mass Conversion and Genealogical Mentalities: Jews and Christians in Fifteenth-Century Spain." *Past and Present* 174 (2002): 3–41.
Peña Rambla, Ferdinand. *La inquisición en las Cortes de Cádiz: un debate para la história*. Universitat Jaume I, 2016.
Peters, Edward. *Inquisition*. The Free Press, 1988.
Prado Moura, Ángel de. *El tribunal de la inquisición en España (1478–1834)*. Actas Editorial, 2003.
Sánchez Moya, Manuel, and Miguel Ángel Moris Dolader. "Autos de fe celebrados por el tribunal del Santo Oficio en Teruel (1485–1487)." *Sefarad* 77 (2017): 315–51.
Radcliff, Pamela Beth. *Modern Spain, 1808 to the Present*. Wiley-Blackwell, 2017.
Rawlings, Helen. *Church, Religion and Society in Early Modern Spain*. Palgrave Macmillan, 2002.
Ray, Jonathan. *Jewish Life in Medieval Spain: A New History*. University of Pennsylvania Press, 2023.

Part I
The Institution

1

Procedures and Goals

Modern readers would be forgiven for presuming that the Spanish Inquisition must have been Spanish in origin. Yet Spaniards did not create the Inquisition's legal standards and procedures, which came instead from ancient Rome. The term "inquisition" in English is derived from the Latin noun *inquisitio*, which simply means "investigation." Significantly, such an investigation depended upon human-generated evidence, arguments, and judgments, and the evidence had to be sensory-based. Furthermore, ancient Roman law had firm standards of proof. A person could be condemned based on two eyewitnesses to the same event, or a confession: Either constituted a full proof. Eyewitnesses to different events amounted only to partial proof, and no quantity of partial proofs was supposed to add up to a full one.

Given Roman law's emphasis on confession, it is perhaps not surprising that the deployment of torture had a place here as well. In the earliest Roman legal codes, slaves could be tortured by their masters, who had an absolute right to do so if the slave had been accused of a crime. As Augustus Caesar (r. 27 BCE–14 CE) solidified his control over Rome, the notion of treason expanded as well, to the point that free Roman citizens could be tortured if they disputed imperial orders. Torture in ancient Rome had two connotations: It could be a form of punishment, but it also could serve an interrogatory purpose, when it was used to move an investigation forward. The process of inquisition involved the latter: Torture could secure a confession, which was a complete proof. A confession obtained under torture in ancient Rome would have to be confirmed or ratified without torture to become legally valid.

Ancient Roman law was gathered and systematized by the Emperor Justinian I in the sixth century CE: The *Institutes* constituted a textbook, while the *Digest* presented the opinions of Roman legal commentators arranged by topic. Taken together, the two were known as the *Corpus iuris civilis*, or body of civil law, and while the collection was circulated throughout Justinian's empire, it had practically no impact on Europe for hundreds of years. Then, things changed. In the twelfth century, medieval kings and popes deliberately revived Roman law because they found it very useful: It allowed rulers to put a single legal system into play, rather than forcing them to cope with a jigsaw puzzle of law codes in the territories they governed.[1] Significantly, the codification of Roman Catholic ecclesiastical law – called canon law – was occurring practically simultaneously. Taken together, Roman law and canon law were known as the *ius commune*, or a common system of legal thought.

The medieval adoption of Roman law had profound implications for European court systems. Before the twelfth century, secular justice in Western Europe involved a private, accusatory process in which the victim bore responsibility for finding the relevant court and swearing an oath that a misdeed had occurred: At that point, the alleged perpetrator would appear in the same court and swear a corresponding oath as to whether the charge was true or false. The oath was the strongest proof; it implied that God was making the decision. Oaths were logically connected to judicial combat and other forms of ordeal in which the litigants and bystanders presumed God would intervene to make known the truth. This system of accusation–oath–ordeal was grounded on a belief that divine intervention in the material world was continuous, and God's judgments, instantaneous.

Beginning around 1100, however, Europeans started to believe that human beings were competent to decide legal cases – to engage, basically, in inquisition, and that belief came directly from the recovery of Roman law. Significantly, the revival of Roman law and inquisition also profoundly affected the investigation into and punishment of Christian error. If such error was intentional, persistent, and public, it was called "heresy," a noun that is derived from the Greek noun *haeresis*: The Greek term originally meant "choice" or "thing chosen," but over time, heresy in Western Europe came specifically to denote an error held by a baptized Christian against some aspect of Christian theology or religious practice.

The phenomenon of heresy did not suddenly appear in the twelfth century: It was present from the very beginning of Christianity, when the Apostle Paul warned the earliest Christians about dissenters who could fracture the unity of their religious communities.[2] By the second century CE, those dissenters were described as heretics, namely, as persons who had chosen a belief or practice that orthodox Christian communities rejected. Early Christians debated and rejected heresy through letters and treatises. The battle became that much more heated after Christianity became the official religion of the Roman empire in 313 CE.

In 325 CE, for example, the Roman emperor Constantine presided over the opening session of the Council of Nicaea: That council had been called to solve the challenge of Arianism, an idea first proposed by Arius of Alexandria asserting that Jesus was created by God rather than divine and co-eternal with God. Attendees at Nicaea condemned Arius and incorporated a nonscriptural word, *homoousios* ("of one substance") into a creed to signify the absolute equality of the Son with the Father in the Christian doctrine of the Trinity. Later in the fourth century CE, another dissenting movement called Donatism in the African Christian Church insisted that the morality of the person administering the church sacraments affected the validity of those sacraments. Meanwhile, the British-born Pelagius (b. 354 CE) insisted that human beings were not inevitably tainted by Adam's original sin but rather had the free will to move themselves toward righteousness. All three groups – Arians, Donatists, and Pelagians – were targeted as heretics and harshly rebuked by early Church Fathers such as Athanasius, Jerome, and Augustine. It is vital to note that categories of heresy could grow or alter over time.[3] Christians had to define what was acceptable before they could define what was unacceptable. Because the boundaries of Christian religious orthodoxy shifted throughout the centuries, so too did Christian ideas about religious dissent.

When it came to penalizing heretics, Roman popes excommunicated them from the fourth century CE on, while bishops and archbishops generally assumed responsibility for correcting religious error and dissent in their dioceses from late antiquity until the twelfth century.

With the adoption of Roman law, however, religious and secular authorities started to voice the same concepts about the damage that heretics caused. In the twelfth century, kings and popes knew that Roman law allowed the death penalty for treason against an emperor; they expanded that connection to ask what heretics were if not traitors to God? They concluded that treason against God was even more important than sedition against an earthly ruler.

Such reasoning was eventually shared by secular and ecclesiastical authorities in the twelfth and thirteenth centuries, which is why they acted in unison against heresy. In 1184, for example, Pope Lucius III and Holy Roman Emperor Frederick I set up inquisitions manned by bishops; Lucius's papal bull said that heretics could be executed by secular authorities, which was called being "turned over to the secular arm." In 1197, King Peter II of Aragon banished all heretics from his domains under threat of confiscation of property and death at the stake. In 1199, Pope Innocent III declared that heretics were traitors to God and directly comparable to traitors against Augustus Caesar; Innocent also noted that land owned by heretics could be confiscated. Finally, from 1220 to 1232, Holy Roman Emperor Frederick II decreed banishment and the confiscation of property for heretics, as well as death for unrepentant ones.

Still, bishops and archbishops remained the primary agents against heresy until 1231, when Pope Gregory IX began to put friars from the Dominican order in charge of discovering, trying, and sentencing heretics. At that moment, Gregory IX started to establish papal "inquisitions," which were spontaneous creations designed to address a particular heresy in a specific area for a certain span of time. It would be misleading to denote a medieval papal inquisition with a capital "I": The papally deputized inquisitors were never integrated into a single unified organization, and they operated independently of each other. They had no special training, whether legal or theological; there was no career path for them in terms of upward mobility. Some were extremely venal, only a few became bishops, and chance probably played a substantial role in their appointment. In theory, papal inquisitors were answerable to the papacy, but in practice they tended to be supervised loosely once they were named.[4] In 1312, at the ecumenical council of Vienne, Pope Clement V openly denounced inquisitorial malfeasance in the bull

Multorum querela, where he also explicitly reinforced a significant role for bishops in the investigation of heresy. Although Clement's bull – which was not put into effect until 1317 – stipulated that bishops and inquisitors were required to work as a team in certain matters, inquisitorial courts usually took precedence over episcopal ones. The inquisitorial and episcopal legal jurisdictions often competed with one another where suspected heretics were concerned.[5]

Once deputized, medieval inquisitors traveled physically to the location in question and began to investigate whether heresy was present and to what degree. They advertised their mission through sermons and promulgations; they could bring in suspects for questioning or listen to witnesses who appeared voluntarily before them. Everyone who appeared before a medieval inquisitor swore oaths to tell the truth. When inquisitors decided they had enough evidence, they shaped the depositions into an accusation against a specific individual, who was subsequently arrested, presented with charges that he or she was expected to answer, and then jailed. One specialist has affirmed that imprisonment after arrest was "one of the [medieval] inquisition's most effective interrogation techniques."[6] No matter where they were operating, papal inquisitors followed certain practices: They declined to identify accusers or other deponents to suspects; they denied suspects the use of an attorney; they mandated secrecy for everyone in their court; finally, they could hear from witnesses who typically would have been barred from testifying, such as other heretics, convicted criminals, and children.

Medieval inquisitors expected suspects to divulge the religious errors of their acquaintances as well as their own faults. They applied Roman legal standards for proof: They wanted two eyewitnesses to the same event, or a confession. While inquisitors themselves did not conduct torture – which was left to professionals – they were present when it was administered. In conformity with Roman law, they required a defendant to later ratify without torture a confession that had occurred during it.

The explicit aim of the medieval papal inquisitions was to reconcile heretics back to the Catholic Church, and there were multiple signs of this religious motivation. Medieval inquisitors always aimed at a confession with the expectation that it would be accompanied by repentance. They called their punishments "penances," which was a reference to one of the Catholic sacraments: Penance "made contrition manifest."[7] Inquisitors were supposed to closely investigate souls of suspected heretics, as were members of the mendicant orders and parish priests who were simply administering the sacrament of penance on a yearly basis. Difficult as it may be for us to grasp, the Dominicans who acted as inquisitors in the medieval epoch conceived of their task as a form of pastoral care, with heresy being a proportionately worse sin than the seven deadly sins of pride, avarice, lust, anger, gluttony, envy, and spiritual sloth.[8]

Inquisition suspects who were proven guilty could be sentenced publicly: These open-air ceremonies featured sermons as well as the recitation of heresies committed and penances mandated.[9] Sentences could range from a requirement to go on pilgrimage, to being forced to wear yellow crosses on one's clothing, to imprisonment, to execution. A heretic could be sentenced to imprisonment and have his house destroyed; he could also be burned posthumously.[10] Executions – typically by means of burning at the stake – were reserved for individuals who refused to repent despite overwhelming evidence, as well as previously convicted heretics who had relapsed. Executions were dramatic public events that could provoke admiration for the steadfastness of the dying as well as horror for the suffering involved.[11] A sentence of death implied that inquisitors had failed in their pastoral objectives.

In the end, suspected heretics could attempt to resist medieval inquisitors by feigning illness to avoid torture; they could pretend to be insane, stupid, or deaf to delay or complicate an interrogation. They could try to intimidate or bribe potential witnesses before their arrest; they could pretend to cooperate and then flee; they might attempt to play one inquisitor against another. More men than women ran away but few of the fugitives escaped capture for long and they did not go far: One scholar has estimated an average maximum distance of some fifty miles.[12]

Still, escape efforts were mostly moot. Medieval inquisitors recaptured the fugitives not only through the help of the secular and episcopal legal jurisdictions but also by deploying the documents preserved in their archives. One of the most remarkable facets of medieval inquisition practice lies not simply in the inquisitors' decisions to record their activities but the ways in which they learned how to recover what they had recorded. Their scribes relentlessly recopied archival documentation to keep it accessible; the inquisitors then arranged that documentation topographically by village, in alphabetical order. These registers of names, crimes, locations, and sentences could become instruments of coercion as well as knowledge, since they allowed the inquisitors to find contradictions in depositions and confessions.[13] Not surprisingly, inquisition archives could become objects of fear and rage from the local populace.

There is no doubt that the Spanish Inquisition, founded in 1478 by King Ferdinand of Aragon and Queen Isabella of Castile, was indebted in multiple ways to its medieval predecessor, even though the Spanish Inquisition was certainly a royal as well as a papal institution. (While the Kingdom of Aragon had experience with medieval inquisitors deputized by the papacy, the Kingdom of Castile did not.) Ferdinand and Isabella received permission from Pope Sixtus IV to name inquisitors on November 1, 1478: That papal authorization was granted in perpetuity and the papal bull's validity could not be blocked by any other ordinance or constitution.[14] The privilege that Ferdinand and Isabella received from Sixtus IV was extraordinary because it gave them the singular ability to put inquisitors into office. The reason the monarchs wanted inquisitors installed in their kingdoms was straightforward: Bishops and archbishops were bound geographically to their dioceses, and hence could not monitor conversos – baptized Christians of Jewish ancestry – who purportedly were continuing to practice Mosaic Law and moving around Castile and Aragon. Such individuals were categorized as heretics because they allegedly practiced a religion other than Christianity despite their Catholic baptisms.

The first Spanish inquisitors were named in 1480: They swore their oaths in the northern city of Medina del Campo but immediately moved south to Seville, where the issue of conversos practicing Judaism seemed to be particularly acute. The earliest inquisitors were supposed to travel constantly, but it soon appeared preferable for them to be based in cities. There was a significant degree of change as inquisition tribunals were founded, moved, and consolidated. Ultimately, the permanent tribunals of the Spanish Inquisition numbered twenty-one in the Spanish empire, which included the islands of Sardinia and Sicily as well as Mexico City, Lima, and Cartagena de Indias. The Spanish Inquisition was never successfully established in the Italian cities of

Milan and Naples, which were under the jurisdiction of Spanish kings; instead, its mission there was overseen by archbishops.

For the first decades of the Spanish Inquisition's existence, it is not clear how or when inquisitors were named; we also have little evidence as to how the Inquisition's councils came into being. The first inquisitor-general, Tomás de Torquemada, a Dominican prior of a convent in Segovia, was appointed in 1483 and was given powers over Aragon as well as Castile. Between 1484 and 1488, Torquemada obtained counselors who formed the "Council of the Supreme and General Inquisition," known by the short title, the Suprema. The number of counselors on the Suprema shifted over time; in the early seventeenth century, it had six, and while the inquisitor-general could suggest candidates for the council, the monarch decided whom to name. The Suprema's responsibilities included responding to questions from the field, vetting challenging cases, and issuing instructions and edicts. The inquisitor-general himself could perform the same tasks, and the hierarchy between the inquisitor-general and the Suprema's members was never explicitly established.[15] An inquisitor-general could act independently from the Suprema, and vice-versa.[16]

The staffing of Spanish inquisition tribunals remained relatively consistent over time in terms of types of employees, though the number of individuals in the various offices could increase. For example, instructions in 1498 told the tribunals to have two inquisitors, a figure that increased to three for the larger tribunals by the end of the sixteenth century. In another example of change over time, Spanish inquisitors shifted from being Dominican friars, to a combination of theologians and jurists, to almost solely canon lawyers.

It also seems clear that the number of men who assisted the inquisitors grew over time as well: Some examples would have been the commissioners (*comisarios*), who could take depositions from suspects and witnesses and forward them to the respective tribunal, as well as the "familiars" (*familiares*) who could not receive witness testimony but who were obliged to assist a particular tribunal in every other way. Significantly, both commissioners and familiars were legally exempt from the secular and episcopal court systems and could only be tried for crimes by the inquisitors who employed them. Moreover, inquisitors needed other consultants who might be in short supply. Locally placed theologians or friars were supposed to weigh the evidence for heresy in ambiguous or difficult cases; they were not employed by the tribunal, and Spanish inquisitors in large or liminal districts, for example, had trouble finding ones who were sufficiently qualified or willing, a problem that could delay trials and sentencing.

Prosecutions in the Spanish Inquisition proceeded through specific steps, but the discretion of the individual inquisitors was always in play in terms of the timing of each stage as well as the questions posed in interrogations. Investigations were provoked by witnesses who appeared voluntarily or who were called. They deposed under oath and then had to ratify their statements before their words could be used at trial. Inquisitors were supposed to tour their districts regularly, and when they were in the field they could promulgate edicts that instructed laypersons to see them. An edict of faith commanded individuals to appear who knew about or were potentially guilty of heresy; it did not promise reconciliation to the Church. In contrast, an edict of grace asked individuals to appear and promised reconciliation if suspects surfaced freely and were sufficiently repentant. In the absence of either sort of edict, individuals who went to inquisition tribunals to confess and beg for mercy were usually reconciled to the Church and given a penance to perform – unless the archives revealed that the person in question had confessed previously to heresy and had relapsed.

Only the inquisitors could decide when the weight of the evidence reached a level to justify an arrest. At that point, the tribunal's constable went out to locate the suspect and bring him to the tribunal's jail, where the accused would remain during trial. Once suspects were in custody, the inquisitors would arrange a sequence of three meetings with them, during which they would order them to say why they might have been arrested and what they might know about others whose Catholic orthodoxy might be doubtful. The inquisitors would tell prisoners that their souls were in danger; they were hoping that verbal psychological pressure would elicit a confession. If no confession were forthcoming, they would instigate a trial.

An inquisition case formally began when the tribunal's prosecutor orally listed charges of heresy in the suspect's presence: Those charges would be written down and given to the defendant, though all identifying marks of the prosecution witnesses would have been omitted. After the oral presentation of charges, the defendant was supposed to respond immediately and verbally to the allegations. Once this spoken interchange had taken place, both sides were received "for proof," which meant each side typically had nine days to present witnesses. Unlike the medieval incarnation of inquisition, the Spanish variety allowed suspects to mount a defense, through an attorney who was paid by the tribunal in question but who often took his job seriously. The prosecutor's witnesses nevertheless were presented first, and the prosecutor could add charges as the trial went on.

As was the case with the medieval papal inquisitions, the Spanish variety allowed less-than-ideal witnesses to testify for the prosecution, including others suspected or convicted of heresy. Nevertheless, there are signs that the inquisitors could recognize and act upon levels of persuasiveness in prosecution depositions: Though Spanish inquisitors rarely laid out their reasons for their legal decisions, sometimes we can intuit connections between the evidence presented and their judgments. When supposed eyewitnesses really testified about the spouses of defendants instead of the defendants themselves, or prosecution witnesses had particularly bad reputations, Spanish inquisitors could limit the weight of the proof. For example, in a trial from 1483 to 1484, witnesses against defendant Pedro Villegas focused on his wife's judaizing, and he was freed without penalty. In a case from 1533, defendant María de Cazalla substantiated the wicked reputation and capital enmity of multiple prosecution witnesses. If a defendant could guess the identity of a prosecution witness and prove that witness wished her dead, that witness's deposition could be nullified: This was a defense strategy called *tachas*, from the Spanish verb *tachar*, "to stain." After Cazalla then withstood torture, the inquisitors and their consultants voted that she should be absolved.[17]

Although defendants were always presumed guilty – as was the case for all legal jurisdictions in this period – proof could end up being more ambiguous than the inquisitors would like. When witnesses were disqualified for enmity, or were suspect or unique, the inquisitors had two solutions. They could call for compurgation, whereby a certain number of witnesses would swear to the defendant's Catholic orthodoxy: After those oaths, the suspect would be absolved and released. The inquisitors could also suspend the case pending further investigation and better witnesses, whereupon the charges could be reinstated or augmented.

If the evidence was ambiguous and the defendant refused to confess, the inquisitors, their theological consultants, and a representative of the local bishop could decide to order a session of torture in the hopes of gaining a confession. As was the case in medieval inquisitions, torture was administered by a professional in a separate room, and it had to be witnessed by at least one inquisitor and a scribe; the scribe was supposed to write down anything and everything the suspect said while the torture was ongoing. There were three forms of torture in the Spanish Inquisition, and they did not change over time. The first was the *toca* or hood: once in a horizontal position, defendants would have a linen cloth placed over the face and large quantities of water were poured over their mouth and nose to simulate drowning. The second was the *potro* or rack, on which the defendant was bound with cords that were tightened. Finally, the Spanish Inquisition could impose the *garrucha* or pulley, in which a defendant's hands were tied behind him and he was raised from the ground by his wrists.

To heighten the possibility of a confession, the defendant would be shown the torture room and its instruments before the torture session began; he also would be admonished to confess from the moment he entered the room, and warned that any physical harm from the torture would be his own fault. If a confession occurred, it would have to be ratified later, in the absence of torture, to be legally binding; if a defendant revoked a confession made under torture, he could be tortured again. Spanish inquisitors did not typically torture the elderly, the disabled, or the infirm. Although torture remains one of the most lurid features of the Spanish Inquisition, modern historians now believe it was deployed relatively infrequently. For the sake of context, it is important to note that torture was also legal in the secular court system throughout most of Western Europe in the sixteenth and seventeenth centuries. While common law prohibited torture in England, it could be permitted via warrants from the royal Privy Council until 1628.

It might seem impossible that any defendant could have fought back against Spanish inquisitors, given the rule of secrecy about prosecution witnesses, the presumption of guilt, and the potential role of torture in confessions. Yet people on trial for heresy in Spanish inquisition tribunals found numerous ways to contest their trials. Like their medieval predecessors, some ran, though it would be impossible to quantify how many; here again, the depth and breadth of the inquisitorial archive allowed so much information-sharing that escape was not necessarily successful.[18] An equally drastic tactic was to plan to kill the inquisition tribunal's jailer and burn the documentation: Inquisitors recognized this risk, which is why they kept their archive locked with multiple keys.

Less dramatic resistance was also plausible and undoubtedly more common. Defendants could present character witnesses to attest their Catholic beliefs and behavior. The longer the degree of acquaintance and the higher the social or ecclesiastical status of the witness, the better. Parish priests, local friars or constables, and a working or religious relationship with the defendant helped a great deal. Defense witnesses could be especially useful if they had spent substantial time in the defendant's home and had observed spiritual and dietary habits.[19] A defendant could also call witnesses to cast doubt on specific accusations, or witnesses who could verify that a particular individual wished the defendant dead, although the rule of secrecy and a corresponding lack of information about dates, times, and the identity of prosecution witnesses made these strategies riskier. In 1494, for example, Marina González panicked over being asked to name witnesses in a compurgation for fear they had testified against her. She failed the process and ultimately was burned at the stake.[20]

Ironically, given the Spanish Inquisition's own obsession with paper, defendants could also submit endless petitions that sapped the tribunal's time and served as relentless distractions. Defendants could dispute whether prosecution witnesses had actually ratified their depositions; they could assert that depositions had not been received within the time allowed; they might highlight every conceivable legal misstep and demand an investigation. The overarching point of such petitions was to slow down the trial process. If a defendant could find a way to communicate with persons inside or outside of prison – and jailed suspects very often found ways to smuggle letters out of prison or talk with one another – she might be able to learn something about the prosecution's witnesses and thereby be in a better position to challenge them.[21] Other tacit defense strategies involved repeatedly mentioning one's highly placed connections, especially in the religious sphere, and noting the excellence of one's own reputation. For example, defendant María de Cazalla repeatedly invoked the spiritual counsel of her brother, a Franciscan friar, as she explained her religious outlook. After his arrest in 1529, inquisition prisoner Friar Francisco Ortiz spoke at length about his fame as a preacher in Toledo's most important churches; in 1532, inquisition prisoner Juan de Vergara underlined his position as secretary to the most important ecclesiastic in Spain, the archbishop of Toledo.[22]

Intention was always supposed to matter to Spanish inquisitors because heresy was not supposed to be inadvertent. Consequently, accidents and contexts could mitigate guilt, and there is no doubt that at least some defendants highlighted the fact that they had made a mistake. It was common for first-time female offenders on trial for judaizing to claim that they had forgotten it was a Friday when they served meat. Women and men throughout the Spanish empire could explain bigamy via the apparent death of a spouse overseas. Blasphemy was more forgivable if it occurred while losing a card game, arguing with a neighbor, or realizing a fishing net had ripped. Younger suspects could claim they had been misled by older relatives or assert they had never been instructed.

Notably, some inquisition defendants turned to a sense of history to dispute the charges. Many knew exactly when Martin Luther had been excommunicated and declared a heretic: They consequently argued that there had been no prohibition on reading Luther's works before January 1521. The same held true for conversations or friendships with individuals who eventually were deemed heretics. If conversations with those current heretics had occurred *before* anyone had realized that heresy was in play, then suspicion or guilt could not be imputed backwards in time, or so defendants often argued.[23]

Crucially, defendants in its courts were not the only ones to resist the Spanish Inquisition. Modern scholars have discovered that the Spanish Inquisition provoked more learned opposition, for a much longer period of time, than we ever imagined. Late fifteenth- and sixteenth-century theological writings, reflections on religious conversion, and interpretations of the New Testament demonstrate that Spanish clerical and legal elites debated how to correct Christian religious error. In the process, they offered an alternative to the inquisitorial model. If Spanish inquisitors promoted a legalistic, lineage-obsessed mentality that demanded public discipline, then certain bishops, Jesuits, missionaries, and preachers of all sorts advanced an ethos of private, fraternal correction based on charity, the equality of all Christians, the values of Saint Paul, and the abandonment of ceremony and gesture.[24]

Nevertheless, the Spanish Inquisition usually prevailed in proving its cases and finding defendants guilty of heresy. The more serious heresies included the continued practice of Islam or Judaism despite being baptized, as well as becoming a Protestant, which the inquisitors conceptualized as being a follower of Martin Luther. (Spanish inquisitors called even the followers of John Calvin *luteranos*.) What modern readers might think of as moral offenses – blasphemy, fornication, bigamy, scandalous statements (*proposiciones*), sodomy, and the solicitation of sexual favors by priests – were treated as lesser heresies: People accused of these were liable to face inquisitorial prosecution under the reasoning that no truly Catholic Christian would engage in such behaviors. The language of the sentences differed between the two categories of heresy. Defendants in the more serious group who confessed and named accomplices were absolved of excommunication and were said to be "reconciled" (*reconciliado*) to the Church. Defendants in the less serious category who confessed and named accomplices were reconciled to the Church as well, but forswore a light (*de levi*) or grave (*de vehementi*) suspicion of heresy, and inquisitors called them "penanced." Both categories were viewed as convicted and individuals in either one were subject to charges of relapse if they reoffended.

The Spanish Inquisition's most notorious punishment was death through burning at the stake, which usually was reserved for people who had been convicted of serious heresy once and then relapsed, or individuals who had refused to confess to serious heresy despite overwhelming evidence against them. Like its medieval predecessor, this penalty was called "being relaxed (i.e. released) to the secular arm," because inquisitors could not personally carry out executions: Instead, defendants condemned to the stake had to be handed over to secular authorities who put the execution into motion. The death sentence always occurred outside of town; it was customary to strangle the victim before lighting the fire, unless the case was especially egregious. If the convicted repented on the way to execution, inquisitors also had the ability to return the individual to the tribunal if they gauged the repentance as sincere. Modern scholars now believe that death at the stake was a relatively rare sentence. Because so many inquisition sources from Spain and its wider empire have not survived, historians now often prefer to engage in qualitative rather than quantitative assessments of its activities and.

More typical punishments – which Spanish inquisitors, like their medieval predecessors, called penances – usually featured some form of public humiliation. When inquisitors had a sufficiently large number of people to sentence, they did so in public ceremonies called *autos de fe* or "acts of faith," which could draw large crowds. (In November 1610, an *auto de fe* in the Logroño inquisition tribunal that featured 29 convicted witches allegedly drew an audience of 30,000.)[25] After a sermon was preached by a local cleric, descriptions of the heresies involved would be read aloud, along with the sentences. The guilty frequently were condemned to publicly wear *sambenitos* – yellow smocks with red crosses – for a length of time, after which the garb would be placed in the offender's parish church with their names and heresies inscribed below. The guilty could be enclosed in a monastery for a period of re-education; they could be sent to "perpetual prison," which was never actually perpetual. They could be ordered to sponsor and attend a certain number of masses, or to perform public penance by kneeling bare-legged in their parish church while Mass was being said. The most severe sentence besides death at the stake was condemnation to row in the king's Mediterranean gallies for a certain number of years.

Defendants in the Spanish Inquisition also had their property sequestered from the moment of their arrest; a tribunal officer took charge of that property while the trial was ongoing. If the defendant was convicted of a major heresy, upon sentencing his property was formally confiscated. Once confiscated, the defendant's movable and immovable goods were turned over to the Inquisition and then sold at public auction.[26] Conviction of a major heresy often carried consequences for a defendant's wider family: The Inquisition could declare the heirs "infamous," whereby they were prohibited from holding public office, possessing luxury items, or entering clerical orders.

Like its medieval, papal counterpart, the Spanish Inquisition was created for an overarching pastoral goal that can seem delusional or simply disingenuous to modern readers: Its mission was to save the souls of those in deliberate theological or ceremonial error by reuniting them with the Catholic Church. Spanish inquisitors were explicitly adjured to balance justice with mercy, and while it is easy to find inquisitors who preferred judgment over compassion, the reverse is also true. That being said, it is impossible to quantify a predilection for justice or mercy on the part of Spanish inquisitors, or their medieval counterparts, for that matter: The sentences that Spanish inquisitors administered cannot be neatly divided into harsh or lenient penalties. After the brutal revolt of the Alpujarras in 1568–71 – when descendants of Islamic converts to Christianity revolted against King Philip II's religious and cultural reforms, were conquered, and then violently displaced – inquisitors asked the Suprema in Madrid if they might privately reconcile two young boys in their tribunal rather than subject them to a public *auto de fe*. The boys had participated in the rebellion but had been absolved sacramentally; they had not committed heresy after the rebellion.[27] In 1611, an inquisitor visited the territory of Navarre, in northern Spain, to examine witchcraft suspects, and the accounts he heard about local violence, forced confessions, and suicide tormented him for years.[28] That inquisitor ultimately convinced the inquisition leadership in Madrid to overturn sentences and even annul prosecutions.

It is important to recognize that the Spanish Inquisition had a great deal of company when it came to attempts to stamp out religious dissent. In the Christian religious polities of early modern Europe, religious variety was hardly tolerated in an official way, though scholars have documented many instances of nonconformists, whether Catholic or Protestant, evading notice as well as individuals who shifted religious affiliation according to circumstances.[29] Anabaptists were regarded as religious enemies by both Protestant and Catholic political entities throughout the sixteenth century: They were drowned in Zurich in the 1520s and executed by the hundreds in Münster in the early 1530s. The French Wars of Religion (1562–98) began when the monarchy attempted to allow some freedoms for followers of John Calvin. King Philip II of Spain refused to endure Dutch Protestants, which became one crucial reason for an eighty-year war (1568–1648). England saw persecution shift according to royal religious identity: Under Queen Mary, almost 300 Protestants were executed in four years; under Queen Elizabeth I, Parliament created aggressive legislation against Catholics, with offenders subjected to forfeiture of property, fines, life imprisonment, exile, and death, and executions were common if not routine.[30] In no way did Spain have a monopoly on religious persecution.

Finally, while the Spanish Inquisition was a royal institution, and its inquisitors would always side with kings rather than popes if they had to choose, it could not have functioned without support from below. Inquisitors relied upon witnesses; the Catholic faith of those witnesses was often startlingly apparent. For example, in 1603 four older women turned in a twenty-four-year-old female for reciting an obscene ditty about the Trinity. In 1604, five male parishioners reported their parish priest to inquisitors: On the Feast of Corpus Christi, the priest and his congregation had been debating whether to sing before a certain altar that held holy relics. The priest opined, "what relics? In Rome, all you have to do is take three donkey heads to the pope, and he'll bless them and given them the saint's name that's requested." Everyone who heard the priest's words was scandalized, "thinking it was offensive to the pope and to the relics of the saints."[31] In 1609, when six Spanish sailors arrived in the French port of La Rochelle, they recognized a friar named Felipe Ribadeneira, who was walking around the city "without his habit, like a Lutheran and an apostate." The sailors grabbed Felipe, put him on their boat, and returned him to Spain, "in order to remove him from his wicked condition"; while on the boat, Felipe told them, "he wished all his siblings could live in La Rochelle, so that they could be removed from Catholicism." Upon landing, the sailors promptly took their prisoner to an inquisition commissioner, who transferred him to the inquisition tribunal in Logroño.[32]

In these three cases, not only was popular investment obvious when it came to the inquisitorial system but the inquisitors in question also understood and followed institutional values. With the young woman, Logroño's inquisitors were able to verify that she had uttered the profane poem multiple times. Treating her "as a minor" – which meant she was assigned a special advisor (*curador*) because she was under twenty-five years of age – the inquisitors "reprehended her seriously" in their courtroom and then exiled her for two months from the village of Salinillas, where her offense had occurred. The blasphemous priest successfully proved capital enmity on the part of one of his accusers; his witnesses verified that he was "a good and virtuous cleric, a good Christian, a clean Old Christian, and the son of an inquisition familiar." Here, Logroño's inquisitors took seriously the defendant's public reputation but at least some of them viewed the charges as weighty. When they could not agree on a sentence, they sent the case to the Suprema in Madrid, which voted to absolve the culprit. Finally, in the case of Felipe, the would-be Lutheran, the inquisitors listened carefully to

> his long speech about his wandering life, wherein he walked around for an extended time without his habit and as an apostate in different provinces and outside Spain, and finally he came to stop in La Rochelle, where he did not mean to leave the Christian (Catholic) faith. Although he pretended to leave it on the outside, he did not do so in his heart, and this was only because he was in need and to cure his lack of health.[33]

In La Rochelle – a hotbed of French Calvinism – Felipe found a doctor who was not only from Spain but had also escaped the Spanish Inquisition after being sentenced to death for Protestantism. Apparently fearing his new physician would not treat him if he realized he were Catholic, Felipe told the inquisitors that he asked the doctor to instruct him in the Protestant religion.

Before Logroño's inquisitors, Felipe "confessed deeds and errors as a heretic [but] denied intention." He declined to mount a defense; the inquisitors voted to put him to the question of torture to sort out the true objective behind his apparent Protestant interests. Felipe then fell into another round of malarial fever, which became so severe that torture could not be carried out.[34]

On the point of death, Felipe asked for an audience: An inquisitor with a notary went to his jail cell. There, he confessed that he had indeed planned to become a Protestant but begged now to be reconciled with the Catholic Church. The inquisitor absolved him from excommunication and administered the Eucharist. After Felipe died, the inquisitors voted to present his effigy, with secular clothing, at an *auto de fe*, but also to give him a Catholic burial. Were they religiously intolerant? Absolutely. Yet they nonetheless operated on the principle that their actions had to balance Felipe's theological errors against his spiritual repentance.[35]

The methods and aims of Spanish inquisitors are difficult to stomach in a modern environment that prizes religious acceptance, noncoercion, and private spiritual beliefs that are not subject to communal evaluation. And yet historical investigations of this notorious institution not only illuminate alterity – meaning, the gap between our values and ones in the past – but also rescue victims from oblivion. The Spanish Inquisition was a controversial institution throughout its existence. Examining opposition to it, as well as its officials' priorities, processes, and literal physical settings, restores nuance to what all too often are impressions drenched in mythology.

Notes

1. On the Kingdom of Aragon and Roman law after 1137, see Marie A. Kelleher, *The Measure of Woman: Law and Female Identity in the Crown of Aragon* (University of Pennsylvania Press, 2010), chapter 1.
2. See, for example, Galatians 1:8–9 and Romans 16:17–18.
3. Christians were not alone in worrying about the orthodoxy of religious belief: Christina Caldwell Ames, *Medieval Heresies: Christianity, Judaism, and Islam* (Cambridge University Press, 2015).
4. James B. Given, *Inquisition and Medieval Society: Power, Discipline, Resistance in Languedoc* (Cornell University Press, 2001), 194.
5. Given, *Inquisition and Medieval Society*, 68.
6. Given, *Inquisition and Medieval Society*, 54.
7. Christina Caldwell Ames, "Does Inquisition Belong to Religious History?" *The American Historical Review* 110 (2005): 20.
8. Ames, "Does Inquisition Belong," 18. Given, *Inquisition and Medieval Society*, 78, disagrees with the weight I give here to pastoral care.
9. Given, *Inquisition and Medieval Society*, 73–5.
10. Given, *Inquisition and Medieval Society*, 68–71.
11. Given, *Inquisition and Medieval Society*, 75–8.
12. Given, *Inquisition and Medieval Society*, 108.
13. Given, *Inquisition and Medieval Society*, 35–9.
14. Lu Ann Homza, ed. and trans., *The Spanish Inquisition, 1478–1614: An Anthology of Sources* (Hackett, 2006), xvi, n19.
15. Ramón Rodríguez Besné, *El Consejo de la Suprema Inquisición: Perfíl jurídico de una institución* (Editorial Complutense, 2000), 173–82.
16. The Suprema was especially involved in conflicts over legal jurisdictions: Rodríguez Besné, *El Consejo*, 187–205.
17. Homza, *The Spanish Inquisition*, 23–4, 151–2.
18. For a two-time escapee who ultimately was burned at the stake, see Angela Selke, "Vida y muerte de Juan López Celain, alumbrado vizcaíno," *Bulletin Hispanique* 62 (1960): 136–62.

19. Homza, *The Spanish Inquisition*, document 4.
20. Homza, *The Spanish Inquisition*, document 5.
21. Lu Ann Homza, *Religious Authority in the Spanish Renaissance* (The Johns Hopkins University Press, 2000), chapter 1.
22. Homza, "How to Harass an Inquisitor-General: The Polyphonic Law of Friar Francisco Ortiz," in John A. Marino and Thomas Kuehn, eds., *A Renaissance of Conflicts: Visions and Revisions of Law and Society in Italy and Spain*, 297–334 (University of Toronto Press, 2004); Homza, *Religious Authority*, 21, 32–3.
23. Homza, *Religious Authority*, 40; Lu Ann Homza, "Webs of Conversation and Discernment: Searching for Spiritual Accompaniment in Sixteenth-Century Spain," *The Catholic Historical Review* 106 (2020): 245–6.
24. Stefania Pastore, *Il vangelo e la spada: L'inquisizione di Castiglia e i suoi critici (1460–1598)* (Storia e Letteratura, 2003).
25. Lu Ann Homza, *Village Infernos and Witches' Advocates: Witch Hunting in Navarre, 1608–1614* (Pennsylvania State University Press, 2022), 40–1.
26. José Martínez Millán, *La hacienda de la Inquisición (1478–1700)* (CSIC, 1984), 59–73. Penitential fines were a different category from the confiscation of goods.
27. Homza, *The Spanish Inquisition*, document 23.
28. Homza, *Village Infernos*, chapter 5.
29. John Martin, *Venice's Hidden Enemies: Italian Heretics in a Renaissance City* (University of California Press, 1993); Mercedes García-Arenal and Gerard Wiegers, *A Man of Three Worlds: Samuel Pallache, a Moroccan Jew in Catholic and Protestant Europe* (The Johns Hopkins University Press, 2007).
30. Diarmaid MacCulloch, *The Reformation: A History* (Penguin Books, 2005), 392.
31. The examples in this paragraph come from a summary of cases heard by inquisitors in Logroño in the early seventeenth century. Madrid, Archivo Histórico Nacional [AHN], Sección de la Inquisición [Inqu.], Legajo [Leg.] 1679, Exp. 2.1, images 522–3.
32. Madrid, Archivo Histórico Nacional, Sección de la Inquisición, Legajo 1679, Exp. 2.1, images 522–3.
33. Madrid, AHN, Inqu., Leg. 1679, Exp. 2.1, image 523.
34. Madrid, AHN, Inqu., Leg. 1679, Exp. 2.1, image 524.
35. Jean-Pierre Dedieu and Gunnar W. Knutsen, "The Trial of Faith in the Spanish Inquisition: Between Law and Repentance," *Annales: Histoire, Sciences Sociales*. Published online 2023:1–26. doi:10.1017/ahsse.2022.27

Suggestions for Further Reading

Ames, Christina Caldwell. "Does Inquisition Belong to Religious History?" *The American Historical Review* 110 (2005): 11–37.

Medieval Heresies: Christianity, Judaism, and Islam. Cambridge University Press, 2015.

Dedieu, Jean-Pierre, and Gunnar W. Knutsen. "The Trial of Faith in the Spanish Inquisition: Between Law and Repentance." *Annales: Histoire, Sciences Sociales* (2023): 1–26. doi.org/10.1017/ahsse.2022.27.

Given, James B. *Inquisition and Medieval Society: Power, Discipline, Resistance in Languedoc.* Cornell University Press, 2001.

Homza, Lu Ann, ed. and trans. *The Spanish Inquisition, 1478–1614: An Anthology of Sources.* Hackett, 2006.

Village Infernos and Witches' Advocates: Witch Hunting in Navarre, 1608–1614. Pennsylvania State University Press, 2022.

MacCulloch, Diarmaid. *The Reformation: A History.* Penguin Books, 2005.

Martin, John. *Venice's Hidden Enemies: Italian Heretics in a Renaissance City.* University of California Press, 1993.

Martínez Millán, José. *La hacienda de la Inquisición (1478–1700).* CSIC, 1984.

Pastore, Stefania. *Il vangelo e la spada: L'inquisizione di Castiglia e i suoi critici (1460–1598).* Storia e Letteratura, 2003.

Bibliography

Ames, Christina Caldwell. "Does Inquisition Belong to Religious History?" *The American Historical Review* 110 (2005): 11–37.

Medieval Heresies: Christianity, Judaism, and Islam. Cambridge University Press, 2015.

Dedieu, Jean-Pierre, and Gunnar W. Knutsen. "The Trial of Faith in the Spanish Inquisition: Between Law and Repentance." *Annales: Histoire, Sciences Sociales* (2023): 1–26. doi.org/10.1017/ahsse.2022.27.

García-Arenal, Mercedes, and Gerard Wiegers. *A Man of Three Worlds: Samuel Pallache, a Moroccan Jew in Catholic and Protestant Europe.* The Johns Hopkins University Press, 2007.

Given, James B. *Inquisition and Medieval Society: Power, Discipline, Resistance in Languedoc.* Cornell University Press, 2001.

Homza, Lu Ann. *Religious Authority in the Spanish Renaissance.* The Johns Hopkins University Press, 2000.

The Spanish Inquisition, 1478–1614: An Anthology of Sources. Hackett, 2006.

"Webs of Conversation and Discernment: Searching for Spiritual Accompaniment in Sixteenth-Century Spain." *The Catholic Historical Review* 106 (2020): 245–6.

Village Infernos and Witches' Advocates: Witch Hunting in Navarre, 1608–1614. Pennsylvania State University Press, 2022.

Kelleher, Marie A. *The Measure of Woman: Law and Female Identity in the Crown of Aragon.* University of Pennsylvania Press, 2010.

MacCulloch, Diarmaid. *The Reformation: A History*. Penguin Books, 2005.
Martin, John. *Venice's Hidden Enemies: Italian Heretics in a Renaissance City*. University of California Press, 1993.
Martínez Millán, José. *La hacienda de la Inquisición (1478–1700)*. CSIC, 1984.
Pastore, Stefania. *Il vangelo e la spada: L'inquisizione di Castiglia e i suoi critici (1460–1598)*. Storia e Letteratura, 2003.
Rodríguez Besné, José Ramón. *El Consejo de la Suprema Inquisición: Perfíl jurídico de una institución*. Editorial Complutense, 2000.
Selke, Angela. "Vida y muerte de Juan López Celain, alumbrado vizcaíno." *Bulletin Hispanique* 62 (1960): 136–62.

KIMBERLY LYNN

2

Inquisitorial Careers

I begin with three sketches. In 1597, an eight-month-long visitation of Córdoba's inquisition tribunal – conducted, as was typical, by an inquisitor from another tribunal (in this case, Valladolid's) – yielded serious questions about the conduct and character of the inquisitor Licentiate Alonso Jiménez de Reinoso. The visitor collected testimonies that he lived a dissolute life, unbecoming to his office, that he abused his judicial authority, and that he had as his servants conversos and Moriscos who had relatives currently undergoing trial, held in the Inquisition's jails. Concerns about him also centered on a reputed sexual relationship with a woman who lived "in the company of some *moriscas*," and with whose family he had first become acquainted in Granada many years before. This particular visitation has attracted scholarly attention in recent years because the famous poet Luis de Góngora was one of those who provided testimony against the inquisitor, written in the poet's own hand.

The charges were taken seriously and, in 1598, the inquisitor-general suspended Inquisitor Reinoso for two years. Yet the judge also seems to have been protected by his brother, Hernando Arenillas de Reinoso, who was then the secretary of the Suprema. The secretary had entered the service of the Suprema in 1566 as a reporter (*relator*), becoming a prosecutor (*fiscal*) of the council in 1578.[1] Inquisitor Reinoso was able to gain a new post in Valladolid's court – effectively a promotion – where he arrived as the fourth inquisitor in 1600. A study of that tribunal describes him as doctor rather than licentiate and as a native of the region of Palencia, noting that his purity of blood investigation had been conducted in 1572. And it supplies a career trajectory that moved from an appointment as *fiscal* in Granada's court to becoming an inquisitor in Valencia in 1580, and from there to Córdoba. Once Inquisitor Reinoso was installed in Valladolid at the turn of the century, the other three inquisitors complained of "the perpetual disagreement between him and us."[2] There were conflicts over his lodging, over the animosity caused by his outranking one of the existing judges, and over reputedly speaking improperly about another inquisitor; suspicions were raised over his handling of secret papers and the inquisitorial archive. The other Valladolid officials fired off complaints about him to the Suprema, and he was almost sent back to Córdoba in 1603. But the transfer never came to fruition and instead he died in Valladolid in 1607, succumbing to an illness that sickened many of the tribunal's officials.[3]

Trying to pursue Inquisitor Reinoso further through the available secondary literature produces intriguing leads and unresolved puzzles. A study of the Cuenca inquisitorial court's personnel indicates that there were two inquisitors Reinoso in the later sixteenth century: It records Alvaro de Reinoso's tenure there as 1569–76, after which time he transferred to the Toledo tribunal; Alonso Jiménez de Reinoso is recorded in Cuenca from 1582 to 1589, and noted as transferring to Córdoba in 1590.[4] Both these figures (who might also have been relatives) were likely associated with investigations of Moriscos and *alumbrados*. For approximately two weeks in the Fall of 1569, during a visitation of Cuenca's district, notary Pablo García and an Inquisitor Licentiate Reinoso stopped in the small town of Deza, on the Castilian-Aragonese border. This was a different kind of inquisitorial visitation, not an inspection of the inquisition tribunal but instead a tribunal's inspection of more remote areas of its district for unreported heresy. They focused their attention on the denunciations of the town's Moriscos, setting in motion events that would unravel that local community. "Beginning in late 1569, about forty-five of Deza's Moriscos were transported to Cuenca for trial."[5] Three would be given capital sentences, one would die in prison, and another six men would die during their sentenced galley service; their confessions would spur further examination of the town's remaining Moriscos. In the early 1580s, when Alonso Jiménez de Reinoso was there, Valencia conducted multiple visitations of its district and became increasingly preoccupied with prosecuting Moriscos and with reported Morisco conspiracies.[6] "It was in 1581, as dozens of Teruel's Moriscos were being brought to trial, that Valencia's Inquisitor Alonso de Reinoso first suggested the idea of expulsion in a letter to the Suprema."[7] In another set of leads, recent work on the circulation of ideas about *alumbradismo* and pursuit of suspected *alumbrado* heretics has found an inquisitor named Reinoso of Toledo forwarding *alumbrado* trials to the Suprema in 1577, and that the two Cuenca inquisitors Reinoso were both sent as additional judges to the tribunal in Córdoba when that court discovered what it believed was a surge of *alumbrado* heretical activity, one in 1575–6 (reporting that he found no *alumbrado* activity), and the other in 1590–2.[8]

I offer now a second sketch. Pedro Sáenz de Mañozca served as the secretary of the Spanish Inquisition's tribunal in New Spain, which was headquartered in Mexico City, for more than twenty years, from 1594 until his death there in 1618. His signature is evident in reams of inquisitorial documentation. He was the official, for example, who soon after his arrival in Mexico would record almost every proceeding in the well-known second trial of Luis de Carvajal the Younger, who was prosecuted for "judaizing," and who was a visionary and prolific writer whom the tribunal sentenced to death for crypto-Judaism, as a relapsed heretic, in December 1596. A native of the Basque Country, Sáenz de Mañozca had spent almost twenty years as a lower-level official in the employ of the Suprema's secretary before crossing the Atlantic in 1594. And Sáenz de Mañozca was at the heart of what would become an inquisitorial dynasty. Various family members' tenure as different kinds of inquisition officials lasted for at least 100 years, mainly in the Americas, but with transatlantic and transpacific dimensions to this network, too. In 1600, he married a young woman whose father was a familiar of the Inquisition in Mexico City. He patronized the career of his sister's son – Juan de Mañozca y Zamora – who would ultimately become an inquisitor in Cartagena de Indias and then in Lima, a councilor of the Suprema, a visitor of the Inquisition tribunal in Mexico, and even the archbishop of Mexico. In 1635, Pedro Sáenz de Mañozca's son Juan Sáenz de Mañozca, too, would start to work for the inquisition, first as an attorney for the Lima tribunal (*abogado del fisco y presos*), which was still writing to the Suprema in praise of the deceased secretary's career as late as 1637. His son would continue his career ascent, in 1640 becoming *fiscal* of New Spain's tribunal and then inquisitor there in short order, remaining in that court until he was made a bishop in 1661. His daughter would marry the constable of the tribunal's jail in Mexico City (*alguacil mayor*), and her sons would be made familiars in the 1640s. Other likely relatives were even appointed familiars in Manila, also in the jurisdiction of New Spain's Inquisition tribunal.[9]

I offer, finally, a third inquisitorial career to consider. Doctor Don Juan Gutiérrez Flores moved from one set of peripheral inquisitorial tribunals to another, from Mediterranean islands to two tribunals in the Americas. Born in Toledo around 1567 to a family associated with the cathedral's administration, the illegitimate son of a cleric, his inquisitorial career seems to have started in Sicily, where he was made a *fiscal* or prosecutor in the Palermo tribunal in 1600. He quickly became embroiled in that tribunal's ongoing jurisdictional battles with the Spanish viceroy in Sicily and returned to the royal court in 1602 to argue the inquisitorial court's case there. His promotion to inquisitor took him next to Mallorca in 1605, where he was again swept up in jurisdictional conflicts with that island's viceroy. In that battle, the viceroy accused the new inquisitor of immorality, including a sexual liaison with a young woman in the city. Gutiérrez Flores sought a way out, requesting a transfer back to Sicily or to Valencia, eventually gaining one to Galicia, but instead acquiring new orders before arriving there and setting out as inquisitor for New Spain in 1613.[10] There are a few traces of him scattered in studies of the Inquisition in each of his postings: In 1614 in the town of Atenango, he ordered the investigation of a cleric, Hernando Ruiz de Alarcón, who was reported to be mimicking inquisitorial procedure and staging his own *autos de fe* to police the faith of the local Indigenous population. Working through a *comisario*, the inquisitors in Mexico City resisted the cleric's encroachment on their authority, yet they also continued to receive information from him about potential heresy in his community for the subsequent decade (and the cleric would go on to publish a 1629 treatise on Nahua ritual as part of a campaign to suppress it).[11] In Mexico, Gutiérrez Flores also intersected with the Mañozca family, if he had not done so already. Those ties would become even closer with his final posts, when he was ordered to Lima on two different inspections in 1623, and ultimately entered that tribunal as inquisitor in 1625. In Lima, Gutiérrez Flores joined Juan de Mañozca in a conflict with Lima's other inquisitor, Andrés Juan Gaitán, and the tribunal's staff filed letters back to the Suprema in Madrid with complaints about Gaitán's mismanagement of the tribunal, insufficient activity, and financial irregularities. Gutiérrez Flores died in Lima in 1631, reportedly with significant debts, and was buried in the tribunal's chapel, dedicated to San Pedro Mártir, patron saint of inquisitorial officials.[12]

The official functions, lived experiences, and career trajectories of the Spanish Inquisition's personnel were both widely varied and shared some common features. Through the multiple centuries of the Spanish Inquisition's existence, there were many thousands of early modern men who held some kind of inquisitorial office. For some, it was a stepping-stone or a brief professional transit, while for others the institution provided a lifetime of employment and a vast social network. I have included the three profiles above – all drawn from the peak decades of the Spanish Inquisition's institutional expansion – to hint at some typical features of inquisitorial careers, as well as some of the methodological issues inherent in studying such careers.

Many of those who worked for the Spanish Inquisition were embedded in family networks that included multiple inquisitorial officials, and often those with other royal or ecclesiastical appointments. Yet the length of time in a particular inquisitorial office could vary widely. Sometimes officials moved quickly between different positions and different tribunals. And some careers, as the examples above suggest, were hypermobile, moving around the Iberian peninsula and far beyond. But others were much more sedentary. Secretary Sáenz de Mañozca, for example, had essentially two twenty-year chapters of his career, one at the Suprema in Madrid, one in the tribunal in Mexico City. Officials were often closely tied both to the places where the tribunals sat and to far-flung networks of family, patronage, and clientage. And, as in these examples, their career trajectories could overlap with one another, as experience circulated through the twenty-one tribunals and the royal council. And while the vast majority of Spanish inquisitors – as well as the commissioners (*comisarios*) they deputized in remote regions or the censors and consultants they relied on to evaluate theological claims – were clerics, and thus meant to be celibate, most of the other officials (including the familiars) were lay people, many of whom married and had children while they worked for the Inquisition.

Inquisitorial tribunals were also, not infrequently, contentious institutions. Inquisitors and other officials, whether inside or outside of their institution, disagreed and came into conflict with one another about the trials of faith they conducted. They also clashed over status, hierarchy, privileges, funds, buildings, jurisdiction, and fitness for office. And those conflicts were often unresolved, as even sanctioned inquisitors such as Jiménez de Reinoso might be reinstated, transferred to another office, or even promoted; similarly, even competing inquisitorial opinions sent to the Suprema for resolution might leave a set of trials or a court operating in considerable ambiguity for long periods of time. I have included the career sketches above to give some sense of the peril and possibility of studying inquisitorial careers. It remains challenging to establish all the inquisitorial personnel involved in a particular trial or enumerate all those who coincided in a tribunal at a particular moment. Recent scholarship has repeatedly demonstrated that it mattered to the conduct of trials who the particular inquisitorial personnel were. The Inquisition's officials had real power to affect who was investigated and when, which crimes and accused criminals were pursued, and which were not. Yet even with the prolific archives the Spanish Inquisition created, it is very challenging to discern the actions of individual officials, and even more fraught to venture interpretations of their reasoning or motivations. While we can see a secretary's signature or identify their handwriting, for example, it is rare to know how they might have shaped a particular case, or to guess what they might have taken from the experience of one case to their subsequent work. Inquisitors' judgements, too, were generally recorded collectively, with rare traces of their individual opinions or their disagreements with one another. We can often summon the names of personnel, but their significance can remain opaque. The sources that give us glimpses of the officials as individuals, moreover, have their own challenges. They were often generated in moments of intense conflict or during inspections of the tribunals, and thus must be evaluated in that light.

Tribunal Personnel

By the middle of the seventeenth century, there were twenty-one regional tribunals of the Spanish Inquisition. The number and placement of the tribunals varied to some extent across the institution's history; the amount of territory each jurisdiction covered varied widely. Each tribunal had, at a minimum, twenty salaried officials who staffed it. And each tribunal had at least a few dozen more additional associates, some who were not inquisitorial personnel but who were appointed to fulfill a specific duty, and many who were inquisitorial officials but were located not in the city where the tribunal sat, but in other places throughout its district. The Inquisition was hierarchically organized, and inquisitorial correspondence offers extensive evidence of how inquisitorial personnel attended carefully to markers of hierarchy and authority. At the top of each tribunal were the inquisitors, the judges who were also the chief administrators of the district courts as institutions. From the start, there were meant to be at least two inquisitors, and by the turn of the seventeenth century, three was the aim, with tribunals sometimes having as many as four or as few as one (or even a total vacancy), depending on conditions.

Another group of inquisitorial officials had to do, primarily, with the conduct of trials. There was a *fiscal*, the tribunal's prosecutor, and a secretary. There were notaries, who recorded testimonies. The notaries generally were divided into those responsible for "the secret" work of the Inquisition (writing the carefully preserved records of the trials of faith, district visitations, and the like), and those who generated records related to goods confiscated from those tried. There could be other attorneys (*abogados*) attached to the tribunal, too, including those assigned to defense, and other secretaries, scribes, reporters, or similar officials, as well. There were regional reasons for variations in personnel; for example, the court in Sicily constantly complained about a lack of qualified secretaries, aiming to have a minimum of four, in significant part because they dealt with correspondence from the Roman Inquisition in the Italian peninsula, which, unlike the Spanish Inquisition, kept its records in Latin.[13] In addition to these appointed officials, other consultants were called in, generally on a short-term basis. Inquisitors sometimes consulted on their trials and the testimonies received in them with a representative of the bishop (*ordinario*) or with others trained in law or theology on more complex issues, either before they decided to initiate a trial or during the proceedings (*consultador, calificador*). Similarly, the Inquisition deputized theologians (often members of the regular clergy) as censors for the work of book censorship. In Mexico, there was a stable cohort of censors (*calificadores*) appointed by the tribunal, and one recent study has uncovered traces of 151 censors nominated between 1571 and 1640; of those, only nine or ten were secular clerics, while all the rest were drawn from the regular clergy, including Franciscans, Dominicans, Augustinians, Jesuits, and Mercedarians.[14]

If one cadre of officials had more to do with the paperwork of the Inquisition and the substance of conducting trials of faith, another was concerned more with the operations of the tribunal. At least one of the inquisitors typically lived in the tribunal building, and the archives were also housed there. There was a receiver (*receptor*) in charge of the finances, and sometimes additional officials dedicated to that work and the confiscation of goods, including a secretary and an accountant (*contador*), and other notaries and attorneys. Crucial to these courts as physical spaces was also the administration of the tribunal jails, so there were personnel primarily concerned with the imprisonment of those undergoing trial – a warden (*alcalde*) and a quartermaster (*despensero*), as well as a nuncio and a constable (*alguacil*) and porters, in addition to various other servants, including, sometimes, a medical doctor (*médico*). This general division in the tribunal's work was mirrored in more remote regions, too. The Inquisition appointed commissioners (*comisarios*), generally clerics, who were deputized to operate in matters of faith (for example, in taking witness testimonies and forwarding them to the tribunal). And they also appointed familiars throughout their districts, laymen who served the Inquisition, who could carry arms and undertake such charges as delivering a prisoner, accused of heresy, from somewhere in the district to the tribunal's jails.[15]

Above the twenty-one district courts was a royal council, the Suprema, and a royal councilor at the head of the institution: the inquisitor-general. The Suprema was effectively an appellate court, with similar staffing: "In each of the years between 1555 and 1565, annual salaries were listed for the inquisitor-general, between four and seven councilors, two to three secretaries of varying degrees of importance, a *fiscal*, a reporter (*relator*) who prepared information for the council, a constable (*alguacil mayor*), a medical doctor, a nuncio, two porters, and an official who was both the receiver and accountant."[16] The inquisitor-general usually controlled the patronage of inquisitorial appointments to the district tribunals; decisions about who would be inquisitor or *fiscal* as well as assignments of visitors of Inquisition tribunals were made at the royal court. Lesser officials and familiars, on the other hand, were generally identified, investigated, and recommended by the local tribunals, who then usually secured the Suprema's license for their choice. There was significant potential for patronage to shape the character of a particular inquisition tribunal. For example, one of the two inquisitors general who was a native of Galicia, Friar Antonio de Sotomayor (1632–45), placed fourteen associates in inquisitorial office in that region's tribunal.[17]

The most expansive view of people connected to the Spanish Inquisition would also take into account the households of inquisitorial officials. And the institution itself considered them to also be in need of vetting and protection. In 1599, before the tribunal secretary Pedro Sáenz de Mañozca married Doña Catalina Murillo, the tribunal also investigated her purity of blood. Inquisitors and other tribunal staff had households not just made up of family members – as early modern officials often brought nephews, for example, along as clients – but also servants and even slaves. Juan de Mañozca included retainers on his requests for licenses to cross the Atlantic.[18] While not themselves inquisitorial officials, these people, too, are significant for how we think about the place of inquisition tribunals in the early modern social fabric. All these human connections and dynamics were, moreover, sometimes quite important for the ways that trials of faith unfolded. While the Inquisition, in theory, kept its proceedings secret and those in its jails isolated, the many different people involved in inquisitorial administration sometimes became conduits for information among jails, courtrooms, and the cities beyond their walls. The Inquisition's archives also leave traces of many instances – and scandals – of messages smuggled in and out of the jails, as well as the manipulation of those on trial by inquisitorial personnel, working with informants or intercepting attempts of the imprisoned to communicate with the world beyond the tribunal walls. For example, the Toledo trial of the Morisco Jerónimo de Rojas, which ended with his execution in 1603, "suffered a strong impact not only from the inquisitors themselves but from the prison warden, Gaspar de Soria, aged sixty, and to a lesser extent from Blas Criado, aged sixty-four, who was Soria's assistant warden and a familiar of the Inquisition."[19]

There are multiple ways to understand the appeal of inquisitorial office in the early modern Hispanic world. Inquisition posts, whether salaried, formally appointed positions or ad hoc, short-term commissions, were potential sources of income and ways of establishing attachment to the royal administration, throughout the monarchy's territories. They were one potential avenue of social mobility and professional advancement, particularly for the growing class of men who earned university degrees in the sixteenth and seventeenth centuries. Inquisitorial officials and familiars also had access to a separate jurisdiction. Any civil or criminal case of theirs belonged first to inquisitorial jurisdiction, rather than to any other royal or ecclesiastical court. These cases – quite different from trials of faith – are a little-studied aspect of the legal history of inquisitions, and potentially a powerful inducement to hold inquisitorial office in the early modern era. In theory, as for clerics, this jurisdictional separation was intended to protect inquisition officials from reprisals by the families or other associates of those tried for heresy. In practice, it had a wide variety of effects. There were regular skirmishes with other courts over jurisdiction, as, for example, when royal courts sometimes sought to try familiars with murder and the inquisition tribunals instead exerted their claim to jurisdiction over their personnel, insisting that they were the appropriate court in which the trial should occur.[20]

With increasing regularity by the last third of the sixteenth century, the Spanish Inquisition investigated the purity of blood (*limpieza de sangre*) of all potential inquisitorial officials and familiars. To do so, tribunals conducted inquiries in the native towns of candidates and corresponded with one another about family histories. There were also exceptions to typical practices – as, for instance, when the inquisition tribunal in Sicily protested that it was too difficult, in its particular circumstances, to hold to the same standards for investigating the backgrounds of familiars as in the Iberian peninsula.[21] The potential spouses of inquisitorial officials were also often investigated. Thus, status as a familiar or tribunal official became one route to demonstrating purity of blood and building social capital, with implications for an entire family network. This inducement to inquisitorial office was further augmented by other institutional practices. Inquisitorial officials established and belonged to a confraternity dedicated to San Pedro Mártir, a murdered thirteenth-century Dominican inquisitor-saint, to whom tribunals had dedicated chapels, and whose standard was often carried in processions of *autos de fe*. And the *auto de fe* was also a forum for the creation of social capital for inquisitorial personnel. For example, the announcement of the upcoming 1639 *auto de fe* in Lima, Peru, involved a procession with familiars on horseback, followed by at least seven officials of the tribunal (nuncio, an attorney responsible for the tribunal's fiscal affairs, notary of the sequestrations, accountant, secretary, general receiver, and chief constable), to the accompaniment of trumpets and drums. The day of the *auto de fe*, a wide array of inquisitorial personnel joined the other elites of the viceregal capital in procession. Their presence there articulated their authority to all those in attendance, and that affiliation to the Inquisition was further extended in printed accounts of this *auto de fe* that included the names and offices of local authorities, a genre of pamphlet that itself became increasingly common in the seventeenth century.[22]

The Inquisitors

Inquisitors were both the tribunal's judges and its chief administrators. At least the most senior inquisitor, and sometimes more, resided in the tribunal building itself. They conducted audiences related to their judicial work in both morning and afternoon. Their work in trials of faith involved questioning the accused or witnesses, listening to the charges of the *fiscal*, consulting with one another or with other authorities, preparing or receiving correspondence, or reviewing materials from the tribunal archives, among other frequent duties. With greatest frequency in the second half of the sixteenth century, they also went periodically on visitations to inspect the districts of their tribunals, tours that often lasted a few months, spreading the Inquisition's definitions of heresy, collecting testimonies and confessions, and absolving some people on the spot. And they were also occasionally deputized to engage in another kind of visitation, sent out to other tribunals to inspect those courts' conduct of trials of faith, their officials, finances, and jails. Inquisitors were among the highest royal and religious authorities in their cities, a status regularly announced to the community on ceremonial occasions, including the tribunals' *autos de fe*.[23]

The number and activity of inquisitors in a tribunal could vary widely. While the number of inquisitors per tribunal reached as high as four in the later sixteenth and seventeenth centuries, tribunals could also be short staffed or without an acting inquisitor for significant periods of time as a result of illness, death, transfer, and delays in travel. Both the available data and the number of inquisitors appointed to different tribunals range widely. Scholars have counted 134 inquisitors appointed to Valencia's court from 1481 to 1818; sixty-one to Toledo's from 1483 to 1620; 73 to Sicily's from 1487 to 1712; with 16 in Mexico from its establishment in 1571 to 1642, and only nine in Lima from 1569 to 1627.[24] An overview of the Cuenca tribunal's key officials between 1489 and 1714 enumerated 107 inquisitors of the tribunal in that period. A large proportion of the judges appear to have spent only a few years in Cuenca; that survey identifies only twelve inquisitors who spent at least a decade as inquisitor in the tribunal. A study of Valladolid's inquisitors in the reign of Philip III (1598–1621) found eleven judges in the court during that time, two of whom served for fifteen years, two more for twelve years, while the others served for ten, seven, five, and four years, with the remainder transiting through the position briefly.[25] Of the fifty inquisitors appointed to the tribunal in Galicia from 1561 to 1700, only seven spent a decade or more in the tribunal, and several served only a few months. The two longest-serving, at twenty-eight and seventeen years, respectively, were natives of Galicia; only one inquisitor without ties to the region would serve anywhere near that long, occupying his post for fifteen years.[26] At the same time, the length of encounters with the Inquisition varied widely. Some self-denunciations and absolutions occurred in one day in the midst of an inquisitor's district visitation; it was also not uncommon for the accused to spend years on trial, held in the inquisitorial jails. Thus, the workings of the Spanish Inquisition were shaped profoundly by variable human dynamics. Inquisitors sometimes sat in the same tribunal for many years, but this was often not the case. The particular relationships between and differences in seniority of members of the panel of judges, and the local or institutional memory of each, could range widely from case to case, or even across different phases of the same trial.

By the early sixteenth century, Spanish inquisitors were almost entirely secular clerics who held a licentiate or a doctoral degree in law. While there had been fifteenth-century guidelines elevating the pairing of a jurist and a theologian, and while the majority of inquisitors in the early decades were Dominican friars, this changed quickly. The architects and theorists of the Spanish Inquisition were well aware that such judicial work left a wide space for the exercise of the judge's discretion and discernment, hence their idea that those appointed inquisitors should be educated and not too young (generally aged over forty), men of "knowledge and conscience."[27] While not exclusively the case, the bulk of inquisitors were also Castilians, and most often from the gentry or lower nobility; purity of blood investigations of candidates for inquisitorial office were only regularly conducted starting in the 1570s.

Typically, inquisitors had held multiple previous positions in universities, cathedrals, inquisitorial tribunals or civil law courts; the inquisition post of *fiscal* was sometimes a stepping-stone to inquisitor. And they were embedded in networks of patronage and clientage that often began with their families, with relatives who held inquisitorial, ecclesiastical, and royal offices. It was also most common for inquisitors to serve in multiple different tribunals, as the examples at the start of this chapter indicated. For the inquisitors in Valladolid in the first two decades of the seventeenth century, their arrival there was effectively a promotion, as they arrived most frequently from the less prominent tribunals of Córdoba and Murcia, as well as from Logroño, Zaragoza, and Valencia.[28] In theory, inquisitors were not meant to have strong ties to the region where they served, while in practice this, too, varied. Eighteen of the fifty inquisitors in Galicia in the sixteenth and seventeenth centuries, including the two longest-serving, were natives of the region.[29] Families such as the Mañozca clan preserved extended networks of clientage and patronage in both their native Basque country and then in Mexico City, where they married into other family networks tied to the Inquisition.

To become an inquisitor in any tribunal was to occupy an elite judicial post. Yet this, too, was sometimes an intermediary step in an upwardly mobile career trajectory. Inquisitors could parlay their position into appointments as bishops or into posts on royal councils, especially a place on the Suprema. They were university graduates and part of lettered networks, and sometimes distinguished also for their learning. The noted Sevillian humanist Diego López de Cortegana (1455–1524) described himself as an affiliate of the Inquisition for thirty years, from scribe in Seville in the early years of the Inquisition to an agent of it in Rome in the 1490s, and eventually to the post of inquisitor, his career moving between the royal court, Seville, Córdoba, and Rome; his other primary support and affiliation was with Seville's cathedral chapter.[30] Some of the principal theorists of inquisitorial law were also inquisitors. The seventeenth-century inquisitor of Valencia, Aragón, and Sicily, Diego García de Trasmiera, who would become a councilor of the Suprema, published legal commentaries (including on inquisitorial law) and two hagiographies, of Neapolitan nun Ursula Benincasa and of Pedro Arbués, an inquisitor murdered in Zaragoza in 1485.[31] Inquisitors participated in elaborating a mythology of their office, seeking to buttress its authority in local contexts and more broadly in print. They created genealogies of their work that stretched back to biblical figures and to the Greco-Roman world. And they, and other officials, sometimes staged and engaged various kinds of publicity around their judicial work, from commissioning pamphlets or selecting preachers for *autos de fe*.[32] Inquisitors were patrons of the arts, as well, commissioning paintings and architecture.

The councilors of the Suprema and Inquisitors General – royal councilors, the institution's chief administrators, and its appellate court – shared many commonalities with tribunal inquisitors, although they were predictably from more elite backgrounds, with a higher representation of the elite nobility. Between 1488 and 1819, 376 men were nominated to the Suprema, while there were forty-six Inquisitors General from 1483 to 1818. By the middle of the sixteenth century, the majority of the councilors of the Suprema had prior experience in inquisitorial office (roughly two-thirds of the nominees from the mid-sixteenth to the mid-seventeenth century), while most of the Inquisitors General had first been members of the Suprema, although they were generally of higher social rank than tribunal inquisitors, and had rarely served first in that office.[33]

Inquisitors brought these complex backgrounds and range of experience to their judicial work. They were products of their social origins, training, and prior experience, and their careers were organized in such a way that there was an ongoing circulation of experience, conversation, and communication in and between the Spanish Inquisition's many district courts and the Suprema. The particular judges in a tribunal could have a considerable effect on the tribunal's activities. Some inquisitors took what could be described as a more pastoral approach.[34] Others were fairly inactive, for a variety of reasons. And sometimes particular spikes in tribunal activity can be traced to the initiatives of a single inquisitor or group in a tribunal at a particular time. Inquisitors General also often set a particular tone or direction in their appointments of inquisitorial personnel, and changes at the top of the institution could have ripple effects throughout. The peak of activity in the tribunal in New Spain around the turn of the seventeenth century has been traced in large part to the inquisitor don Alonso de Peralta y Robles, a Creole born in Peru who first entered the Inquisition's orbit in service of the Suprema, before gaining the post of inquisitor, his career intersecting with that of the secretary Pedro Sáenz de Mañozca on both sides of the Atlantic. Peralta also became remarkably wealthy during his time in Mexico City, capitalizing on the powers of his office, while also seeking to bolster the institution's authority and activity.[35] Scholars have shown some of the influences on inquisitorial decisions and charted moments when they decided to act or, equally significantly, not to act, upon suspicions about *alumbrado* heresies.[36] Some inquisitors doggedly pursued particular kinds of perceived crimes, communities, or networks. The Cuenca inquisitor Pedro Cortés dramatically increased that tribunal's activity during his twenty-year tenure, from his arrival in 1535 to his death in 1555. Even more strikingly, he focused the tribunal's attention on conversos of the bishopric of Sigüenza, in a violent episode of persecution that ultimately resulted in an astonishing 572 trials of that population during his time in office.[37]

Other Tribunal Personnel

The prosecutor (*fiscal*) typically had a similar social and educational profile to the inquisitors, and, depending on the tribunal staffing, inquisitors sometimes shifted to performing the duties of the prosecutor, or vice versa. These officials were second only to the inquisitors in terms of their authority, prestige, and duties within the court. In the tribunal in New Spain, the prosecutors typically served quite briefly (a few years), and the post of *fiscal* was not infrequently vacant, making it necessary for one of the inquisitors to act as prosecutor instead of judge.[38] In Cuenca, from 1489 to 1714, the tenure in office was similarly short, as only five of the forty-four prosecutors served in that office for a decade or longer. Several of these officials also worked simultaneously as inquisitor and prosecutor, and in a few instances, the most senior secretary was even appointed to serve as *fiscal*. Some men moved from one tribunal to another in the post of *fiscal*, which was also a stepping-stone to appointment as an inquisitor. Nearly half of Cuenca's prosecutors became inquisitors, promoed seemingly with increasing frequency throughout the seventeenth century. Sixteen were promoted in the same tribunal, while one rose to the rank of inquisitor in Granada, one in Llerena, and two in Murcia.[39]

From the middle of the sixteenth century, the Spanish Inquisition deliberately sought to extend and regularize its local networks of officials, made up principally by *comisarios* and familiars, sometimes assisted by notaries and *alguaciles*. These officials did not receive inquisition salaries, although the commissioners were arguably one of the most important categories of inquisitorial personnel. They were the delegates of the inquisitors themselves, although without their full powers. Usually they were secular clergy, often parish priests, and they had a mandate to investigate heresy in lieu of the inquisitor, questioning the accused or witnesses and receiving testimony, but explicitly not judging cases. The investigative work of the commissioners dramatically increased the number of trials that inquisition tribunals could conduct. At its most expansive in the first half of the seventeenth century, for example, the Cuenca inquisition tribunal had commissioners in approximately sixty-five different places around its district. "In addition to gathering evidence . . . They published the inquisitors' edicts, investigated the background of candidates to inquisitorial office, supervised the familiars, and collected and censored the publications that had been placed on the *Index of Prohibited Books*."[40] The Galicia tribunal listed 110 locations with commissioners in 1611.[41] Recent research has also stressed the importance of the commissioners in the enormous inquisition districts in the Americas, and the significant variability in their activities. The commissioner sent to the province of Michoacán in the 1570s was repeatedly blocked from his work and even assaulted by established local authorities.[42] The Franciscan Diego Muñoz, active from 1588 to 1626, on the other hand, "would go on to be one of the most prolific, wide-ranging *comisarios* of New Spain, sending hundreds upon hundreds of letters, depositions, and investigations about suspicious religious activities in rural Michoacán."[43]

To take another example, the commissioners of Córdoba del Tucumán, in Lima's inquisition district, created a significant surviving archive. After the establishment of a commissioner there in 1616, there were two long-serving office holders in the seventeenth century. One, Adrian Cornejo, was born in the city and amassed great wealth and a prestigious series of ecclesiastical posts; as commissioner, he collected denunciations of prominent conversos in the district during the intense global persecution of the 1640s.[44]

Another part of that widespread network – the familiars – have often featured in the Inquisition's mythology. Scholarship now shows that the "familiar acted as the inquisitors' helpmate, whose primary function was to deliver messages and occasionally to capture and house prisoners."[45] Only in very rare cases did the familiars denounce people for heresy. They sometimes served as bodyguards or servants for the inquisitors. In principle, they were to be married laymen of good character, Old Christians, and over the age of twenty. Their numbers could vary widely and there were debates about tribunals that were perceived to have too many of them. In Galicia, a 1641 census established 218 familiars.[46] In New Spain, there were meant to be twelve or more in Mexico City, four in each cathedral city, and at least one in every other Spanish town.[47] There were 144 familiars appointed in Mexico City between 1577 and 1646. Secular officials in Sicily complained about the Inquisition's "army of familiars," and about how many local nobles were appointed to the position; there were special permissions granted in Sicily not to have to conduct the same purity of blood investigations as other tribunals did. They probably reached a peak number in 1575, when 1,572 familiars were reported attached to the Inquisition's tribunal in Sicily. And the jurisdictional benefits of office were clearly an important attraction: There were nearly 500 criminal trials of familiars in Sicily from 1595 to 1634.[48]

Overall, throughout the Spanish Inquisition's many locations, the familiars – their number and their behavior – were a recurring refrain of criticism and contestation, both between the Suprema and the district tribunals and especially in the skirmishes between the Inquisition and other local, royal, or ecclesiastical authorities; such conflicts were already in evidence in the early sixteenth century. To be a familiar offered meaningful social status and potential mobility, and they came from a wide variety of social backgrounds and occupations. Their numbers increased notably in the middle of the sixteenth century, reaching a maximum around century's end, and falling off by the middle of the seventeenth century, mapping the trajectory of the Inquisition's institutional expansion and contraction more generally. While familiars do not seem to have increased the judicial activity of the tribunals, they were crucial to the ability of tribunals to conduct their work. And the appointment of familiars seems, most of all, to have been an important way of building the Inquisition's local authority, and thus establishing its ability to conduct cases.[49]

Sources, Studies, and Conclusions

A rich array of recent scholarship has demonstrated the importance of attending to inquisitorial personnel. The particular officials in place (or not) in a particular moment often made the difference as to whether or not inquisitorial tribunals pursued particular cases or kinds of transgressions. As the editor of this book has comprehensively demonstrated, conflict and different commitments among the Logroño inquisitors, the tribunal's notaries, a familiar, a commissioner, the bishop, and local clerics all profoundly shaped the infamous Navarrese witch hunt of 1608 to 1614.[50] But unraveling those human dynamics behind inquisitorial proceedings remains challenging. Studies of personnel remain highly variable and still divided by locality. Despite the massive amount of surviving inquisitorial documentation, many tribunals' records have been lost. It remains difficult, as the example of the inquisitor Reinoso indicates, to trace an inquisitorial career through the available scholarly literature, and even through the surviving archives. And the archival sources are more often than not opaque as to the decision-making or agency of individual officials. Moreover, the conflicts that tended to generate the most documentary traces – disagreements among inquisitors over cases, lawsuits, and visitations – have their own challenging conflictual dynamics, and do not always shed light on specific trials of faith. The experiences, attitudes, commitments, beliefs, relationships, and conversations of inquisitorial personnel shaped the Spanish Inquisition's activities in profound ways, but we are still only beginning to grasp the full extent of how they did so.

Notes

1. Amelia de Paz, ed., *Góngora y el Señor Inquisidor: Un autógrafo inédito de Don Luis en edición facsímil* (Minsterio de Educación, Cultura y Deporte y Sociedad Estatal de Acción Cultural, 2012), 9; Amelia de Paz, "Ascenso y caída del ínclito doctor Reinoso, gallo de las bravatas," *Boletín de la Real Academia de Córdoba* 97 (2018): 310–34; Alejandro López Álvarez, "Hernando Arenillas de Reynoso," *Diccionario Biográfico Electrónico*, Real Academia de la Historia, dbe.rah.es/biografias/28945/hernando-arenillas-de-reynoso
2. María del Carmen Sáenz Berceo, "Los inquisidores del Tribunal de Valladolid durante el reinado de Felipe III," *Revista de la Inquisición* 8 (1999), 55.
3. Sáenz Berceo, "Los inquisidores del Tribunal de Valladolid," 52, 54–9.
4. Victor Sánchez Gil, "El tribunal de la Inquisición de Cuenca: notas para un catálogo de sus miembros (1489–1714)," *Archivo ibero-americano* 40 (1980): 12–13.
5. Patrick O'Banion, *Deza and Its Moriscos: Religion and Community in Early Modern Spain* (University of Nebraska Press, 2020), 60; the record of the visitation is translated in Patrick O'Banion, ed., *This Happened in My Presence: Moriscos, Old Christians and the Spanish Inquisition in the Town of Deza, 1569–1611* (University of Toronto Press, 2017), 3–54. O'Banion identifies the inquisitor as the same Alonso Jiménez de Reinoso who would eventually arrive in Córdoba, and describes him as part of Toledo's court in 1569: O'Banion, *This Happened*, lxxiv.
6. Ricardo García Cárcel, *Herejía y Sociedad en el Siglo XVI: La Inquisición en Valencia, 1530–1609* (Ediciones Península, 1980), 91–113.
7. Stephen Haliczer, *Inquisition and Society in the Kingdom of Valencia, 1478–1834* (University of California Press, 1990), 265, cited in O'Banion, *This Happened*, xxxvi.

8. Jessica J. Fowler, "Illuminating Heretics: Alumbrados and Inquisition in Sixteenth-Century Cuenca," MA thesis, University of Georgia, 2009, 53–5; Jessica J. Fowler, "Illuminating the Empire: The Dissemination of the Spanish Inquisition and the Heresy of Alumbradismo, 1525–1600," Doctoral dissertation, University of California-Davis, 2015, 111, 129.
9. Kimberly Lynn, *Between Court and Confessional: The Politics of Spanish Inquisitors* (Cambridge University Press, 2013), 243–4, 267, 276–7; Solange Alberro, *Inquisition et Société au Mexique, 1571–1700* (Centre d'Études Mexicaines et Centramericanes, 1988), appendix I.8. On the Carvajal case and family, see Miriam Bodian, *Dying in the Law of Moses: Crypto-Jewish Martyrdom in the Iberian World* (Indiana University Press, 2007), chapter 3.
10. Mateu J. Colom Palmer, "El Tribunal de la Inquisición de Mallorca (1578–1700)," Doctoral dissertation, Universitat de Barcelona, 2015, 368, 392–401. On the Sicilian conflict through the prism of a different inquisitorial career, Lynn, *Between Court and Confessional*, 165–77.
11. Richard Greenleaf, "The Inquisition and the Indians of New Spain: A Study in Jurisdictional Confusion, *The Americas* 22 (1965): 146–7.
12. Lynn, *Between Court and Confessional*, 261–3; María del Pilar Pérez Canto, "La Crisis del Santo Ogivio (1621–1700): Tribunal de Lima," in Joaquín Pérez Villanueva and Bartolomé Escandell Bonet, eds., *Histoira de la Inquisición en España y América* Vol. 1 (Biblioteca de Autores Cristianos/Centro de Estudios Inquisitoriales, 1984), 1134.
13. Lynn, *Between Court and Confessional*, 158.
14. Martin A. Nesvig, *Ideology and Inquisition: The World of the Censors in Early Mexico* (Yale University Press, 2009), 214–15, 261–8.
15. See, for example, the overviews in Francisco Bethencourt, *The Inquisition: A Global History* (Cambridge University Press, 2009), 83–104, 134–73; John F. Chuchiak IV, *The Inquisition in New Spain, 1536–1820: A Documentary History* (The Johns Hopkins University Press, 2012), 12–29; Lu Ann Homza, ed. and trans., *The Spanish Inquisition, 1478–1614: An Anthology of Sources* (Hackett, 2006), xxii–xxv; Gretchen D. Starr-LeBeau, *Seven Myths of the Spanish Inquisition* (Hackett, 2023), 74–80; Robin Vose, "V. Familiars and Officials," in *Inquisitio: Hesburgh Libraries of Notre Dame, Department of Rare Books and Special Collections*, University of Notre Dame, 2010, inquisition.library.nd.edu/genre-familiars-and-officials-introduction.
16. Lynn, *Between Court and Confessional*, 25.
17. Contreras, *El Santo Oficio de la Inquisición de Galicia, 1560–1700: poder, sociedad y cultura* (AKAL Editor, 1982), 208–15.
18. Lynn, *Between Court and Confessional*, 243, 261.
19. Mercedes García-Arenal and Rafael Benítez Sánchez-Blanco, *The Inquisition Trial of Jerónimo de Rojas, a Morisco of Toledo (1601–1603)*, trans. Consuelo López-Morillas (Brill, 2022), 61.

20. Examples in Lynn, *Between Court and Confessional*, 164, 208–9.
21. Lynn, *Between Court and Confessional*, 158.
22. Fernando de Montesinos, *Auto de la fe, celebrado en Lima a 23 de enero de 1639*, ed. Marta Ortiz Canseco (Iberoamericana Editorial and Vervuert, 2016) 43, 50–7.
23. Lynn, *Between Court and Confessional*; Kimberly Lynn, "Judges and Shepherds: Inquisitions," in *Judging Faith, Punishing Sin: Inquisitions and Consistories in the Early Modern World* (Cambridge University Press, 2017); Jean-Pierre Dedieu, "Inquisitore," in Adriano Prosperi, with Vincenzo Lavinia and John Tedeschi, eds., *Dizionario Storico dell'Inquisizione*, Vol. 1 (Edizioni della Normale, 2010).
24. Lynn, "Judges and Shepherds," 119.
25. Sánchez Gil, "El tribunal de la Inquisición de Cuenca," 9–20; Sáenz Berceo, "Los inquisidores del Tribunal de Valladolid," 68–69.
26. The three long careers were, respectively: Lic. Antonio Ozores Sotomayor (1639–67); Dr. Matías Flores de Mora (1683–1700); Lic. Antonio Zambrana de Bolaños (1663–78). Contreras, *El Santo Oficio de la Inquisición en Galicia*, 189–90.
27. "ciencia y conciencia," quoted in Contreras, *El Santo Oficio de la Inquisición en Galicia*, 184.
28. Sáenz Berceo, "Los inquisidores del Tribunal de Valladolid," 68.
29. Contreras, *El Santo Oficio de la Inquisición en Galicia*, 189–90.
30. Francisco J. Escobar Borrego, Samuel Díez Reboso, and Luis Rivero García, eds., *La Metamorfosis de un Inquisidor: El Humanista Diego López de Cortegana (1455–1524)* (Universidad de Huelva, 2012).
31. Lynn, *Between Court and Confessional*, 317–18; Isabel Mendoza García and Teresa Sánchez Rivilla, "Diego García de Trasmiera," *Diccionario Biográfico Electrónico*, Real Academia de la Historia, dbe.rah.es/biografias/30992/diego-garcia-de-trasmiera.
32. Lynn, "Inquisitors, Print, and Publication"; Kimberly Lynn, "Was Adam the First Heretic? Diego de Simancas, Luis de Páramo, and the Origins of Inquisitorial Practice," *Archiv für Reformationsgeschichte/Archive for Reformation History* 97 (2006): 184–210.
33. Teresa Sánchez Rivilla, "Inquisidores Generales y Consejeros de la Suprema: documentación biográfica," in Joaquín Pérez Villanueva and Bartolomé Escandell Bonet, eds., *Historia de la Inquisición en España y América* Vol. 3 (Biblioteca de Autores Cristianos & Centro de Estudios Inquisitoriales, 2000); Lynn, "Judges and Shepherds," 120.
34. See, for example, my study of Cristóbal Fernández de Valtodano, Lynn, *Between Court and Confessional*, chapter 1.
35. John F. Chuchiak IV, "Corruption and Careerism in New Spain: don Alonso de Peralta y Robles, Creole Inquisitor," *Colonial Latin American Review* 2 (2020): 376–97.

36. Jessica J. Fowler, "Assembling Alumbradismo: The Evolution of a Heretical Construct," in Mercedes García-Arenal, ed., *After Conversion: Iberia and the Emergence of Modernity* (Brill, 2016); Jessica J. Fowler, "Process and Punishment: Alleged *Alumbrados* Before the Mexican Holy Office, 1593–1603," *Colonial Latin American Review* 29 (2020): 357–75; Alison Weber, "The Inquisitor, the Flesh, and the Devil: Alumbradismo and Demon Possession," in Hans de Waardt, Jüren Michael Schmidt, H. C. Erik Midelfort, Sönke Lorenz, and Dieter R. Bauer, eds., *Demonic Possession: Interpretations of a Historico-Cultural Phenomenon* (Verlag für Regionageschichte, 2005).
37. Sara T. Nalle, "A Forgotten Campaign against the Conversos of Sigüenza: Pedro Cortés and the Inquisition of Cuenca," in Kevin Ingram and Juan Ignacio Pulido Serrano, eds., *The Conversos and Moriscos in Late Medieval Spain and Beyond. Vol. III: Displaced Persons* (Brill, 2015). Another study hinging on the career of Inquisitor Cortés that closely follows inquisitorial personnel is Sara T. Nalle, *Mad for God: Bartolomé Sánchez, the Secret Messiah of Cardenete* (University Press of Virginia, 2001). For other studies of inquisitors who were responsible for extensive persecution of conversos see the early sixteenth-century example of Inquisitor Lucero in Córdoba: John Edwards, "Trial of an Inquisitor: The Dismissal of Diego Rodríguez Lucero, Inquisitor of Córdoba, in 1508," *Journal of Ecclesiastical History* 37 (1986): 240–57. On Juan de Mañozca and mid seventeenth-century trials of conversos in both Lima and Mexico City, see Lynn, *Between Court and Confessional*, chapter 5, and Ferry, "The Inquisitor and the Virgin: A Study in Personality and Circumstance," *Colonial Latin American Review* 29 (2020): 434–60.
38. Chuchiak, *Inquisition in New Spain*, 15–16.
39. Sánchez Gil, "El tribunal de la Inquisición de Cuenca," 21–6.
40. Nalle, "Inquisitors, Priests, and the People," 566. See also López-Vela, "Commissario," in Adriano Prosperi, with Vincenzo Lavinia and John Tedeschi (eds.), *Dizionario Storico dell'Inquisizione*, Vol. I (Edizioni della Normale, 2010).
41. Contreras, *El Santo Oficio*, 169–71.
42. Martin A. Nesvig, *Promiscuous Power: An Unorthodox History of New Spain* (University of Texas Press, 2018), chapter 4.
43. Martin A. Nesvig, *Forgotten Franciscans: Works from an Inquisitorial Theorist, a Heretic, and an Inquisitional Deputy* (Pennsylvania State University Press, 2011), 79.
44. Federico Sartori, "El Comisario de la Inquisición, el capitán portugués y un secreto bien guardado en los confines del Imperio," *Colonial Latin American Review* 29 (2020): 461–94; Federico Sartori, "Tan a banderas

desplegada: el poder de un comisario inquisitorial americano del sglo XVII," *Colonial Latin American Review* 24 (2015): 356–82.
45. Nalle, "Inquisitors, Priests, and the People during the Catholic Reformation in Spain," 559; Jaime Contreras, "Social Infrastructure of the Inquisition: Familiars and Commissioners," in Ángel Alcalá, ed., *The Spanish Inquisition and the Inquisitorial Mind* (Social Science Monographs, distributed by Columbia University Press, 1987).
46. Contreras, *El Santo Oficio*, 171–5.
47. Chuchiak, *Inquisition in New Spain*, 21–2.
48. Lynn, *Between Court and Confessional*, 164–5; Alberro, *Inquisition et Société*, 340–3.
49. Rafael Carrasco, "Los familiares del Santo Oficio, un dispositivo problemático," *Estudis: Revista de historia moderna* 49 (2023): 139–75; Ana Cristina Cuadro García, "Familiari, Spagna," in Adriano Prosperi with Vincenzo Lavinia and John Tedeschi, eds., *Dizionario Storico dell'Inquisizione* (Edizioni della Normale, 2010).
50. Lu Ann Homza, *Village Infernos and Witches' Advocates: Witch-Hunting in Navarre, 1608–1614* (Pennsylvania State University Press, 2022).

Suggestions for Further Reading

Bethencourt, Francisco. *The Inquisition: A Global History, 1478–1834.* Cambridge University Press, 2009.

Chuchiak, John F., IV. "Corruption and Careerism in New Spain: Don Alonso de Peralta y Robles, Creole Inquisitor, 1594–1610." *Colonial Latin American Review* 29 (2020): 376–97.

Chuchiak, John F., IV, ed. and trans. *The Inquisition in New Spain, 1536–1820: A Documentary History.* The Johns Hopkins University Press, 2012.

Ferry, Robert J. "The Inquisitor and the Virgin: A Study in Personality and Circumstance." *Colonial Latin American Review* 29 (2020): 434–60.

Fowler, Jessica. "Assembling Alumbradismo: The Evolution of a Heretical Construct." In Mercedes García-Arenal, ed., *After Conversion: Iberia and the Emergence of Modernity.* Brill, 2016.

Homza, Lu Ann. *Village Infernos and Witches' Advocates: Witch-Hunting in Navarre, 1608–1614.* Pennsylvania State University Press, 2022.

Lynn, Kimberly. *Between Court and Confessional: The Politics of Spanish Inquisitors.* Cambridge University Press, 2013.

Nalle, Sara T. "A Forgotten Campaign against the Conversos of Sigüenza: Pedro Cortés and the Inquisition of Cuenca." In Kevin Ingram and Juan Ignacio Pulido Serrano, eds., *The Conversos and Moriscos in Late Medieval Spain and Beyond.* Vol. 3: *Displaced Persons.* Brill, 2015.

"Inquisitors, Priests, and the People during the Catholic Reformation in Spain." *Sixteenth-Century Journal* 18 (1987): 557–87.

Nesvig, Martin Austin. *Ideology and Inquisition: The World of the Censors in Early Mexico*. Yale University Press, 2009.

Bibliography

Alberro, Solange. *Inquisition et Société au Mexique, 1571–1700*. Centre d'Études Mexicaines et Centramericanes, 1988.

Bethencourt, Francisco. *The Inquisition: A Global History, 1478–1834*. Cambridge University Press, 2009.

Bodian, Miriam. *Dying in the Law of Moses: Crypto-Jewish Martyrdom in the Iberian World*. Indiana University Press, 2007.

Caro Baroja, Julio. *El Señor Inquisidor y Otras Vidas por Oficio*. Alianza Editorial, 1968.

Carrasco, Rafael. "Los familiares del Santo Oficio, un dispositivo problemático." *Estudis: Revista de historia moderna* 49 (2023): 139–75.

Chuchiak, John F. IV, ed. and trans. *The Inquisition in New Spain, 1536–1820: A Documentary History*. The Johns Hopkins University Press, 2012.

"Corruption and Careerism in New Spain: Don Alonso de Peralta y Robles, Creole Inquisitor, 1594–1610." *Colonial Latin American Review* 29, no. 3 (2020): 376–97.

Colom Palmer, Mateu J. "El Tribunal de la Inquisición de Mallorca (1578–1700)." Doctoral dissertation, Universitat de Barcelona, 2015.

Contreras, Jaime. *El Santo Oficio de la Inquisición de Galicia, 1560–1700: poder, sociedad y cultura*. Akal Editor, 1982.

"The Social Infrastructure of the Inquisition: Familiars and Commissioners." In Ángel Alcalá, ed., *The Spanish Inquisition and the Inquisitorial Mind*, 133–58. Social Science Monographs, distributed by Columbia University Press, 1987.

Cuadro García, Ana Cristina "Familiari, Spagna." In Adriano Prosperi with Vincenzo Lavinia and John Tedeschi, eds., *Dizionario Storico dell'Inquisizione*. volume 2. Edizioni della Normale, 2010.

Dedieu, Jean-Pierre. "Les inquisiteurs de Tolède et la visite du district. La sédentarisation d'un tribunal (1550–1630)." *Mélanges de la Casa de Velázquez* 13 (1977): 235–56.

L'Administration de la foi: l'Inquisition de Tolède, XVI-XVII siècle. Casa de Velázquez, 1989.

"Inquisitore." In Adriano Prosperi, with Vincenzo Lavenia and John Tedeschi, eds., *Dizionario Storico dell'Inquisizione*, Vol. 2, 800–3. Edizioni della Normale, 2010.

Domínguez Salgado, María del Pilar. "Inquisidores y fiscales de la Inquisición de Corte (1580–1700)". *Revista de la Inquisición* 4 (1995): 205–47.

Edwards, John. "Trial of an Inquisitor: The Dismissal of Diego Rodríguez Lucero, Inquisitor of Córdoba, in 1508." *Journal of Ecclesiastical History* 37, no. 2 (1986): 240–57.

Escobar Borrego Francisco J., Samuel Díez Reboso, and Luis Rivero García, eds. *La Metamorfosis de un Inquisidor: El Humanista Diego López de Cortegana (1455–1524)*. Universidad de Huelva, 2012.

Ferry, Robert J. "The Inquisitor and the Virgin: A Study in Personality and Circumstance." *Colonial Latin American Review* 29, no. 3 (2020): 434–60.

Fowler, Jessica J. "Illuminating Heretics: Alumbrados and Inquisition in Sixteenth-Century Cuenca." MA thesis, University of Georgia, 2009.

"Illuminating the Empire: The Dissemination of the Spanish Inquisition and the Heresy of Alumbradismo, 1525–1600." Doctoral dissertation, University of California, Davis, 2015.

"Assembling Alumbradismo: The Evolution of a Heretical Construct." In Mercedes García-Arenal, ed., *After Conversion: Iberia and the Emergence of Modernity*. Brill, 2016.

"Process and Punishment: Alleged *Alumbrados* Before the Mexican Holy Office, 1593–1603." *Colonial Latin American Review* 29, no. 3 (2020): 357–75.

García-Arenal, Mercedes, and Rafael Benítez Sánchez-Blanco. *The Inquisition Trial of Jerónimo de Rojas, A Morisco of Toledo (1601–1603)*, trans. Consuelo López-Morillas. Brill, 2022.

García Cárcel, Ricardo. *Herejía y Sociedad en el Siglo XVI. La Inquisición en Valencia, 1530–1609*. Ediciones Península, 1980.

Greenleaf, Richard. "The Inquisition and the Indians of New Spain: A Study in Jurisdictional Confusion." *The Americas* 22, no. 2 (1965): 138–66.

Haliczer, Stephen. *Inquisition and Society in the Kingdom of Valencia, 1478–1834*. University of California Press, 1990.

Henningsen, Gustav. *The Witches' Advocate: Basque Witchcraft and the Spanish Inquisition (1609–1614)*. University of Nevada Press, 1980.

The Salazar Documents: Inquisitor Alonso de Salazar Frías and Others on the Basque Witch Persecution. Brill, 2004.

Homza, Lu Ann, ed. and trans. *The Spanish Inquisition, 1478–1614: An Anthology of Sources*. Hackett, 2006.

Village Infernos and Witches' Advocates: Witch-Hunting in Navarre, 1608–1614. Pennsylvania State University Press, 2022.

López Álvarez, Alejandro. "Hernando Arenillas de Reynoso." *Diccionario Biográfico Electrónico*. Real Academia de la Historia. dbe.rah.es/biografias/28945/hernando-arenillas-de-reynoso

López-Vela, Roberto. "Commissario del Sant'Uffizio, Spagna." In Adriano Prosperi, with Vincenzo Lavenia and John Tedeschi, eds. *Dizionario Storico dell'Inquisizione*. Edizioni della Normale, 2010.

Lynn, Kimberly. "Was Adam the First Heretic? Diego de Simancas, Luis de Páramo, and the Origins of Inquisitorial Practice." *Archiv für Reformationsgeschichte/Archive for Reformation History* 97 (2006): 184–210.

Between Court and Confessional: The Politics of Spanish Inquisitors. Cambridge University Press, 2013.

"Spanish Inquisitors, Print, and the Problem of Publication." In *The Early Modern Hispanic World: Transnational and Interdisciplinary Approaches*, ed. Kimberly Lynn and Erin Kathleen Rowe, 220–42. Cambridge University Press, 2017.

"Judges and Shepherds: Inquisitions." In *Judging Faith, Punishing Sin: Inquisitions and Consistories in the Early Modern World*, ed. Charles H. Parker and Gretchen D. Starr-LeBeau, 116–27. Cambridge University Press, 2017.

Mendoza García, Isabel, and Teresa Sánchez Rivilla. "Diego García de Trasmiera." *Diccionario Biográfico Electrónico*. Real Academia de la Historia. dbe.rah.es/biografias/30992/diego-garcia-de-trasmiera.

Monter, E. William. *Frontiers of Heresy: The Spanish Inquisition from the Basque Lands to Sicily*. Cambridge University Press, 1990.

Montesinos, Fernando de. *Auto de la fe, celebrado en Lima a 23 de enero de 1639*, ed. Marta Ortiz Canseco, coord. Esperanza López Parada. Iberoamericana Editorial and Vervuert, 2016.

Nalle, Sara T. "Inquisitors, Priests, and the People during the Catholic Reformation in Spain." *Sixteenth-Century Journal* 18, no. 4 (1987): 557–87.

Mad for God: Bartolomé Sánchez, the Secret Messiah of Cardenete. University Press of Virginia, 2001.

"A Forgotten Campaign against the Conversos of Sigüenza: Pedro Cortés and the Inquisition of Cuenca." In Kevin Ingram and Juan Ignacio Pulido Serrano, eds., *The Conversos and Moriscos in Late Medieval Spain and Beyond. Vol. 3: Displaced Persons*. Brill, 2015.

Nesvig, Martin A. *Ideology and Inquisition: The World of the Censors in Early Mexico*. Yale University Press, 2009.

Forgotten Franciscans: Works from an Inquisitional Theorist, a Heretic, and an Inquisitional Deputy. Pennsylvania State University Press, 2011.

Promiscuous Power: An Unorthodox History of New Spain. University of Texas Press, 2018.

O'Banion, Patrick J., ed. *This Happened in My Presence: Moriscos, Old Christians and the Spanish Inquisition in the Town of Deza, 1569–1611*. University of Toronto Press, 2017.

Deza and Its Moriscos: Religion and Community in Early Modern Spain. University of Nebraska Press, 2020.

Pastore, Stefania. *Il Vangelo e la Spada: L'Inquisizione di Castiglia e i Suoi Critici (1460–1598)*. Edizioni di Storia e Letteratura, 2003.

Paz, Amelia de, ed. *Góngora y el Señor Inquisidor. Un autógrafo inédito de Don Luis en edición facsímil*. Ministerio de Educación, Cultura y Deporte and Sociedad Estatal de Acción Cultural, 2012.

"Ascenso y caída del ínclito doctor Reinoso, gallo de las bravatas (1597)." *Boletín de la Real Academia de Córdoba* 97, no. 167 (2018): 319–34.

Pérez Canto, María del Pilar. "La Crisis del Santo Oficio (1621–1700). Tribunal de Lima." In Joaquín Pérez Villanueva and Bartolomé Escandell Bonet, eds., *Historia de la Inquisición en España y América* Vol. 1. Biblioteca de Autores Cristianos/Centro de Estudios Inquisitoriales, 1984.

Rivero Rodríguez, Manuel. "La Inquisición Española en Sicilia." In Joaquín Pérez Villanueva and Bartolomé Escandell Bonet, eds., *Historia de la Inquisición en España y América* Vol. 3. Biblioteca de Autores Cristianos/Centro de Estudios Inquisitoriales, 2000.

Sáenz Berceo, María del Carmen. "Los inquisidores del Tribunal de Valladolid durante el reinado de Felipe III." *Revista de la Inquisición* 8 (1999): 43–83.

Sánchez Gil, Victor. "El tribunal de la Inquisición de Cuenca: notas para un catálogo de sus miembros (1489–1714)." *Archivo ibero-americano* 40 (1980): 3–36.

Sánchez Rivilla, Teresa. "Inquisidores Generales y Consejeros de la Suprema: documentación biográfica." In Joaquín Pérez Villanueva and Bartolomé Escandell Bonet, eds., *Historia de la Inquisición en España y América* Vol. 3. Biblioteca de Autores Cristianos/Centro de Estudios Inquisitoriales, 2000.

Sartori, Federico. "Tan a banderas desplegada: el poder de un comisario inquisitorial americano del siglo XVII." *Colonial Latin American Review* 24, no. 3 (2015): 356–82.

"El Comisario de la Inquisición, el capitán portugués y un secreto bien guardado en los confines del Imperio." *Colonial Latin American Review* 29 (2020): 461–94.

Starr-LeBeau, Gretchen D. *In the Shadow of the Virgin: Inquisitors, Friars, and Conversos in Guadalupe, Spain*. Princeton University Press, 2003.

Seven Myths of the Spanish Inquisition. Hackett, 2023.

Vose, Robin. "V. Familiars and Officials." In *Inquisitio: Hesburgh Libraries of Notre Dame, Department of Rare Books and Special Collections*. University of Notre Dame, 2010. inquisition.library.nd.edu/genre-familiars-and-officials-introduction.

Weber, Alison. "The Inquisitor, the Flesh, and the Devil: Alumbradismo and Demon Possession." In Hans de Waardt, Jürgen Michael Schmidt, H. C. Erik Midelfort, Sönke Lorenz, and Dieter R. Bauer, eds., *Demonic Possession: Interpretations of a Historico-Cultural Phenomenon*. Verlag für Regionalgeschichte, 2005.

JOSÉ LUIS LORIENTE TORRES
TRANSLATION BY LU ANN HOMZA

3

Pursuing Life Stories: Inquisitors and Suspects

Introduction[1]

More than a century and a half ago, Jacob Burckhardt launched the myth of modern individualism with the following proposition: "In the Middle Ages both sides of human consciousness – that which was turned within and that which was turned without – lay as though dreaming or half-awake beneath a common veil [. . .]. Man was conscious of himself only as a member of a race, people, party, family, or corporation—only through some general category. It is in Italy that this veil dissolved first [. . .]; and at the same time the subjective side asserted itself with corresponding emphasis. Man became a spiritual individual and recognized himself as such."[2] He posited that during the Renaissance, there was a gap between medieval man, anchored in a sense of community, and modern man, who possessed a greater awareness of himself. Since then, many researchers have nuanced Burckhardt's idea, either by anticipating its emergence and moving it earlier in chronological time, or not perceiving a true break at all. In the mid-sixteenth century in the Iberian peninsula there was an explosion of autobiographical texts that seems to coincide with the Burckhardtian myth. Pioneering works in the first person such as *El Lazarillo de Tormes* (1554) or *El libro de la Vida* de Teresa de Jesús (1562) appeared, but so too did all kinds of self-referential texts. In the midst of this autobiographical whirlwind, Inquisitor-General Fernando de Valdés promulgated a new regulation for the Spanish Inquisition in 1561. The new mandate established that everyone accused of heresy by an inquisition tribunal had to declare, in their first hearing before the inquisitors, an account of their lives from birth to the very moment of their deposition.[3] It is difficult to think that the two things were not related.

To some extent, the appearance of this autobiographical requirement order has puzzled the few researchers who have considered the surviving statements in a self-referential way.[4] They have asked about Valdés's motives for launching the new requirement. They have wondered why he decided to do so at this particular moment, thought about antecedents and motives, and pondered in particular what such required statements might mean for the concept of autobiography. Could all of this be related to the myth of modern individualism?

The Development of Autobiographical Consciousness in the Sixteenth Century

It is challenging to explain the burst of self-referential publications in sixteenth-century Spain. Perhaps the most plausible reason is the one proposed by Peter Burke: The emerging publishing industry made available to readers an unprecedented catalogue of autobiographical models, who then decided to follow suit.[5] Undoubtedly, this must have happened in the case of Teresa de Jesús, whose work provoked a powerful imitation effect, although other factors must also be taken into account. But what I would like to highlight here is less a mechanistic and inevitable emulation and more the development of an "autobiographical consciousness." That is, throughout the sixteenth century there was a gradual increase in the practice of speaking and writing about oneself. Thus, to the flood of first-person literary works, we should add the appearance of all kinds of self-narratives and "personal documents" – such as proofs of merit, penned by conquistadores and royal officials; memorials that explained past actions; women's spiritual literature, the lives of soldiers, or urban chronicles. Many of these genres share a series of common characteristics that both unifies them and transcends the strictly literary.[6] Due to the concurrence of dates and details, the "inquisitorial autobiography" constitutes one aspect of this phenomenon.[7]

Proof of the development of an autobiographical consciousness is the appearance in Castilian, and its expansion throughout the sixteenth century, of the expression "discourse of life" (*discurso de la vida*). The first time we find a definition of the term "discourse" is in Covarrubias's *Tesoro de la Lengua* (1611): "from the Latin, *discursus*, the flow from one thing to another; it is the way of proceeding in treating some point or subject, through different propositions and various concepts."[8] But it was not until the *Diccionario de Autoridades* (1732) that the full phrase appeared with an unequivocal autobiographical meaning in a lexico-grammatical compendium: "DISCURSO. It is also taken for distance that runs or passes from one time to another, or from one thing to another [...]. [Example:] And hence in the discourse of my life, I knew many of those named in history."[9]

Nevertheless, the expression "discurso" was already used much earlier, both to refer to the life course of any person and to the act of narrating such a story. So we find it in Teresa de Jesús, who appealed "for the love of the Lord, [...] whoever will read this *discourse of my life*, which has been so ruinous that I have not found a holy person who can console me, among those who turn themselves to God."[10] Or in *La Vida y Cosas Notables del Señor obispo de Zamora don Diego de Simancas*, Simancas stated, "If anyone would like to know the *discourse of my life*, together with some particularities worthy of memory, they will find it here, all truthfully set down, with the brevity and distinction that I have always used in all my writings."[11]

If we turn to the Diachronic Corpus of Spanish – *Corpus Diacrónico del Español*, or CORDE – we can gain a clear picture of the appearance and diffusion of the term "discurso," which appears fifty-one times in thirty-eight documents in the sixteenth century:

- four between 1531 and 1550
- five between 1551 and 1570
- eight between 1571 and 1590
- up to twenty-two between 1591 and 1600.[12]

The results are more abundant, albeit similar, for the search term "discourse of his life," producing 186 instances in 109 documents. Here, the search dates the appearance of the longer phrase to the 1520s, with the first occurring in the anonymous work, *Chrónica del rey Don Guillermo*.[13] This presence of "discourse of his life" increases gradually throughout the entire period: six instances in the 1530s; another four between 1540 and 1554; five in the 1560s; rising in 1570 with fifteen appearances; eighteen more in 1580; fourteen in 1590; and finally, forty-five in the 1600s.

Some Characteristics of the "Autobiographical Culture" of the Sixteenth Century

Descriptive phrases that have been applied to inquisition-mandated autobiographies are "eclectic" and "lacking in structure."[14] Both comments are true, whether from a formal or thematic point of view. Autobiographical statements produced in inquisition contexts range from thirteen words to more than 6,500, though the average is 350: our evidence base here consists of 2,725 trials with 424 autobiographical statements from the Toledo tribunal, dated 1561 to 1819. Thematically, the statements are also wide-ranging and not at all limited to the crime or heresy allegedly committed.[15] Their content spans from the most common details of everyday life to lengthy doctrinal digressions. For example, Teresa García, accused of sorcery in 1716, told the inquisitors that one night, she dined on "chestnut stew" while her friend Felipa consumed "some cat soup."[16] Girarlo París, prosecuted in 1603, was convinced that he could explain to the tribunal "the virginity of Our Lady before childbirth, in childbirth, and after childbirth."[17] Yet for all their variability, a basic choice can be observed: Authors either spoke of the reasons for bringing them before the tribunal, or they remained totally silent about the reality of their arrests, as if they were not really speaking in an inquisition tribunal before inquisitors.[18] A crucial context for their speech acts was the fact that inquisitors were seeking details as well as the names of potential accomplices, while defendants were both attempting to minimize their culpability and often, to shield acquaintances or family members (Figure 3.1).

That being said, these narratives were very repetitive, perhaps because of the way they were composed. These were oral statements put in writing by an inquisitorial notary.

> And the notary before whom the questioning occurs writes down everything that the inquisitor or inquisitors say to the prisoner, and what the prisoner says in return ... and once the hearing is over ... the notary

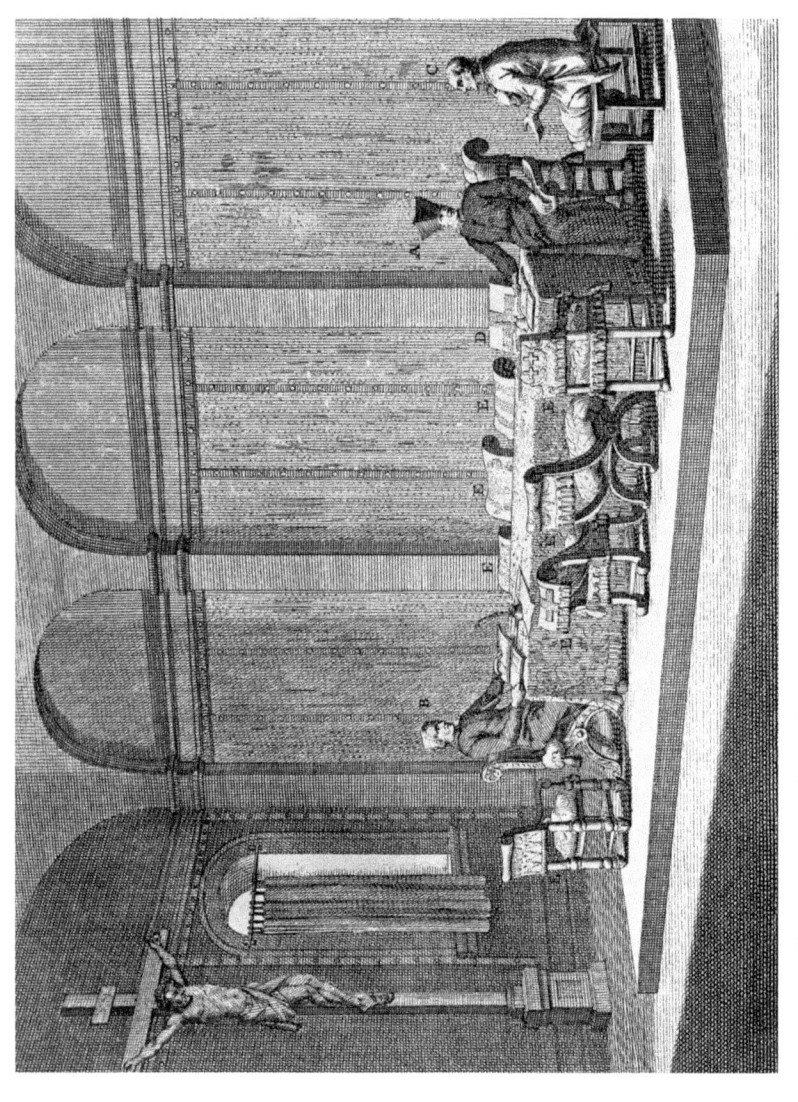

Figure 3.1 Bernard Picart. "The Inquisition Room." Engraving, 1722. Source: DEA Picture Library/Getty Images.

reads back everything he has written down, so that the prisoner can, if he wishes, add or amend something...[19]

Although the surviving documentation has not left many clues as to exactly how the scribes worked, it may be that the accused received some kind of instruction or hints while declaring the "discourse of their lives," or so Valdes's *Instructions* and Garcia's *Orden de procesar* lead one to believe. Still, close inspection of the statements gives the impression that they were spontaneous. For example, this is how the declaration of Antonio Márquez, accused of "dishonesty" in 1565, begins:

> Asked for the discourse of his life. He said that he was raised in his parents' house until he was ten years old and in this time he learned to read and write and was an altar boy there in his village; and from that age he went with his father to the Kingdom of Valencia and there he lodged with one Juan Alemán, a notary of the archbishop, whom he served for two years; and from there he went to Arriola which is in the Kingdom of Valencia and served there Alonso Guillén, a cleric, for three years...[20]

There is no evidence in Márquez's opening that he was prompted for more information or interrupted.

When it comes to questions of interference or independence vis-à-vis the suspects' narratives, we have not reached a consensus. One scholar believes that the very term "discourse of life" is misleading. He argues that, instead, the suspects' statements were simply a combination of various pieces of information, an amalgam that must have resulted from a questionnaire which in turn was grounded on inquisitorial instructions. The questionnaire could have been assembled in some way by the notaries.[21] This supposed process is based upon the similarities between the defendants' narratives and the inquisitorial mandates. Still, the extant discourses of lives do not appear to have undergone any manipulation after they were transcribed; another expert believes that the official instruction from Valdés opened an "autobiographical space" that the declarants could fill in "freely," which would explain the variability of the depositions. The truth probably lies somewhere in between the two possibilities and depends upon whether we wish to emphasize sameness or difference. It will always be impossible to know for sure, not least because we cannot assume that the same processes – whether intervention or interference or free narration – took place in every tribunal with every defendant.

Defendants usually began their statements by talking about the place where they were born and raised, identifying their parents, and highlighting the moment when they left their family home to go out into the world. Variability then ensues, but the suspects nevertheless consistently "tracked" the places they had gone and the people with whom they had had some kind of relationship, which was exactly what inquisitorial instructions demanded. Again, we circle back to the problem of who was taking the initiative in creating these narratives. The declarants could have been encouraged to add information as they spoke, such as details as to what they did in such and such a place, where they went afterwards, whom they met there, and so on. Yet even that sort of direction cannot nullify the self-referential nature of the statements because the defendants exercised some control over them. There was no minimum or maximum amount of space on a manuscript page that they had to fill. They were free to add or contradict information they had given; they could direct their deposition where they wanted it to go.

In fact, many under arrest took advantage of the self-narrative to compose exculpatory or justificatory stories, try to convince their interrogators of their innocence or to obtain their mercy. For example, after Maria Calzada was accused of scandalous propositions for questioning Mary's virginity in 1591, she limited herself in the "discourse of her life" to declaring dramatically that "she was born in Bustarviejo, and there she grew up in her parents' house, bringing bundles of firewood and making a living with great misery to support her mother, because her father died eleven years ago, and she has never left the said place."[22] How could such a wretched woman sin? And if she had sinned, had she not already atoned through her sorrow over such a miserable life?

In addition to their form of composition, another possibility is that these elements were part of the "autobiographical culture" of the declarants. With this expression I refer to the set of ideas, expressions, elements, rhetoric, forms, and all the other elements that a person – from this or any other historical period – used to narrate the story of his or her life. The notion of an autobiographical culture helps, in a practical and concrete way, to analyze a self-referential source whose origin was not exclusively literary.

Several researchers have already pointed to the similarity between some early self-referential sources and the materials under assessment here. One scholar of women's spiritual literature, Sonja Herpoel, tied feminine spiritual literature to inquisitorial autobiographies via the phrases "autobiographies by mandate" or *picaresque a la divina*.[23] Another expert, searching specifically for the origins of the picaresque novel, established that it could be a subversion of the crucial narratives produced during inquisitorial interrogations.[24] Finally, one historian has seen similarities among the picaresque novel, inquisition autobiographies-by-mandate, and memorials of services performed.[25] It is certainly true that some of the inquisition narratives read like a picaresque work.

As was the case for the *Life* of Teresa de Jesús or *Lazarillo de Tormes*, the inquisition texts were addressed to a higher authority than the one that provoked the narration. Unlike later examples of the autobiographical genre, in no way do these early modern, self-referential narrators describe how they feel: instead, feelings must be inferred from the events being relayed. On the other hand, parents and ancestors are of vital importance in these life stories, since all defendants begin by talking about them. Likewise, the defendants are composing "narratives in motion" in which they relay places they have been, and people they have known in those places, coinciding with the structure of "a servant of many masters" that was characteristic of the picaresque novel. Finally, all these stories contain material about confession, which we will discuss below.

The Appearance of the Injunction to Tell a Life Story before Inquisitors

Part of the confusion surrounding the 1561 requirement for modern historians has been provoked by the different ways in which the mandate was presented in formal inquisitorial instructions or regulations, as opposed to the way it was framed in the trial records. In 1561, Valdés's new instructions ordered inquisitors to ask the defendant "where he was raised, and with what persons, and if he has studied any university subject, and if he has left these kingdoms, and in what sort of company."[26] In principle, these questions did not imply or require any kind of autobiographical account. Yet in the surviving inquisitorial interrogations, we find that defendants were asked directly about the discourse of their lives: It looks as if that phrase suddenly appeared with no clue as to its origin.

To add to the ambiguity, we do not find an explicit mention of "discourse of life" in any inquisition treatise until the manual of Pablo García, which reads: "[The accused] shall be asked for the discourse of his life. He shall say where he was born, etc. He shall declare where he has been raised, and the places where he has resided, and with whom he has dealt and communicated, and all of it should be very extensive and very detailed."[27] García's own comments were a reflection of what we find in Valdés's 1561 instruction. Traditionally, scholars have thought that its first edition appeared in 1591.[28] Therefore, it had been thought that thirty years elapsed between the appearance of the requirement in Valdes's instructions and the appearance of the instruction in Garcia's treatise. Now we can confirm that both occurred almost simultaneously, because Garcia's treatise actually had a small print run in 1565.

As to why García believed he needed to repeat Valdés's instruction, that detail could be explained by the different nature of the two works. Valdés's manual was a set of instructions for inquisitors everywhere and hence had a normative character, while García's manual was supposed to be an addition to inquisition tribunals. Valdés's work was intended to be complete, whereas Garcia's was intended to be practical: The latter was composed to assist inquisition notaries in their duties, explaining what to do, say, or write at each moment of the process. Thus, García's recapitulation describes what Valdés's instruction on upbringing, persons, and places was thought to mean at the time, and he was setting down all the elements that every discourse of life should, or in fact did, have. That circumstance would explain the appearance of the expression in the inquisitorial treatise and help us to understand the autobiographical culture of the time.

At the same time, it is important to note that this autobiographical mandate was not entirely new. Until Valdés's reforms, Spanish inquisitors were governed by custom, the advice given in Nicolau Eymerich's inquisitorial manual, written in the fourteenth century, and instructions compiled after the inquisition was established in 1478. Eymerich had already suggested the convenience of putting the same questions to defendants: where they had grown up, with whom they had communicated, whether they had moved about and why.[29] Yet Eymerich's counsel in this regard was not repeated in the earliest formal, printed instructions for Spanish inquisitors, which were first produced in 1484, and then expanded in 1485, 1488, 1498, 1503, 1504, and 1516.[30] Valdés's novelty, in short, consisted in writing down the obligation to systematically request autobiographical information.

Valdés's Motives and the Real Author behind the 1561 *Instructions*

The overarching purpose of Valdés's revisions to existing inquisitorial procedures and practices was to unify the inquisitorial process in the different courts of the Spanish empire. There is no doubt that his work in this regard was affected by his experiences in the anti-Lutheran trials of 1557–62. He also wished to retroactively justify some of the measures he pursued and authorized against Archbishop Bartolomé de Carranza of Toledo, whose trial was the most notorious prosecution of the Spanish Inquisition in the sixteenth century.[31]

As far as the autobiographical mandate is concerned, scholars disagree on why Valdés suddenly included it; they attribute more or less sinister motives to its presence. Some experts think the request amounted to a trap for defendants: They point out that the questions could induce overfamiliarity and confidence, at which point defendants might let their guard down or become less vigilant in their comments.[32] Others pay more attention to the Spanish Inquisition's pastoral purpose of reconciling those in error to the Church: They think the autobiographical questions, which were supposed to occur in the very first hearing, should be interpreted as "a sign of familiarity and trust offered by the judges, which could facilitate a sincere confession."[33] Every expert agrees that the questions helped the inquisitors to gain a first impression of the accused.[34]

At the same time, questioning Valdés's motives ends up taking us in the wrong direction, since Diego de Simancas, not Valdés, was the author of the 1561 *Instructions*. Simancas had a peculiar career. After finishing his legal studies in Valladolid in 1545, he began to work as a consultant for the inquisition tribunal in the same city, which meant that he conferred with inquisitors about the appropriateness of their verdicts. His first royal appointment was as a judge in Valladolid's royal chancery court, which was one of Spain's two highest courts of appeal. Simancas held that position from 1548 to 1559, and he and his colleagues could trumpet an incredible record of case completion: In 1558, for example, they issued 432 definitive sentences in twenty-seven days.

Yet Simancas never served as an inquisitor in a tribunal before being appointed to the Supreme Council of the Inquisition, the Suprema, as a counselor, on April 20, 1559. He turned out to be a pivotal advisor on the inquisition's cases against Protestants between 1559 and 1562. His brilliance led Inquisitor-General Valdés to put him in charge, along with Cristóbal Hernández Valtodano, of the inquisition trial against Archbishop Carranza in 1561.[35] His works – *Institutiones Catholicae* and *La vida y cosas notables del señor obispo de Zamora Don Diego de Simancas* – can help us understand his priorities, though neither text explicitly relays why he included the autobiographical question in inquisitorial instructions.[36]

Simancas's *Institutiones Catholicae* is an inquisitorial treatise very similar to other examples of the genre. It credits Simancas as an expert jurist, familiar with both Eymerich's work and legal and confessional texts in general. Simancas's *Vida* is an early example of the autobiographical genre, and identifies him as the true author of the 1561 inquisitorial instructions:

> While the Archbishop came from Santiago, Valtodano and I made ninety-one chapter[s] of the processes that the Inquisitors should observe in their activities. Though the old instructions had ordered everyone to follow them, such was not the case, which was greatly inconvenient. These chapters were printed in the name of the Inquisitor-General [Valdés], and I gave them to Pope Gregory XIII for the [Roman] inquisitors of Italy, who had most need of them, and he enjoyed them.[37]

Simancas's *Vida* also indicates that he met the archbishop of Valencia, Martín Pérez de Ayala, and their interactions could have been provocative in terms of finding a common pastoral ground. Simancas became bishop of Ciudad Rodrigo in 1564, the same year Pérez de Ayala was named archbishop of Valencia. While Simancas "spent only a small fraction of his career" as a resident bishop – he moved from Ciudad Rodrigo to Badajoz to Zamora before his death in 1583 – "he tried to identify with episcopal ideals."[38]

Meanwhile, Archbishop Pérez de Ayala was a model Catholic bishop to his core. He composed a formal autobiography in which he described his participation in all three sessions of the Council of Trent.[39] He wrote a confessors' manual that drew many parallels between the sacrament of penance and autobiography.[40] Though he died after only fifteen months in his archepiscopal office, Pérez de Ayala limited the Inquisition's prosecutions of Moriscos in Valencia, targeted the secular clergy for reform, and printed a bilingual Spanish-Arabic catechism.[41]

The Sacrament of Penance and an Inquisition Trial

More than fifty years ago, a specialist in Renaissance history explored the relationship between modern autobiography and the sacrament of penance, one of the seven sacraments in Catholicism and a rite that required the confession of sins and transgressions to a priest or friar.[42] In the early Middle Ages, penance involved a public confession and public expiation for sins confessed. In the course of the twelfth century, however, penance evolved into a primarily private rite between priests and penitents. That change was accompanied by a new emphasis on motives and contrition in the confession of sins, which in turn was linked to the revival of interest in Aristotle because his treatises elevated the link between cause and effect. The context for and process of sin became that much more important. And with a new stress on incentives and sorrow, the clerics hearing confessions saw their responsibilities grow, since they now had to know the mental, emotional, and circumstantial landscape behind what the penitent recounted.

In 1215, Pope Innocent III and the Fourth Lateran Council formally codified the development of the sacrament of penance with the canon *Omnis utriusque sexus*. Penance was now at least an annual obligation for all Christians who had reached the age of discretion, or six to seven years of age; ideally, penance would be received before the holiest days of Christianity, the three-day period known as the *Triduum* or Easter. Modern historians and medieval theologians concur on the effects of *Omnis utriusque sexus*: The canon immediately enlarged the number of individuals who were interested in confessing to a priest or friar and wished to be reconciled to the Church for their sins. The rise in penitents produced in turn a flood of confessors' manuals, which in Latin were called *summa de casibus* or *summa confessorum*, meaning a "compendium of cases of conscience" or "a summary of confessors."

(The formal title *summa confessorum* did not come into use until after 1280.) Medieval confessors' manuals were inevitably written in Latin, and they blended legal and pastoral care. They were supposed to teach the clergy how to weigh the gravity of various sins; they typically also relayed Christian doctrine in case the clerical readers in question were not particularly educated in theology.

Scholars have posited that the sacrament of penance after 1215 created an obligation for introspection that might have contributed in a fundamental way to the awakening of self-awareness: Hence an earlier historian tied penance to Burckhardt's thesis about the emergence of modern individualism. Crucially, confessors' manuals were published increasingly in vernacular languages after 1500, and of course, the fact that they could be printed simply amplified their presence and reach. Vernacular confessors' manuals were cheap; evidence from sixteenth-century bookstore inventories in Spain proves they were widely available. Remarkably, the authors of the vernacular manuals often explicitly included the laity as part of their audience. It seems likely that by the first few decades of the sixteenth century, ordinary Spaniards understood how to examine their consciences.[43]

Confessors' manuals in Spanish were detailed when it came to explaining introspection and how to achieve it. For example, one work advised:

> At least three days before confessing, the penitent should devote himself to a great deal of study and recollection. He should free himself from other matters in order to reduce to memory the sins he has committed, going over the places, times, persons, and business in which he has been occupied since his last confession, either doing this on his own or through a confessors' manual.[44]

Self-scrutiny within the sacrament had been implicit and desirable from the twelfth century on, but the Council of Trent made it obligatory in 1551 in its fifteenth session. Trent's mandate was then incorporated into authoritative confessors' manuals such as Cajetan's, published in Spanish translation in 1557 with a prologue by Luis de León:

> The first condition that the confession must have is to reflect a diligent examination of conscience, as stated in the [decrees] of the Council of Trent ... where these words are found, "The penitent is to examine

himself and think over his sins, searching all the corners of his heart." From this phrase it is inferred, that if the penitent has left many sins out of the confession because he has not performed this diligence, the confession must be done over again. For which reason no penitent shall be admitted to confession (unless he is at the point of death) without having sufficiently run through his memory to remember his sins.[45]

The manuals not only advised – or required, after Trent – that such an examination of conscience should occur but also offered concrete details on how to carry it out by means of detailed signs and mnemonic recommendations. In his confessors' manual, published in 1579, Bartolomé de Medina noted:

> To confess well, [these] points must be considered ... First, decide to withdraw [from the world] and recollect oneself for a few days, in order to think and examine one's paths and weaknesses ... Third, reduce to memory the time that has passed since our last confession, thinking hard if we have forgotten anything [...]. Fifth, it is necessary to remember our sins through the companions with whom we have interacted, those with whom we have had dealings, because this will help us to remember our offenses.[46]

The following quotation, though coming from an eighteenth-century manual, illustrates the point even more clearly. In 1794, Manuel de Arceniega advised:

> In order to make this examination properly, the following steps must be taken ... to more easily bring to mind each and every one of his sins, he must reflect on the places he has been, the persons with whom he has dealt, the business matters he has been involved with, and the positions and jobs he has held.[47]

The Inspiration for the 1561 Injunction

Until now, no one has noticed the similarities between these confessors' manuals and the inquisition treatises reviewed above. When Medina's 1579 work talks about "examining paths" or "the companions with whom we have interacted," it matches to a degree the *Instructions* of Valdés, which asked the defendant "where he has been raised, and with what persons [...], and if he has left these kingdoms, and with what companions." Medina's counsel also recalls Pablo García's *Orden de*

Processar, which mentions that the accused should declare "the places where he has resided, and with whom he has dealt and communicated." If we compare the inquisitorial treatises with Arceniega's manual, they seem to be a direct match. Thus, we end up in the same place via both kinds of literature: A thorough confession was the objective behind the inquisition mandate to engage in an autobiographical statement, as was the injunction in the confessors' manual to study one's past.

In fact, the heart of Inquisition was doctrinally based on the sacrament of penance.[48] In the mentality of the ancien régime, categories of heresy, sin, and crime could be entangled and, to a certain extent, interchangeable with each other.[49] Heretics were sinners and rebels who violated the political and social order as well as the religious one. In the early modern Catholic world, confessors were judges, and inquisitorial judges were also confessors. Both functions were mechanisms to "reconcile" the sinner with the community, and they could have two different impacts: experienced as a relief for the person who confessed, and experienced as a tool for social control. Likewise, both judging and confessing were strengthened by the Council of Trent, which approached the sacrament of penance from the same perspective: as consolation for the soul and as the exercise of disciplinary power.

The processes of inquisition and penance had doctrinal and practical similarities: Both were designed to make the accused confess all his sins, in order to punish and reconcile him. It is an open question as to whether Spanish inquisitors realized over time what their autobiographical mandate was doing, that is, whether it lost its original function toward confession and became simply a ruse. While the Inquisition's "discourses of life" provided a lot of useful information for the prosecution, deciding that it was always only a trap is overly teleological and reflects modern sensibilities.[50]

Conclusion

Jacob Burckhardt probably did not think of inquisitorial writings when looking for sources that might tell him about the alleged birth of modern individualism. While most modern scholars would dispute that such a change even occurred in the early modern period, or happened in the way Burckhardt proposed it did, what did emerge was an "autobiographical consciousness." That is, increasingly people were talking or writing about themselves and the course of their lives. Proof of this lies in the endless number of self-referential texts that were composed in this historical period: from accounts of one's merits, memorials to justify or explain one's past, literature to demonstrate spiritual gifts or challenges, or even picaresque novels. The discourses of life produced in Spanish Inquisition trials undoubtedly should be counted as part of this phenomenon.

No one has yet been able to explain the reasons why a supposedly "sudden" interest arose in inquisition circles about the lives of those accused of heresy. In fact, that question is *mal posée*. The discourse of a life in an inquisition trial was always there; its origins and its function in the process stem from the sacrament of penance. At the same time, the sacrament was behind the more general autobiographical impulse, either helping to create a system of introspection or serving as a model for it. Appreciating the connections among these spheres – pastoral and judicial, penitential and inquisitorial – adds to our understanding of Spanish inquisitors.

Notes

1. This work is part of the research project "Social Transformations in Madrid and the Hispanic Monarchy in the Modern Age: Upward and Downward Movements between Changes and Resistances" (PID2022-142050NB-C22), funded by the Ministry of Science and Innovation.
2. Jacob Burckhardt, *The Civilization of the Renaissance in Italy*, trans. S. G. C. Middlemore, revised and edited by Irene Gordon, 1st ed. 1860 (The New American Library, 1961), 88.
3. Fernando Valdés, *Copilación de las instrucciones del Oficio de la Santa Inquisición hechas en Toledo año de mil y quinientos y sesenta y sesenta y uno* (Toledo, 1561). The instructions are reproduced in Miguel Jiménez Monteserín, *La Inquisición Española: Documentos básicos* (Universitat de València, 2020).
4. Primarily the works of Richard L. Kagan and Abigail Dyer, *Inquisitorial Inquiries: Brief Lives of Secret Jews and Other Heretics* (The Johns Hopkins University Press, 2004); James S. Amelang, "Tracing Lives: The Spanish Inquisition and the Act of Autobiography," in Arianne Baggerman, Rudolf Dekker, and Michael Mascuch, eds., *Controlling Time and Shaping the Self* (Brill, 2011).

5. Peter Burke, "Representations of the Self from Petrarch to Descartes," in Roy Porter, ed., *Rewriting the Self. Histories from the Middle Ages to the Present* (Routledge, 1997).
6. On autobiography in the early modern period, see James S. Amelang, *The Flight of Icarus: Artisan Autobiography in Early Modern Europe* (Stanford University Press, 1998).
7. Kagan and Dyer, *Inquisitorial Inquiries*, 4.
8. Sebastián de Covarrubias y Orozco, *Parte primera del Tesoro de la Lengua Castellana o Española* (Melchor Sánchez, 1611), 322.
9. *Diccionario de Autoridades* – Tomo III (1732), apps2.rae.es/DA.html.
10. Teresa de Jesús, *Libro de la vida de Santa Teresa de Jesús [Manuscript]*, BNE, Mss/2601, f. 1r.
11. We know the work from Manuel Serrano y Sanz, *Autobiografías y memorias de españoles de los siglos XVI y XVII* (Bailly-Bailiere, 1905), 151–210 (151). The text circulated mostly in manuscript form, of which a copy is preserved in the Biblioteca Capitular de Sevilla, Mss. 84-6-29.
12. www.rae.es/banco-de-datos/corde. CORDE yields some incorrect data, so the figures should be taken with caution; however, they are undoubtedly indicative of a trend.
13. "... because he who does not know more than the things that happen in the *speech of his life*, a beginner child can be said ...": *Chrónica del rey Don Guillermo, rey de Ynglaterra y duque de Angeos, y de la reina Doña Beta, su mujer* (s.n., 1526), fol. 1v., BNE, R/2965.
14. Kagan and Dyer, *Inquisitorial Inquiries*, 6; Amelang, "Tracing Lives," 40.
15. José Luis Loriente Torres, "Los 'discursos de la vida' de la documentación inquisitorial como manifestaciones autobiográficas," Doctoral dissertation, Universidad Autónoma de Madrid, 2023, 115–26.
16. AHN, Inq., leg. 87, exp. 2, fol. 97r.
17. AHN, Inq., leg. 100, exp. 21, fols. 18r–20r.
18. Loriente, "Los 'discursos de la vida' de la documentación inquisitorial," 159–85.
19. Gaspar Isidro de Argüello, *Instrucciones del Santo Oficio de la Inquisición, sumariamente, antiguas y nuevas* (Imprenta Real, 1630), fol. 29v. There is an intense historiographical debate about the accuracy and fidelity of inquisition transcriptions.
20. AHN, Inq., leg. 72, exp. 41, fol. 3r. The punctuation marks have been added by us.
21. Jean-Pierre Dedieu, "The Archives of the Holy Office of Toledo as a Source for Historical Anthropology," in Gustav Henningsen, John Tedeschi, and Charles Amiel, eds., *The Inquisition in Early Modern Europe: Studies on Sources and Methods* (Northern Illinois University Press, 1986), 165.
22. AHN, Inq., Leg. 200, Exp. 21.

23. Sonja Herpoel, *In the Wake of St. Teresa: Autobiographies by Mandate* (Rodopi, 1999).
24. Antonio Gómez-Moriana, "The Subversion of Ritual Discourse: An Intertextual Reading of Lazarillo de Tormes," *Canadian Journal of Hispanic Studies* IV (1980): 133–54.
25. David Gitlitz, "Inquisition Confessions and Lazarillo de Tormes," *Hispanic Review* 68 (2000): 53–74.
26. Valdés, *Copilación de las instrucciones del Oficio de la Santa Inquisición*, fols 29r–29v.
27. Pablo García, *Orden que comunmente se guarda en el Santo Oficio de la Inquisición acerca del processar en las causas que en él se tratan conforme à lo que está proueydo por las instructiones antiguas y nueuas* (Pedro Madrigal, 1591), fols. 10r–10v.
28. Bárbara Santiago Medina, "La burocracia inquisitorial: escrituras y documentos," Doctoral dissertation, Universidad Complutense de Madrid, 2016, 119–25.
29. Nicolau Eymerich and Francisco Peña, *Directorium inquisitorum F. Nicolai Eymerici Ordinis Praed. Cum commentariis Francisci Pegnae* . . . (in aedibus Populi Romani apud Georgium Ferrarium, 1587), 421.
30. Argüello, *Instrucciones*. Also see Lu Ann Homza, ed. and trans., *The Spanish Inquisition, 1478–1614: An Anthology of Sources* (Hackett, 2006), 61–79.
31. Valdés, *Copilación de las instrucciones del Oficio de la Santa Inquisición*, fol. 27v. José Luis González Novalín, "Las instrucciones de la Inquisición española: de Torquemada a Valdés (1484–1561)," in José Antonio Escudero López, ed., *Perfiles jurídicos de la Inquisición española* (Complutense University of Madrid. Instituto de Historia de la Inquisición, 1986), 103.
32. Werner Thomas, *Los protestantes y la Inquisición en España en tiempos de Reforma y Contrareforma* (Leuven University Press, 2001), 173; David L. Graizbord, *Souls in Dispute: Converso Identities in Iberia and the Jewish Diaspora, 1580-1700* (University of Pennsylvania Press, 2004), 109–12 Amelang, "Tracing Lives," 37.
33. González Novalín, "Las instrucciones," 105.
34. Antonio Gómez-Moriana, "Autobiography discurso ritual: problemática de la confesión autobiográfica destinada al tribunal Inquisitorial," *Imprevué* 1 (1983): 110.
35. Kimberly Lynn, *Between Court and Confessional: The Politics of Spanish Inquisitors* (Cambridge University Press, 2013), 88–139.
36. Diego de Simancas, *Institutiones Catholicae quibus ordine ac brevitate diseritur quicquid ad praecanendas & extirpandas haereses necessarium est*, ed. Egidio de Colomies (ex officina Aegidii de Colomies typographi . . ., 1552); *La vida* is published in Serrano y Sanz, *Autobiografías y memorias de españoles de los siglos XVI y XVII*, 151–210, with a manuscript copy

preserved in the Biblioteca Capitular de Sevilla, Mss. 84-6-29 (microfiche 58-5-23).
37. Serrano y Sanz, *Autobiografías y memorias de españoles de los siglos XVI y XVII*, 158.
38. Lynn, *Between Court and Confessional*, 127.
39. *Discurso de la vida del Iltmo. y Rmo. Sr. Dn. Martín de Ayala*, also reproduced in the work of Serrano y Sanz, just after that of Simancas (211–88); the original manuscript is in Biblioteca Valenciana Digital, Fondo Antiguo, Mss/787. Adriano Prosperi, *Tribunali della coscienza. Inquisitori, confessori, missionari* (Einaudi, 1996), 270–6.
40. Martín Pérez de Ayala, *Breve compendio para bien examinar la consciencia en el juyzio de la confesión sacramental* (Christoual Plantino, 1574).
41. Benjamin Ehlers, *Between Christians and Moriscos: Juan de Ribera ad Religious Reform in Valencia, 1568–1614* (The John Hopkins University Press, 2006), 19–20; Daniel I. Wasserman-Soler, *Truth in Many Tongues: Religious Conversion and the Languages of the Spanish Empire* (Pennsylvania State University Press, 2020), chapter 3.
42. T. Price Zimmermann, "Confession and Autobiography in the Early Renaissance," in Anthony Molho and John A. Tedeschi, eds., *Renaissance Studies in Honor of Hans Baron* (Northern Illinois University Press, 1971).
43. Lu Ann Homza, *Religious Authority in the Spanish Renaissance* (The Johns Hopkins University Press, 2000), chapter 5; Antonio González Polvillo, *Análisis y repertorio de los tratados y manuales para la confesión en el mundo hispánico (ss. XV–XVIII)* (Universidad de Huelva, 2010), 80 ff.
44. *Confessionario breve y muy prouechoso con el vita Christi con una instrución para los que nuevamente se convierten a nostra santa fe cathólica hecho por vn deuoto religioso de la orden de los predicadores* (Toledo, n.d.), onb.digital/result/1083FD51.
45. Thomas de Vio and Paulo de Palacio, *Suma Caietana, sacado en lenguaje Castellano: Con Annotationes de muchas dubdas y casos de consciencia. By M. Paulo de Palacio, etc.* (in the house of Ioannes Blauio de Colonia, 1557), fol. 91r.
46. Bartolomé de Medina, *Breue instructión de cómo se ha de administrar el Sacramento de la Penitencia, etc* (Herederos de M. Gast, 1579), fols. 288v–289r.
47. Manuel de Arceniega, *Método práctico de hacer fructuosamente confesión general de muchos años: útil para confesores y penitentes* . . . (in the printing house of Ramón Ruiz, to be found in the bookstore of Don Valentín Francés, 1794), 129.
48. Adriano Prosperi, "L'Inquisitore come confesore," in Paolo Prodi and Carla Penuti, eds., *Disciplina dell'anima, disciplina del corpo e disciplina della società tra medioevo ed Età Moderna* (Il Mulino, 1994).
49. Francisco Tomás y Valiente, "El proceso penal," *Historia 16*, 1 (1986): 15–28.

50. By the adjective "teleological," I am referring to a reductive approach in which, for example, we decide the purpose of the Inquisition lay only in persecution, and disregard the causes and contexts behind its creation and survival.

Suggestions for Further Reading

Amelang, James S. *The Flight of Icarus: Artisan Autobiography in Early Modern Europe*. Stanford University Press, 1998.
    "Tracing Lives: The Spanish Inquisition and the Act of Autobiography." In Arianne Baggerman, Rudolf Dekker, and Michael Mascuch, eds., *Controlling Time and Shaping the Self*. Brill, 2011.
Burckhardt, Jacob. *The Civilization of the Renaissance in Italy*. Trans. S. G. C. Middlemore, Irene Gordon, revised and ed. 1st edition 1860. The New American Library, 1961.
Dedieu, Jean-Pierre. "The Archives of the Holy Office of Toledo as a Source for Historical Anthropology." In Gustav Henningsen, John Tedeschi, and Charles Amiel, eds., *The Inquisition in Early Modern Europe: Studies on Sources and Methods*. Northern Illinois University Press, 1986.
Herpoel, Sonja. *In the Wake of St. Teresa: Autobiographies by Mandate*. Rodopi, 1999.
Jiménez Monteserín, Miguel. *La Inquisición Española: Documentos básicos*. Universitat de València, 2020.
Kagan, Richard L. and Abigail Dyer. *Inquisitorial Inquiries: Brief Lives of Secret Jews and Other Heretics*. The Johns Hopkins University Press, 2004.
Prosperi, Adriano. *Tribunali della coscienza. Inquisitori, confessori, missionari*. Einaudi, 1996.
Zimmermann, T. Price. "Confession and Autobiography in the Early Renaissance." In Anthony Molho and John A. Tedeschi, eds., *Renaissance Studies in Honor of Hans Baron*. Northern Illinois University Press, 1971.

Bibliography

Amelang, James S. *The Flight of Icarus: Artisan Autobiography in Early Modern Europe*. Stanford University Press, 1998.
    "Tracing Lives: The Spanish Inquisition and the Act of Autobiography." In Arianne Baggerman, Rudolf Dekker, and Michael Mascuch, eds., *Controlling Time and Shaping the Self*. Brill, 2011.
Anónimo. *Chrónica del rey Don Guillermo, rey de Ynglaterra y duque de Angeos, y de la reina Doña Beta, su mujer*. s.n., 1526.
Arceniega, Manuel de. *Método práctico de hacer fructuosamente confesión general de muchos años: útil para confesores y penitentes … en la*

imprenta de Ramón Ruiz, se hallará en la librería de don Valentín Francés, 1794.

Burckhardt, Jacob. *The Civilization of the Renaissance in Italy*. Trans. S. G. C. Middlemore, and Irene Gordon, revised and ed. 1st edition 1860. The New American Library, 1961.

Burke, Peter. "Representations of the Self from Petrarch to Descartes." In Roy Porter, ed., *Rewriting the Self: Histories from the Middle Ages to the Present*. Routledge, 1997.

Castiglione, Baldassarre y Juan Boscán. *Los quatro libros, del cortesano compuestos en italiano por el conde Balthasar Castellón, y agora nueuamente traduzidos en lengua castellana por Boscán*. Pedro Monpezat, 1534.

Confessionario breve y muy prouechoso con el vita Christi con una instrución para los que nuevamente se convierten a nostra santa fe cathólica hecho por vn deuoto religioso de la orden de los predicadores. Toledo: ND.

de Argüello, Gaspar Isidro. *Instrucciones del Santo Oficio de la Inquisición, sumariamente, antiguas y nuevas*. Imprenta Real, 1630.

de Covarrubias y Orozco, Sebastián. *Parte primera del Tesoro de la Lengua Castellana o Española*. Melchor Sánchez, 1611.

de Medina, Bartolomé. *Breue instructión de cómo se ha de administrar el Sacramento de la Penitencia, etc.* Herederos de M. Gast, 1579.

de Vio, Thomas, and Paulo de Palacio. *Suma Caietana, sacada en lenguaje Castellano: Con Annotationes de muchas dubdas y casos de consciencia. Por el M. Paulo de Palacio, etc.* en casa de Ioannes Blauio de Colonia, 1557.

Dedieu, Jean-Pierre. "The Archives of the Holy Office of Toledo as a Source for Historical Anthropology." In Gustav Henningsen, John Tedeschi, and Charles Amiel, eds., *The Inquisition in Early Modern Europe: Studies on Sources and Methods*, 158–89. Northern Illinois University Press, 1986.

Ehlers, Benjamin. *Between Christians and Moriscos: Juan de Ribera and Religious Reform in Valencia, 1568–1614*. The John Hopkins University Press, 2006.

Eymerich, Nicolau, and Francisco Peña. *Directorium inquisitorum F. Nicolai Eymerici Ordinis Praed. Cum commentariis Francisci Pegnae . . .* in aedibus Populi Romani apud Georgium Ferrarium, 1587.

García, Pablo. *Orden que comunmente se guarda en el Santo Oficio de la Inquisición acerca del processar en las causas que en él se tratan conforme à lo que está proueydo por las instructiones antiguas y nueuas*. Pedro Madrigal, 1591.

Gitlitz, David. "Inquisition Confessions and Lazarillo de Tormes." *Hispanic Review* 68 (2000): 53–74.

Gómez-Moriana, Antonio. "La subversión del discurso ritual: una lectura intertextual del Lazarillo de Tormes." *Revista Canadiense de Estudios Hispánicos* IV (1980): 133–54.

"Autobiografía y discurso ritual: Problemática de la confesión autobiográfica destinada al tribunal inquisitorial." *Imprevué* 1 (1983): 107–27.

González Novalín, José Luis. "Las instrucciones de la Inquisición española. De Torquemada a Valdés (1484–1561)." In José Antonio Escudero López, ed., *Perfiles jurídicos de la Inquisición Española*, 91–110. Universidad Complutense de Madrid. Instituto de Historia de la Inquisición, 1986.

González Polvillo, Antonio. *Análisis y repertorio de los tratados y manuales para la confesión en el mundo hispánico (ss. XV–XVIII)*. Universidad de Huelva, 2010.

Graizbord, David L. *Souls in Dispute: Converso Identities in Iberia and the Jewish Diaspora, 1580–1700*. University of Pennsylvania Press, 2004.

Guevara, Antonio de. *Libro llamado relox de principes en el qual va encorporado el muy famoso libro de Marco aurelio*. por maestre Nicolas tierri imp[re]ssor . . ., 1529.

Herpoel, Sonja. *In the Wake of St. Teresa: Autobiographies by Mandate*. Rodopi, 1999.

Homza, Lu Ann. *Religious Authority in the Spanish Renaissance*. The Johns Hopkins University Press, 2000.

The Spanish Inquisition, 1478–1614: An Anthology of Sources. Hackett, 2006.

Jiménez Monteserin, Miguel. *La Inquisición española. Documentos básicos*. Universitat de València, 2020.

Loriente Torres, José Luis. Los "discursos de la vida" de la documentación inquisitorial como manifestaciones autobiográficas. Doctoral thesis, Universidad Autónoma de Madrid, 2023.

Lynn, Kimberly. *Between Court and Confessional: The Politics of Spanish Inquisitors*. Cambridge University Press, 2013.

Pérez de Ayala, Martín. *Breve compendio para bien examinar la consciencia en el juyzio de la confesión sacramental*. Christoual Plantino, 1574.

Prosperi, Adriano. "L'Inquisitore come confesore." In Paolo Prodi and Carla Penuti, eds., *Disciplina dell'anima, disciplina del corpo e disciplina della società tra medioevo ed Età Moderna*. Il Mulino, 1994.

Tribunali della coscienza. Inquisitori, confessori, missionari. Einaudi, 1996.

Santiago Medina, Bárbara. "La burocracia inquisitorial: escrituras y documentos." Doctoral thesis, Universidad Complutense de Madrid, 2016.

Serrano y Sanz, Manuel. *Autobiografías y memorias de españoles de los siglos XVI y XVII*. Bailly-Bailiere, 1905.

Simancas, Diego de. *Institutiones Catholicae quibus ordine ac brevitate diseritur quicquid ad praecanendas & extirpandas haereses necessarium est*. ex officina Aegidii de Colomies typographi . . ., 1552.

Thomas, Werner. *Los protestantes y la Inquisición en España en tiempos de Reforma y Contrarreforma*. Leuven University Press, 2001.

Tomás y Valiente, Francisco. "El proceso penal." *Historia* 16 (1986): 15–28.

Valdés, Fernando. *Copilación de las instrucciones del Oficio de la Santa Inquisición hechas en Toledo año de mil y quinientos y sesenta y uno.* Toledo, 1561.

Zimmermann, T. Price. "Confession and Autobiography in the Early Renaissance." In Anthony Molho and John A. Tedeschi, eds., *Renaissance Studies in Honor of Hans Baron.* Northern Illinois University Press, 1971.

LU ANN HOMZA AND
AMANDA L. SCOTT

4

Scandals

No matter what their socioeconomic or intellectual class, people who lived in early modern Europe shared a concept of scandal, though they undoubtedly had different senses of its possible degrees and attached it to dissimilar offenses. Something "scandalous" carried a sense of disgrace, outrage, shock, or wickedness; the adjective intensified the transgression and implied that the wrongdoing was known to and disapproved of by others. When people did disorderly and reckless things, they knew they were risking public opprobrium, but it was their neighbors who felt the brunt of these actions and complained they had been "scandalized" by others' misbehaviors.

In legal records from early modern Spain, scandal was invoked as an aggravating factor when infants were abandoned, parish priests had concubines, widows were assaulted, married people had affairs, and insults were repeated in public. For example, in 1603, Ramón de Irarte, who lived in the Navarrese village of Uscarrés, greatly scandalized his neighbors as well as residents of surrounding villages because he was sleeping with a married woman. Ramón and his lover had been caught in bed the year before, when village officials became so disturbed that they purposely spied on the couple. Now, villagers were saying that Ramón was having sex with his lover's daughter as well.[1] Scandal occurred when honorable women had their headdresses knocked off in public by enraged husbands. A woman who would not stop calling another one a witch, or women who came to blows over who took precedence in church, incurred scandal as well.[2]

In 1609, the mayor and constable of Vera launched a criminal complaint against a neighbor, Martín Sanz de Taberna, for not wishing to assume responsibility for a three-month-old infant left at his front door. When confronted by village officials, Martín denied the infant was his. The formal charge against him noted that he had impregnated and abandoned other girls and their babies, that he was a man who did not want to do his job as a royal notary, and that he had been residing in the house of María de Apestegui for some years, causing great scandal and harmful gossip. The village asked that Martín be harshly penalized as a warning to others.[3] Finally, parish priests who liked to pawn church valuables, dance in the streets, or fish in the nude could also incur charges of scandal.[4]

Given their sense of privilege, attention to status, potential lack of vocation, and probable absence of oversight, it should not be surprising that Spanish inquisitors as well as their staff could provoke scandals. Spanish inquisitors could commit moral offenses, avoid responsibilities, or watch misconduct happen under their noses; the people they employed could also flout procedures and norms, or ignore supervision. Crucially, inquisitors and their employees were subject only to the inquisitorial legal jurisdiction: In theory and almost always in practice, this condition meant that badly behaving inquisitors were subject to discipline by their supervisors – the inquisitor-general and the Suprema – while inquisitorial notaries, jailers, commissioners, familiars, and receivers of sequestered or confiscated goods from suspected or convicted heretics were subject to discipline by the inquisitors of their specific tribunal. It was not particularly unusual for bishops to attempt to intervene with their own courts when inquisitorial staff committed crimes, but the staff knew they had the right to be prosecuted by their inquisitor-employers. In fact, that jurisdictional privilege was a major incentive for pursuing employment with an inquisition tribunal.[5] Inquisitors had economic privileges as well. They were exempt from royal taxes, sales taxes, and the requirement to lodge soldiers. In 1505, Ferdinand II of Aragon signed a royal decree stipulating that inquisitors would be the judges in civil or criminal cases affecting their officials.

There is no doubt that inquisitors could argue with, shout at, and insult one another in their tribunals, as well as ignore the wrongdoings of their personnel. The Logroño tribunal, for example, seems to have had a significant history of bad behavior on the part of its inquisitors. Between 1610 and 1613, the three stationed there raged about each other to Inquisitor-General Bernardino de Sandoval y Rojas: They complained about canceled vacations, overly lengthy deliberations, inappropriate clothing choices, and arrogance.[6] Over the same four years, they also disregarded improprieties committed by the notaries *del secreto*, who were responsible for taking down witness testimony. Those notaries were seldom in the tribunal, where they belonged: Instead, they were out gathering genealogies, for private customers, in their native lands. Those customers wanted inquisitorial employment; they paid Logroño's notaries to hide information if they had Jewish or Muslim ancestry, which was disqualifying. When the notaries finally returned home, they exaggerated the extent of their journeys and inflated what they were owed as compensation.[7]

Awareness of inquisition-generated scandal often came to the Suprema's knowledge when inquisition tribunals were formally visited and inspected. For example, in 1619, a formal visitation of the Logroño tribunal was mandated by the Suprema and carried out by Inquisitor Martín Cardillo y Aldrete, who was stationed in the inquisition tribunal in Santiago de Compostela. The Suprema ordered Cardillo y Aldrete to see whether "some inquisitors and [their] officials are worthy of sanction or punishment."[8] The Suprema also provided Carillo y Aldrete with a list of questions to pose during his inspection. Some queries asked whether there was "peace and concord" among the inquisitors, and whether "they lived honestly without public concubines and without having access to female prisoners, or the daughters or relatives of prisoners." Certain inquiries questioned whether the inquisitors had "failed to attend acts which they should personally witness," such as sessions of torture; another wondered whether "through friendship or money, has some legal action been quashed regarding the reconciled heretics who are in perpetual prison."[9]

The questionnaires that guided a visitation to an inquisition tribunal were standardized to some extent, but sometimes they provide clues about the specific issues afflicting a tribunal. Documents authorizing a visitation may reveal problems as well. For example, in 1596 Inquisitor-General Pedro de Portocarrero received inside information that two inquisitors in the Santiago tribunal were exhibiting loose morals with women and had nearly come to blows over a certain servant girl. The official visitor to the tribunal discovered that inquisitors Alonso Blanco and Juan Ortiz de Matienzo had been involved in a tempestuous love triangle with a servant named María. A local priest testified that two years earlier, on the feast of Corpus Christi, Matienzo suspected that his colleague Blanco was hiding María in his house. When Matienzo confronted Blanco at the latter's front door, Blanco refused to admit him, and the two men did not speak for five months. The same priest confirmed that María had returned to her native village, but he also noted that Blanco had another new servant girl who was extremely attractive: This one traveled by horseback and was dressed like a lady, with a white headdress. The whole city was gossiping about her.[10]

Of course, other employees of the Spanish Inquisition could also provoke scandal via sex, as well as violence and money. Inquisition commissioners and familiars could be prosecuted by the tribunals that had hired them when they indulged in concubinage or committed rape.[11] In 1538, a judge in charge of the Inquisition's confiscated goods was turned in by his son for having a long-term sexual relationship with a "white morisco slave."[12] In 1602, inquisitors in Logroño sentenced Juan Melón for entering the inquisition's house of penance, where convicted heretics were confined, in order to have sex with a servant of the warden there.[13] Finally, a massive trial survives from 1630 in Seville, in which inquisitors tried one of their own prison lawyers for concubinage and illicit relationships with the city's nuns.[14]

Homicide in inquisition circles was not unknown. In 1569, inquisition familiar Francisco Núñez Tenorio protested being sentenced *in absentia* to a fine of 500 ducats for the alleged murder of Juan Gutierrez: He denied his guilt, but more importantly, he adamantly asserted that his case belonged to the Inquisition, not to a judge appointed by King Philip II.[15] The inquisitors of Seville backed up Francisco's story and provided him with a signed document written on parchment, which verified that he was an inquisition familiar. The inquisitors threatened the secular judges with excommunication if they continued to pursue Francisco's case. Not surprisingly, the secular jurisdiction countered: Its officials noted that Francisco had accomplices who were not familiars and who needed to be pursued; moreover, the case belonged to them because the murder involved premeditation.[16] Such jurisdictional conflicts were not unusual. In 1661, for instance, a lawsuit was filed by the royal justice of Aragon, which protested the Inquisition's jurisdiction over a familiar who was accused of banditry along with murdering the nephew of Aragon's vice-chancellor.[17]

Inquisition prisons could also turn into sites for scandal. Juan de Vergara, secretary to the archbishop of Toledo, subverted an inquisition case against his older half-brother from 1530 to 1533 with bribes, promises, and secret communication techniques that infiltrated the inquisitors' jail.[18] Once Vergara himself was detained, he leaned out the windows of his cell and spoke to bystanders, thereby breaking the code of silence that always applied in inquisition procedure; the inquisitors responded by nailing his windows shut. From 1609 to 1611, witch suspects imprisoned in Logroño, who were Basque speakers, were pressured into naming false accomplices by Basque translators hired by the tribunal. The inquisitors there – or anywhere in the Spanish empire, for that matter – did not understand Basque and had no idea what was transpiring.[19] In 1620, a familiar and notary of Madrid's inquisition tribunal, Alonso de Paredes, was accused of abetting the escape of Carlos de Arellano as Paredes transported Arellano to Toledo. Paredes was condemned to a year of exile, deprived of his title as a familiar, and ordered to pay a fine. In 1633, the jailer of the inquisition tribunal in Cuenca was prosecuted by his employers on the demand of Isabel de la Mota: The jailer fell under suspicion because Mota's husband had been murdered by an inquisition familiar who used keys to escape the tribunal's prison. Finally, in 1668, the Suprema in Madrid ordered an investigation into one of Barcelona's inquisitors for having assisted the flight of Joseph Guinart and Joseph Mofat, who were on trial for having murdered the receiver of sequestered goods for the Barcelona tribunal. Guinart and Mofat had tried to break out more than once; they had communicated with persons on the outside; inquisitor Francisco Saravia was suspected of aiding and abetting them.[20]

Money could figure in inquisition scandals as well, as the death of the Barcelona receiver of goods implies. An inquisitorial receiver of sequestered goods in Zaragoza started a criminal investigation in 1589 after he noticed that money was missing from the "ark of the three keys in the

Secret Chamber" of the tribunal; the defendant ended up being the notary who tracked the sequestrations. The opportunity to squeeze also could prove irresistible. Like their counterparts in Logroño, Toledo's notaries *del secreto* were accused in 1618 of wringing money out of individuals who hoped to become employees of the tribunal.[21]

Concubines, rape, pregnancies, homicide, assault, flight from prison, theft, extortion: Inquisitors and their employees were deeply embedded in local circumstances; they certainly could forget their obligations, with scandal as a result.[22] Notably, however, legal privilege and the rule of secrecy meant that inquisitorial employees did not inevitably have their misdeeds proclaimed in a public space. Furthermore, because inquisitors were punished by their governing supervisors – the Suprema and the inquisitor-general – their own potential misdeeds were not necessarily made public, either. That sort of confidentiality could fall to pieces, however, if inquisitors and their employees ended up in civil lawsuits, where there was no principle of secrecy at all, or if inquisitors-general and the Suprema commuted or revoked sentences, which could have become common knowledge within a community.[23]

An analogous situation in terms of hiding scandal occurred with another crime prosecuted by the Spanish Inquisition: that of "solicitation," which modern readers might link to prostitution, but which in early modern Catholic countries meant the solicitation of sexual contact by a priest during the sacrament of penance. For centuries, clergy who misbehaved sexually belonged to the legal jurisdiction of bishops. They became a problem for the Spanish Inquisition in 1561, when Pope Pius IV promulgated a bull that condemned the sexual solicitation of female penitents by their confessors and handed the responsibility to prosecute to Spanish inquisitors. Sexual solicitation during penance was heretical because it disrespected that sacrament. The offending clerics injected the sacrament with sin, abused their office, misappropriated sacred space, and, knowingly or not, assisted Protestants, who enjoyed seeing Catholics deface their own sacred rituals.[24]

Still, Pius's 1561 bull was confined in scope: It limited the heresy of solicitation to sexual words or actions that only occurred while the sacrament was literally in progress. Modern scholars think that Spanish clerics quickly understood the question of timing and acted accordingly: If they decided to approach their female penitents, they made sure to do it before the penitent had made the sign of the Cross, or after the penitent had been absolved. Penitents also could appear for confession, only to have their confessors tell them not to engage in it at that particular moment. Such loopholes were closed in 1622, when Pope Gregory XV widened the scope of the heresy via a papal bull. Now, solicitation could happen outside the formal space for confession, and before or after the sacrament took place. It also could occur if confession was simply a pretext for a sexual overture.

At its core, solicitation was understood by inquisitors and other legal and ecclesiastical authorities as a perversion in the exchange of absolution of sin for sexual favors. Solicitation often went hand in hand with auricular confession, which in the Catholic tradition, was a key element of absolution: Earlier medieval penance was harsh, public, and often excruciating, but its effective completion was essentially in the hands of the individual sinner; in the twelfth century the focus shifted more to the priests' ability to offer absolution for deeply felt contrition, thus recasting the relationship between the penitent and the priest, and placing the penitent in a state of moral dependency upon the (male) confessor.[25] The shift toward clerical supremacy in matters of absolution further solidified the relationship as unequal. Priests were in positions of power with their superior education and often higher social standing. They could leverage their power to forgive or deny absolution.

Of course, medieval and early modern authorities did not view solicitation in terms of power dynamics. Instead, they worried that priests who solicited sexual favors would cause the laity to esteem them very little and perhaps even abandon this sacrament all together. In the worst-case scenario, abused or disillusioned penitents might seek consolation instead from heretics and Protestants, or might at least be more receptive to their message that the Catholic clergy was thoroughly corrupt.

Nonetheless, more frequently the problem was that priests took advantage of vulnerable penitents. In solicitation cases handled by the Spanish Inquisition, prosecutors often alleged that priests used the confessional setting to meet women, attempted to find out where they lived, and then tried to meet up with them later. Other clerics tried to convince penitents to make their confessions at the priests' homes, or in other covert locations. Some of the most vivid episodes detail priests who made penitents come to their houses for confession, only for the penitent to discover that the priest wanted to hear their confessions from his bed.[26] Licensed confessors assigned to convents raised a host of other problems; contemporary commentators such as Alonso de Andrade, for instance, warned of situations in which nuns became so enthralled by the intellectual superiority of their confessors that they developed unhealthy obsessions with them.[27] On the other hand, bored, competitive, and/or vocationally unfit nuns might attempt to harass, tease, and assault their own confessors, as did the nuns of La Concepción in Madrid in 1607. In this case, which would have been at home in Boccaccio's *Decameron*, when the overqualified Don Pedro de Villanueva arrived at La Concepción, the nuns there began to torment and provoke him, calling him "a saint or else hardly a man," as well as cold and impotent. To regain his masculine honor, Villanueva eventually solicited three nuns, who cooperated until they grew jealous of his attentions to a fourth nun and subsequently denounced him to the Inquisition.[28]

Clerical solicitation was a difficult heresy for inquisitors to prosecute, both legally and socially. The Spanish Inquisition's ideals of proof rested on a confession or two eyewitnesses to the same event. Given that solicitation occurred within a sacrament involving only two people, it was basically impossible to find two eyewitnesses to the offense. As far as denunciations were concerned, scholars have hypothesized that women were generally loath to complain about their confessors to inquisitors or inquisitorial employees who were deputized to take sworn testimony. The women could be married; they might risk the honor of their household by deposing, despite the Inquisition's rule of secrecy. Though the Inquisition published edicts of faith that mentioned solicitation as a heresy that must be decried, one modern scholar has asserted that out of 560 witnesses to solicitation, a mere fifteen, or 4 percent, said they had come forward because of inquisitorial edicts.[29]

Yet earlier historians have missed two crucial and contradictory facts about the Inquisition's prosecution of solicitation. First, inquisitors routinely sentenced clergy guilty of this heresy to penalties that took them out of their communities. Inquisitors forced *solicitantes* into exile, seclusion in monasteries, or into the royal Mediterranean galleys. Furthermore, inquisitors usually delivered the sentences against soliciting clergy in private rites of reconciliation and thereby avoided broadcasting what the malefactors had done. The inquisition's sensitivity to scandal in this regard was notable; inquisitors were not eager to have Catholic clerics suffer public shame. Their desire to protect sinful clergy could be interpreted as having a silencing effect.[30]

Significantly, when Spanish Inquisition studies surged after the death of Spanish dictator Francisco Franco in November 1975, scholars in the 1980s and 1990s still neglected the inquisition's prosecution of solicitation because they were more interested in patterns of repression and religious minorities. Even more recent studies have focused on how inquisitors and other religious authorities sought to curb this crime from an educational or prosecutorial angle. Far less attention has been paid to how victims fit into this process.

One telling example of such neglect concerns a 1793 inquisition trial from the Spanish city of Valladolid, which was taken out of Spain at some point in the late nineteenth century by a naval officer, eventually ending up at the United States Naval Academy in Annapolis, Maryland. The prosecution features the depositions of twenty women against a Capuchin friar, Miguel Coreses: He had been arrested by Valladolid's inquisitors on charges of groping, soliciting, and otherwise assaulting nearly an entire convent of nuns, as well as other women in Rueda, Valladolid, and Madrid. Coreses's advances were as extreme as they were varied. He touched women through the confessional screen, put his hands on their legs, caressed their faces, and masturbated while he heard their confessions. One nun testified that Coreses had attempted multiple times to "stick his tongue in her mouth while touching her breasts and playing with himself." Another woman testified that Coreses had explicitly refused to hear her confession unless she let him touch her; he had also insinuated that he wanted to go further and was seeking "carnal acts." These were not isolated instances: Coreses had been soliciting single women and nuns for at least seven years. The Naval Academy archivist dismissed the Coreses case as unworthwhile and tedious: His comments noted "I have reviewed this trial," "it is nothing special," and "this trial can tell us nothing new about the Spanish Inquisition."[31]

Nevertheless, if the Spanish Inquisition's sentencing of solicitating clergy was deliberately private, its interest in such cases also complicates our assumptions about power dynamics, because inquisitorial prosecutions in this instance can flip the victim–oppressor template we are usually primed to notice in inquisition history. It turns out that the Spanish Inquisition was uniquely suited to prosecuting clerical sexual misconduct and providing a platform in which victims could discretely and safely call out their abusers.

Women – not their male relatives – made the denunciations about clerical sexual overtures to inquisition tribunals throughout the Spanish empire, and the willingness of the Spanish Inquisition to let female victims speak freely is striking.[32] Inquisitorial hearings proceeded in secrecy; female victims were more shielded and may have felt more protected, and this condition positively affected the efficacy of bringing a solicitation cases.

Such conditions did not hold when women in early modern Spain tried to complain about sexual overtures or attacks in other legal jurisdictions. In this honor-based culture, victims had to consider often life-changing harm to their own and their family's honor when reporting and pursuing charges against their assailants, though as one scholar has forcefully argued, victims (and their families) could also recoup a substantial portion of honor simply by making a legal complaint.[33] Participants in nonmarital consensual sex also put their honor at risk, to the point that historians have framed lawsuits over broken promises to marry as attempts to recast sexual conduct in financial terms.[34] Importantly, cases over any kind of sexual affront handled by the secular legal jurisdiction were almost exclusively brought at the behest of male relatives of female victims – and there was no rule of secrecy in any respect.[35] In these cases, the woman's testimony was filtered through her male relative's voices; male relatives' narrations of the events were recorded as the woman's testimony, even if she was not present for the deposition.

The venue in which victims could testify and how they did so vis-à-vis depositions by male relatives is an important difference between inquisitorial trials and cases of rape or assault handled by secular jurisdictions. The Archivo General de Navarra, for instance, holds an astonishing 1,318 cases of *estupro* occurring between the years 1575 and 1650, forty-seven of which involved force, meaning they were probably rapes or assaults rather than seductions. *Estupro forçado* almost always relied on second-stage testimony by relatives of the accused, who described physical signs, circumstances, and the character of each person involved; in only a few of these cases did the women themselves testify.[36] Where they did testify – as in the case of fifteen-year-old Ana de Gascon, who was raped in 1578 in a field by an itinerant traveler while she tended her family's livestock – they did so under the close supervision of their fathers, who were present at all stages of the inquest.[37] This is even clearer in the case of Gracia de Muto, who was also raped while she tended her family's cows in 1581: Though the notarized witness testimony seems to be hers, it was actually a statement made by her father in her name.[38]

Even more striking are cases of rape by priests handled by the diocesan court in Pamplona. These are rare, namely because few rape victims fell directly under the jurisdiction of the diocese, as opposed to the secular courts, but the diocese did claim control over allegations of sexual assault brought by *seroras*, who were devout laywomen employed by the diocese to care for shrines and parish churches.[39] Though perhaps only four such trials exist, they are noteworthy primarily because of the consistent failure of the diocesan court to rule in favor of the victims (though underreporting means that more rapes might have occurred).[40]

In 1618, for instance, Don Miguel de Gorrosari was criminally charged with "punching the [serora] in the public plaza and calling her many ugly and injurious words." These crimes were exacerbated by the fact that the "two were illicit lovers and living together, to the great scandal of the villagers," though their relationship seems to have been far from loving and consensual.[41] In 1643, Elena de Erauso, serora in Urnieta, Gipuzkoa, was raped repeatedly by the parish priest, Don Andrés de Ierategi. Upon discovering she was pregnant, Elena confronted her assailant, but Don Andrés "punched her in the stomach, and as a result, she lost the child." Later, Don Andrés tried to "pay her so that she would remain silent," and arranged for his cousins to harass her and intimidate her into signing a document stating that the two had had no relationship. Unable to work due to the injuries Don Andrés had inflicted upon her, Elena approached a number of other clergy in Urnieta, telling them what had happened and asking that they intervene on her behalf. Not one of them was willing to take up her case; instead, several reportedly took the opportunity to spread rumors that she was mentally unstable. Finally, Elena journeyed to Pamplona where she presented her case in person and initiated her own lawsuit against her rapist. Unfortunately for Elena, the bishop's attorney seemed to have come to the same conclusion as Urnieta's clergy. Elena's lawsuit led to no real or meaningful punishment. Instead, claiming that there was not enough proof to rule in favor of one side or the other, the bishop absolved Don Andrés. Elena, on the other hand, was fined three ducats – for bringing what the ecclesiastical tribunal ruled were "false" charges – and sentenced to three months reclusion in her shrine.[42]

These cases exemplify the haphazard and often ambivalent approach townspeople and diocesan authorities took to prosecuting rape or assault. Privileging male religious celibacy over women's celibacy was standard practice, and women – seroras, female servants, and townswomen alike – were regularly held responsible for male clerics' sexual misbehavior.[43] The male clergy were likely to receive minimal censure for sexual misconduct, while the rumor (and scandal) of the same misconduct stuck to women far more easily than it did to men. Indeed, the most common reprimand for priests accused of sexual misconduct amounted to instructions from the bishop to henceforth live with honesty, "and refrain from talking to, dealing with, or communicating with the woman with whom he is accused of having joined himself with in suspicious locations." Bishops were upfront about their intentions with these reprimands. They preferred to think about allegations of sexual misconduct as uncertain rumors; in the end, they just wished their priests to stop doing suspicious things "so that the murmuring will cease."[44] Like inquisitors, bishops also feared scandal.

These responses help us to see why bringing a charge of sexual misconduct in an inquisitorial court might be attractive to victims. In solicitation cases before inquisitors, female victims took the initiative to file complaints and then were given secrecy: They were theoretically shielded from the knowledge or awareness of husbands, fathers, or parishioners. Furthermore, women complaining about solicitation often raised further abuses by the priests or friars in question that had not occurred during the sacrament of penance.

In the 1793 Coreses case from Valladolid, for instance, the women listed one violation after another that had occurred outside of penance. A similar phenomenon occurred when the Cuenca inquisition tribunal investigated Don Diego de Quiroga in Requena in 1613: During the investigation, multiple women came forward to describe how Quiroga had actually gotten on *his* knees during confession, begged them for their friendship, and exposed himself to them.[45] In 1589, the Toledo inquisition tribunal investigated rumors that one Don Juan Jacome, friar of the order of St. Bernard and native of Eboli, Naples, and confessor in the parish of Sanct Yuste in Madrid, had been propositioning various female penitents. A total of thirteen women testified against Jacome, detailing the abuses they had suffered, from groping to harassing language. María de la Torre, for instance, testified "that while she was making her confession," the friar had told her "he wanted to be her friend, and he would treat her better than any other man on this earth." On hearing this, María laughed and "took it for a joke," but the "friar grabbed her hands and lunged towards her, and then she jumped up, as if burned, and the friar kissed her on the mouth and grabbed her belly, and told her that they needed to be close friends." María testified that she had avoided the confessor ever since.

Other women reported nearly identical attacks at the hands of Jacome: The confessor reportedly told Marina de Madrigal that "she had pretty hands," and "that she shouldn't confess with anyone else." He also asked where she lived, only to "go [later] to the said house, stand out front, and walk [back and forth] in front of it." Geronima Rodrigues testified that Jacome also asked her where she lived, "offered to buy her a [better] house," and then "grabbed her breasts." Iñes de Ortiz, a widow, reported that Jacome took her hands "and placed them on his shame," at which point she declared she had nothing more to confess and left. In his own defense, Jacome claimed that the entire pack of women amounted to unreliable witnesses, due "to their youth, qualities, and sex, and [because of this] . . . [they] are inclined to false testimony, traitorous actions and convictions, lies, fraud, and every category of mischief." Significantly, he also contended that "[the things they claim to have happened] are impossible and could not have happened . . . because of the [short time it takes to make a] confession, as well as the public place in which it occurs." Jacome received six years of monastic reclusion; he also was forbidden to hear the confessions of anyone, women or men. The sentence was upheld through appeal.[46]

The patterns evinced in the Jacome case recur in other locations and centuries. The quantity of witnesses and details mattered; defense claims about the witnesses' characters did not necessarily carry weight even when the women were deposing about dishonorable events. In a 1693–4 case from the Canary Islands against a Franciscan friar,

Domingo Mireles, two women had denounced Mireles to inquisition personnel, which resulted in his prosecution.[47] Josepha Ramirez, aged twenty-two, had Mireles as her confessor for two years: During that time, he repeatedly solicited her when she was on her knees, which was a sign that the sacrament of penance was about to commence. When the prosecutor asked Josepha for the form of solicitation that Mireles used, she relayed both verbal and physical acts. Josepha said that Mireles used love language with her, calling her "my life and little sister," and asking "when will we have the chance to fulfill the desire I have for you?" Mireles put his hands under her cloak; he touched her face, throat, and breasts, and said he could not eat or sleep for love of her.

Mireles's language toward Josepha was extravagant and explicit. If she got cold at night, he would be happy to warm her up; he wanted her uncle and brother to be asleep constantly, so they could not gaze upon her; if it were possible, he would enclose her in a little cloud, where only he could see her. When Josepha told him that she had heard an inquisitorial edict about solicitation, and was worried about her conscience, he replied "what they read out at church is just to put fear into the faithful."

Mireles's treatment of Francisca de Artacho, aged thirty-three, was no better.[48] Francisca was a third-order Franciscan. When she deposed before the inquisition's commissioner, she said she had Mireles as her confessor and spiritual father (*padre espiritual*) for a year and a half. Once, she went to him for the sacrament of penance: When he told her not to confess, she asked why. At that point, "he put his hands under her cloak and sought hers, with caressing words, telling her he had dreamed about her." Francisca responded by chastising him, saying "Look, you are here in God's place." Another time, he caressed her face, and when she told him not to do it, he replied, "oh, don't be so scrupulous." Finally – and here, Francisca said Mireles must have been armed by the devil – he put his foot under the edge of her skirt and touched her leg. At that point, Francisca retired to a corner of the church to cry, believing that God wanted to mortify her through such experiences.

Mireles's defense was short; it consisted of a character statement, without defense witnesses.[49] He had only used amorous language with Josepha, the unmarried twenty-two-year-old, as a means of persuading her to enter a convent. As far as the *beata* Francisca was concerned, he did not move his foot in order to touch her leg; he might have been bitten by a flea, which caused his leg to jerk forward. Besides, how could he have put his leg under Josepha's skirt while she was kneeling? In kissing her sleeve, his mouth could have ended up on her face. Mireles reported that he had not thought the inquisition edicts were relevant for his female penitents because he had never had any intention of offending God. Though he and his lawyers told the tribunal that it could not possibly have a "full and exuberant proof" to convict him with only two witnesses, it did so. Mirales was secluded in his Franciscan monastery, prohibited from any sort of vote on monastic matters, and ordered to remain silent about the cause of his arrest, as well as anything else he might have learned while staying in the inquisitors' jail.[50]

It was routine for women denouncing clerics for solicitation before the Spanish Inquisition to have their own characters investigated by the relevant tribunal. The results of those investigations were written into the margins of the trial manuscripts, though the questions and answers were not reproduced, nor were the witnesses named. Mirales opined that Josepha and Francisca might have been conducting a conspiracy against him; the inquisitors did not buy that line of reasoning; they finally removed and silenced him from his worldly and monastic communities. Meanwhile, Josepha and Francisca thought it was worthwhile to speak voluntarily to inquisition commissioners about the ills they had suffered at Mirales's hands. Their sense of physical and spiritual violation outweighed concerns about their personal or familial honor. While they might have been encouraged or coached by family members, they deposed alone, without intervention. Questions of scandal – whether committed by the clergy, inquisitors, inquisitorial staff, or inquisition prisoners – thus leave modern readers in an appropriately complicated place, interpretatively. When it came to the Spanish Inquisition, privilege, jurisdiction, and honor mattered, but so too did shame, crimes, and character.

Notes

1. Archivo Real y General de Navarra, Tribunales reales [hereafter AGN], sig. 266131 (1603), fol. 1r-v.
2. AGN, sig. 212327 (1581–83), fol. 1r-v; Lu Ann Homza, *The Child Witches of Olague* (Pennsylvania State University Press, 2024), 114–15. Scott Taylor, *Honor and Violence in Golden-Age Spain* (Yale University Press, 2008), 157.
3. AGN, sig. 284949 (1609), fol. 1r-v.

4. Archivo Diocesano de Pamplona, Tribunal eclesiástico [ADP], C/669, N. 26 (1615), fol. 1r; ADP, C/207, N. 1 (1606), fol. 3r.
5. For an enlightening discussion of the jurisdictional rights of familiars, which were controversial, Ángel de Prada Moura, *El tribunal de la Inquisición en España (1478–1834)* (Actas Editoriales, 2003), 42–4.
6. Lu Ann Homza, *Village Infernos and Witches' Advocates: Witch-Hunting in Navarre, 1608–1614* (Pennsylvania State University Press, 2022), 154–65.
7. Homza, *Village Infernos*, 165–72, 178–9.
8. Archivo Histórico Nacional [AHN], Sección de la Inquisición [Inqu.], Legajo [Leg.] 1683, Image 61.
9. AHN, Inqu., Leg. 1683, Images 66–75 for the entire interrogatory.
10. AHN, Inqu., Leg. 2043, Expediente [Exp.].2, Images 3, 11–13.
11. For example, AHN, Inqu., Leg. 2142, Exp.3 (1583–84); Inqu., Leg. 2043, Exp. 4 (1611–12); Inqu., Leg. 2145, Exp. 2 (1627); Inqu., Leg. 1818, Exp. 26 (1629–32); Inqu., Leg. 4586, Exp. 24 (1705–8).
12. AHN, Inqu., Leg. 1972, Exp. 1.
13. AHN, Inqu., Lib. 835, ff. 63–88.
14. AHN, Inqu., Leg. 1085, Exp. 4.
15. AHN, Inqu., Leg. 2055, Exp. 4, image 3.
16. AHN, Inqu., Leg. 2055, Exp. 4, images 9, 23, 27.
17. AHN, Inqu., Leg. 1788, Exp. 10.
18. Lu Ann Homza, *Religious Authority in the Spanish Renaissance* (The Johns Hopkins University Press, 2000), chapter 1.
19. Homza, *Village Infernos*, 82–4; Peio J. Monteano Sorbet, *El iceberg Navarro: Euskera y castellano en la Navarra del siglo XVI* (Pamiela, 2017).
20. AHN, Inqu., Leg. 2091, Exp. 6; AHN, Inqu., Leg. 1927, Exp. 2; AHN, Inqu., Leg. 1592, Exp. 24.
21. AHN, Inqu., Leg. 1806, Exp. 2; AHN, Inqu., Leg. 2104, Exp. 10.
22. Kimberly Lynn, *Between Court and Confessional: The Politics of Spanish Inquisitors* (Cambridge University Press, 2013).
23. Lu Ann Homza, "When Witches Litigate: New Sources from Early Modern Navarre," *Journal of Modern History* 91 (2019): 245–75; Homza, *Village Infernos*, chapter 5. See, too, the "Registro del Secreto de los Inquisidores Generales" of 1695–1703, which contains commutations and revocations of sentences for particular tribunals: AHN, Inqu., Leg. 407.
24. Stephen Haliczer, *Sexuality in the Confessional: A Sacrament Profaned* (Oxford University Press, 1996); Adelina Sarrión Mora, *Sexualidad y confesión: la solicitación ante el tribunal del Santo Oficio (siglos xvi–xix)* (Alianza Editorial, 1994); Juan Antonio Alejandre, *El veneno de Dios: La inquisición de Sevilla ante el delito de solicitación en confesión* (Siglo XXI de España Editores, S.A., 1994), and Eduardo Galván Rodríguez, "La praxis inquisitorial contra confesores solicitantes (tribunal de la inquisición de Canarias, 1601–1700)," *Revista de la Inquisición* (1996): 103–85.

25. Haliczer, *Sexuality in the Confessional*, 7–8; Rob Means, *Penance in Medieval Europe, 600–1200* (Cambridge University Press, 2014); Jodi Bilinkoff, *Related Lives: Confessors and Their Female Penitents, 1450–1750* (Cornell University Press, 2005).
26. For example, see the case of Pedro de Orezqueta, suspected of lechery among other crimes, in Gascueña in 1672. Archivo Diocesano de Cuenca [ADC], Sección de Inquisición [Inqu], Leg. 538, N. 6819 (1672), fol. 1v.
27. Alonso de Andrade, *Libro de guía de la virtud y de la imitación de Nuestra Señora*, book 2 (Francisco Moroto, 1644), uvadoc.uva.es/handle/10324/34747.
28. AHN, Inqu., Leg. 233, exp. 9.
29. Haliczer, *Sexuality in the Confessional*, 53.
30. Celeste I. McNamara, "Priests Behaving Badly: The Problem of Scandal in the Early Modern Catholic Church," *The Journal of Modern History* 96 (2024): 47–77.
31. United States Naval Academy Museum Archives [USNA], FICM.D27.0116.
32. Archivo de la Real Chancellería de Valladolid, Sala de Vizcaya (ARCV), 174, 3/177, 1 (1580), fols. 17r–v, 57r–58r, 71r, and 550r; and ARCV, 3156, 4 (1622).
33. Taylor, *Honor and Violence*, 55, 93, 188.
34. Abigail Dyer, "Seduction by Promise of Marriage: Law, Sex, and Culture in Seventeenth-Century Spain," *The Sixteenth Century Journal* 34, no. 2 (2003): 439–55.
35. See many examples of this at the appellate level in Renato Barahona, *Sex Crimes, Honour, and the Law in Early Modern Spain: Vizcaya, 1528–1735* (University of Texas Press, 2003).
36. See among others, AGN, sig. 074685 (1636); AGN, sig. 011319 (1578); AGN, sig. 29844 (1642); AGN, sig. 29577 (1604); AGN, sig. 212853 (1594); AGN, sig. 11427 (1580) (note: this case is mistakenly cataloged as the rape of a man, but actually pertains to an assault against him coupled with the rape of his sister); AGN, sig. 11197 (1576); and AGN, sig. 14598 (1619–20).
37. AGN, sig. 011319 (1578), fols. 1v–3v.
38. AGN, sig. 056284 (1581), fols. 3r–v.
39. Amanda L. Scott, *The Basque Seroras: Local Religion, Gender, and Power in Northern Iberia, 1550–1800* (Cornell University Press, 2020).
40. See for instance ADP, C/1100 (1674), N.10.
41. ADP, C/638 (1618), N.18, fols. 1r and 16r.
42. Scott, *The Basque Seroras*, 135–6; ADP, C/767, N.18 (1643), fols. 5r–13r, 46r–47r, 49r, and 243v.
43. On the difficulties of erasing the clerical wife, see Dyan Elliot, *Fallen Bodies: Pollution, Sexuality, and Demonology in the Middle Ages* (University of Pennsylvania Press, 1999), 81–4; on canonical norms and clerical celibacy, James A. Brundage, *Law, Sex, and Christian Society in Medieval Europe* (The University of Chicago Press, 1987); on the normalcy of clerical

concubinage, as well as the perceived linkage between faltering service and concubinage in medieval Italy, Daniel Bornstein, "Priest and Villagers in the Diocese of Cortona," *Richerche Storiche* 27 (1997): 93–106; and on clerical sexuality and masculinity, Michelle Armstrong-Partida, *Defiant Priests: Domestic Unions, Violence, and Clerical Masculinity in Fourteenth-Century Catalunya* (Cornell University Press, 2017).

44. ADP, C/676, N. 28 (1617), no folio numbers.
45. ADC, Leg. 382, N. 5424 (1613), fols. 2r–5v.
46. AHN, Inqu., Leg. 228, Exp. 1.
47. AHN, Inqu., Leg., 1825, Exp. 6.
48. AHN, Inqu., Leg., 1825, Exp. 6; her testimony begins on Image 7.
49. AHN, Inqu., Leg., 1825, Exp. 6, Images 42–3.
50. AHN, Inqu., Leg., 1825, Exp. 6, Image 43.

Suggestions for Further Reading

Alejandre, Juan Antonio. *El veneno de Dios: La inquisición de Sevilla ante el delito de solicitación en confesión*. Siglo XXI de España Editores, S.A., 1994.

Barahona, Renato. *Sex Crimes, Honor, and the Law in Early Modern Spain: Vizcaya, 1528–1735*. University of Texas Press, 2003.

Galván Rodríguez, Eduardo. "La praxis inquisitorial contra confesores solicitantes (tribunal de la inquisición de Canarias, 1601–1700)." *Revista de la Inquisición* 5 (1996): 103–85.

Haliczer, Stephen. *Sexuality in the Confessional: A Sacrament Profaned*. Oxford University Press, 1996.

Homza, Lu Ann. *Village Infernos and Witches' Advocates: Witch-Hunting in Navarre, 1608–1614*. Pennsylvania State University Press, 2022.

Lynn, Kimberly. *Between Court and Confessional: The Politics of Spanish Inquisitors*. Cambridge University Press, 2013.

McNamara, Celeste I. "Priests Behaving Badly: The Problem of Scandal in the Early Modern Catholic Church." *The Journal of Modern History* 96 (2024): 47–77.

Sarrión Mora, Adelina. *Sexualidad y confesión: la solicitación ante el tribunal del Santo Oficio (siglos xvi–xix)*. Alianza Editorial, 1994.

Bibliography

Alejandre, Juan Antonio. *El veneno de Dios: La inquisición de Sevilla ante el delito de solicitación en confesión*. Siglo XXI de España Editores, S.A., 1994.

Andrade, Alonso de. *Libro de guía de la virtud y de la imitación de Nuestra Señora*. Francisco Moroto, 1644.

Armstrong-Partida, Michelle. *Defiant Priests: Domestic Unions, Violence, and Clerical Masculinity in Fourteenth-Century Catalunya*. Cornell University Press, 2017.

Barahona, Renato. *Sex Crimes, Honour, and the Law in Early Modern Spain: Vizcaya, 1528–1735*. University of Texas Press, 2003.

Bornstein, Daniel. "Priest and Villagers in the Diocese of Cortona." *Richerche Storiche* 27, no. 1 (1997): 93–106.

Brundage, James A. *Law, Sex, and Christian Society in Medieval Europe*. The University of Chicago Press, 1987.

Bilinkoff, Jodi. *Related Lives: Confessors and Their Female Penitents, 1450–1750*. Cornell University Press, 2005.

Dyer, Abigail. "Seduction by Promise of Marriage: Law, Sex, and Culture in Seventeenth-Century Spain." *The Sixteenth Century Journal* 34 (2003): 439–55.

Elliot, Dyan. *Fallen Bodies: Pollution, Sexuality, and Demonology in the Middle Ages*. University of Pennsylvania Press, 1999.

Galván Rodríguez, Eduardo. "La praxis inquisitorial contra confesores solicitantes (tribunal de la inquisición de Canarias, 1601–1700)." *Revista de la Inquisición* 5 (1996): 103–85.

Haliczer, Stephen. *Sexuality in the Confessional: A Sacrament Profaned*. Oxford University Press, 1996.

Homza, Lu Ann. "When Witches Litigate: New Sources from Early Modern Navarre." *Journal of Modern History* 91 (2019): 245–75.

Religious Authority in the Spanish Renaissance. The Johns Hopkins University Press, 2000.

Village Infernos and Witches' Advocates: Witch-Hunting in Navarre, 1608–1614. Pennsylvania State University Press, 2022.

Lynn, Kimberly. *Between Court and Confessional: The Politics of Spanish Inquisitors*. Cambridge University Press, 2013.

McNamara, Celeste I. *The Bishop's Burden: Reforming the Catholic Church in Early Modern Italy*. The Catholic University of America Press, 2020.

"Priests Behaving Badly: The Problem of Scandal in the Early Modern Catholic Church." *The Journal of Modern History* 96 (2024): 47–77.

Means, Rob. *Penance in Medieval Europe, 600–1200*. Cambridge University Press, 2014.

Monteano Sorbet, Peio J. *El iceberg Navarro: Euskera y castellano en la Navarra del siglo XVI*. Pamiela, 2017.

Prada Moura, Ángel de. *El tribunal de la Inquisición en España (1478–1834)*. Actas Editoriales, 2003.

Sarrión Mora, Adelina. *Sexualidad y confesión: la solicitación ante el tribunal del Santo Oficio (siglos xvi-xix)*. Alianza Editorial, 1994.

Scott, Amanda L. *The Basque Seroras: Local Religion, Gender, and Power in Northern Iberia*. Cornell University Press. 2020.

Part II

Targets

5

Conversos

On June 15, 1492, Abraham Seneor found himself standing at the church in Guadalupe, Castile, awaiting the final step in his conversion from Judaism to Christianity. But this was no ordinary baptism, and don Abraham was no ordinary convert. He was not an infant or child, but eighty years old. The priest conducting the baptism was the primate of all Spain. His godparents were Isabella, queen of Castile, and Ferdinand, king of Aragon, and don Abraham Seneor was one of their most important tax farmers and advisors. He had also served as chief rabbi of Castile. The church in Guadalupe was equally distinguished. It held an image of the Virgin Mary that was the object of the most important pilgrimage in Iberia in the fifteenth century. Her importance came in part from her role in redeeming captives held by Muslims, and redeemed captives sometimes brought their chains to the church in recognition of the Virgin's intercession on their behalf. Furthermore, the wealthy Jeronymite friars who controlled the town and managed the church were, like don Abraham, key supporters of Isabella. During the recent civil war in which Isabella fought her half-sister for control of Castile, they had provided safekeeping for some of her wealth, and they continued to support the Catholic monarchs.

The friars had also recently hosted a yearlong inquisitorial investigation of conversos (converts from Judaism to Christianity and their descendants) only a few months after Inquisitor-General Tomás de Torquemada issued the inquisitors' initial Instructions (now known as the Old Instructions). In a highly unusual move, the inquisitors sent by Torquemada were joined in their work by the prior, a friar named

Diego de París. During the year 1485, the prior and his fellow inquisitors investigated more than 200 residents of the town and almost two dozen brethren from the friary itself. Normally, those found guilty by the Holy Office of the Spanish Inquisition had all their possessions seized by the Inquisition, and the proceeds from the sale of those goods funded the institution. But in this case, in return for the friars' early welcome of their controversial new institution (the only institution that spanned both monarchs' kingdoms), Isabella and Ferdinand granted to the friars the goods seized by the Inquisition, rather than leaving them in the possession of the Holy Office. In turn, the friars used these gains to build Ferdinand and Isabella a palace that they could use on their visits to Guadalupe. Indeed, it is possible that the monarchs and don Abraham Seneor used this residence when they visited Guadalupe for don Abraham's baptism.

In other words, everything about this baptism sent a powerful, multilayered message to those in attendance and to those who heard about it later. The church, the Virgin, the friars, the primate, the monarchs, and don Abraham Seneor himself – their presence reinforced both royal approbation bestowed on those Jews who converted to Christianity and the penalties for those who thwarted the royal will, or who converted insincerely. Guadalupe's history sent a none-too-subtle message to all in attendance, including the baptizant and those Jews who looked to him for guidance, that conversions from Judaism to Christianity must be sincere and followed with correct Christian practice. Converts who attempted to observe Judaism in secret ran the risk of investigation, a loss of all worldly possessions, and even execution.

For those of us considering this event centuries later, don Seneor's baptism also can serve as a nexus point – a hinge in Spanish history between, on the one hand, the earlier history of the appearance of conversos and the modern inquisition in Spain, and, on the other, the expansion of the investigation and punishment of Jewish converts and their descendants in early modern Iberia and its global colonies – investigations that occurred in lands from which Jews had been expelled. Inquisitorial investigations of so-called New Christians had already begun about a decade before Abraham Seneor's conversion, as Guadalupe's own history with the Spanish Inquisition indicates. And those investigations would continue after 1492 – with greater and lesser intensity, in some places more than others – into the eighteenth century. This chapter briefly reviews that history, beginning with the peripatetic existence of descendants of Jews and Jewish converts beginning in the fifteenth century, and the ambiguity of defining who exactly was a descendant of Jewish converts to Christianity in Spain. Next, the chapter examines the kinds of accusations made against Jewish converts to Christianity and their descendants in the first four decades of the Spanish Inquisition's activity, from approximately 1484 to 1525, and considers the gendered nature of these accusations, as well as the range of potential motivations of accusers. After a discussion of the veracity of inquisition records regarding claims of judaizing, the chapter moves to a comparison of trials from the first years of the Spanish Inquisition and trials of descendants of Jewish converts for most of the Inquisition's history, from the mid-sixteenth century onward. One of the most notable qualities of inquisition trials against conversos from the later sixteenth century on was the prominence of descendants of Jewish converts from Portugal, so the chapter continues by examining these accusations. These trials demonstrate the complicated, ongoing interactions among Jews, New Christians, and so-called "Old Christians" throughout the Spanish empire and around the world. The end of the chapter notes the decline of trials for judaizing in the eighteenth century.

I also want to add a note about terminology. Scholars recognize that the terms people used at the time for Jewish converts to Christianity and their descendants often carried negative connotations. "Marrano" is uncommon in contemporary English-language scholarship for this reason. Yet we now know that even more apparently neutral terms, such as "New Christian" or "converso" also carried political meanings, and even who was included in the definition of these terms changed over time.[1] The category of accusation under discussion in this chapter is judaizing, that is, practicing Judaism as a baptized Christian, and I use that term here to refer to the charges made in inquisitorial tribunals, as well as to Jewish practices observed by baptized Christians. To refer to the people who fell under investigation for the charge of judaizing, I use the phrase "descendants of Jewish converts to Christianity," "converso," or "New Christian." It is important to remember that the large majority of those tried were not themselves converts from Judaism but had been born into families of baptized Christians identified as descended from Jews. The Spanish Inquisition did not have jurisdiction over non-Christians (or Indigenous peoples in the Americas).

Abraham Seneor's baptism did not occur in a vacuum. It was the culmination of decades of pressure on Jewish communities in Castile and Aragon – Isabella and Ferdinand's realms that became the Kingdom of Spain. Jewish communities survived and in some instances even thrived in their last century before the expulsion, but the pressure on Jews to convert to Christianity was significant. Some families resisted this pressure and stayed put, maintaining their community structures until the expulsion order of 1492. Other families had some family members (or some branches of the family) who converted to Christianity, while others remained Jewish. This may have reflected deeply felt religious sentiment, but it also provided families with social, political, and economic links across the Jewish-Christian religious divide. By contrast, some family members emigrated to Portugal or across the Mediterranean – a phenomenon that began shortly after the forced conversions in 1391 and continued through the end of the fifteenth century.[2] Indeed, one of the most prominent emigrants was don Isaac Abravanel, don Seneor's coreligionist and fellow royal advisor, who left the Iberian peninsula rather than convert and who wrote bitterly about his experience.

Migration continued to be a marker of New Christian experiences throughout the early modern period. When Ferdinand and Isabella issued their 1492 order of expulsion or conversion for all of Spain's Jews, each family was forced to make the choice either of Abravanel or Seneor, but for many in Spain's Jewish community it was a series of choices, rather than a singular decision. Many of those who emigrated to North Africa, for example, faced harsh conditions and persecution, and some ultimately returned to Spain and to life as Christians. Others traveled to Portugal or Spanish Navarre to preserve their faith, only to undergo forced conversion at the order of the Portuguese king, Manoel I, in 1497, or in Navarre in 1499. Others landed in the Low Countries, on the Italian peninsula, or in the Ottoman eastern Mediterranean. Even after the turn of the sixteenth century and the end of expulsion orders, some Jewish converts to Christianity and their descendants continued to travel widely. Some crossed back and forth over the shifting Spanish-Portuguese border, either for reasons of trade, or family connections, or the changing dynamics of converso prosecutions in these two countries. Others continued a generations-long progression eastward across the Mediterranean to Ottoman-controlled territory. Some even migrated to the Americas (though this was technically forbidden by the Spanish crown) or Asia.[3]

This extensive travel among some conversos had significant repercussions for the reputations of all descendants of Jewish converts and their encounters with inquisitors. Some locations, such as southern France, the Netherlands, or Venice, turned a blind eye to baptized Christians of Jewish descent who practiced Judaism and lived as Jews in their territories. Whether reluctantly or willingly, some conversos might live as practicing Christians in Spain and Portugal, and as practicing Jews in France and the Netherlands. Not all New Christians led lives of such entangled religious identities; other Spanish descendants of Jewish converts to Christianity assimilated into the broader Christian community and are largely lost to the view of historians.

The imprecision of who was a converso and what a converso believed was equally unsettled and unsettling in this early phase of the Inquisition's activity. Recent scholarship has highlighted that the term "converso" was not a neutral term in the fifteenth century, and reflected a larger debate over who should be considered a newcomer to the faith. The imagined opportunistic mutability of converso beliefs and practices also generated fear in some quarters. Infamously, an anonymous fifteenth-century tract compared New Christians to the hybrid animal which Muslims believe carried the Prophet Muhammad to heaven on his Night Journey, the al-buraq, or Alborayque in Spanish (Figure 5.1). Neither fully Christian nor fully Jewish, Jewish converts to Christianity and their descendants observed an unholy, heretical mixture of Christian and Jewish practices that was unrecognizable as orthodox in either community. Such blended practices suggested to some critics the intentional rejection of Christian doctrine that is part of the theological definition of heresy, rather than an ignorant confusion that is incorrect but not technically heretical.[4]

The ambiguous and shifting religious affiliations of some New Christians were not the only challenges for inquisitors in identifying and rooting out what they considered to be heresy. Even defining normative Christian belief could be challenging. Some points of doctrine were debated by theologians; there was no simple right answer. Furthermore,

Figure 5.1 Tunisian al-buraq. Glass painting. Source: DEA/Archivio J. Lange/ Getty Images.

Christians who were not of Jewish descent held a range of attitudes and beliefs, some of them quite common but not canonical. In this environment, identifying and defining judaizing as distinct from customary Christian practice could be difficult.[5] In effect, the boundaries between Judaism and Christianity (and Islam) were not as fixed as people liked to imagine.[6] Finally, how converso behavior was interpreted by authorities depended in part on other political, religious, or economic pressures that might have little direct connection to deep-seated religious belief.

In short, inquisitorial prosecution of judaizing did not appear out of nowhere. It was the result of years of pressure on Jews to convert to Christianity and the resulting suspicion among some so-called Old Christians toward these New Christians after they converted. Like other Christians, Jewish converts and their descendants held to a range of beliefs and practices. Many converts were also highly mobile, which generated suspicion as well. These suspicions had political and economic as well as religious origins. Together, these multiple lines of concern led to the prosecution of judaizing by the newly formed Spanish Inquisition.

Approximately the first forty years of inquisitorial activity focused almost exclusively on Jewish converts to Christianity and their descendants, which is not surprising given the intertwined history of the establishment of the early modern Spanish Inquisition and concerns about conversos (described in more detail in the Introduction to this volume). There was significant debate among theologians about converts and descendants of converts who remained connected to Jewish family members and the Jewish community, and those debates spilled into the political arena as well. In a world of corporate, collective Christian salvation, rather than individual, personal salvation, the religious practices of one's neighbor could endanger the salvation of the kingdom as a whole.

Yet there were also political and social concerns associated with New Christians in these early years of the Inquisition. Converts and their descendants had intermarried with elite Castilian families, and factions among governing urban elites sometimes divided along New Christian/Old Christian lines and opportunistically used the religious heritage of others as a political tool for their own advancement. When Isabella and Ferdinand established the Spanish Inquisition, they were also still in the latter stages of establishing control over the Kingdom of Castile, as well as at the beginning of an expensive war with the Muslim state of Granada on the southern tip of the Iberian peninsula. As a result, the queen and king remained focused on quelling resistance and political unrest among a nobility accustomed to significant power, some of whom descended from converts or supported those descendants. Across Spain, some people argued that the Inquisition was a *sacadinero*, a "money-grab" from wealthy conversos, rather than a religious tribunal. At the same time, like European monarchs generally, Ferdinand and Isabella understood their authority to have a divine imprimatur, and the pope had awarded them the title of Catholic monarchs. Since conversos were a religious minority who some people feared would falsely claim fidelity to Christianity, converts and their descendants also potentially undermined the religious foundation of Isabella and Ferdinand's rule. Some Old Christians, therefore, saw conversos as politically and religiously dangerous.[7]

Inquisitorial prosecutions for judaizing in the early decades of the Spanish Inquisition's history reflected these twin religious and political concerns. Many investigations centered on religious practice and theological questions. Accusations of Jewish observance were precise and specific, not surprising in a time when most New and Old Christians had a lived memory of Jewish practice on the Iberian peninsula – even if the conversos themselves had been born into a Christian family. One category of accusations charged conversos with participation in Jewish life-cycle events, such as circumcision, Jewish wedding rituals, and Jewish burial and mourning rituals. Another category of accusations involved the Jewish liturgical year. Most prominently this included Yom Kippur, the annual day of fasting and repentance. But conversos also faced charges of observing Passover, as well as participating in the harvest festival of Sukkot, known in Spanish as the *fiesta de las cabañuelas*. Hanukkah was traditionally a minor holiday and does not appear in inquisition records, but Jewish penitential Monday and Thursday fasts are frequently mentioned in these early decades.[8]

Judaizing practices that appear in inquisition records particularly highlight Jewish women's religious activity. This is due to the circumstances surrounding secretive Jewish practices by baptized Christians, as opposed to the practices of openly observant Jews. Male Jewish ritual activity focused on activity in the synagogue, ritual slaughtering of meat, and circumcision – all activities that were almost entirely curtailed by conversion to Christianity and the loss of synagogue life. Typical charges against converso men might include collecting and reading Jewish prayers, or seeking out correct information about the Jewish liturgical calendar, but otherwise their judaizing activities depended upon the conversa women in their lives. By contrast, other than the mikveh baths that re-established Jewish women's ritual purity, and which are mentioned infrequently, most ritual activity for Jewish women involved domestic activities that could continue after conversion. Maintaining a kosher household and preparing food according to the laws of kashrut was one central and abiding concern of women charged in the first decades of the Spanish Inquisition. Accusers looked with suspicion on women who cooked without pork or lard (pork fat, commonly known as lard, was cheaper and more common than olive oil at least into the sixteenth century). Old Christian servants complained when their mistresses had them throw a small lump of dough into the fire as a "challah offering." And nosy neighbors, always keenly aware of goings-on in the small communities or neighborhoods where most people lived, questioned why some women cleaned their cooking pots in the fire, rather than scrubbing them as most women did. One accused woman said that this was how her mother had taught her to clean cooking implements, but the prosecuting attorney described this as a Jewish method of cleaning, and in fact it is a way to make a cooking pot ritually clean after being used with pork fat or other non-kosher foods. At Passover, some women were accused of making matzo bread in observance of the special dietary rules for that holiday.[9]

Observing the Jewish Sabbath was another aspect of ritual practice particularly associated with women. Preparations began on Friday afternoon, when women and girls swept out the house, and everyone put on clean clothes. Women also used Friday afternoon to prepare special dishes for Shabbat, when work – including cooking and lighting fires – was forbidden. By far the most common Shabbat dish mentioned in inquisition records was *adafinas*, a kind of stew that was prepared in advance and could be left over a low flame throughout the Sabbath. References to adafinas occur throughout inquisition records, and the dish also appears in Jewish communities in North Africa. Finally, women lit the pair of Shabbat candles to welcome in the Sabbath at sundown on Friday. Accusers before the Spanish Inquisition describe these as oil lamps, not wax candles, and voiced particular criticism over lamps being left unattended to burn out on their own. Some women mentioned putting the oil lamps in a shallow dish of water to help prevent the spread of fire in case of accidents. Once the Shabbat candles were lit, no family members did any work until the end of the Jewish Sabbath on Saturday at sundown. New Christian women understood that, just as they did not want their own family to work on the Jewish Sabbath, they likewise could not ask their Old Christian servants to work on the Christian Sabbath, that is, Sunday. They did not understand, however, that Christians considered Sunday after sundown still to be a part of the Christian Sabbath. Many servants complained bitterly about having to work on Sunday evenings.[10]

Other accusations, even in these early years of the Spanish Inquisition, reflected an understanding of Judaism inflected by Christian theology. This was not surprising, given that New Christians were Christians, baptized and raised in a Christian community, even if their families hoped to maintain a secret affiliation with Judaism. For example, the Monday and Thursday Jewish penitential fasts mentioned above figured frequently in early inquisition trials of Judaizers. In their own statements they emphasized the importance of penance in their salvation, a distinctly Christian interpretation of this Jewish practice. In one particularly striking example, a young conversa woman named Inés of Herrera had a series of visions. Visionary young female mystics were not uncommon in the early modern Christian world, but they were virtually unheard of among Jews. Furthermore, her visions incorporated hybrid Jewish and Christian elements. Her deceased mother appeared to Inés in one vision, saying that she was in purgatory and that she benefited from her daughter's righteous judaizing acts. In her most dramatic vision, Inés foresaw a glorious future, not for Jews, but for judaizing martyrs, who would achieve glory in heaven in a coming messianic age.[11]

Some accusations were not indicative of an active attempt to observe Judaism so much as a neglect or rejection of Christian practices. One frequent accusation, for example, was the avoidance of Christian fast days. Christian fasts required abstinence from meat (but not fish) and dairy products on Fridays and other fast days spread throughout the year. By some estimates the number of fast days at this period could extend to up to a third of the year. Many accusations centered on conversos who ate meat on fast days, sometimes claiming illness or family pressure as an excuse. Other New Christians were charged with questioning Christian doctrine such as the Virgin birth of Jesus, or the idea that salvation could be achieved only through Christianity. Yet attitudes such as these were not limited to New Christians. Old Christians might have evinced similar doubts about Christian doctrines, but in the case of conversos inquisitors read uncertainties as markers of secret Jewish belief rather than inconsistent Christian belief. This ability to define, redefine, and classify individuals in a binary system as heretics or good Christians allowed inquisitors to create certainty; it also provided them with a power rooted in definition. That power gave inquisitors and the Catholic monarchs an increasing control over Jewish converts to Christianity and their descendants. By extension, the exercise of authority over local factions and local communities gave them increasing power over Old Christians as well.

In other words, throughout these early trials, inquisitors, accusers, and the accused all attempted to deploy or resist the definitional power of the Spanish Inquisition. Individuals sought to use that power for political and religious reasons. They attempted to identify themselves and others as good Christians, faithfully judaizing conversos, or good Jews. Moreover, they understood everyone involved, as well as their motivations and acts, in gendered terms. This definitional power was incomplete, but that did not make it any less compelling.

Of course, this definitional power existed whether or not the accusations were true, and whether or not witnesses testified honestly. For example, when Juana González was threatened with torture during her inquisitorial trial in Guadalupe in 1485, she began to speak at length, reciting a prayer and claiming to have participated in other judaizing practices. As her testimony continued, Juana sounded increasingly desperate. Eventually, she asserted that she disbelieved in key Christian doctrines such as the eternal virginity of the Virgin Mary. Yet six days later, when inquisitors asked her to affirm her testimony, Juana claimed not to believe the theological heresies she uttered under threat of torture – though she did confirm the heretical practices that she admitted to in her testimony.[12] More than 500 years later, it is impossible to determine whether she was lying under threat of torture or lying after the immediate threat of torture had passed – or whether elements of both statements were true. In Juana's case, it was an accused person who made conflicting statements about her beliefs, but prosecution witnesses also lied to inquisitors. During the many investigations of converted Jews and their descendants in Ciudad Real during the first years of the Spanish Inquisition, one conversa testified against several women in town. María González (no relation to Juana) had been accused of Jewish practices, and she defended herself in part by hurling specific, damaging accusations, which demonstrated her penitence by naming other heretics. Yet several of her accusations were eventually deemed untrue because the inquisitors overseeing the case detected enmity between María and those she had named. As a result, the inquisitors charged her with lying to the Holy Office, which was itself a heretical act. Ultimately, María was found guilty of judaizing and lying under oath, and was sentenced to death.[13]

The self-interested nature of María González's false testimony is clear, and Juana González's desperate attempt to say whatever she thought inquisitors might want to hear so she could avoid torture seems similarly motivated. Accusers, too, might lie out of self-interest. In one case from 1631 to 1638, a woman testified against her former employer, Ana Gómez, claiming that she kept a kosher home. Like many trials after the first generation of inquisition cases, her accusation is relatively unspecific, but it reflected the kinds of practices described by inquisitors in their sermons. It failed to persuade the inquisitors, however, for two reasons. First, her testimony was uncorroborated by eyewitnesses. Several other servants confirmed her statement, but they worked in other households and were dependent upon what they had heard the witness tell them. Second, Ana Gómez successfully proved that her accuser had malicious intent toward her (a process called *tachas*, described in the Introduction). The maid who accused her former employer had been sacked for stealing, and right before making her accusation to inquisitors she had lost a civil case against her former employers. As a result, the inquisitors rejected her testimony and paused the proceedings – effectively an acquittal.[14] Of course, these are only a few examples of cases in which the inquisitors themselves determined that prosecution or defense testimony was untrue; there likely were many more instances of falsehoods that are invisible to us today. For the Spanish Inquisition, it seems reasonable to assume that testimonies were neither entirely true nor entirely false – that some elements of the trials reflected to some degree the experience of some converted Jews and their descendants. But whatever the veracity of statements made before the inquisitors, prosecution and defense testimony can tell us what witnesses thought inquisitors wanted to hear, what they thought might sound plausible, and what made a narrative persuasive. Both prosecution and defense witnesses, like inquisitors, attempted to make some use of the definitional power of the Holy Office, even if it was only to save themselves from a death sentence.

That power to define and hence exercise more control over Spain's Christians was a political power as well as a religious one, and testifiers sometimes attempted to claim that power for themselves, either to defend their own position or to challenge someone else's place in the community. For instance, some accusations veered to more thoroughly political statements, or to defending the testifier's own newly established status in society. Some judaizing accusations bore little or no theological weight at all, such as the man who accused a neighbor of setting inappropriately high prices in his shop. Other people denounced neighbors and acquaintances for complaining about the Inquisition, or testified falsely to aggrandize themselves, as in the case of María González above.

In short, scholars recognize that Spanish inquisitorial records, like all legal records, cannot be used uncritically. They also emphasize the importance of considering the political, social, and religious context in which cases occurred. That context changed significantly by the mid-sixteenth century, after the first few decades of trials. Understanding the difference between early trials (before about 1525) and trials during the bulk of the Spanish Inquisition's existence (from about 1525 through the eighteenth century) is key to making sense of trials of descendants of Jewish converts to Christianity overall.

Both the Spanish Inquisition itself and the political and religious circumstances in which it operated changed as the first wave of cases faded in the 1520s. The range and specificity of accusations of judaizing practices declined over time. At the same time, the more idiosyncratic format of the early trials disappeared within a few decades. Partly, this was because conventions and norms of inquisitorial practice only became established over the first several decades of the institution's existence. Also, the early mass trials, where inquisitors traveled to a city for a few months or years and then left, generated different kinds of evidence and led to different outcomes than later trials held at established tribunals. For example, when a short-term tribunal arrived in a new city, they encouraged all converts from Judaism to Christianity and their descendants to come forward and confess before the inquisitors during a grace period. Many people voluntarily confessed, likely in the hope that such a confession would protect them from further accusations. Instead, those confessions could become the starting point for trials by the prosecuting attorney (the *promotor fiscal*), if he argued that the confessions were incomplete, insincere, or false. The initial confessions also served to give the inquisitors and the prosecuting attorneys a list of names of potential Judaizers to investigate, as well as possible prosecution witnesses; the same statements were preserved in the tribunals' archives and could jump-start a later prosecution. In short, inquisitors and prosecuting attorneys in the early decades of the Spanish Inquisition pursued entire networks of extended families, business partners, and friends, all in a relatively short period of time.

The abbreviated, concentrated nature of these early trials also affected how conversos attempted to defend themselves before inquisitors. The intensely local nature of these series of trials, and the large networks of defendants, meant that the accused could be more aware of the development of prosecutions. They knew who had been tried and who had been executed or otherwise punished. They also knew whether the Holy Office was investigating friends and neighbors who were already deceased. Secrecy was a key goal from the very first inquisition trials, but this was more difficult to maintain during early mass trials. As a result, many accused people defended themselves by blaming any judaizing practices on those who were beyond the reach of the inquisitors – deceased parents or spouses, or those who had fled town. For example, Andrés González de la República said that if he had eaten meat on days prohibited by the Catholic Church, it was because his deceased mother Mari Flores had prepared it for him.[15] Early trials were also more ad hoc affairs, making use of available spaces rather than building new structures designed to accommodate the tribunal's purposes.

One effect of this was that inquisitorial prisoners might be housed in large spaces that held many people, rather than smaller cells with only a very small number of other prisoners. In these large cells, prisoners talked together about the progress of their trials and their experiences before inquisitors. In some cases, prisoners may have changed their defense strategies as a result. Mari Ruiz shared a prison cell with Mari Sánchez and many other women in Guadalupe. Mari Ruiz was present when Mari Sánchez returned from being tortured for refusing to admit to any heresy. And she would also have learned about Mari Sánchez's resulting death sentence. When Mari Ruiz appeared before the inquisitors for her own sentencing, she burst into tears, changed her statement, admitted everything, and begged for mercy. And the inquisitors granted it, sparing her life and sentencing her to a sentence of perpetual imprisonment, which was commuted after three years.[16]

Mari Sánchez was not particularly unusual in receiving a death sentence, though torture was uncommon. Over the entire span of the Spanish Inquisition's activity, death sentences (and torture) were unusual. But the earliest years of the Inquisition's activity differed from what came later. Death sentences were more common from 1478 to 1525, though still not the verdict in a majority of trials. Still, our knowledge of sentencing in the earliest decades of the Spanish Inquisition, like much about these early trials, is incomplete. It seems likely that thousands of conversos were tried and many hundreds, or even thousands, condemned to death. Death sentences included a significant percentage of posthumous death sentences (victims' bones were exhumed and burned in effigy), as well as the living, some of whom were present and some of whom were tried and sentenced in absentia. The first four decades of the Spanish Inquisition are the years about which we know the least, and much documentation was lost. In fact, it is not clear that inquisitors even began compiling their archive until the sixteenth century – nearly two decades after trials began. The records of the trials in Guadalupe remained with the Jeronymite friars for over a decade before the tribunal established in Toledo asked for them to be sent there. For most of the history of the Spanish Inquisition, scholars can compensate for lost documents to some extent by making use of the case summaries that inquisitors sent to the Suprema (the supervisory council and effective appellate court of the Spanish Inquisition). These summaries enabled twentieth-century scholars to analyze patterns of accusations for most of the history of the Holy Office. But the Suprema did not begin to require that regional tribunals send summaries until the mid-sixteenth century, decades after the first phase of accusations against descendants of Jewish converts to Christianity ended. According to those case summaries, there were approximately 4,400 trials of Judaizers between 1540 and 1700, around 10 percent of the total number of extant summaries.[17] Trials of Judaizers continued into the mid-eighteenth century, though the Inquisition overall was less active.

After this first wave of prosecutions, trials for judaizing became less frequent, though they continued into the eighteenth century. These later trials, like all trials in the Spanish Inquisition after the first few decades, were distinct from the first wave of prosecution for judaizing in several respects. First, by the mid-sixteenth century the Spanish Inquisition had become a more bureaucratized institution. Ad hoc, itinerant tribunals had given way to formal districts, each with its own tribunal. A system of regional assistants (*comisarios* and *familiares*) assisted in the work of each tribunal, and the inquisition had begun setting up a system of censors. The Suprema began requiring summaries of trials from the various districts and eventually exercised oversight of decisions to torture defendants. By 1561, a set of guidelines, known as the "New Instructions" to distinguish them from the "Old Instructions" of 1484, helped guide inquisitorial practices, and provided some consistency across the various tribunals, though that consistency was never complete. Furthermore, there were many fewer sentences of execution after the first wave of trials ended.[18]

Second, for descendants of Jewish converts to Christianity, this bureaucratization meant that their trials resembled contemporaneous trials for other charges more than they resembled judaizing trials from the late fifteenth and early sixteenth centuries. Because short-term, mass trials had ended, New Christians were tried individually or in smaller groups. As a result, there were fewer prosecution witnesses available to testify. Furthermore, in later trials of descendants of Jewish converts to Christianity there were fewer, and less specific, charges. Early trials for judaizing often listed many distinct Jewish practices, such as several specific aspects of observing the Jewish Sabbath or burial practices. But in later trials there might only be a few specific accusations, or a general claim of following the Law of Moses while falsely claiming to adhere to Christianity.

To compensate for the decreasing number of charges and the decreasing number of witnesses, other elements of the trial expanded. After being arrested, but before being charged, the accused was visited in prison multiple times (in theory three times, but in practice sometimes more or less) and warned to admit to all wrongdoing. Inquisitors also instituted a requirement that the accused provide a narrative of their lives, known as a *discurso de la vida* (see Chapter 3), to help prosecutors identify both heretical practices and people who might have influenced the accused in wrongdoing. In effect, both these elements increased the pressure on the accused to confess to wrongdoing, a useful legal tactic as the number of corroborating witnesses declined. On the other hand, defendants also seem to have learned more about inquisitorial procedures, and the use of *tachas* as a mode of self-defense became somewhat more common, though still unusual.

A third quality distinguishes trials of descendants of Jewish converts to Christianity before and after 1525, namely, the shifting beliefs and practices of these individuals. The challenge of identifying the beliefs of Jewish converts to Christianity and their descendants existed throughout the history of the Spanish Inquisition, but it became increasingly acute after the first decades of trials ended. There is little definitive evidence, but it seems that – to the extent that there had been individuals attempting to maintain Jewish practices after baptism as Christians – that practice was in decline after forty years of fierce inquisitorial investigation in Spain. It is difficult to be definitive, since inquisition records were not designed to identify and record the existence of converts and their descendants who adopted Christian beliefs and practices and assimilated into the larger Christian community. For example, St. Teresa de Jesús's converso ancestry might have influenced how she lived in Ávila or understood Christianity, but it would strain credulity to argue that she was anything other than a devout Christian. Yet unlike Teresa, other devoutly Christian converts from Judaism and their descendants are largely hidden from view. Francisco Bethencourt suggests that converso elites had a broad range of beliefs, not all of them consistent, and that their elite status – and concomitant pressure – encouraged both Christian devotion and judaizing.[19] In any case, prosecutions for judaizing occurred into the eighteenth century, and entangled religious and political motivations likely continued to influence prosecutions.

Even if inquisitorial activity suppressed judaizing among some conversos, it is possible that inquisitors inadvertently taught Jewish practices to new generations of descendants of Jewish converts through their sermons and through the *autos de fe* that publicized punishment of the guilty. Even for descendants of Jewish converts whose families had adopted normative Christian practices, the memory of their status as conversos lingered in community memory and, more tangibly, in the penitential garments that hung from the walls of churches, identifying their heretical ancestry. In the light of persistent suspicion over one's converso status, it is plausible that some conversos raised with Christian practices chose to pursue knowledge of Judaism. The memory of Jewish ancestry in the larger community might also cause an ambivalent act such as image desecration, which was predominantly carried out by Old Christians, to be "reread" as an act of judaizing. Similarly, converso ancestry could provide a convenient weapon when local political hostilities or anxieties emerged. Two rival elite families in the province of Murcia, for example, used the local tribunal of the Inquisition as one field for their ongoing conflict, since one of the two families was of converso ancestry.[20]

Changes in the structure of the Spanish Inquisition's operations, as well as changes in the circumstances of descendants of Jewish converts, resulted in different accusations and different inquisitorial prosecutions from the mid-sixteenth century on. But perhaps the primary difference between the first wave of trials for judaizing and later trials has to do with the political and cultural history of Spain – specifically, the relationship of the Spanish kingdom and its residents with the neighboring state and people of Portugal.

After King Manoel I's forced conversion of Portugal's Jews in 1497, he then decreed that Jewish converts to Christianity and their descendants would receive a grace period of twenty-five years before they could be investigated for heresy. By all accounts, there was little effort made to educate converts in their new faith. Furthermore, once the Portuguese established their own Inquisition in 1536, it quickly developed a reputation for harshness toward conversos that exceeded that of the Spanish Inquisition. Unlike the Spanish Inquisition, the Portuguese Inquisition focused more exclusively on descendants of Jewish converts. It also did not follow the same procedural rules as the Spanish Inquisition, and transcripts of its investigations are more formulaic than those of the Spanish institution.

In short, while it is just as difficult to evaluate the religious beliefs of Portuguese conversos as it is to evaluate Spanish conversos, the circumstances of Portuguese New Christians differed from their Spanish counterparts, and by the 1530s they faced greater scrutiny and harsh penalties. They also shared significant familial and social bonds across the Spanish-Portuguese border – bonds that only increased when the Spanish king, Philip II, claimed the throne of Portugal in 1580 as Portuguese Philip I. Throughout the late sixteenth century and through the first half of the seventeenth century, Spanish and Portuguese descendants of Jewish converts moved freely across the border for family or for reasons of trade, and their work took them across the Iberian peninsula and into southern France, where some descendants of Iberian Jews lived in the Jewish community as Jews. They also traveled across the united Spanish and Portuguese empires to the Americas and Asia, though technically conversos were not permitted to immigrate to the American colonies.[21]

This mixed group of Portuguese and Spanish conversos, moving across political borders – and potentially across religious borders, as well – raised great concerns among some Spaniards. These concerns were in part political, because Portuguese elites remained a reluctant part of the Spanish empire, and Portuguese immigrants raised fears among Spaniards of political unrest. At the same time, the economic role of the *nação*, or Portuguese nation, generated suspicion that these merchants were weakening the Spanish economy and undermining its foundations. Others feared that all Portuguese immigrants were conversos and Judaizers, weakening the Spanish monarchy religiously, as well as politically and economically. The slippage of these categories and the anxieties associated with them can be seen in the terms "Portuguese," "businessmen" (*homes de negocios*), and "Jews," all of which were used interchangeably in this period.[22]

These concerns increased after 1580, when there seems to have been a significant movement of Portuguese conversos across the border in response to the increased opportunities and the less-virulent Inquisition available in Spain. Prosecutions for judaizing increased in the later sixteenth century as a result. Some descendants of Jewish converts voluntarily denounced themselves before Spanish inquisitors when they crossed the border into Spain as a means of demonstrating their Christian orthodoxy and inoculating themselves from further inquisitorial harassment. Yet the relationship between so-called "Old Christian" anxieties about New Christians on the one hand, and the lived experience of converso political, economic, and religious life is unclear. Some descendants of Jewish converts to Christianity felt equally pressured to live as Jews by Jewish relatives, and to live as Christians by others.[23]

Much of the Spanish Inquisition's work globally in the seventeenth century involved adjudicating these questions. With the increasing economic pressures and deteriorating social and economic conditions of the 1630s and 1640s, Portuguese women and men in Spain and in Spain's colonies faced increasing suspicion. Some of those accused were political and economic elites, such as Mencía de Almeida, whose son, Sebastián López Hierro de Castro, was a key financier of the king. Some were Portuguese, but not of Jewish descent, like María de Albín, who was able to prove her Christian devotion to the satisfaction of the inquisitors. Some individuals in Spain were prosecuted because their relatives named them under questioning by Portuguese inquisitors (the Portuguese Inquisition had a practice of copying statements implicating people living in Spain, and forwarding the denunciations to local Spanish tribunals). Though the Spanish and Portuguese Inquisitions remained separate even during the decades when Spain and Portugal were united, they were both global institutions, and they did collaborate by sharing statements and information – not only between Spain and Portugal, but even as far afield as Manila (under the authority of the Mexican tribunal of the Spanish Inquisition) and Goa (one of the tribunals of the Portuguese Inquisition). At various times, the Spanish and Portuguese Inquisitions also extradited individuals to their home tribunals, almost always for charges of judaizing.[24]

Individual inquisitors also paid close attention to conversos across multiple postings over the course of their careers. One inquisitor, Juan de Mañozca y Zamora, was connected to some of the most notorious prosecutions of conversos in the Americas – mass trials of descendants of Jewish converts in Cartagena in the early 1620s, Lima in the 1620s and 1630s, and Mexico City in the 1640s. In Lima he tried conversos for participation in what became known as "The Great Conspiracy" (*gran complicidad*), a fear that conversos of the *nação* were planning to attack the colony and give it to the Dutch. The *gran complicidad* trials in Peru did not follow appropriate procedures, and the Lima tribunal was penalized, but Juan de Mañozca y Zamora went on to serve as inquisitor in Mexico City, where some victims of the Lima trials had fled, and where Mañozca believed that he found a second "great conspiracy" to prosecute.[25]

The Mexican "great conspiracy" trials occurred as Portugal rose up in rebellion against Spanish authority, and as the king's most prominent advisor and supporter of conversos, the Count-Duke of Olivares, was ousted from power. In the wake of the successful Portuguese war for independence, combined with the conclusion to the Thirty Years' War and a suppressed rebellion by the Catalans, Portuguese trade in Spanish territory diminished, and trials against Judaizers declined. A few final trials for judaizing in the 1720s and 1730s were the end of prosecutions of conversos by the Spanish Inquisition.

Jewish converts to Christianity and their descendants were the first targets of the Spanish Inquisition, and they remained in the sights of inquisitors into the eighteenth century. Yet that apparent continuity obscures the variability of accusers' interests and motivations, which might range from theological concerns to economic and political ones. It also obscures the intermittent nature of inquisitorial attention, which rose in some times and places and fell to relative indifference in others.

Variability and diversity also marked the religious practices of some Jewish converts to Christianity and their descendants over the centuries. Individual conversos might hold a variety of religious points of view simultaneously, and certainly during a lifetime. Their practices were situationally determined, and experiences in and out of Spain could influence their attitudes and beliefs, which might range from devout Christianity to devout Judaism, and difficult-to-define points in between. Contact with Jewish communities in Spain until 1492, and out of Spain in later centuries, also influenced conversos and their trials before inquisitors. Throughout, inquisitors worked to define and create theological and juridical certainty from the incomplete, indeterminate evidence they collected.

When don Abraham Seneor made the decision to convert to Christianity toward the end of his life, his motivations – like the motivations of many other converts – were undoubtedly varied, and his initial unwillingness to convert suggests a reluctance that was likely shared by other Jewish converts to Christianity in late fifteenth-century Spain. But the repercussions of the decisions that he and others made would affect his descendants, and the descendants of other Jewish converts to Christianity, for centuries to come.

Notes

1. Yosi Yisraeli and Yanay Israeli, "Defining 'Conversos' in Fifteenth-Century Castile: The Making of a Controversial Category," *Speculum* 97, no. 3 (July 2022): 609–48.
2. See Mark D. Meyerson, "Aragonese and Catalan Converts at the Time of the Expulsion," *Jewish History* 6 (1992): 131–49; and Jonathan Ray, *After Expulsion: 1492 and the Making of Sephardic Jewry* (New York University Press, 2013).

3. See Francesca Trivellato, *The Familiarity of Strangers: The Sephardic Diaspora, Livorno, and Cross-Cultural Trade in the Early Modern Period* (Yale University Press, 2009).
4. David M. Gitlitz, "Hybrid Conversos in the 'Libro llamado el Alboraique,'" *Hispanic Review* 60, no.1 (1992): 1–17.
5. John Edwards, "Faith and Doubt in Late Medieval Spain: Soria *circa* 1450–1500" *Past & Present* 120 (1988): 3–25.
6. On religious boundaries, see Mercedes García-Arenal and Gerard Wiegers, eds., *Polemical Encounters: Christians, Jews, and Muslims in Iberia and Beyond* (Pennsylvania State University Press, 2019).
7. Gretchen D. Starr-LeBeau, *Seven Myths of the Spanish Inquisition* (Hackett, 2023), 21.
8. David Gitlitz, *Secrecy and Deceit: The Religion of the Crypto-Jews* (Jewish Publication Society, 1996).
9. Renée Levine Melammed, *Heretics or Daughters of Israel? The Crypto-Jewish Women of Castile* (Oxford University Press, 1999).
10. Gretchen D. Starr-LeBeau, *In the Shadow of the Virgin: Inquisitors, Friars, and* Conversos *in Guadalupe, Spain* (Princeton University Press, 2003): 53–89.
11. Sharon Faye Koren, "A Christian Means to a Conversa End," *Nashim* 9 (2005): 27–61.
12. Starr-LeBeau, *In the Shadow*, 263–75.
13. Lu Ann Homza, ed. and trans., *The Spanish Inquisition, 1478–1614: An Anthology of Sources* (Hackett, 2006), 50–60.
14. Starr-LeBeau, *Seven Myths*, 109–10.
15. Starr-LeBeau, *In the Shadow*, 100–1.
16. Gretchen D. Starr-LeBeau, "Writing (for) Her Life: *Judeo-Conversas* in Early Modern Spain," in Maria V. Vicente and Luis R. Corteguera, eds., *Women, Texts, and Authority in the Early Modern Spanish World* (Ashgate Press, 2003), 57–72.
17. Jaime Contreras and Gustav Henningsen, "Forty-Four Thousand Cases of the Spanish Inquisition (1540–1700): Analysis of a Historical Data Bank," in Gustav Henningsen and John Tedeschi, with Charles Amiel, eds., *The Inquisition in Early Modern Europe: Studies on Sources and Methods* (Northern Illinois University Press, 1986), 114.
18. Jaime Contreras and Jean Pierre Dedieu, "Geografía de la inquisición española: La formación de los distritos, 1470–1820," *Hispania* 40 (1980): 37–93; the New and Old Instructions are available in translation in Homza, *Spanish Inquisition*, documents 7 and 20.
19. Francisco Bethencourt, *Strangers Within: The Rise and Fall of the New Christian Trading Elite* (Princeton University Press, 2024): 9, 460.

20. Yosef Haim Yerushalmi, *From Spanish Court to Italian Ghetto: Isaac Cardoso: A Study in Seventeenth-Century Marranism and Jewish Apologetics* (Columbia University Press, 1971); on the trials in Murcia, see Jaime Contreras Contreras, *Sotos contra Riquelmes. Regidores, inquisidores y criptojudíos* (Anaya & Muchnik, 1992).
21. Starr-LeBeau, *Seven Myths*, 41–2.
22. Irene Silverblatt, *Modern Inquisitions: Peru and the Colonial Origins of the Civilized World* (Duke University Press, 2004).
23. Bruno Feitler, *Inquisition, juifs et nouveaux-chrétiens au Brésil: Le Nordeste XVIIe et XVIIIe siècles* (University Press of Louvain, 2003).
24. For Mencía de Almeida, see Starr-LeBeau, *Seven Myths*, chapter 4; for María de Albín, see Starr-LeBeau, *Seven Myths*, 109. For interactions between the Spanish and Portuguese inquisitions, see François Soyer, "An Example of Collaboration between the Spanish and Portuguese Inquisitions: The Trials of the *Converso* Diogo Ramos and his Family (1680–1683)," *Cadernos de Estudos Sefarditas* 6 (2006): 317–40.
25. On Juan de Mañozca y Zamora, see Kimberly Lynn, *Between Court and Confessional: The Politics of Spanish Inquisitors* (Cambridge University Press, 2013).

Suggestions for Further Reading

Bethencourt, Francisco. *Strangers Within: The Rise and Fall of the New Christian Trading Elite*. Princeton University Press, 2024.

Bodian, Miriam. *Dying in the Law of Moses: Crypto-Jewish Martyrdom in the Iberian World*. Indiana University Press, 2007.

Graizbord, David L. *Souls in Dispute: Converso Identities in Iberia and the Jewish Diaspora, 1580–1700*. University of Pennsylvania Press, 2004.

Graizbord, David L., and Claude Stuczynski, eds. "Special Issue on Portuguese New Christian Identities, 1516–1700." *Jewish History* 25 (2011).

Pastore, Stefania. *Una herejía española. Conversos, alumbrados e inquisición (1449–1557)*. Marcial Pons, 2010.

Starr-LeBeau, Gretchen D. *In the Shadow of the Virgin: Inquisitors, Friars, and* Conversos *in Guadalupe, Spain*. Princeton University Press, 2003.

Wachtel, Nathan. *The Faith of Remembrance: Marrano Labyrinths*. University of Pennsylvania Press, 2013.

Yisraeli, Yosi, and Yanay Israeli. "Defining 'Conversos' in Fifteenth-Century Spain: The Making of a Controversial Category." *Speculum* 97, no. 3 (2022): 609–48.

Bibliography

Bethencourt, Francisco. *Strangers Within: The Rise and Fall of the New Christian Trading Elite*. Princeton University Press, 2024.

Contreras, Jaime. *Sotos contra Riquelmes. Regidores, inquisidores y criptojudíos*. Anaya & Muchnik, 1992.

Contreras, Jaime, and Jean Pierre Dedieu. "Geografia de la inquisición Española: La formación de los distritos, 1470–1820." *Hispania* 40 (1980): 37–93.

Contreras, Jaime, and Gustav Henningsen. "Forty-Four Thousand Cases of the Spanish Inquisition (1540–1700): Analysis of a Historical Data Bank." In Gustav Henningsen and John Tedeschi with Charles Amiel, eds., *The Inquisition in Early Modern Europe: Studies on Sources and Methods*. Northern Illinois University Press, 1986.

Feitler, Bruno. *Inquisition, juifs et nouveaux-chrétiens au Brésil: Le Nordeste XVIIe et XVIIIe siècles*. University Press of Louvain, 2003.

García-Arenal, Mercedes, and Gerard Wiegers, eds. *Polemical Encounters: Christians, Jews, and Muslims in Iberia and Beyond*. Pennsylvania State University Press, 2019.

Gitlitz, David M. "Hybrid Conversos in the "Libro llamado el Alboraique." *Hispanic Review* 60, no. 1 (1992): 1–17.

Secrecy and Deceit: The Religion of the Crypto-Jews (Jewish Publication Society, 1996).

Homza, Lu Ann, ed. and trans. *The Spanish Inquisition, 1478–1614: An Anthology of Sources*. Hackett, 2006.

Edwards, John. "Faith and Doubt in Late Medieval Spain: Soria *circa* 1450–1500." *Past & Present* 120 (1988): 3–25.

Lynn, Kimberly. *Between Court and Confessional: The Politics of Spanish Inquisitors*. Cambridge University Press, 2013.

Koren, Sharon Faye. "A Christian Means to a Conversa End." *Nashim* 9 (2005): 27–61.

Melammed, Renée Levine. *Heretics or Daughters of Israel? The Crypto-Jewish Women of Castile*. Oxford University Press, 1999.

Meyerson, Mark D. "Aragonese and Catalan Converts at the Time of the Expulsion." *Jewish History* 6 (1992): 131–49.

Ray, Jonathan. *After Expulsion: 1492 and the Making of Sephardic Jewry*. New York University Press, 2013.

Silverblatt, Irene. *Modern Inquisitions: Peru and the Colonial Origins of the Civilized World*. Duke University Press, 2004.

Soyer, François. "An Example of Collaboration between the Spanish and Portuguese Inquisitions: The Trials of the *Converso* Diogo Ramos and his Family (1680–1683)." *Cadernos de Estudos Sefarditas* 6 (2006): 317–40.

Starr-LeBeau, Gretchen D. *In the Shadow of the Virgin: Inquisitors, Friars, and Conversos in Guadalupe, Spain*. Princeton University Press, 2003.

"Writing (for) Her Life: *Judeo-Conversas* in Early Modern Spain." In Maria V. Vicente and Luis R. Corteguera, eds., *Women, Texts, and Authority in the Early Modern Spanish World*. Ashgate Press, 2003.

Seven Myths of the Spanish Inquisition. Hackett, 2023.

Trivellato, Francesca. *The Familiarity of Strangers: The Sephardic Diaspora, Livorno, and Cross-Cultural Trade in the Early Modern Period*. Yale University Press, 2009.

Yerushalmi, Yosef Haim. *From Spanish Court to Italian Ghetto: Isaac Cardoso: A Study in Seventeenth-Century Marranism and Jewish Apologetics*. Columbia University Press, 1971.

Yisraeli, Yosi, and Yanay Israeli, "Defining 'Conversos' in Fifteenth-Century Castile: The Making of a Controversial Category." *Speculum* 97, no. 3 (July 2022): 609–48.

STEPHANIE M. CAVANAUGH

6

Moriscos

The Muslims of Spain converted to Catholicism under coercion in the early sixteenth century. As Christian converts from Islam, this population and their descendants became known as Moriscos and came under the jurisdiction of the Spanish Inquisition. For more than a century, Catholic authorities worried about Moriscos adhering to their former religion and being Christian in name only; inquisitors investigated Moriscos and prosecuted them for practicing Islam. The number of trials reached a high point in the second half of the sixteenth century and only dropped when the monarchy expelled the Moriscos from the Spanish kingdoms between 1609 and 1614. This chapter explores how the Spanish Inquisition constructed a model of Islamic heresy that encompassed Morisco cultural traditions. It surveys the rise in inquisitorial prosecution of this population across many regions. It also considers Morisco responses to the Inquisition, including strategies of petitioning and financial negotiation. Overall, this chapter considers what inquisition records can reveal about Morisco histories, attending to the richness and limitations of this archive, as well as methods for reading beyond inquisitorial perspectives.

There is no single history of the Inquisition and the Moriscos. Their entwined histories encompass multiple regional contexts, local politics and power dynamics, and – crucially – diverse Morisco communities, beliefs, and sociocultural traditions. Despite this diversity, the Inquisition's persecution of Moriscos contributed to the idea that Moriscos were all the same: all potential Muslims and dissidents, all possible threats to Catholic Spain. Moriscos were baptized Christians and were already integrated into society in many ways, yet many did not thoroughly profess Catholicism or meet the requirements of conversion. Their encounters with the Inquisition reveal how complex the processes of conversion really were, and illustrate how the Spanish church and state defined and policed the boundaries of Catholic society. Inquisitorial activity took place in the context of overlapping debates concerning the validity of baptism, the efficacy of conversion, and proper methods of evangelization. How should Catholic authorities measure religious sincerity? What was the relationship between spiritual belief and cultural practices? Could Moriscos assimilate into Christian society? Overall, these inquisitorial histories form part of a longer trajectory of religious conflict and coexistence in Spain.

Becoming Moriscos

The Moriscos' confrontations with the Spanish Inquisition were preceded by eight centuries of Christian–Muslim coexistence in the Iberia peninsula. The medieval kingdoms of Spain and Portugal were populated by people of three monotheistic faith traditions: Judaism, Christianity, and Islam. Catholic and Muslim rulers fought for territorial control from the time of the Islamic conquest of Iberia in 711. These periodic wars ended in 1492, when Ferdinand II of Aragon and Isabella I of Castile accepted the surrender of Muhammad XII, known as Boabdil, who was the last Muslim ruler in Iberia. The terms of surrender for the conquered Kingdom of Granada included freedom of religion, which meant that Muslims there could continue to practice Islam legally. The same protection was already given to Muslims throughout Catholic Spain, just as Christians and Jews had been protected minorities in Islamic Spain. Nevertheless, the conquered Muslims in Granada soon faced pressure to convert to Christianity. They responded with rebellion, namely the Granadan War of 1499–1501, which ended in royal victory. As a result, the Catholic monarchs rescinded the freedom to practice Islam. In 1502, they ordered all Muslims living in the Crown of Castile (into which the Kingdom of Granada had been incorporated) to leave the Spanish kingdoms, or else convert to Christianity. As the terms of exile were extremely restrictive, most of this population had no choice but to accept baptism. In effect, they underwent a forced religious conversion.

The order of 1502 did not apply in the Crown of Aragon, which was united with Castile by the marriage of Ferdinand and Isabella but governed separately. Muslims in the Crown of Aragon had long enjoyed freedom of religion as a right guaranteed by treaty. This legal protection never precluded religious violence or intolerance – the same was true in Castile – but it did shield Aragonese Muslims from forced conversion. This right was upheld in 1502 and again in 1510, when Ferdinand reaffirmed it at the Cortés of Aragon in Monzón. His successor, grandson Charles I, also swore to uphold the same religious protection for Aragonese Muslims. In 1521, however, the *Germanías* rebellion in Valencia ended the Muslims' security. This popular revolt targeted Muslims with violent attacks, the destruction of communities, and forced baptisms. The rebels' actions reveal both anti-Muslim sentiment and the intent of weakening the Valencian nobility, whose estates relied on the labor of their Muslim vassals. After the rebellion was subdued, Catholic authorities had to determine the validity of the coerced baptisms that had occurred. The inquisitor-general himself directed a commission that ultimately found the baptisms legitimate.[1] Following this decision, the remaining Muslim population of the Crown of Aragon was compelled to accept baptism. This obligation was imposed by royal order in 1525, with many conversions taking place the following year. The early decades of the sixteenth century thus marked the end of the legal practice of Islam in Spain and the beginning of what modern scholars refer to as the Morisco century.

The word Morisco refers to "moorish" origins, as the Muslims of Spain and other Mediterranean regions were historically described as "Moors." Moriscos were also called New Christians. This term was more than an allusion to recent baptism; rather, it marked convert status that was inheritable. This New Christian category was first created to identify converts from Judaism, called conversos. Violence and forced baptism had also instigated the conversion of the Jewish population of Spain, notably during the 1391 pogroms in Seville and then again after waves of anti-Jewish preaching and legislation in the early fifteenth century. Iberian Catholics who claimed only Christian ancestry deemed themselves Old Christians to distinguish themselves from New ones. This distinction, which centered on genealogical proximity to Judaism, was codified in legal statutes regarding *limpieza de sangre*, meaning "purity of blood." This was not a single law that was applied across the Spanish kingdoms. Rather, individual institutions – universities, municipal councils, the Inquisition, and others – could require evidence of their members' ancestry. Limpieza statutes were a way to exclude converts and their descendants from honorable positions and upward social mobility; it also theoretically prohibited them from emigration to overseas Spanish colonies.[2] The concept of blood purity was also applied to the Moriscos in the sixteenth century, by which time any non-Christian ancestry was considered proof of impurity.

Envisioning Heresy

The Spanish Inquisition sought evidence that Moriscos lived as Muslims. The records this institution produced (including visitation reports, correspondence, trial documents, and inquisitors' manuals) describe patterns of sociocultural behaviors and religious professions that fit the inquisitorial profile of Islamic heresy. In other words, through surveillance and prosecution, the Inquisition shaped ideas about Moriscos as secret Muslims.

Inquisition records contain descriptions of a wide range of actions that Catholic authorities understood to be evidence of adhering to what they often called the "sect of Muhammad" (*secta de Mahoma*). Of primary concern was any evidence of Islamic religious belief. In Islam, the central profession of faith is the *shahada* – "There is no god but God, and Muhammad is the Prophet of God" – which is the first of the five pillars of Islam. While evidence of belief was difficult to ascertain, inquisitors sought confessions or denunciations that provided evidence of Islamic faith, such as prayer. The second pillar of Islam is the *salat*, to pray five times each day while facing the direction of Mecca, the birthplace of the Prophet Muhammad and the holiest city in Islam. Another common charge against Moriscos was bathing, which Catholic priests and inquisitors viewed as evidence of ritual purification for Islamic prayer.

Church authorities were also aggrieved when Moriscos did not fulfill the duties of good Christians, such as attending Mass, learning Catholic prayers, confessing before a priest, and partaking of the Eucharist, the sacrament also called Holy Communion. Parish priests commonly reported Moriscos' failures regarding Catholic sacraments and practices as evidence of their resistance to Christianity. Moriscos also were accused of working on Sundays and feast days. Parish priests feared Moriscos would replace their children's Christian names with Arabic ones after baptism.

Moriscos sometimes told priests and inquisitors that they sinned out of ignorance rather than malice. The Moriscos of Valladolid made this claim in 1566 when they collectively petitioned for a royal pardon to alleviate inquisitorial prosecution.[3] It is worth remembering that a lack of knowledge and compliance were not problems only among New Christians; Old Christians also routinely failed to meet the religious requirements prescribed by the Catholic Church, as evidenced in the records of the Inquisition itself.

Ultimately, religious and cultural factors merged in the Spanish Inquisition's assessment of the Moriscos. Food was a major issue. Inquisitors looked for evidence that Moriscos were adhering to dietary requirements that were *halal* (permissible) in Islam, which included slaughtering animals according to Islamic law, and recorded when Moriscos did not eat pork or drink wine. Moriscos were suspected of fasting and giving to charity in observance of the Muslim holy month of Ramadan. Inquisitors also looked for evidence of Arabic texts, particularly for anything with religious meaning. Written and spoken Arabic were associated with Islam. So, too, was any form of traditional dress or personal grooming customary in Muslim Spain. It was problematic to practice circumcision; music, celebrations, and ceremonies such as marriage or burial rites could also raise concerns if they followed the Moriscos' pre-conversion traditions. Community ties and residential patterns were also perceived as evidence of religious allegiance; living among and only interacting with other Moriscos could be counted as signs of "poor conversion." In the eyes of Christian authorities, any pre-conversion customs signaled a lack of assimilation into Catholicism. Contemporary debates over the problem of Morisco conversion addressed this overlap between tradition and faith. Did language, food, dress, and bathing belong to the realm of culture and regional tradition? Or were these traditions manifestations of religious identity, ways to abide by ancestral faith, and linked to spiritual convictions at odds with Iberian Catholicism?

Lists of activities deemed heretical were read out in the announcement of edicts of faith. These edicts were declared at the start of inquisitorial visitations before church congregations. The manifestos invited people to make confessions about themselves or denunciations about others pertaining to any word or act that deviated from Catholicism. The confessions or denunciations could pinpoint evidence of Judaism, Islam, Protestantism, or anything else in the realm of sacrilege and heterodoxy. Denunciations could be about individuals or groups of people; sometimes, local religious authorities could accuse entire Morisco communities. In the fall of 1569, for example, inquisitors arrived in Deza, a Castilian town near the Aragonese border. Among the many who responded to the edict of faith was the local parish priest, Miguel Bonito: "He said that in order to unburden his conscience, he declares that most of Deza's New Converts – the ones that were formerly Moors – neither eat pork nor drink wine. And ... they also keep their children from eating or drinking."[4] Bonito went on to accuse individual Moriscos of specific infractions regarding food, weddings, burial practices, and problematic discussions about the Christian sacraments. Other accusations included pettier details. During the same visitation in 1569, a woman named Mari Rodríguez reported speaking to a Morisco man after his son had sneezed repeatedly: "She said to Román Ramírez, 'He's sneezed so many times, and you didn't say, 'Jesus,' or cross yourself or commend yourself to God even once.' Román Ramírez replied, 'Cross yourself, Miss Holier-than-thou.'"[5]

The fear that Moriscos were potentially secret Muslims was fueled by the cohesiveness of many Morisco communities. Inquisitors targeted Morisco community leaders as well as anyone suspected of teaching Islam to others. Their aim was to uncover Morisco networks or supposed conspiracies of Muslim activity. Moriscos often married and lived among other Moriscos. Church leaders and inquisitors believed that close family and community ties could facilitate the secret practice of Islam, and modern studies have demonstrated how domestic spaces could be crucial to the preservation of Islamic traditions. Morisca women played a central role in maintaining religious and cultural customs within the home. They could teach Islam and Arabic to children, continue pre-conversion traditions for family celebrations, and prepare food in keeping with Islamic law.[6]

Hearts and minds were even more difficult for inquisitors to police than the interiors of Morisco homes. What increased the inquisitors' concern was their awareness of the concept of *taqiyya*. Meaning precaution or prudence in Arabic, *taqiyya* was the principle that Moriscos could observe Islam via intention and, when possible, through concealed religious practice, while acting outwardly as Christians. Such concealment was authorized by Islamic leaders as a way for forcibly converted Moriscos to survive in Catholic Spain without abandoning their Muslim faith and identity. In the words of the mufti of Oran, directed to the Moriscos in the early sixteenth century, "God is not concerned with your exterior attitude, but with the intention of your hearts . . . And if they tell you to denounce Muhammad, denounce him by word and love him at the same time in your heart."[7] In essence, Moriscos who wanted to retain their Islamic faith could do so inwardly, in their hearts, while outwardly complying with the Catholic duties imposed upon them by their baptism.

It is impossible, of course, to uncover a "true" religious identity of Moriscos because they did not have one: There was no single Morisco identity. The category of Morisco was imposed on diverse people from different regions who held a multitude of opinions. They shared a religious background of forced conversion and Muslim ancestry, yet they were not limited to a single set of beliefs. Their diversity grew even more complex as generations passed, which is why the very historical category of Morisco has limitations. Many Moriscos actively practiced some form of Islam or sought to retain elements of Muslim culture while resisting full assimilation into Christianity. Other Moriscos observed elements of both faith traditions, enacting a religious and cultural hybridity that troubled Catholic authorities. Still other Moriscos professed sincere Catholicism. At the time of the Morisco expulsion in the early seventeenth century, bishops were ordered by the king to investigate whether any Moriscos in their jurisdictions were earnest Christians. The bishop of Valladolid submitted witness testimony substantiating that some Moriscos conducted themselves as

Catholics and lived among Old Christians.⁸ This should not be surprising because, over time, Catholic knowledge became common among Moriscos. In Valencia in the early seventeenth century, for example, "even among the Moriscos tried by the Holy Office, it was becoming difficult to find those who did not perform basic Christian observances (Mass, confession) or recite basic Christian prayers (Our Father) and the articles of faith."⁹

At the same time, some Moriscos grappled with doubt or identified with different religions as time went on. For example, when Román Ramírez – the son of the Morisco man denounced in the 1569 visitation of Deza, described above – confessed to inquisitors in 1570, he portrayed his religious state in the following way:

> At [this] point, he truly desired and wanted to convert to our holy Catholic faith and he went more than twenty years without performing any Moorish ceremonies. Yet in his heart he was always inclined to be a Moor, and he vacillated within himself over which was the better law, that of the Moors or of the Christians, and in which one he would be saved.¹⁰

Ramírez's confession illustrates doubt, spiritual struggle, personal identity, and transformation. His and many other stories of people "caught between two laws" are preserved in trial records; their statements challenge us to weigh not only personal intention but also rhetorical expectations when inquisitors and their staff were present and acting as mediators.¹¹

How much knowledge of Islam did Moriscos have? The surviving evidence is mixed. Modern historians have pointed to a decline in Arabic and Islamic knowledge in early modern Spain, especially in the decades after the first forced baptisms.¹² Yet extant testimony also points to the survival of that knowledge, and the Qur'ān was both a touchstone text and a source of controversy when it was translated into Castilian.¹³ Moreover, one recent scholar has affirmed that *jofores* – prophetic messages written in Aljamiado, meaning Castilian or Aragonese languages in Arabic script – circulated widely.¹⁴ Such textual and linguistic clues point to Morisco resistance and wide circulations of knowledge in the early modern Mediterranean world.

Inquisition after Conversion

Like other targeted populations, Moriscos were subject to all phases of inquisitorial activity: surveillance and investigation; denunciation and confession; imprisonment and torture; trial and sentencing; penance and punishment. Yet if the history of the Inquisition's prosecution of Moriscos was different in each region for peninsular Spain, what all the inquisition tribunals had in common was that their prosecution rates rose over the course of the sixteenth century. In general, Moriscos were not subjected to intense inquisitorial scrutiny in the first years following their conversions. There was a commonly held view that patience was required for Moriscos to learn the tenets of their new faith; it was expected that the newly converted would need time to assimilate.

Early examples of inquisitorial action against Moriscos in Castile occurred in the town of Daimiel in 1509, and in Toledo and Valladolid in 1509–10.[15] The Inquisition arrested Moriscos in Segovia in 1523. Trials took place in larger numbers in the 1530s. Some of the earliest episodes of amplified investigation were connected to so-called Morisco conspiracies in the 1540s. In that decade, inquisitors found what they believed to be a network of Moriscos engaged in crypto-Islamic heresy throughout old Castilian towns, including Arévalo and Medina del Campo. Denunciations led to a rush of arrests, raising the alarm in the tribunals of Valladolid, Toledo, and Córdoba, as well as the Suprema.[16]

Complaints that the Inquisition was too harsh in its treatment of the Moriscos came from various corners. Castilian Moriscos made a collective complaint to the Suprema in 1524. They reported unfair treatment, including prosecution for minor offenses and insufficient witness testimony. In response, the Suprema ordered inquisitors to act with more restraint, to prosecute only when evidence of heresy was certain, and to send a report about the trials before confiscating Morisco property.[17] Protest also came from governing bodies. In 1533, the Cortés of Aragon complained to the king about the Inquisition and specifically criticized it, stating:

> Your Reverence knows well the way in which [the Moriscos] were "converted," and the little or no teaching or instruction in our Holy Catholic faith which has been given them, and the lack of churches in the

places where they live. Yet despite this lack of teaching and instruction, they are being proceeded against as heretics.[18]

The Inquisition continued to investigate and prosecute Moriscos despite the criticism sometimes leveled against the institution and its officers. Significantly, inquisition leadership could also provoke changes in the rhythm of prosecution: once the relatively moderate Inquisitor-General Alonso Manrique lost influence in 1533, the Inquisition began to pursue Moriscos with greater severity.[19]

In some cases, legal arrangements restrained the Inquisition's prosecution of Moriscos. These were normally financial exchanges for specific protections. For example, in 1525, twelve Muslim leaders in Valencia tried to persuade Charles V not to enforce baptism; they offered 50,000 ducats in this bargain but were unsuccessful. In 1526, those same leaders negotiated an agreement, called a *concordia*, in which the Muslim leaders agreed to facilitate mass conversion for the original 50,000 ducats; in return, the Valencian Inquisition would treat this newly converted community with lenience. The period of clemency would last for forty years in cases of minor infractions, with Muslim dress and the Arabic language being permitted for ten years.[20] The Inquisition's religious and fiscal motivations were both apparent in this deal. Still, by the 1560s Valencia's Moriscos were experiencing "a new wave of prosecution."[21] After further bargaining, Inquisitor-General Diego de Espinosa agreed in 1571 to accept an annual payment of 2,500 ducats, in exchange for which Valencia's Moriscos would not have their property confiscated.[22]

Negotiations between the Inquisition and the Morisco communities routinely included financial offers and settlements. Regional inquisition tribunals were usually short of the funds required to pay salaries and maintain their offices. Tribunals relied on the income derived from a common inquisitorial punishment: property confiscation. Protecting property became a common point of negotiation for Moriscos, who in many places retained the community structure and leadership for collective action. Such was the case in 1557, when Moriscos from neighboring Castilian towns took collective action to secure this protection from the Valladolid inquisition tribunal.[23] Legal compromises could be advantageous for both sides. Inquisition tribunals profited from annual payments; the Moriscos who entered these agreements chose controlled, predictable spending over sporadic, unpredictable confiscations of property. There was historical precedent for arranged payments throughout the medieval Spanish kingdoms, whereby religious minorities of Muslims and Jews paid special taxes and tribute in exchange for royal protection. While financial settlements with the Spanish Inquisition in the sixteenth century could still cause financial hardship for Morisco communities, collective negotiation allowed communities to exert agency as they made specific requests.

The Inquisition's Morisco Era

Over time, however, priests and inquisitors grew less inclined to ignore what they perceived as signs of the Moriscos' "poor conversion" to Catholicism, not least because King Philip II promulgated the decrees of the reform-minded Council of Trent after that gathering formally concluded in 1563. Morisco inquisition trials were most numerous from the 1560s to 1614, dropping off sharply after the Moriscos' expulsion from Spain, which began in 1609 and lasted five years. Experts in this field of study call these decades the "anti-Morisco phase of the Inquisition."[24] Moriscos under the jurisdiction of the tribunals of Valencia and Zaragoza endured the most prosecution, with inquisition cases being numerous after 1570. The surviving records indicate that in Valencia, the inquisition tribunal had 724 Morisco prosecutions out of 774 total cases between 1591 and 1595. In Zaragoza, the inquisition tribunal heard 579 Morisco cases out of 683 total cases between 1606 and 1610.[25]

The question of Morisco rebellion increased political and religious tensions. To the Spanish monarchy, Moriscos posed a threat not only as potentially insincere Christians but also as potentially disloyal subjects. Fears that Moriscos could ally with the Ottoman empire affected royal policy toward this religious minority.[26] The Ottoman empire was a powerful Islamic state that had been moving westward into the Mediterranean since the fifteenth century; it was one of Hapsburg Spain's major enemies. There were also fears that Moriscos living on the Mediterranean coast might join or collaborate with corsairs, who engaged in kidnapping Christians for ransom or for sale into slavery.

The Inquisition's increasingly harsh prosecution of Moriscos was enacted in the context of these religious and political perils. Church and state wanted the Morisco population under surveillance, and argued that full religious conversion must go hand in hand with social assimilation for Catholic safety.

Emblematic of these rising tensions was the Second War of the Alpujarras, which occurred from 1568 to 1570 in Granada and began as a Morisco rebellion against the Spanish monarchy. The Inquisition played a central role in creating the conditions that sparked the rebellion, including high rates of prosecution and anti-Morisco sentiment. The uprising also came in reaction to a royal edict that targeted Granadan Morisco culture, traditions, and the Arabic language. The edict had first been written in 1526, but Charles V retracted it in exchange for a payment of 80,000 ducats from Morisco leaders. Suspended for four decades, the royal edict was finally reissued on January 1, 1567, by Philip II.[27]

The edict was a direct attack on Moriscos and Granadan culture, a hardline attempt to force their assimilation. Granadan Moriscos were ordered to learn Castilian Spanish within three years and to stop speaking, reading, and writing in Arabic.[28] The language requirement had wide-reaching implications: Legal contracts in Arabic would eventually become invalid; all books written in Arabic had to be submitted for inspection. Granada's Moriscos were also ordered to stop making clothing in the style they wore when they were Muslims, and to make all new clothing in the style of Christians. Existing clothing could be worn for another one to two years. The Moriscos were forbidden from using Muslim names. Morisca women were banned from veiling and were required to keep their faces uncovered; they could not use henna on their skin or hair. The order also banned baths, as Catholic authorities believed Moriscos bathed for ritual purposes in observance of Islam. Moriscos in Granada had to keep the doors of their homes open while they celebrated weddings and festival days, as well as on Fridays, to ensure that they were not engaging in the dancing and music (*zambras* and *leilas*) "that they had used during the Muslim period."[29] Violators would be subjected to fines, imprisonment, exile, or five years in the galleys.

This list of prohibitions reflects an endorsement among royal, ecclesiastical, and inquisitorial authorities of the principle that outward appearance and external actions could be reliable markers, of religious belief. Yet the association of Morisco cultural traditions and the Arabic language with Islam was not universally accepted. A key dissenting point of view was expressed by a Granadan Morisco elder named Francisco Núñez Muley. He wrote a detailed defense of the Moriscos and their customs, which remains important as a counterpoint to royal and inquisitorial thinking.[30]

Núñez Muley addressed his memorandum to the president of the Royal Audiencia of Granada, Pedro de Deza Manuel, a man known for his strict anti-Morisco policies. Núñez Muley argued that traditional Morisco culture was neither proof of Islam nor at odds with Catholicism. He defended Morisco dress and baths as necessary for safety, modesty, and cleanliness. He pointed out the impossibility of enforcing the king's edict and outlined the harm to property and industry that would result from its implementation. Núñez Muley described the level of inquisitorial scrutiny his people faced, and argued that the king's order would:

> cause only tremendous personal and material losses, as have begun to be seen in the places and towns outside Granada, where it is an everyday occurrence to hear questions such as, "Are you unveiled?" and "Did you shut your doors?" as well as questions regarding the use of Morisco names. I beg Your Lordship, for the love of God ... to look with merciful eyes to the natives of this kingdom, as they are loyal servants of His Majesty [King Philip II] in all things and in all ways.[31]

Dissenting voices did not persuade the king to change course. Philip II issued the order, and Núñez Muley's predictions proved true. It took approximately a year for Granada's Moriscos to move into armed insurrection, forming themselves into bands in the Alpujarras mountains. Royal forces won the ensuing war, but only after years of violent fighting. In response to their rebellion, the king ordered the deportation of nearly all Moriscos from the Kingdom of Granada. An estimated 80,000 deportees were resettled throughout the lands of Andalucia and Castile. Thousands of captured Moriscos were sold into slavery; while the enslavement of Morisco adults was deemed legal because of the rebellion, the king ordered that captured Morisco children should be freed.[32]

Religious and secular authorities were ordered to keep the deportees under surveillance, to restrict them to the places where they were resettled, to enforce prohibitions on religious and cultural behavior, and to issue regular reports to the Crown. The deportation and atmosphere of heightened surveillance affected levels of inquisition activity, too. Granadan Moriscos had been prosecuted for years at a high rate, with their trials constituting between 78 and 85 percent of all extant inquisition cases in Granada from 1561 to 1575, including 425 out of 499 from 1566 to 1570, and 186 out of 249 from 1571 to 1575. Those rates dropped after the Moriscos were deported, but inquisition tribunals in other places stepped up their prosecution of the resettled population. Morisco trials increased fivefold in the tribunal of Cuenca, for example.[33]

Accounting for the Expulsion

The Inquisition's high number of Morisco trials dropped abruptly in the second decade of the seventeenth century because the Moriscos were forcibly removed from the Spanish kingdoms. Philip II's son and heir, Philip III, ordered the expulsion of the Moriscos between 1609 and 1614 in a sequence of regional deportations. Approximately 300,000 Moriscos went into exile, most eventually settling in North Africa under the Ottoman empire. The overall violence of the expulsion was inestimable. It was the monarchy (the king and his advisors) and not the Inquisition that made the formal decision to expel the Moriscos from the Spanish kingdoms.[34] Yet if the leadership of the Spanish Inquisition did not take part in the decision to expel the Moriscos, the Inquisition certainly played a central role in creating the climate that led to the expulsion – a climate of suspicion and surveillance, of persecution, of constant impetus to uncover so-called crypto-Islamic threats. The Spanish Inquisition was instrumental in creating an image of Moriscos as a threat to Catholic Spain. Decades of inquisitorial prosecution of Moriscos contributed to the prejudicial view that was used to justify the expulsion. Those justifications relied on the imagery of cleansing Spain of heresy.

The impact of the Moriscos' expulsion was felt throughout Spanish society. Local effects of population loss differed by region; Moriscos had constituted 20 percent of the population in parts of Aragon, while they had comprised closer to 2 percent of the overall population of Castile.[35] Scholars debate the degree to which each region experienced social and economic effects from the expulsion. The loss of laborers and tax revenue was higher in some areas than in others, to say nothing of the social, cultural, and human loss of expelling people from their homeland. Among other consequences, the expulsion removed a major target population from the grasp of the Spanish Inquisition. This changed the nature of inquisitorial activity, as there were very few trials for practicing Islam after the expulsion. In the tribunal of Valencia, where prosecution of Moriscos had been the main focus for decades before 1614, there were only thirteen cases against Moriscos from 1700 to 1820.[36]

To an even greater degree, the loss of the Moriscos affected the financial status of many inquisition tribunals, due to losses of confiscated property as well as payments for leniency. Inquisitors made this financial hardship clear in reports to the monarchy. In a letter to the king written on June 22, 1610, leaders of the Inquisition explained the loss of revenue experienced in the tribunals of Valencia and Zaragoza. The inquisitors described how "despite the great quantity of newly converted [Moriscos] who were regularly punished for the crime of heresy, we did not confiscate their property"; their actions complied with a royal order, with Moriscos instead paying huge annual sums to those tribunals as recompense. That cash flow had now run dry. "With this expulsion, the rents that the said two Inquisitions had have ceased," the inquisitors explained, leaving them short 7,500 ducats every year and thus unable to pay the salaries of their officials. As this situation threatened their ability to continue "such a holy ministry," they asked for aid from the king. They proposed that help could come from the property left behind by the deported Moriscos.[37]

Inquisitors were not the only complainants on this matter. In 1611, Moriscos in Valladolid successfully petitioned the king to break their obligation to pay the local tribunal of the Inquisition on an annual basis (a payment called the *situado*, in effect since 1558). Such a measure would free Morisco property from this tax and cut future revenue to the Inquisition, while leaving the Moriscos free to sell their own property before they left.[38] Disputes over property and money dragged on as the expulsion unfolded. The vast majority of Moriscos were forced out of Spain by 1614. The Spanish Inquisition was not abolished until 1834.

Reading the Inquisition

Records produced by the Spanish Inquisition documented the Moriscos and their encounters with religious authorities from limited and heavily prejudiced points of view. Histories of religious minorities have traditionally been told from the perspective of the dominant group. Early studies of the Spanish Inquisition replicated its own questions: Were Moriscos sincere Catholics or secret Muslims? Could they be Christians? Currently, most modern scholars no longer focus on determining religious sincerity, nor do they study the history of the Moriscos using only sources created by a persecuting institution. While inquisition records certainly reflect the aims and opinions of the inquisitors, they do not contain irrefutable evidence of Morisco identities, actions, or lived experiences.

One recent historian has found sources that reveal complex histories of Morisco assimilation and agency. He has called for a careful reading of sources produced by institutions of power, stating:

> It is high time, therefore, to begin to mistrust the official version of events, to put the stereotypes to one side, to look for signs of coexistence and cooperation between Morisco and Old Christian rather than hatred and separation, to judge the Moriscos not just as imagined crypto-Muslims and therefore an inassimilable fifth column but also as political and socio-economic entities fully involved in the communities which surrounded them and in which they played their part, religious as well as social.[39]

In order to demonstrate how the category of Morisco heresy was created and the ways in which it did not match lived realities, the records of the Spanish Inquisition must be read in combination with other sources.

Historians often refer to reading their materials "against the grain." This phrase can have many meanings: to identify the dominant point of view, to analyze biases, to consider alternate and multiple perspectives, to take missing information into account, to ask new questions of old problems, and so on. All these methods are important for reading texts left behind by the Spanish Inquisition. For instance, scholars can consider modes of being and belief beyond the Inquisition's binary model of religious identity. To heed the words of historian Mercedes García-Arenal, a leading expert in this field, "We need to reread Inquisition trial records without attending so much to Inquisition classifications; in the process, we may be able to restore the fuzziness to forms of religiosity that otherwise will be misperceived, if perceived at all."[40] Moreover, "while the Inquisition constituted a powerful weapon for silencing dissent, this does not mean that dissent did not exist."[41] In many instances, Moriscos responded to the prosecution they faced. Some of their responses are illustrated in this chapter, including petitioning and financial negotiation. These were actions of legal self-defense that highlight the aims and agency of different Morisco communities. Dissimulation and covert observance of prohibited practices (religious, cultural, and linguistic) can also be considered forms of dissent in inquisitorial Spain.

Finally, primary historical sources can be used for purposes beyond the intention of their creators. The archive of the Inquisition contains a plethora of data regarding Morisco property, which was routinely confiscated or taxed. As such, it was listed in registries that provide access to information about Morisco finances, land ownership, demographics, residency patterns, and legal disputes. Morisco petitions and the Inquisition's reports of their negotiations offer the names of leaders who acted on behalf of Morisco communities, evidence of communication between groups in different places, and specific requests related to local dynamics. Moriscos also engaged in forms of resistance that are recorded in different archives, such as the records of local and royal governance or the Royal Chancery courts of appeal of Valladolid and Granada. From these sources come histories – some detailed, others fragmentary – of the ways in which Moriscos claimed privileged status to seek relief from persecution.

For example, after their deportation from Granada, judges received petitions from Morisco individuals requesting legal recognition of their claims to Old Christian status, stating that they had inherited the title and privileges from a forefather, usually a voluntary convert from Islam with a record of service to the Spanish crown. If this inheritable status was confirmed in court, it would exempt the claimant and their relatives from the forced relocation and prohibitions placed upon deported Granadans.[42] Moriscos in the town of Hornachos and in the five towns of the Campo de Calatravas pursued collective claims to Old Christian status on the basis of law and hereditary status, not according to the parameters of *limpieza de sangre*.[43] Their efforts not only expand our grasp of disparate Morisco identities but also illustrate limits to the Spanish Inquisition as a legal institution.

The Morisco century lasted from the forced baptisms of the early sixteenth century until the forced deportations of the early seventeenth century. The Spanish Inquisition targeted this population with increasing intensity over the course of the intervening decades and in a variety of regional patterns. The Inquisition prosecuted Moriscos for a range of beliefs and practices that it deemed Islamic heresy. This inquisitorial profile of Moriscos shaped the systemic prejudice they faced in Spanish society and governance. Moriscos faced extraordinary violence in this system but were not merely victims. While Morisco histories are entwined with that of the Spanish Inquisition, they also encompass stories of resistance, community, and survival.

Notes

1. Stephen Haliczer, *Inquisition and Society in the Kingdom of Valencia, 1478–1834* (University of California Press, 1990), 246.
2. Nevertheless, some Moriscos emigrated: Karoline P. Cook, *Forbidden Passages: Muslims and Moriscos in Colonial Spanish America* (University of Pennsylvania Press, 2016).
3. Archivo Histórico Nacional [AHN], Sección Inquisición [Inqu.], Lejago 2108, expediente 16c.
4. Patrick O'Banion, ed., *This Happened in My Presence, Moriscos, Old Christians, and the Spanish Inquisition in the Town of Deza, 1569-1611*, 9.
5. O'Banion, ed., *This Happened in My Presence*, 34.
6. Mary Elizabeth Perry, *The Handless Maiden: Moriscos and the Politics of Religion in Early Modern Spain* (Princeton University Press, 2005), 53, and see chapter 3, "Dangerous Domesticity."
7. Perry, *The Handless Maiden*, 80.
8. Archivo General de Simancas [AGS], Sección Estado, Legajos 224 (s.f.) and 225 (ff. 49–50), August 1610.

9. Haliczer, *Inquisition and Society*, 252.
10. O'Banion, ed., *This Happened in My Presence*, 129.
11. Karoline P. Cook, "Navigating Identities: The Case of a Morisco Slave in Seventeenth-Century New Spain," *The Americas* 65 (2008): 79.
12. Haliczer, *Inquisition and Society*, 251.
13. Mayte Green-Mercado, *Visions of Deliverance: Moriscos and the Politics of Prophecy in the Early Modern Mediterranean* (Cornell University Press, 2019), 56–9; Claire M. Gilbert, *In Good Faith: Arabic Translation and Translators in Early Modern Spain* (University of Pennsylvania Press, 2020); Daniel Wasserman-Soler, *Truth in Many Tongues: Religious Conversion and the Languages of the Early Spanish Empire* (Pennsylvania State University Press, 2020).
14. Green-Mercado, *Visions*, 4.
15. Rafael Benítez Sánchez-Blanco, "La Inquisición ante los Moriscos," in Bartolomé Escandell Bonet and Joaquín Pérez Villanueva, eds., *Historia de la Inquisición en España y América*, Vol. 3 (Biblioteca de Autores Cristianos/Centro de Estudios Inquisitoriales, 2000), 705–6.
16. Serafín de Tapia Sánchez, *La comunidad morisca de Ávila* (Universidad de Salamanca, 1991), 226–30.
17. Tapia Sánchez, *La comunidad morisca*, 223.
18. Henry Kamen, *The Spanish Inquisition: A Historical Revision* (Yale University Press, 1998), 80.
19. Mercedes García-Arenal and Rafael Benitez Sánchez-Blanco, *The Inquisition Trial of Jerónimo de Rojas, a Morisco of Toledo (1601–1603)* (Brill, 2022), 93; see also Haliczer, *Inquisition and Society*, 258–60.
20. Benjamin Ehlers, *Between Christians and Moriscos: Juan de Ribera and Religious Reform in Valencia, 1568–1614* (The Johns Hopkins University Press, 2006), 16–17.
21. Haliczer, *Inquisition and Society*, 261.
22. Henry Charles Lea narrates these events in *A History of the Inquisition in Spain*, Vol. 3 (Macmillan, 1906-7), 345–62.
23. Tapia Sánchez, *La comunidad morisca*, 241–51.
24. García-Arenal and Benitez Sanchez-Blanco, *The Inquisition Trial of Jerónimo de Rojas*, 95.
25. Benítez Sánchez-Blanco, "La Inquisición ante los Moriscos," 733–6.
26. A classic article on this topic is Andrew C. Hess, "The Moriscos: An Ottoman Fifth Column in Sixteenth-Century Spain," *The American Historical Review* 74 (1968): 1–15.
27. Lea, *A History of the Inquisition in Spain*, 336.
28. Gilbert, *In Good Faith*, 47–8.
29. Luís de Mármol Carvajal, "Historia del rebellion y castigo de los moriscos del Reino de Granada," in Francisco Núñez Muley and Vincent Barletta,

A Memorandum for the President of the Royal Audiencia and Chancery Court of the City and Kingdom of Granada (The University of Chicago Press, 2007), 106.
30. Gilbert, *In Good Faith*, 48–51.
31. Núñez Muley, *A Memorandum*, 95–6.
32. Stephanie Cavanaugh, "Litigating for Liberty: Enslaved Morisco Children in Sixteenth-Century Valladolid," *Renaissance Quarterly* 70, no. 4 (Winter 2017): 1282–1320.
33. Kamen, *The Spanish Inquisition*, 244.
34. This decision was not unanimous; see Nicole Reinhardt, *Voices of Conscience: Royal Confessors and Political Counsel in Seventeenth-Century Spain and France* (Oxford University Press, 2016).
35. Bernard Vincent, "The Geography of the Morisco Expulsion: A Quantitative Study," in Mercedes García-Arenal and Gerard A. Wiegers, eds., *The Expulsion of the Moriscos from Spain* (Brill, 2014), 19.
36. Haliczer, *Inquisition and Society*, 270.
37. British Library, Egerton MS 1834, fols. 7–8. My translation.
38. AHN, Inquisición, Legajo 2109.2 (s.f., June 17, 1611). My translation.
39. Trevor J. Dadson, *Tolerance and Coexistence in Early Modern Spain: Old Christians and Moriscos in the Campo de Calatrava* (Boyd & Brewer Ltd, 2014), 121.
40. Mercedes García-Arenal, "A Catholic Muslim Prophet: Agustín de Ribera, 'The Boy Who Saw Angels,'" *Common Knowledge* 18 (2012): 269.
41. Mercedes García-Arenal, "Religious Dissent and Minorities: The Morisco Age," *The Journal of Modern History* 81 (2009): 896.
42. Santiago Otero Mondéjar, "'Que siendo yo cristiano viejo la justicia procedió contra mi . . .' La instrumentalización de la imagen del morisco," *Historia y Genealogía* 1 (2001): 125–7.
43. Dadson, *Tolerance and Coexistence*, 200–1.

Suggestions for Further Reading

Benítez Sánchez-Blanco, Rafael. "La Inquisición ante los Moriscos." In Joaquín Pérez Villanueva and Bartolomé Escandell Bonet, eds., *Historia de la Inquisición en España y América* Vol. 3. Biblioteca de Autores Cristianos/Centro de Estudios Inquisitoriales, 2000.

Cardaillac, Louis, ed. *Les morisques et l'inquisition*. Publisud, 1990.

Dadson, Trevor J. *Tolerance and Coexistence in Early Modern Spain: Old Christians and Moriscos in the Campo de Calatrava*. Boydell & Brewer, 2014.

Domínguez Ortiz, Antonio, and Bernard Vincent. *Historia de los moriscos: vida y tragedia de una minoría*. Revista de Occidente, 1978.

García-Arenal, Mercedes. "The Inquisition and the Search for Qur'ans." In Mercedes García-Arenal and Gerard Wiegers, eds., *The Iberian Qur'an: From the Middle Ages to Modern Times*. De Gruyter, 2022.

García-Arenal, Mercedes, and Rafael Benitez Sanchez-Blanco. *The Inquisition Trial of Jerónimo de Rojas, A Morisco of Toledo (1601–1603)*. Brill, 2022.

Green-Mercado, Mayte. *Visions of Deliverance: Moriscos and the Politics of Prophecy in the Early Modern Mediterranean*. Cornell University Press, 2019.

Núñez Muley, Francisco, and Vincent Barletta. *A Memorandum for the President of the Royal Audiencia and Chancery Court of the City and Kingdom of Granada*. The University of Chicago Press, 2007.

O'Banion, Patrick J., ed. *This Happened in My Presence: Moriscos, Old Christians, and the Spanish Inquisition in the Town of Deza, 1569–1611*. University of Toronto Press, 2017.

Perry, Mary Elizabeth. *The Handless Maiden: Moriscos and the Politics of Religion in Early Modern Spain*. Princeton University Press, 2005.

Bibliography

Benítez Sánchez-Blanco, Rafael. "La Inquisición ante los Moriscos." In Bartolomé Escandell Bonet and Joaquín Pérez Villanueva, eds., *Historia de la Inquisición en España y América* Vol. 3. Biblioteca de Autores Cristianos/Centro de Estudios Inquisitoriales, 2000.

Cook, Karoline P. *Forbidden Passages: Muslims and Moriscos in Colonial Spanish America*. University of Pennsylvania Press, 2016.

Cook, Karoline P. "Navigating Identities: The Case of a Morisco Slave in Seventeenth-Century New Spain." *The Americas* 65, no. 1 (2008): 63–79.

Dadson, Trevor J. *Tolerance and Coexistence in Early Modern Spain: Old Christians and Moriscos in the Campo de Calatrava*. Boydell & Brewer, 2014.

Ehlers, Benjamin. *Between Christians and Moriscos: Juan de Ribera and religious reform in Valencia, 1568–1614*. The Johns Hopkins University Press, 2006.

García-Arenal, Mercedes, "A Catholic Muslim Prophet: Agustín de Ribera, 'the Boy Who Saw Angels.'" *Common Knowledge* 18 (2012): 276–91.

"Religious Dissent and Minorities: The Morisco Age." *The Journal of Modern History* 81 (2009): 888–920.

García-Arenal, Mercedes, and Rafael Benitez Sanchez-Blanco. *The Inquisition Trial of Jerónimo de Rojas, A Morisco of Toledo (1601–1603)*. Brill, 2022.

Gilbert, Claire M. *In Good Faith: Arabic Translation and Translators in Early Modern Spain*. University of Pennsylvania Press. 2020.

Green-Mercado, Mayte. *Visions of Deliverance: Moriscos and the Politics of Prophecy in the Early Modern Mediterranean.* Cornell University Press, 2019.

Haliczer, Stephen. *Inquisition and Society in the Kingdom of Valencia, 1478–1834.* University of California Press, 1990.

Hess, Andrew C. "The Moriscos: An Ottoman Fifth Column in Sixteenth-Century Spain." *The American Historical Review* 74 (1968): 1–15.

Kamen, Henry. *The Spanish Inquisition: A Historical Revision.* Yale University Press, 1998.

Lea, Henry Charles. *A History of the Inquisition in Spain*, Vol. 3. Macmillan, 1906–7.

Núñez Muley, Francisco, and Vincent Barletta. *A Memorandum for the President of the Royal Audiencia and Chancery Court of the City and Kingdom of Granada.* The University of Chicago Press, 2007.

O'Banion, Patrick J., ed. *This Happened in My Presence: Moriscos, Old Christians, and the Spanish Inquisition in the Town of Deza, 1569–1611.* University of Toronto Press, 2017.

Otero Mondéjar, Santiago, "'Que siendo yo cristiano viejo la justicia procedió contra mí...' Lainstrumentalización de la imagen del morisco." *Historia y Genealogía* 1 (2001): 113–31.

Perry, Mary Elizabeth. *The Handless Maiden: Moriscos and the Politics of Religion in Early Modern Spain.* Princeton University Press, 2005.

Reinhardt, Nicole. *Voices of Conscience: Royal Confessors and Political Counsel in Seventeenth-Century Spain and France.* Oxford University Press, 2016.

Tapia Sánchez, Serafín de. *La comunidad morisca de Ávila.* Universidad de Salamanca, 1991.

Vincent, Bernard. "The Geography of the Morisco Expulsion: A Quantitative Study." In Mercedes García-Arenal and Gerard A. Wiegers, eds., *The Expulsion of the Moriscos from Spain.* Brill, 2014.

Wasserman-Solier, Daniel. *Truth in Many Tongues: Religious Conversion and the Languages of the Early Spanish Empire.* Pennsylvania State University Press, 2020.

Wright, Elizabeth. *The Epic of Juan Latino: Dilemmas of Race and Religion in Renaissance Spain.* University of Toronto Press. 2018.

JESSICA J. FOWLER

7

Alumbrados

The heresy of *alumbradismo* – with its practitioners known as *alumbrados* – was unique among offenses persecuted by the Spanish Inquisition. Meaning "the enlightened" or "the illuminated," the term *alumbrado* first surfaced among the laity in villages around Toledo in the early sixteenth century.[1] At first, the name was a term of derision wielded against those who claimed to have such a close relationship with God that the mediating rituals and sacraments of the Catholic Church were unnecessary for their salvation. Significantly, the Spanish Inquisition adopted the same insult as an appropriate moniker for what they deemed to be a novel form of heresy. The inquisitors' careless use of language was a clue as to how the Inquisition as an institution would formulate who *alumbrados* might be as well as what they believed. Over the next two centuries, the Spanish Inquisition found itself repeatedly confronting *alumbrados* and sometimes being forced to re-envision the meaning and content of this heresy. Yet the heresy of *alumbradismo* only exists in documents by, for, or about the Spanish Inquisition. The lack of corroborating sources, beyond those geared toward or influenced by persecution, demonstrates how the Inquisition was able to construct a lurking heretical menace out of disparate individuals who could be aligned in cohorts in some specific times and places, but remained unconnected to their alleged partisans in other moments and locations.

Modern researchers have often dismissed *alumbradismo* as a "catch-all" charge, one that was too expansive and all-encompassing to be taken seriously. Nonetheless, when tracing its prosecution across the sixteenth and seventeenth centuries, there was always a certain inquisitorial logic and understanding of what it constituted. While the charge certainly evolved over time and its affinity to other crimes against the faith (such as judaizing, false sanctity, and fraud) shifted in response to changing spiritual climates, it never became meaningless. In fact, it was this malleability that allowed it to remain relevant across two centuries as the Inquisition's fourth heresy of concern, as listed in general edicts of faith.

Still, the idea that the hundreds of individuals charged with this heresy across Spain, Peru, Mexico and even the Philippines somehow constituted a "sect" was a bogeyman of the Inquisition's own creation. Defendants charged as *alumbrados* were indeed often acting beyond the pale of orthodox Spanish Catholicism. However, the idea that they were members of an organized group – despite lacking any self-formulated doctrine or teachings, much less a means for global communication or dissemination of their ideas – was a stretch of logic that validated inquisitorial persecution but fails to adhere to modern historians' concepts of proof. While there are a few instances of mobile *alumbrado* defendants, they remained exceptional; they cannot explain the volume of cases that appeared across the entirety of the Spanish empire. Rather, it was the Inquisition's persecutorial discourse and bureaucracy that brought this phantom to life on the backs of hundreds of defendants across the globe, providing the connective threads for this "sect" when the *alumbrados* themselves failed to do so.

This chapter introduces the interactions of Spanish inquisitors with *alumbradismo* by first providing an overview of the who, what, where, and when of suspects across two centuries, followed by descriptions of three key moments in which the Inquisition defined – or tried to define – this heresy. The crux of the heresy of *alumbradismo* was always an emphasis on an interior piety that made the rituals and rites of the Catholic Church unnecessary, and which could imbue the practitioner with a state of impeccability. However, establishing the specificities and contours of this doctrine was a fraught endeavor. *Alumbrados* never seem to have formulated any sort of confession of faith or specific tenets that could be used as evidence to prove their deviation from Catholicism. Thus, the Inquisition was left to assemble a supposed statement of belief and doctrine for them by cobbling together the disparate testimony of unlearned witnesses and, later, learned religious men bent on the *alumbrados*' persecution.

Further complicating the Spanish Inquisition's efforts to delineate *alumbradismo* was the fact that this was the first "major heresy" that the institution had to define, and it was forced to do so without guidance from Rome. The Catholic Church had centuries of practice condemning the errors of both Jews and Muslims, whom its authorities viewed as infidels: When those Jews and Muslims were baptized as Christians, willingly or forcibly, they became heretics if they continued to practice their former faiths. The Protestant Reformation, spurred on by the Lutheran challenge, also received plenty of attention and clear condemnation from the pope as a threat to Catholicism. On the other hand, *alumbradismo* was so tied to Spain that neither the papacy nor any church council ever provided a clear foundation or precedent for its condemnation.[2] Therefore, in its efforts to define and add this novel heresy to its own catalog of offenses, the Spanish Inquisition was, itself, on novel – and perhaps even shaky – ground.

The very singularity of *alumbradismo* and the fact that it was a construct of the Spanish Inquisition is also what makes it a particularly fascinating heresy. Lacking the support of Rome or any clear statement of doctrine provided by the alleged heretics, proving the accuracy and truth of the Inquisition's own claims about the heresy fell solely on the Inquisition itself. Fortunately for this institution, its own practices and procedures were capable of doing exactly that. Once defined as a heresy, the Spanish Inquisition set in motion a cycle that, while self-referential, proved the existence of this novel sect and once activated, was largely self-perpetuating. The incorporation of this new category of heresy into general edicts of faith meant that the inquisitorially constructed definition of this sect was disseminated to the widest possible public in hopes of encouraging denunciations while also codifying this heresy as fact among learned religious circles. When denunciations were inevitably provided, the Inquisition prosecuted these suspects and presented those found guilty to the public in an *auto de fe* as *alumbrados*, proving that, indeed, an *alumbrado* sect did exist. In this way, the Inquisition demonstrated the reality of its heretical construction through its own methods and procedures. As increasing numbers of *alumbrados* were tried and punished it became harder to deny the existence of such a heretical sect.

This is not to say that this cycle of validation could not be stopped once set in motion. While obviously an institution designed for the prosecution of heretics, the men staffing the Inquisition were some of the most learned in the Spanish realms, and although some were zealots, most were capable of rational and critical appraisal of reports and denunciations. This did not mean that they could not be swayed to certain opinions based on their own career aspirations, particular loyalties, or other personal affinities, but rather that they continued to act with individual agency and, in doing so, sometimes chose to refuse the identification of certain deviants with particular heresies. These men did not doubt that *alumbradismo* existed and was a heresy, but they did not always concede that *alumbrado* was an appropriate label for the heterodox individuals brought before them.[3] It was these men in the employ of the Spanish Inquisition who could derail the self-affirming and self-replicating cycle set in place by the identification of *alumbrados* as heretics, and they did so regularly throughout the history of the charge. Thus, it was the interplay of instigators and skeptics, most often within the Inquisition itself, that dictated the identification, evolution, and future of the charge of *alumbradismo*.

Alumbrados were identified, at some point, in most tribunals in both Spain and its colonial holdings. It is perhaps no coincidence that those tribunals with the most impoverished archival remains also seem to have the fewest, if any, *alumbrado* cases. However, the two tribunals with the largest collection of extant documents, Toledo and Mexico, are also where historians find the most *alumbrados*. The responsibility of the Mexican tribunal for policing the orthodoxy of Spanish settlers in Manila also resulted in occasional accusations of *alumbradismo* appearing in the Philippines, the farthest outpost of the Spanish empire.

While many people were accused of being *alumbrados*, culprits often fell into identifiable types. The archetypal *alumbrado* was a *beata*, a laywoman who had taken informal religious vows but lived outside a convent. Some of these women chose a life in the world; however, many had no alternative, lacking the dowry required to enter a convent or constrained by family obligations. Although the ideal for the life of a *beata* was to emulate Catholic models of devotion, many ecclesiastical authorities feared that these women, unrestrained by either cloister or husbands, were dangerously free of male supervision. When such women began to develop cohorts of spiritual followers who believed they were divinely inspired and thus capable of discussing and teaching spiritual matters, and even providing spiritual guidance, they became a threat to the patriarchal Catholic Church. In the wake of the Council of Trent (1545–63), efforts were made to force these women into convents. Nonetheless, *beatas* remained an active part of Spanish religious life for decades and, thus, continued to be suspected as *alumbrados*. Although less frequently than *beatas*, nuns also could face charges as *alumbrados*. The continual surveillance of their religious lives by their conventual sisters and confessors, however, offered a wealth of opportunities to correct errant nuns before they fell into heresy.

Alumbradismo is often considered a heresy dominated by women, but men were also regularly indicted. These defendants were typically priests, those who had taken holy orders, or occasionally laymen who had assumed a religious vocation without formal vows. Such men often found themselves enthralled by a charismatic woman, typically a *beata*; believing themselves fortunate to have encountered a truly blessed and saintly individual, such men regularly became her greatest advocates and propagandists. Thus, while the central figure of many *alumbrado* cohorts was a woman, the number of men she attracted to her following could result in a higher preponderance of male defendants. Although less frequent, occasionally religious men did assume a leading role in *alumbrado* cohorts.

Alumbradismo was a Spanish heresy and, even when it began to appear in Spain's colonial holdings, it was predominantly Spaniards who remained suspect, with Portuguese and Mestizo defendants appearing only periodically. In the rare case that an Indigenous person, typically a woman, was accused of this heresy, the Inquisition found itself incapable of proceeding against her. As neophytes, Indigenous people remained beyond the reach of the Inquisition and thus, the inquisitors' only recourse, if they wished to see her disciplined, was to report her to other ecclesiastical authorities.

Regardless of their identity, *alumbrados* typically received relatively lenient punishments, considering the options available to the Inquisition. Most *alumbrados* would be presented to the public in an *auto de fe* and sentenced to some sort of reclusion, for instance in a convent or hospital where they would serve the sick. Defendants were also regularly exiled from where they had been renowned for their spiritual gifts, sometimes for a few years and other times permanently. Depending on the notoriety they had garnered before prosecution, they could also be paraded through the streets as an act of public shaming, or even be whipped. Pecuniary punishments occasionally also accompanied sentencing. Only in the most exceptional cases were *alumbrados* ever sent to the stake.

These generally benign punishments reflected the fact that *alumbrados* never fully rejected Catholicism, instead embracing certain aspects of the faith, such as the Eucharist or saintly models, while renouncing those ceremonies that they believed impeded their direct connection to and experience of God. Although dismissing the need for intermediaries between themselves and God, their visions and raptures were populated by the full cast of Catholic celestial figures: God, Jesus, and the Virgin Mary as well as a full panoply of saints and angels. In fact, many of those accused as *alumbrados* yearned to be regarded as saintly, feigning holy gifts – such as raptures, ecstasies, and visions – experienced by women held up by the church as paradigms, such as St. Teresa of Ávila or Catherine of Siena. Although rejecting a number of the sacraments, by the end of the sixteenth century *alumbrados* were often characterized by their fervent devotion to the power of the Eucharist, even if they did not believe it required consecration by the clergy. When forced to face inquisitors, *alumbrados* typically, although not always quickly, would confess to a litany of individual transgressions while rejecting the overarching claim that they were an *alumbrado* or a member of any sect. Such deference in the face of authority surely contributed to the lenience of the Holy Office in its handling of these defendants.

While it is easy enough to pinpoint the emergence of the heresy of *alumbradismo* and its later redefinition, it is significantly less clear how it evolved in case law over time and when it ceased being considered a real threat. *Alumbradismo*, as a heresy defined by the Spanish Inquisition, originated in 1525 before the tribunal of Toledo. However, only in 1574 was a revised definition of its alleged doctrine, and its classification as a sect, added to general edicts of faith. While *alumbradismo* could always be used as a singular charge, inquisitors also used it alongside other accusations. Thus, *alumbradismo* became a regular bedfellow of less serious religious crimes such as hypocrisy, fraud, suspect propositions, feigning sanctity, or even being possessed by the devil. The listing of these crimes in addition to the charge of *alumbradismo* indicates that these remained distinct offenses that were not inherently included as part of this heresy. In turn, these other charges could also be deployed independently of *alumbradismo*.

Which additional charges were likely to appear alongside *alumbradismo* varied widely over time. A rather sweeping and broad generalization of this chronology begins in the first decades of the sixteenth century when *alumbrados* were most likely to face additional charges as Lutherans and Erasmians. By the end of that century and into the next, the Inquisition considered *alumbrados* as potential victims of demonic possession (*endemoniadas*). During much of the seventeenth century, *alumbradismo* was regularly accompanied by accusations of religious fraud, imposture, or feigned sanctity. However, by roughly the middle of that century there was the increasing appearance of the charge of "*iluso*." This ill-defined offense would eventually become a stand-alone accusation, although leaving behind a linguistic legacy of "*illuminismo*" or "*illuminados*" to occasionally still accompany *alumbradismo*. In the closing decades of the seventeenth century, *alumbradismo* became most closely associated with the newly minted charge of "*molinosismo*," the heresy attributed to followers of the recently censured Miguel de Molinos and his iteration of Quietism, the religious movement then sweeping Europe. By the beginning of the eighteenth century, *alumbradismo*, when used at all, most often appeared as a secondary or even tertiary charge accompanying accusations against *ilusos* or followers of Molinos.

The de facto utilization of *alumbradismo* traced above, however, was not reflected in the Spanish Inquisition's de jure definition of the heresy. As a juridical category, *alumbradismo* was first described in 1525 and then redefined in 1574. Despite efforts to drastically expand the bounds of the heresy in 1623, the latter would remain the definitive version. The remainder of this chapter will focus on these key moments – 1525, 1574, and 1623 – and their role in the evolution of the charge. Despite adjustments to certain aspects of its definition over time, *alumbradismo* remained a heresy grounded in interior piety, claims to impeccability, defense of one's personal relationship with God, and the dismissal of certain key Catholic precepts, prescriptions, and rituals.

The birth certificate of the heresy of *alumbradismo* appeared in 1525 as an edict of faith directed to the archbishopric of Toledo, the result of the Inquisition's efforts to corral a group of lay religious individuals – a handful of *beatas*, a lay preacher, and their various followers – who were based in the area.[4] However, what inquisitors perceived as a cohort of like-minded individuals with shared spiritual teachings was, in fact, a fractious group, its members by that time often competing and even publicly disparaging each other, including before inquisitors. Indeed, the earliest denunciation of this group was provided by a woman familiar with the members' various spiritual circles who found herself on the outs with the leading figures and chose to denounce them to inquisitors. Thus, any effort to formulate a shared doctrine from this clearly polyphonic group was going to be tricky.

The appearance of this first group of *alumbrados* in a particularly fraught religious moment only further complicated the Inquisition's efforts to parse their doctrine. That many of these first defendants were conversos made them particularly suspicious to an institution founded for the sole purpose, at least initially, of rooting out judaizing. Despite the dogged efforts of the prosecutor, any affinity to judaizing was ultimately dismissed and in the future *alumbrados* would rarely be conversos. Additionally, the suspects' renunciation of exterior manifestations of faith spurred the Inquisition to question if they were Lutherans. While the first edict describing *alumbrados'* beliefs would attribute certain propositions to Lutheran errors, these earliest suspects would eventually be cleared of any such connection.[5] After all, the *alumbrados* in question had been disseminating their beliefs years before Luther burst on to the European religious scene.

Rather than deriving from other heresies, the spirituality posited by these *alumbrados* was instead inspired by a Spanish religious climate that embraced Desiderus Erasmus, the Reformed Franciscans, and mystical literature in the vernacular, all under the patronage of the highest Catholic authority of the land, Archbishop and Cardinal Francisco Jiménez de Cisneros of Toledo. Rather than Luther, it was the writings of Erasmus that inspired at least some of these earliest *alumbrados*, but they were far from alone. The Dutch humanist had enjoyed immense popularity for decades, even being invited to Spain, an invitation he perhaps presciently never accepted, given that certain of his works would be banned by mid-century. However, when these earliest *alumbrados* were reading and discussing Erasmus's work, it was not a crime but rather a predilection shared by much of the Spanish Church. Another key influence on these earliest *alumbrados* was the attempt by the Reformed Franciscans to return their order to the discipline and rules upon which it had been founded, shunning the riches and laxity that had overtaken so many religious orders by that time. This effort also emphasized religious meditation and contemplation, *recogimiento*, which would inspire the earliest *alumbrados* to see interior prayer as a key spiritual practice. Additionally, Cardinal Cisneros was also a supporter and patron of vernacular spiritual literature, including texts related to the mystical experiences of women who were later canonized, such as Catherine of Siena and Angela of Foligno. These various sources provided rich fodder from which the earliest *alumbrados* plucked their own preferences for a more interiorized Catholicism.[6]

Amid this already charged religious climate, the Inquisition in Toledo found that the *alumbrado* suspects had no fixed statement of doctrine or clearly articulated belief system and was thus forced to rely on the claims of witnesses to piece together what this group allegedly believed. The edict of faith of 1525 was the result of cobbling together the statements of lay individuals – many of them unlettered and none possessing theological training – and proffering these to the public as if it were a systematic theological overview of a novel form of heresy. While problematic in its compilation, the 1525 edict nonetheless pointed to certain religious ideas that would certainly have been anathema to the church.

The defining characteristic of these heretics, both at the time and in the future, was an emphasis on interior religious experience, especially mental prayer, which would lead toward the abandonment of one's soul in God. Upon achieving this state of union, the practitioner became incapable of sin and freed from the requirement to perform many of the works, rituals, and acts stipulated by the Catholic Church to achieve salvation. Allegedly, these *alumbrados* declared exterior acts of prayer unnecessary, chided those who lamented their sins as "penance-addicts," reminded those adoring the Cross that it was merely wood, called those processing in the streets with the Virgin Mary idolators, and laughed at those who venerated statues of the Lord since these were "simply sticks." The edict stated that the *alumbrados* also decried papal bulls as unnecessary, dismissed the need for fasts and acts of charity, and believed that "it was not good for men to become monks." It also claimed that *alumbrados* rejected the idea that knowledge of God or Scripture was the sole provenance of learned men, believing instead that God would bestow upon them what He desired them to know. However, while this edict included a coherent thread of antinomian dismissal of Catholic practice, it was also littered with miscellaneous assertions that did not fit this mold but clearly contradicted Catholic theology, for example, that the world would end in twelve years, that hell was a bogeyman meant to scare people, that one should never swear an oath, and that married people were more united to God when making love than when in prayer.[7]

The earliest *alumbrados* were arrested, prosecuted, and penanced by Spanish inquisitors between 1524 and 1534. Still, the charge of *alumbradismo* continued to lurk alongside concerns about Erasmians and Lutherans in the following decades. Indeed, there were clear familial connections between the earliest *alumbrados*, such as María de Cazalla, penanced in 1534, and certain so-called Lutherans who would be burned by mid-century, such as Agustín de Cazalla, executed in 1559.[8] In 1558, the royal governing council of the Spanish Inquisition, called the Suprema, highlighted potential links between the Toledo area's *alumbrados* from the 1520s and the suspected Lutherans currently on trial in Valladolid and Seville.[9] Still, while inquisitors in the 1550s might have wanted to make historical connections to earlier *alumbrados*, the men and women burned at the stake between 1559 and 1562 were executed for their endorsement of Protestantism as well as to set an example.[10]

Some four decades after the first *alumbrados*' arrests, a second group was identified and the heresy redefined to accommodate their prosecution by the Inquisition. If the heresy was first codified by Spanish inquisitors in the 1520s, it would be the 1570s that provided the decisive definition, through at least the mid-eighteenth century, of what its practitioners allegedly believed. The Inquisition became aware of this 1570s group thanks to the dogged efforts of a Dominican friar named Alonso de la Fuente, who seems to have imagined himself as a sort of crusader against *alumbrados*.[11] This dynamic, of a certain persecutorial protagonist instigating or encouraging the Inquisition to action against alleged *alumbrados*, would be a recurring feature of the heresy in the future.[12] The fact that the men who played this role were nearly always associated with or aspiring to work in the Inquisition indicates the power of this institution to encourage the identification of those heresies which it sought and, in doing so, reaffirm the validity of its heretical constructions.

Unfortunately, the cases against the 1570s defendants from the region of Extremadura are no longer extant. Thus, the historian is left to piece together how the transformation in the definition of *alumbradismo* occurred based on inquisitorial correspondence and the extensive, although clearly biased, writings of de la Fuente. By his own telling, he encountered a suspicious religious group upon his arrival in Badajoz, in southern Spain, where he was to take up his post as preacher in a Dominican convent. The deviants were led by a priest who had a number of *beata* followers; the *beatas* received the Eucharist daily, practiced contemplation, and experienced raptures. Horrified that uneducated lay people claimed to experience such divine gifts, de la Fuente undertook a dual-purpose campaign of preaching and investigation in the area. (It is imperative to remember that what we know of this period of discovery and pursuit is indebted to what de la Fuente told King Philip II in a 1575 report, which recounted his efforts that began five years earlier.) When his efforts to alert the local inquisition tribunal in Llerena proved fruitless, he decided to consult with his Dominican colleagues in Seville. One of these men, Juan de Ochoa, had previously acted as a theologian in the cases of the earlier *alumbrados* of Toledo, and he informed de la Fuente that what he had uncovered was "a portrait of what the *alumbrados* of Toledo taught."[13] With this information de la Fuente was able to convince the Suprema that he had indeed identified a threat to orthodoxy, and this body, in turn, ordered the previously apathetic tribunal of Llerena to take immediate action. In fact, de la Fuente's letter to Inquisitor General Gaspar de Quiroga resulted in his own appearance before the Suprema. He so impressed that council that he was allowed to single out its own prosecutor, Juan López de Montoya, who was then promoted to inquisitor and instructed to return with de la Fuente to Extremadura to investigate.

To address this newest appearance of *alumbrados* the Suprema released an amended and adjusted edict of faith in 1574, which de la Fuente and López de Montoya carried with them.[14] Compared to its 1525 predecessor, this document halved the number of propositions attributed to these heretics and despite its less detailed descriptions, offered a more coherent overview of *alumbradismo* while adding important new components. Mental prayer remained the cornerstone of the heresy; the dismissal of corporal exercises, virtuous works, and the veneration of images of the saints also endured. While the earlier edict had spoken of *alumbrados* chastising an individual for moving to better see the consecration of the Eucharist, by 1574 they had a more ambivalent attitude toward this sacrament. Supposedly, they claimed that one could take communion with simple bread but that if it were to be consecrated then they should close their eyes during this act. At the same time, *alumbrados* were now accused of taking communion in many forms, convinced that in doing so they received greater grace.

Additionally, the 1574 edict outlined how *alumbrado* teachers now demanded strict obedience from their followers as well as a monopoly on their confessions. In return, devotees were assured that once they reached a certain state of grace that they would see marvelous things, such as the divine essence of God and the mysteries of the Holy Trinity. In such moments, the Holy Spirit would immediately govern their souls and they could experience certain raptures and ecstasies that were the product of God's love for them and proof that they were in a state of grace.

When it came to more earthly matters, *alumbrados* in 1574 allegedly believed they should neither marry nor join religious orders; they also were freed from obeying the mandates of any religious authority or family member who dared to interrupt their hours of prayer and contemplation. While the suspects described by the 1574 edict of faith were, in many ways, distinct from those identified in 1525, the Inquisition believed them similar enough to require just a simple redefinition of the tenets of the heresy of *alumbradismo* to better accommodate these latest defendants.

While this 1574 edict of faith was initially written for and directed to the specific jurisdiction of the Llerena tribunal, it would soon find its way, in a slightly condensed format, into the general edicts of faith released to all tribunals under the heading "sect of *alumbrados.*" In doing so, the Inquisition transformed *alumbradismo* from a site-specific threat, to be addressed when and where it appeared, into a more generalized menace that threatened to appear anywhere at any time. Additionally, it was only upon this heresy's inclusion into general edicts of faith that it was formally identified by the Inquisition as a "sect," a designation absent from the 1525 and 1574 edicts directed at Toledo and Extremadura respectively. When the *alumbrados* of 1574 were publicly sentenced in an *auto de fe* in Llerena in 1579, their category of heresy was reified. Nineteen individuals were judged guilty "for the sect and doctrine of *alumbrados*," a statement that provided yet further public proof that this heresy had indeed coalesced into a faction opposed to Spanish Catholicism. What began as a singular appearance of a group of deviants around Toledo in the 1520s, and then reappeared in Extremadura, now warranted the designation of a sect, a much more sinister threat to Catholic orthodoxy. *Alumbradismo* now required the vigilance of all inquisition tribunals, and the general edicts of faith informed them of exactly that.

The next major appearance of the heresy, which would result in further efforts to redefine and expand it, occurred in Seville in the 1620s.[15] Once again, it was certain inquisitorial instigators who fomented a sense of impending danger posed by an *alumbrado* menace. This role was taken up with zeal by Inquisitor Alonso de Hoces and the Dominicans of the San Pablo convent who together spurred the Suprema to action. The first arrests were made by 1622. Based on the ensuing interrogations the tribunal, with the diligent assistance of the Dominicans, sent the council a dossier proposing a new edict of grace. Demonstrating their assiduous study of the heresy, this portfolio included a copy of the 1525 edict of faith, now nearly a century old, multiple copies of the general edicts of faith, and a list of seventy propositions that they believed were needed to update this heretical category.[16] Inquisitor General Andrés Pacheco rapidly approved the release of an edict of grace, copied nearly wholesale from the suggestions provided in the dossier. Significantly, inquisitorial edicts of grace offered reconciliation to the Church for individuals who confessed before inquisitors and expressed repentance. The response to

Pacheco's edict would soon swamp the tribunal, and the redefinition of *alumbradismo* would soon flounder.

The 1623 edict of grace attempted not only to redefine but to expand what *alumbradismo* constituted. While adopting nearly wholesale the tenets of the 1574 edict of faith as its first fifteen propositions, the later document ballooned to more than seventy propositions. While many of these additional propositions had been hinted at or cursorily addressed in the 1574 edict, they were more fully developed and expounded upon in 1623. A practice of interior prayer and piety remained foundational to the heresy, as did the belief that such devotion freed its practitioners from certain Catholic rituals. Venerating saints, attending Mass, abstaining from meat on certain days: According to the definition of *alumbradismo* in 1623, none of these acts were necessary.

At the same time, *alumbrados* in 1623 exhibited what Catholic authorities deemed to be an overly zealous fixation on the Eucharist that exceeded the limits of religious orthodoxy. While still deeming it superfluous to witness the moment of consecration, a tenet from the 1574 edict, by 1623 *alumbrados* allegedly were demanding to receive the Eucharist regularly in multiple forms, claiming that in this way, more of God remained within them. They purportedly believed that their reception of the Eucharist in this fashion would allow them to reach a state of spiritual union with the divine, which would manifest in raptures and similar somatic experiences during which they would see God.

The state of grace the *alumbrados* were claiming to achieve implied an inability to sin, which in turn would free them from fault when they engaged in lascivious and carnal behaviors, another regular feature of *alumbradismo* according to the edict of 1623. Their impeccable state also liberated them from any need to abide by the censures of religious authorities: It made them immune to excommunication and incapable of suffering the pangs of purgatory. Additionally – in a clause that harkened back to 1525 – the *alumbrados* in 1623 challenged the common understanding of certain biblical passages offered by theologians and preachers. They believed instead that they could understand Scripture better than learned men, a claim reminiscent of the abilities attributed to *alumbrados* around Toledo in the 1520s and 1530s.

In the 1574 edict against the *alumbrados*, they supposedly posited that salvation was reserved for those following *alumbrado* masters. The

1623 edict amplified the degree of the same offense: Now, *alumbrados* allegedly took strict vows of obedience to their masters, who could absolve all manner of sins. The 1623 edict also asserted that *alumbrados* strayed even farther from Catholic orthodoxy by believing that women could act as spiritual masters. The closing section of the edict specifically warned of how this heresy allowed *beatas* to lead spiritual circles, a concern that also had been present in 1525, although it was never articulated in the edict from that period.

The 1623 edict heightened the sexual and rebellious implications of *alumbradismo* by positing that the sect's spiritual leaders, whether male or female, supposedly held nocturnal conventicles and convened "congregations" to whom they would preach and with whom they discussed spiritual matters. An analogy with the concept of the witches' sabbat is obvious, as is the idea of an anti-Church. Furthermore, male *alumbrados* now enjoyed complete control over their female followers' lives by rejecting the authority of anyone else who might lay claim to these women's allegiance, including parents or husbands. Finally, in 1623 the descriptions of the *alumbrados*' heresy also included contradictory propositions: Masters told their young female followers to both become nuns and reject religious vows, directives that could not be followed simultaneously.

The radical expansion of what constituted *alumbradismo* in the 1623 edict of grace and the internal conflicts within this document did not go unnoticed or uncontested. Juan Dionisio Fernández Portocarrero, at the time employed as an assistant to the archbishop of Seville, promptly penned a rebuttal that found its way to the Suprema.[17] He argued that this edict of grace was so expansive as to condemn orthodox Catholic practice and that it would sow confusion among the laity. Fernández Portocarrero claimed that condemning interior prayer and raptures *in toto* meant censuring the teachings and experiences of Catholic saints. Although not stated directly, he certainly had in mind Teresa of Ávila and Ignatius of Loyola, both canonized the year prior to the edict's release, as well as those female saints whose prayer and raptures had been decisive to their canonization. Furthermore, many saintly women were known to have offered vows of obedience to their confessors: How, then, could doing so constitute a religious failing, as the edict indicated? Fernández Portocarrero also reminded his audience that condemning women as spiritual leaders neglected the long history of certain Catholic women as paragons of virtue, orthodoxy, and even saintliness. He continued that it was a disservice to the faith to ban "congregations" from discussing religious matters, even if these groups were composed only of the laity. Finally, many of the propositions that the edict identified as religious error he found merely ill-advised, vain, or presumptuous, and thus not substantial enough to be used as indicators of heresy. While the bulk of his concerns were theological, Fernández Portocarrero was not above pointing out more careless aspects of the edict including repetitive claims, contradictory propositions – whether a woman should be a nun or shun the convent – the misspelling of words (*ractos* when they meant *raptos*), and instances in which the meaning of certain propositions was unclear.[18]

Ultimately, the 1623 edict of grace proved to be a failed attempt to redefine this heresy. It is hard to imagine that Fernández Portocarrero's critique did not play some role in this. Shortly after penning it, rather than being reprimanded, as one might expect from an institution that often jealously guarded its prerogatives, Fernández Portocarrero was promoted to the rank of inquisitor. He was eventually even sent to preside over the tribunal of Seville, which remained mired in the cases spurred by the very definition he had criticized. By that time Inquisitor Hoces, who had helped instigate these cases, had been reassigned to another tribunal. Although Fernández Portocarrero's appointment occurred after the 1624 *auto de fe*, in which eleven defendants were sentenced as *alumbrados*, under his auspices the remaining cases, including that of the two *alumbrado* leaders, were brought to a fairly rapid conclusion with limited fanfare and mild penances.

It seems telling that the Suprema of the Spanish Inquisition chose to replace an instigator of *alumbrado* cases with a skeptic once the denunciations and accusations of this heresy had spiraled beyond credibility. Furthermore, the definition proffered in the 1623 edict of grace never culminated in a new edict of faith against *alumbrados* nor were its claims codified in the general edicts of faith. Thus, while causing no small amount of drama and excitement in Seville initially, the expanded definition failed to fundamentally reformulate this heresy for the Spanish Inquisition. If we assess the description of the "sect of *alumbrados*" as presented in the general edicts of faith before and after, it was as if the 1623 edict of grace had never been issued.

And yet – ironically – the Suprema proved helpless to stop the 1623 edict's dissemination. When it became clear that printed copies of it were circulating in Córdoba and possibly Granada, the Consejo ordered them immediately confiscated, but any hope of reining in their spread proved illusory. A printer in Spain released a French translation of the edict, presumably to be sent abroad.[19] The 1623 edict also appeared in the records of the Portuguese Inquisition.[20] (It is unclear if this copy arrived with or without the approval of the Spanish Holy Office since the two institutions were known to collaborate at times.) The release of such an expansive definition of the heresy of *alumbradismo* thus spread further than ever intended, even if its revised version was rejected for inclusion in the Inquisition's general edicts of faith.

The 1623 edict of grace was the final, and arguably most spectacular, effort to redefine *alumbradismo*, and it failed. Nevertheless, individuals suspected of *alumbradismo* continued to appear in tribunals across the Spanish empire for the rest of the seventeenth century. Between 1600 and 1650, inquisition tribunals from Lima to Toledo had to determine whether defendants were *alumbrados* or were engaging in some other form of religious deviance.[21] The tribunal in Mexico City found itself mired in *alumbrado* cases in the middle of the seventeenth century; although not involving nearly as many defendants, Valencia was also sorting through a cadre of culprits at the same time.[22] Concerns about *alumbradismo* in the Pacific world were mostly relegated to the seventeenth century.[23] Perhaps the most famous Spanish *auto de fe*, held in the Plaza Mayor in Madrid in 1680, attended by King Charles II and immortalized in the painting by Francisco Rizi, also included *alumbrados*, though in effigy.[24] The closing decades of the seventeenth century saw *beatas* judged for this heresy in both Lima and Murcia.[25] By 1700 *alumbradismo* had mostly receded into the background, a supporting charge used against those accused as *ilusos* or followers of the Quietism of Molinos, though it would make surprise appearances as late as the 1790s. Indeed, given its continued incorporation in general edicts of faith, it was nearly impossible for it to ever completely disappear.

Alumbradismo was a unique charge in the annals of the Spanish Inquisition. The epitome of an inquisitorially constructed heresy, one formulated on less-than-firm foundations, it nonetheless proved capable of surviving centuries of inquisitorial practice around the world. Thanks to the Spanish Inquisition's redefinition of *alumbrados* as a sect in 1574, as well as the inclusion of this heresy in the general edicts of faith, inquisitors were mandated to remain ever vigilant against its appearance. While the heresy certainly evolved over the course of its existence, this evolution remained temporal rather than geographic. For example, *alumbrados* prosecuted in the mid-seventeenth century were charged with having committed remarkably similar acts whether they were tried in Mexico City, Toledo, or Manila. While there were certain local adaptations within *alumbrados*' claims or visions, their overarching qualities and characteristics remained comparable due to the shared inquisitorial definition of this heresy that set their persecution in place. Thus, even beyond the borders of Spain, the Spanish Inquisition perpetuated a consistent vision of *alumbradismo* across the farthest reaches of the empire.

The claim that *alumbrado* defendants – spread across such immense spans of time and geography, without any agreed upon doctrine, statement of faith, founding figure, or even connection to other *alumbrados* – constituted a sect fails all modern conceptions of proof. But the Spanish Inquisition was not beholden to such criteria. In this case, the "reality" of the *alumbrado* sect was "proven" by evidence manufactured by inquisitorial investigation, claims to be able to identify a system of beliefs, and the ability to find defendants to describe as *alumbrados*. Once this cycle had been set in motion, no one argued that *alumbrados* were not a heretical sect; instead, debate remained confined to whether or not particular defendants were members of that sect. Researchers studying inquisitions in general are cognizant of how such institutions constructed forms of deviance and heresy. *Alumbradismo* was the Spanish Inquisition's example par excellence of this process, while also providing a unique example of just how long such constructs could endure and how far they could reach.

Notes

1. The author would like to thank the Women's Studies in Religion Program at Harvard Divinity School for providing her with the time and space to write this piece.

2. The most similar heresy beyond Spain would be "feigned sanctity," persecuted in Italy. However, the timing, motivations, and juridical understandings of these heresies remain quite distinct. Anne Jacobsen Schutte, *Aspiring Saints: Pretense of Holiness, Inquisition, and Gender in the Republic of Venice, 1618-1750* (The Johns Hopkins University Press, 2001).
3. For an example, see Jessica J. Fowler, "Process and Punishment: Alleged Alumbrados before the Mexican Holy Office, 1593-1603," *Colonial Latin American Review* 29 (2020): 357-75.
4. For an English translation of this edict as well as excerpts from some trials, see Lu Ann Homza, ed. and trans., "The Alumbrados in Castile, 1525-1532" in *The Spanish Inquisition, 1478-1614: An Anthology of Sources* (Hackett, 2006), 80-152.
5. Alastair Hamilton, "Merciful Inquisitors: Disagreements within the Holy Office about the Alumbrados of Toledo," in Michael Erbe et al., eds., *Querdenken. Dissens und Toleranz im Wandel der Geschichte* (Palatium Verlag im J & J Verlag, 1996), 132.
6. Alastair Hamilton, *Heresy and Mysticism in Sixteenth-Century Spain: The Alumbrados* (University of Toronto Press, 1992).
7. For an examination of this earliest group, Antonio Márquez, *Los alumbrados. Orígenes y filosofía, 1525-1559* (Taurus, 1972).
8. Homza, *The Spanish Inquisition*, docs. 12, 17.
9. Homza, *The Spanish Inquisition*, 176-8, 187-9.
10. Homza, *The Spanish Inquisition*, 192-7.
11. The work of de la Fuente is meticulously analyzed in Alvaro Huerga, *Historia de los Alumbrados* Vol. 1: *Los alumbrados de Extremadura* (Fundación Universitaria Española, 1978).
12. For additional examples, Jessica J. Fowler, "Assembling Alumbradismo: The Evolution of a Heretical Construction," in Mercedes García-Arenal, ed., *After Conversion: Iberia and the Emergence of Modernity* (Brill: 2016), 251-82.
13. Alvaro Huerga, *Historia de los Alumbrados* Vol. 1: *Los alumbrados de Extremadura* (Fundación Universitaria Española, 1978), 340.
14. A copy of this edict is in Huerga, *Historia de los Alumbrados* Vol. 5: *Temas y personajes* (Fundación Universitaria Española, 1994), 401-2.
15. Alvaro Huerga, *Historia de los Alumbrados* Vol. 4: *Los alumbrados de Sevilla* (Fundación Universitaria Española, 1988).
16. Archivo Histórico Nacional (Madrid), Inquisición, Leg. 3716, exp. 14. A transcription of this edict is in Huerga, *Historia de los Alumbrados* Vol. 5: *Temas y personajes* (Fundación Universitaria Española, 1994), 423-30.
17. A transcription of this document is in Alvaro Huerga, *Historia de los Alumbrados*, vol. 5, *Temas y personajes* (Fundación Universitaria Española, 1994), 430-37.

18. Jessica J. Fowler, "Questioning the 1623 Edict of Grace: Differentiating Between Orthodox and Heterodox Interiority." *Culture & History: A Digital Journal* 6 (2017).
19. Biblioteca de la Real Academia Española, RM VAR-665.
20. Archivo Nacional/Torre do Tombo, Manuscritos da Livraria, no. 1056, ff.337–345.
21. René Millar Carvacho, *Santidad, falsa santidad y posesiones demoniacas en Perú y Chile, siglos XVI y XVII: Estudios sobre mentalidad religiosa* (Ediciones UC, 2009), 227–66; Andrew Keitt, *Inventing the Sacred: Imposture, Inquisition, and the Boundaries of the Supernatural in Golden Age Spain* (Brill, 2005).
22. Adriana Rodriguez Delgado, *Santos o embusteros: Los alumbrados novohispanos del siglo XVII* (Gobierno del Estado de Veracruz, 2013); Francisco Pons Fuster, *Místicos, beatas y alumbrados. Ribera y la espiritualidad valenciana del S. XVII* (Institució Valenciana d'estudis i investigación, 1991).
23. For one example, Jessica J. Fowler, "Illuminated Islands: Luisa de los Reyes and the Inquisition in Manila," in Alison Weber, ed., *Devout Laywomen in the Early Modern World* (Routledge, 2016).
24. "Relación histórica del auto general de fe que se celebro en Madrid este ano de 1680 . . . por José del Olmo." Impreso por Roque Rico de Miranda, 1680.
25. Millar Carvacho, *Santidad, falsa santidad,* 227–66; Cayetano Mas Galvañ, "Un grupo de alumbrados en el sur valenciano durante el siglo XVII (Novelda y Alicante, 1579-1682)," *Revista de Historia Moderna: Anales de la Universidad de Alicante* 21 (2003): 7–51.

Suggestions for Further Reading

Ahlgren, Gillian T. W., ed. and trans., *The Inquisition of Francisca: A Sixteenth-Century Visionary on Trial.* The University of Chicago Press, 2005.

Fowler, Jessica J. "Assembling Alumbradismo: The Evolution of a Heretical Construct." In Mercedes García-Arenal, ed., *After Conversion: Iberia and the Emergence of Modernity.* Brill, 2016.

Hamilton, Alastair. *Heresy and Mysticism in Sixteenth-Century Spain: The Alumbrados.* University of Toronto Press, 1992.

Homza, Lu Ann, ed. and trans. *The Spanish Inquisition, 1478–1614. An Anthology of Sources.* Hackett, 2006.

Huerga, Alvaro. *Historia de los Alumbrados,* 5 vols. Fundación Universitaria Española, 1978–1994.

Jaffary, Nora. *False Mystics: Deviant Orthodoxy in Colonial Mexico.* University of Nebraska Press, 2004.

Bibliography

Fowler, Jessica J. "Assembling Alumbradismo: The Evolution of a Heretical Construction." In Mercedes García-Arenal, ed., *After Conversion: Iberia and the Emergence of Modernity*. Brill, 2016.
"Illuminated Islands: Luisa de los Reyes and the Inquisition in Manila." In Alison Weber, ed., *Devout Laywomen in the Early Modern World*. Routledge, 2016.
"Questioning the 1623 Edict of Grace: Differentiating between Orthodox and Heterodox Interiority." *Culture & History: A Digital Journal* 6 (2017).
"Process and Punishment: Alleged Alumbrados before the Mexican Holy Office, 1593-1603." *Colonial Latin American Review*, 29 (2020): 357-75.
Hamilton, Alistair. *Heresy and Mysticism in Sixteenth-Century Spain: The Alumbrados*. University of Toronto Press, 1992.
"Merciful Inquisitors: Disagreements within the Holy Office about the Alumbrados of Toledo." In Michael Erbe et al., eds., *Querdenken. Dissens und Toleranz im Wandel der Geschichte*, 123-33. Palatium Verlag im J & J Verlag, 1996.
Homza, Lu Ann, ed. and trans. *The Spanish Inquisition, 1478-1614: An Anthology of Sources*. Hackett, 2006.
Huerga, Alvaro. *Historia de los Alumbrados* Vol. 1: *Los alumbrados de Extremadura*. Fundación Universitaria Española, 1978.
Historia de los Alumbrados Vol. 4: *Los alumbrados de Sevilla*. Fundación Universitaria Española, 1988.
Historia de los Alumbrados Vol. 5: *Temas y personajes*. Fundación Universitaria Española, 1994.
Keitt, Andrew. *Inventing the Sacred: Imposture, Inquisition, and the Boundaries of the Supernatural in Golden Age Spain*. Brill, 2005.
Márquez, Antonio. *Los alumbrados. Orígenes y filosofía, 1525-1559*. Taurus, 1972.
Millar Carvacho, René. *Santidad, falsa santidad y posesiones demoniacas en Perú y Chile, siglos XVI y XVII: Estudios sobre mentalidad religiosa*. SantiEdiciones UC, 2009.
Mas Galvañ, Cayetano. "Un grupo de alumbrados en el sur valenciano durante el siglo XVII (Novelda y Alicante, 1579-1682)." *Revista de Historia Moderna: Anales de la Universidad de Alicante* 21 (2003): 7-51.
Schutte, Anne Jacobsen. *Aspiring Saints: Pretense of Holiness, Inquisition, and Gender in the Republic of Venice, 1618-1750*. The Johns Hopkins University Press, 2001.

DORIS MORENO-MARTÍNEZ
TRANSLATED BY LU ANN HOMZA

8

Protestants

News of Lutheranism reached Spain quickly, first with reports of Luther's censorship by the University of Louvain in 1519 and then with information about his papal condemnation via bulls issued by Leo X in 1520.[1] The German reformer was a protagonist in conversations among Spain's intellectual, religious, and political elites. The first direct contacts that Spaniards had with Protestantism occurred at the Diet of Worms, when Luther appeared before Charles V in 1521. In those initial moments of information and contact, he aroused sympathy for his criticism of the corruption of the Church and the abuses of the papacy. As a contemporary said: "At first, when Luther only touched on the need for the reform of the Church and the corruption of morals [*corruptionem morum*], everyone approved of him."[2] That positive opinion quickly shifted. In 1521, in the middle of a popular rebellion against King Charles V of Spain, the inquisitor-general and the Admiral of Castile urged Charles to punish Luther severely, fearing contagion. Two years later, in 1523, the Spanish ambassador in Rome told the pope that the bishop of Zamora, one of the rebellion's leaders, had been "another Luther."[3] The echoes from Germany resounded in Castile.

The eruption of Lutheranism coincided with a time of crisis in the trajectory of the Spanish Inquisition. The period 1516–20 was decisive. Trials against judaizing conversos seemed to have been exhausted after decades of terrible persecution since the first public sentencing in Seville in 1480. The tremendous abuses of Inquisitor Lucero in Córdoba (1504–8) intensified criticism of the Holy Office. The Flemish entourage of the new monarch, Charles V, proposed a possible reform that was quickly stopped by Inquisitor-General Cardinal Francisco de Cisneros. But the voices against the Holy Office were heard in the meetings of the Cortes, both in Castile and Aragon. In this context, it could be said that the outbreak of Lutheranism reactivated the Inquisition and helped to justify its existence.

The first notices about Luther in Spain coincided with the rise of followers of Desiderius Erasmus there, along with a remarkable number of internal spiritual currents that had synthesized diverse influences – Savonarola, the *Devotio moderna*, Franciscan spirituality – and clamored for a reform of the Church and its members, customs and morals, and even the experience of Christian faith itself. Likewise, the discovery of America inspired and stimulated new mystical and prophetic hopes.

Erasmus's works were warmly welcomed in Spain with the support of Charles V and some of the most influential people of the court and the ecclesiastical hierarchy, such as the imperial chancellor, Mercurino Gattinara, and Inquisitor-General Alonso Manrique. The numerous translations and editions of Erasmus's writings demonstrate his success, which included a popular audience. Erasmus proposed a return to the scriptures and a Christian life of more devotional, less ritualized piety. Meditation on the Passion of Christ, mental prayer, and the practice of the virtues were the elements of an authentic Christian discipline that should be within reach of all Christians, not just members of the clergy. His subtle irony and critiques of Rome's abuses and the corruption of the clergy also provoked great approval.

Some historians have suggested that the success of Erasmus in Spain in the 1520s kept the Spanish from taking an interest in Lutheranism in those years.[4] Nevertheless, there undoubtedly was Spanish curiosity about the writings of Luther and his followers. In Castile, at the University of Alcalá, groups of clergymen and students were in favor of the Christian humanism of Erasmus, yet read the works of Protestant reformers at the same time. In 1529, Juan de Valdés, brother of Alfonso de Valdés, Charles V's secretary, published in Alcalá a manual of doctrine inspired by Erasmus with borrowings from Luther, Oecolampadius, and Melanchthon.[5] He fled Spain and settled in Naples, where he died in 1541; he never broke with the Roman Church. He was undoubtedly an Erasmian and while some historians have emphasized Juan de Valdés's Protestant leanings others have tied him more closely to *alumbradismo*, but all agree on his originality and influence.[6]

Alumbradismo was derived from Franciscan spirituality and insisted that Christians must abandon themselves to the love of God (*dexamiento*). From 1510, according to inquisitorial sources, a growing number of people in Castile became interested in putting into practice a more authentic interior religiosity, following the masters of late medieval mysticism. Some of the elements of *alumbradismo* were close to Lutheranism, such as the pivotal role of God's grace in salvation, along with the denial of ecclesiastical celibacy and the sacramental character of marriage. But *alumbradismo* was above all an eclectic current that embraced diverse sensibilities.[7] Codified as a heresy in an inquisition edict of faith of 1525, *alumbradismo* alarmed Spanish inquisitors when they realized the subversive power of some of its propositions and its social influence outside learned circles. The first trials of *alumbrados* took place between 1524 and 1529: They paralleled a growing campaign against Erasmianism, as well as a moment when Luther's ideas were becoming better known and Lutheran books were found crossing Spanish borders.[8]

Where Protestantism was concerned, the first worry in the 1520s was to prevent the entry of the texts of Luther and his followers. In 1521, some informers warned that there were plans in Flanders to translate some of his works into Spanish, a project that appeared to be financed by the converso community.[9] The same year, Luther's works were banned in Spain and inquisitorial inspectors began to find them as soon as they started to look. In 1525, a conference of theologians decided that the first *alumbrados* on trial could be tied to Lutheran ideas, and that conclusion was included in an edict of faith the same year. Printed books about doctrinal controversies were also banned, because of the danger they could pose by publicizing Lutheran theses.

In these years the Inquisition started to burn books that were intended for distribution across frontiers, whether terrestrial or maritime. In 1525, texts of some Protestant reformers were found at the University of Alcalá, where some academic circles endorsed Erasmus's ideas. In 1531, in Salamanca, a peddler sold, among other things, Luther's books in Spanish, in small formats that were easy to handle and hide.¹⁰ There undoubtedly was interest in Spain in reading Luther and his followers because, in the end, they were offering new interpretations of topics that were hotly debated at the time among intellectuals and theologians, with which Spanish elites were also certainly concerned: Such subjects included justification by faith, the value of works for eternal salvation, the real presence of Jesus in the Eucharist, the scope of papal authority, and so on.

It seems that the first Spaniard condemned to the stake for Lutheranism was a painter from Mallorca, named Gonsalvo, in 1523, who never admitted to being Lutheran. The Spanish Inquisition in this period did not confront any organized Protestant group, nor did the accused seem to have a deep knowledge of Protestant doctrines or even a strong adherence to them. Condemnations to the stake were rare; far more common were penances, which mostly featured spiritual or economic penalties, or exile.¹¹

These first prosecutions took place at a critical moment between 1523 and 1533, when there was a struggle for control of the Supreme Council of the Inquisition – called the Suprema – between two political factions with very different religious positions. In very general terms, one side defended a rigid Catholicism, with little tolerance for conversos and the new spiritual currents but more attentive to the external conventions of Catholicism. The other side was more flexible, open to patient strategies of evangelization and acculturation of conversos, with a more internalized religiosity and an inquisition that was more pastoral and "gentle." One of the most important leaders of the second faction was Inquisitor-General Alonso Manrique, archbishop of Seville, who sympathized with Spanish Erasmians, many of whom shared his priorities, albeit not all.¹²

Significantly, even a Spanish inquisitor-general could not necessarily dictate tolerance toward a favorite author. In 1527, anti-Erasmian theologians forced Manrique to convene a congregation to evaluate Erasmus's works, which had been labeled heretical.¹³ The congregation was suspended without reaching a definitive conclusion. Erasmus won a short-lived victory. Two years later, the Erasmian circles of the imperial court left for Italy with Charles V and Erasmus's main supporters dispersed. This power vacuum was exploited by the anti-Erasmian party, which from this moment on controlled the government of the Holy Office.[14] From Bruges in 1534, Renaissance humanist Juan Luis Vives complained of "these difficult times in which one cannot speak or remain silent without danger."[15] In 1536, Erasmus's *Colloquies* were banned in Spain. His works appeared in indices of prohibited books published in Spain in 1551, 1559, 1583, and 1612, although not all his works were banned, as occurred in the indices of the Roman Inquisition.

From the 1530s onward, questions about Lutheranism became more prominent in inquisitorial interrogations, and the accusation of this heresy was made more frequently by inquisition prosecutors, although the charge was not always present in the final sentences. This gap between accusation and sentence seems to indicate that the inquisitors had sufficient means to check whether the prosecutor had really proved a charge of Lutheranism or not. For example, María de Cazalla, who was of converso origin, was accused by Toledo's inquisitors in 1532 of endorsing or repeating several Lutheran propositions: In her 1534 verdict, they stated that they had not been able to prove those specific charges sufficiently.[16] In this complex framework, it must be kept in mind that Spanish inquisitors considered Erasmianism, *alumbradismo*, and Protestantism as intrinsically suspicious because of the presence of conversos in all three movements. The Spanish Inquisition was originally founded in 1478 to investigate and prosecute conversos who allegedly continued to practice Judaism. Its officials made connections between their original targets and Lutheranism when they believed they found conversos promoting and practicing the latter.

In the decade of the 1530s, the news about Protestantism coming from northern Europe and Rome continued to alarm Spanish inquisitors and more conservative theologians and statesmen, but infiltration of actual Protestants into the peninsula was rare. Nevertheless, the inquisitorial machine continued to monitor the scene and take aim at potential Protestant suspects. In 1531, Pope Clement VII granted specific powers to Spain's inquisitor-general and his representatives to persecute Luther and his followers. From that year on, specific edicts against Lutheranism were published. The 1525 prohibition on owning or reading Lutheran books was renewed in 1531, 1532, 1535, and 1536. Letters from the Suprema to the inquisition tribunals multiplied, especially for ones located on frontiers, asking their inquisitors to watch especially for the entry of forbidden books.[17]

In the following decades, the Spanish Inquisition's efforts against Protestantism took place in the context of failures to reunite Catholics and Protestants. In 1541, the Diet of Ratisbon collapsed. In 1542, the Roman Inquisition was recreated and soon fell upon sectors of the Roman Curia most prone to dialogue between Catholics and Protestants. In 1546, the Schmalkaldic War broke out in Germany between the emperor and most of the Lutheran principalities of the Holy Roman Empire. In 1547, Luther died. Calvinism became institutionalized in Geneva and began to spread to other parts of Europe such as France, the Netherlands, and northern Italy. Protestantism began to permeate the circles of Spanish students and merchants in Paris, Montpellier, Louvain, Naples, and Rome, although this process has only been lightly investigated until now.[18] From Rome, Pope Paul III convoked the Catholic Church Council that finally began in Trent in 1545: It was designed not to reconcile Protestants with Catholics but to redefine Catholicism itself. Two years later, the Tridentine decrees on justification by faith, penance, and confession were published; the dogmatic frontier against Protestantism, a source of inquisitorial activity, was being drawn.

In Spain, from the beginning of the 1540s the presence of Protestants became commonplace in the summaries that Spanish inquisitors sent to the Suprema about their cases, especially for frontier tribunals such as Zaragoza, Calahorra-Logroño, Barcelona, and so on. Although the defendants were still mostly foreigners, their sociological profile worried the authorities. Clergymen, grammar teachers, university graduates, some medical doctors – all were educated people who could have a greater social impact due to their professions and their social status. The men of the Holy Office began to become aware of the institution's structural weaknesses when it came to facing a challenge that might have seemed somewhat marginal but was nevertheless persistent. The most outstanding inquisition personality in these years was Fernando de Valdés, appointed inquisitor-general in 1547 by King Philip II. Under his authority, the Inquisition strengthened its bureaucratic and administrative structures.[19] Likewise, procedures and personnel for censorial vigilance were developed, establishing processes such as the inspection of printing presses and libraries. Then came the first indices of banned books, such as that of 1551, indebted to a 1550 index from Louvain, as well as the general censorship of bibles in 1552, with its prohibition of reading vernacular translations of the scriptures. The year 1559 saw the first official index of banned books created by the Spanish Inquisition. Modern historians disagree about the effectiveness of these censorship efforts.

One area in which we can see the common efforts of Spanish kings and inquisitors to sideline Lutheranism is in the search, identification, return, and prosecution of Spanish Protestants outside the borders of Spain itself. For example, inquisitors could send a relative or friend to try to convince a Protestant sympathizer to return to Spain: In 1532, inquisitors in Zaragoza did exactly that by ordering Juan Servetus to go in search of his brother Miguel (1511–53). The aim was for Juan to persuade Miguel to return to Spain. The "Servetus case" is well known. A humanist of varied interests, as well as a theologian and medical doctor, Miguel eventually scandalized both Catholics and Protestants with his denial of the dogma of the Trinity. Though the Spanish Inquisition failed to catch him, he was burned alive in Calvinist Geneva in 1553.[20]

Likewise, in 1546, the ecclesiastic Alfonso Díaz unsuccessfully tried to take his brother Juan Díaz back to Spain: After studying in Paris, Juan had converted to Lutheranism and was living in Neuburg an der Donau in Germany. When Juan refused to go, Alfonso hired an assassin, who killed his brother on March 27, 1546. Though arrested and imprisoned, the assassins were never brought to trial. The story of Juan's murder spread widely in Europe thanks to an account written by another Spaniard, Francisco de Enzinas, who also had converted to Protestantism.[21]

When relatives were missing or reluctant, Spanish inquisitors and kings used their own agents to recapture and punish suspected Protestant heretics. In the last years of his reign, Charles V knitted together an international network of spies and informers that was consolidated in the reign of his son and heir, Philip II. Linked to their country's diplomatic embassies, the Spanish espionage network had tentacles in the main European capitals, in addition to ports and other strategic places, including Genoa, Rome, Paris, London, Antwerp,

Brussels, Milan, Vienna, Naples, Constantinople, and Venice.[22] The Inquisition used this spy network for its own purposes, with remarkable success; when suspects did not voluntarily accept return, inquisitors sought repatriation in order to apply an exemplary punishment. For example, merchant Francisco de Sanromán, who converted to Protestantism in 1540 in Bremen, went shortly afterwards to Emperor Charles V in Regensburg to try to convince him of the need for religious reform in Spain. He was imprisoned and sent to Spain, where he was tried by the Holy Office and condemned for Lutheranism. In 1542, he was burned alive in an *auto de fe* celebrated in Valladolid.

Another extreme case is that of Casiodoro de Reina, a former Hieronymite monk who fled Seville in 1557 when inquisitors there suspected his monastery was full of Protestant heretics.[23] A network of spies managed to get an informer into de la Reina's house in London in 1561, bribed a family to falsely accuse him of sodomy, and monitored his travels as he moved around England, France, and Flanders. He was burned in effigy in an inquisitorial *auto de fe* in 1562, but died of natural causes in Frankfurt in 1594, despite the fact that Philip II had put a price on his head.

In these decades, those tried for Protestantism continued to be mostly foreigners, although there was no shortage of distinguished Spaniards as well.[24] Juan Gil, alias Dr. Egidio, stands out for his extensive influence. An influential professor at the University of Alcalá, and later a canon of the cathedral of Seville, Egidio suffered two inquisition trials after being accused of Lutheranism: He was forced to abjure in 1552.[25] As a result of his preaching and influence, several groups came together in Seville for the purpose of forming a "tiny church": though their members had different emphases, their founding principle was the doctrine of justification by faith alone.[26] During the time Egidio was in the inquisitorial jails, several of his followers fled. Prominent among them was the ecclesiastic Dr. Juan Pérez de Pineda, who played a fundamental role in organizing the networks of Spanish Protestants in exile, in cities such as Paris, Geneva, and Frankfurt. Pérez de Pineda continued to have contact with Spanish Protestants who remained in Spain in Seville, Zaragoza, and elsewhere, and played a crucial role in the publication and dissemination of Protestant texts in Spanish.[27]

At the same time, Protestantism was not perceived as an overwhelming threat by the Spanish Inquisition until the discovery of centers of *"luteranos"* in Seville and Valladolid in 1557 and 1558. These were relatively organized groups, not isolated individuals; they had a strong record of proselytizing, nourished by the readings of John Calvin, Martin Luther, Bernardino Ochino, Philip Melanchthon, and Juan de Valdés. Their members were capable of great fervor and dynamism, while socially they transversed numerous groups, attracting a more popular sector in Seville and a more aristocratic one in in Valladolid. Some had relatives who had been tried for *alumbradismo* twenty years earlier; many belonged to converso families, such as the Cazalla. The participation of women in these Protestant circles was very high in both cities: They acted as leaders in the diffusion of religious dissidence.[28]

The discovery of these Protestant sects stunned Spanish inquisitors. Adding to the Inquisition's shock was the fact that the various groups held periodic meetings and had read books, letters, biblical commentaries, and other texts by Protestant reformers. In Seville, the movement seemed to have its roots in the preaching of Dr. Egidio, and appeared to have maintained regular contact with Spanish Protestant exiles.

The reaction to these discoveries was one of panic, for several reasons. Members of these Protestant circles were numerous: Between Seville and Valladolid, more than 200 people were prosecuted. In contrast to the predominance of foreigners condemned for Lutheranism up to that time, now the suspects were almost all Spaniards. Most alarming, many belonged to privileged sectors: they were high nobility, servants of the Crown, accountants, counselors, knights of the religious orders, famous preachers who had been close to the emperor, such as Constantino de la Fuente or Agustín de Cazalla, or middle managers of town councils and cities.

Furthermore, until 1557, most of those tried for Protestantism had been found in frontier or border zones, but now they were located close to the heart of the monarchy. Seville and Valladolid were two key cities in Spain's political and economic framework. The former was the gateway to the Indies and a commercial hub of international scope, while the latter was at this time the political center for Spain's royal court. Finally, witness testimony and the defendants' own declarations revealed a highly articulate theological discourse in which the key elements of Protestantism were present: justification by faith alone, the singular power of divine grace, sacred scripture as the only source of religious authority, the rejection of the visible church, the denial of indulgences and the Catholic penitential system, the disavowal of the adoration of images, the refutation of the mediation of the Virgin and the saints, and the acceptance of only two sacraments whose scriptural provenance was clear, baptism and communion.

The political reaction was immediate. Charles V, retired in the monastery of Yuste, demanded an exemplary and expeditious punishment, without exception. A general alert was proclaimed, in the fullest sense of the term. Philip II immediately ordered increased vigilance at the border with France and wrote more than 200 royal provisions to all the sections of the monarchy, including prelates, heads of religious orders, the nobility, and those in charge of high administrative positions. The king demanded that each and every one of them become actively concerned with Protestant heresy. Addressing the prelates, Philip asked for vigilance in their bishoprics, with greater supervision and control of preachers, the teachers of children, and the moral life of the diocesan clergy. Of the priors general of the religious orders, he demanded that they check their monastic and convent libraries, and that their confessors tell the Inquisition of any suspicion aroused by hearing a confession. The nobles he instructed to watch over their territories and give every assistance to inquisition commissioners.

In July 1559, Philip II warned his bishops in the Americas of the Lutheran danger; the same year, a royal decree forbade students to study in foreign universities, with the exception of Bologna, Coimbra, Naples, and Rome, an order that was repeated in 1568. The objective of the king's strategy was very clear: First, to involve every possible political and religious authority in the fight against Protestantism; second, to demonstrate the monarchy's complete support for the Inquisition and to warn that in case of suspicion, no one could avoid an inquisitorial investigation or trial.

As Philip II was making his position known, another extraordinary element came into play – namely, requests for changes in the Inquisition's legal principles. In September 1558, the Suprema sent an account of the "Lutherans" to Pope Paul IV: It wrote that the Protestant heresy amounted to a sort of sedition or mutiny by aristocratic figures whom ordinary people would be happy to emulate. The Suprema suggested that nobles sentenced to penances or imprisonment would find a way to evade them; consequently, it asked the pope to grant an apostolic brief that would permit inquisitors to exercise "exemplary justice," regardless of the defendant's "secular, pontifical, or ecclesiastical rank."[29]

In January 1559, Inquisitor-General Fernando de Valdés and Philip II followed up on the Suprema's report and asked Pope Paul IV for two new, temporary, apostolic briefs. In reply, the pope authorized Spanish inquisitors to release to the secular arm all condemned dogmatizers even if they showed repentance, if the inquisitors suspected their contrition was not sincere.[30] Then, the pope allowed the Spanish Inquisition to sentence anyone to death, irrespective of dignity and status. As a result, defendants accused of Protestantism between 1557 and 1562 very often ended up burned at the stake, despite public atonement and noble birth. Inquisitor-General Valdés's Instructions of 1561 returned inquisitorial jurisprudence to reconciliation for suspects who atoned, a development that underlines how exceptional Pope Paul IV's brief had been.[31]

The repression was fierce. The most important *autos de fe* were held in Seville and Valladolid between 1559 and 1562. The spectacle and drama of the sentencing were carefully designed; the Inquisition sought maximum exemplarity. The reports of the *autos* that have been preserved illustrate the enormous social and religious excitement provoked by the Inquisition's performances. Perhaps the most stunning of these public ceremonies took place in Valladolid before the royal family. On May 21, 1559, with regent Doña Juana of Austria, Prince Don Carlos, and the noble and ecclesiastical elite present, thirty people were sentenced for Protestantism, fourteen of whom were condemned to the stake. Five members of the Cazalla family – three brothers, a sister, plus the bones of their mother – were among the latter. In the *auto de fe* of October 8 of the same year, presided over by Philip II, twenty-six people were sentenced for Protestantism and twelve relaxed to the secular arm, including four nuns. Among those condemned to death in October, royal administrator and Italian Don Carlos de Seso stood out: Having refused to repent, and repeating the truth of his Protestant beliefs on the scaffold, he was burned without being strangled first. In

Valladolid and Seville between 1559 and 1562 dozens of Spaniards convicted of Protestantism died and hundreds convicted or suspected of Protestantism were penanced.[32]

The impact of these events was enormous. The descriptions of what had occurred at the *autos de fe* reached all corners of Spain as well as royal European courts. Many accounts emphasized that if Spain had managed to survive the cancer of heresy, it was only due to the righteous actions of the Spanish Inquisition. As a result, the Inquisition increased its credibility and prestige; its position as the guarantor of orthodoxy was even more firmly established.

At the same time, criticism of the Spanish Inquisition and the Spanish monarchy – which already had a substantial history via the complaints of expelled Jews and exiled conversos from the end of the fifteenth century – was galvanized by the accounts of the Protestant deaths, especially in Protestant countries. A fundamental role was played by the book entitled *Artes de la Inquisición Española,* signed by Reginaldus Gonsalvius Montano, probably a pseudonym for Antonio del Corro and Casiodoro de Reina and also, perhaps, Juan Pérez de Pineda.[33] Published in Heidelberg in 1567, this work had enormous publishing success in the following decades, with translations into English, French, Dutch, and German. It recounted fifteen exemplary lives of those condemned to death in Seville. Some of those narratives were collected in the most famous and popular Protestant martyrologies of the following centuries, such as those of the French Calvinist Jean Crespin or the Englishman John Foxe, giving these cases an enormous diffusion.

This was the historical and religious context in which the archbishop of Toledo, the Dominican friar Bartolomé de Carranza, was imprisoned by the Inquisition at the end of August 1559. Carranza was accused of Lutheranism on account of his friendships and sympathies with some of the defendants of Valladolid, some of whom viewed him as a spiritual guide. The inquisitorial prosecution also singled out censures that were made against Carranza's *Commentaries on the Christian Catechism*, published in Antwerp in 1558. Carranza's inquisition trial lasted 17 years, from 1559 to 1576, and ended up turning into a formidable power struggle between Philip II and the papacy as to which authority had legal precedence. The case was finally transferred to Rome in 1567; for the next nine years, two popes attempted to issue a verdict while Philip II sent advisors and censures to block Carranza's absolution. Pope Gregory XIII ultimately pronounced sentence on April 14, 1576. Carranza had to abjure sixteen different propositions and a vehement suspicion of heresy; he was also suspended from his diocese of Toledo for five years, which had been without a bishop since his arrest.[34] He died three weeks later. Though he had managed to successfully recuse Inquisitor-General Valdés for personal enmity in his case's first year, his trial made it clear that no one could be out of danger where the Inquisition was concerned.[35]

There has been much debate in modern historical scholarship as to whether the Spaniards charged with Protestantism in the late 1550s truly held Protestant beliefs.[36] Recent studies have demonstrated that several of the defendants shared a coherent religious doctrine, group identity, and willingness to proselytize covertly. Some preferred to die rather than betray their beliefs. Others were persecuted for scattered ideas, for their personal links with other suspects, or for imprudent comments suspected of heterodoxy.[37]

When the Seville groups were discovered in 1557, a number of their adherents managed to escape the long arm of the Holy Office, and yet the situations of Spanish religious exiles in Protestant Europe were very diverse. Some were integrated into existing local Reformed churches; others joined churches for refugees or created ones themselves. Some found their beliefs closer to Lutheranism, others to Calvinism; some had more radical positions, as was the case with the Seville silversmith Pedro de Sosa, who was condemned to death in Antwerp as an Anabaptist. Still others oscillated among the different Protestant confessions. Former monks Casiodoro de Reina and Antonio del Corro were first Calvinists but ended their days as Lutheran and Anglican, respectively; they were two figures of enormous intellectual stature who participated in the ideological and religious debates of their time.[38] Casiodoro de Reina translated the Bible into Spanish from its original languages and printed it in Basel in 1569. It is known as the *Bear Bible*.

Political and social alarm over Spanish Protestantism remained active in the years after 1562. The detection of crates of forbidden books in the northern ports was frequent throughout this decade. In 1565, the Spanish ambassador in Paris warned of the preparation of a massive shipment of heretical books to Spain. The pressure on the land frontier was felt with greater intensity in those years. It must not be forgotten that over Christmas 1561, the princess of Béarn, Jeanne d'Albret, proclaimed Calvinism as her territory's religion, and in 1562 the wars of religion began in France, which intensified immigration into Spain by a population that was already viewed with suspicion. In 1563, information reached the Suprema that groups of French clergymen were traveling through Navarre, Murcia, and Aragon and preaching the Protestant faith. They had been commissioned by a preacher of Jeanne d'Albret.

Between 1557 and 1571 small Protestant groups could still be found in Spain, namely in Valencia, Toledo, Aragon, Logroño, Cuenca, and Barcelona. From 1560 onward, three small groups were discovered in Valencia, the most important of which involved the Valencian nobleman Gaspar de Centelles, who died at the stake in 1564. In Teruel, a group of Protestant Spaniards and Frenchmen was discovered, who were reconciled or burned in several *autos de fe* between 1567 and 1571. In Toledo in the mid-1560s, a network of about forty people came to light, French artisans who were also a reception point for French immigrants passing through: Most managed to flee. In Cuenca, a group of six or seven Frenchmen was discovered. In Aragon, two small and interrelated nuclei were discovered, with the standout prisoner being rector Miguel Monterde of Villanueva de la Huerva, who also held a prebend in Zaragoza's cathedral. Monterde had been an old student of Dr. Egidio as well as a correspondent of Pérez de Pineda. He was prosecuted for those contacts by Zaragoza's inquisition tribunal in 1558. Another dozen clergymen and students were also penanced in those years in Zaragoza's *autos de fe*.[39]

If we analyze the Inquisition's case summaries (*relaciones de causas*) as a whole for this period, we see that in the decade prior to 1559, the average number of individuals sentenced for Protestantism was ten per year; from 1559 until 1575, the average rose to ninety-three per year. Thus, while the discoveries of Protestant cells in 1558–9 marked a serious crisis, the Protestant problem continued for fifteen more years. Moreover, in the *autos de fe* from 1559 to 1562, the majority of those prosecuted for Lutheranism were Spaniards, ranging from 55.2 to 73.5 percent of all those tried for this heresy.[40] Notably, however, from 1563 on, the percentage of Spaniards prosecuted for Protestantism progressively decreased while the number of foreigners increased. The repression of foreigners was especially intense in the courts of the Crown of Aragon because of a notorious presence of French immigrants.[41] In this period, Protestant suspects frequently were relaxed to the secular arm, though they also could be sentenced to the galleys or banished.

From the 1570s onward, inquisitors continued to be interested in Protestantism but the number of those prosecuted decreased and they were almost exclusively foreigners. The Inquisition no longer searched for assemblies, only specific individuals. One worth mentioning was the Catalan humanist Pere Galès, who traveled to Italy where he was prosecuted by the Roman Inquisition and lost an eye through torture. He fled to Geneva and occupied the chair of philosophy at the university. He then argued bitterly with the Calvinists and traveled to Bordeaux, where he was imprisoned by members of the Catholic League and, after many vicissitudes, handed over to the Spanish Inquisition in 1593. Prosecuted by the tribunal of Zaragoza, he died before his trial was concluded. His effigy was burned in 1597.[42] The only option for Spanish Protestants after the sixteenth century was exile.

Toward the end of the sixteenth century, the Spanish Inquisition was forced to modify its policy toward foreigners suspected of heterodoxy. Its actions were affected by diplomatic pressure from foreign ambassadors and consuls, as well as the increasingly pressing political and economic needs of a monarchy in crisis. The first sign of these changes was the signing of the Alba-Cobham Treaty in December 1574, which designated that English merchants could trade with Spain without inquisitorial interference over matters of faith. If Englishmen were prosecuted and convicted, only their personal belongings could be confiscated, with ships and cargo remaining off-limits. In turn, the English were to show respect for Catholic symbols, rites, and buildings, and should demonstrate reverence for the Eucharist. Some years later, in 1597, Spain signed a commercial treaty with the Hanseatic cities that included similar clauses.

The clauses of the Alba-Cobham Treaty were updated in the Treaty of London of 1604, in which the Spanish monarchy recognized the right of English Protestants passing through Spain to practice their religion.

That being said, their worship was supposed to occur in the strictest privacy. The Treaty of London affected transient English merchants, but indirectly it also changed the fate of English residents. The number of English prisoners decreased and the penalties were softened, with the most common being banishment from Spain or repatriation in an attempt to avoid diplomatic problems. Distant from local pressures and more sensitive to political situations, the Suprema became the guarantor of the treaty's interpretation. William Chapindar, an Englishman who had resided in Malaga since 1606, was betrayed to inquisitors in 1617; accusations of Chapindar's Protestantism were proven. Being a resident, he could not take advantage of the 1604 treaty's clauses, but after the Suprema's intervention, he was simply warned that he should not cause scandal or polemicize in religious matters.

In practice, the Treaty of London meant that English Protestants disappeared from the inquisitors' courtrooms in Spain.[43] As for the Dutch, in 1609 the Twelve Years' Truce was signed, which reproduced the clauses of the English treaty. After several vicissitudes, the Peace of Munster (1648) guaranteed for the Dutch what English subjects already enjoyed under the Treaty of London.

Such measures paved the way for a very limited religious toleration. Although there were no diplomatic agreements that protected French subjects, it seems that there was a mirror effect, whereby the signing of the treaties about the English and Dutch also diminished the number of French defendants and softened their sentences. For example, a French sailor, Martin de Occasso, who traveled to Santander in 1630 to pursue a lawsuit, was asked by some neighbors about his Calvinist faith. Occasso not only explained his outlook but also harshly criticized Catholicism. The Inquisition imprisoned him: While he showed signs of conversion to Catholicism, he managed to flee on two occasions. Seized for a third time, he admitted that he had feigned conversion. He was subjected to torture. In 1631, inquisitors condemned him to a public *auto*, reconciliation with confiscation of goods, the wearing of a *sambenito*, five years in the galleys, and upon his return life imprisonment. The Suprema, however, decreed that he should be privately absolved with a caution (*ad cautelam*) and given religious instruction.

At first, Luther was simply a heretical prospect for the Spanish Inquisition, whose officials viewed Protestantism as a distant problem that might result in contagion. Consequently, the Inquisition's first measures were focused on the surveillance of the circulation, purchase, and reading of the texts of the reformers. The conjunction of Lutheranism, Erasmianism, *alumbradismo*, and fear of conversos in the inquisitorial imagination determined the direction of the anti-Lutheran persecutions of the Holy Office in those early years.

In the 1540s, however, there was a notable turning point. The fracture between Catholics and Protestants seemed irremediable and the decrees of the Council of Trent in 1547 drew the dogmatic border from which inquisitors would develop the persecution in a more sophisticated way. The number of Spanish defendants increased, although foreigners were still in the majority. Inquisitor-General Valdés worked deliberately to strengthen the Inquisition's bureaucracy and reach; he also developed new policies, such as censorship via the publication the indices of forbidden books. All these changes were put to the test with the discovery of Protestant centers in Seville and Valladolid, which had an enormous, immediate impact on elites and Spanish society as a whole. Suppression was ferocious, to the point that over the next two centuries, Spanish inquisitors mostly found Protestants in the shape of foreigners who were in transit across Spain or who resided there.

Finally, despite the many advances in recent years in the study of the Reformation in Spain, there is still a great deal of research to be done. We need more precise information about the theological and social profiles of individuals and groups accused of Protestant beliefs; there undoubtedly is more to discover about the communication networks between those Spaniards accused of Protestantism and the wider European and American world. Only in this way will it be possible to adequately assess the circulation of ideas, books, and people, and gauge the potential impact that these networks could have had on the political and intellectual debates of their time.

Notes

1. The inquisitors often used the term "Lutherans" to describe all Protestants. This study is part of the project *Inquisition and Networks: Communities,*

Actors and Power in the Iberian World of the Modern Age (PID2021-123816NB-100), funded by the Ministry of Science, Innovation and Universities of the Government of Spain.
2. Cited in Marcel Bataillon, *Erasmo y España* (Fondo de Cultura Económica, 1956), 454.
3. Augustine Redondo, "Luther et l'Espagne de 1520 a 1536," *Mélanges de la Casa de Velázquez* 1 (1965): 124.
4. Henry Kamen, "Spain," in Robert Scribner, Roy Porter, and Mikuláš Teich, eds., *The Reformation in National Context*, 202–14 (Cambridge University Press, 1994), 203.
5. Carlos Gilly, "Juan de Valdés, traductor y adaptor de los escritos de Lutero en su *Diálogo de doctrina christiana*," in Luis López Molina, ed., *Miscelánea de estudios hispánicos: homenaje de los hispanistas de Suiza a Ramón Sugranyes de Franch* (Abadía de Montserrat, 1975), 91–9.
6. Massimo Firpo, *Entre alumbrados y "espirituales": Estudios sobre Juan de Valdés y el valdesianismo en la crisis religiosa del '500 italiano* (Fundación Universitaria Española, 2000).
7. Thus, a significant number of defendants accused of *alumbradismo* were deeply indebted to Erasmus: Such was the case for Maria de Cazalla.
8. Stefania Pastore, *Una herejía española: Conversos, alumbrados e Inquisición (1449–1559)* (Marcial Pons, 2010).
9. John E. Longhurst, "Luther in Spain: 1520–1540," *Proceedings of the American Philosophical Society* 103 (1959): 66.
10. Redondo, "Luther et l'Espagne," 154.
11. John E. Longhurst, *Luther's Ghost in Spain (1517–1546)* (Coronado Press, 1969), 41–5.
12. José Martínez Millán, "Corrientes espirituales y facciones políticas en el servicio del emperador Carlos V," in W. Blockmans and N. Mout, eds., *The World of Emperor Charles V* (Royal Netherlands Academy, 2005), 97–126.
13. Lu Ann Homza, *Religious Authority in the Spanish Renaissance* (The Johns Hopkins University Press, 2000), chapter 2.
14. Miguel Avilés Fernández, "El Santo Oficio en la primera etapa carolina," in Joaquín Pérez Villanueva and Bartolomé Escandell Bonet, eds., *Historia de la Inquisición en España y América* Vol. 1 (Biblioteca de Autores Cristianos/Centro de Estudios Inquisitoriales, 1984), 454–5.
15. Ángel Alcalá, "El control inquisitorial de intelectuales en el Siglo de Oro," in Joaquín Pérez Villanueva and Bartolomé Escandell Bonet, eds., *Historia de la Inquisición en España y América* Vol. 3 (Biblioteca de Autores Cristianos/Centro de Estudios Inquisitoriales, 2000) 847.
16. Milagros Ortega-Costa, *El proceso de la Inquisición contra María de Cazalla* (Fundación Universitaria Española, 1978), 497.
17. Longhurst, "Luther in Spain," 71–2.

18. José Ignacio Tellechea Idígoras, "Los españoles en Lovaina, 1551–1558," *Revista española de Teología* 23 (1963): 21–45; Ignacio García Pinilla, "*Aperiat oculos Hispania*: Los disidentes españoles exiliados del siglo XVI como activistas," in Francisco José Aranda Pérez and José Damião Rodrigues, eds., *De Re Publica Hispaniae: Una vindicación de la cultura política en los reinos ibéricos en la primera modernidad* (Silex, 2008), 187–209.
19. Jaime Contreras, "The Impact of Protestantism in Spain, 1520–1600," in Stephen Haliczer, ed., *Inquisition and Society in Early Modern Europe* (Croom-Helm, 1987), 47–63.
20. For a deep investigation into the relationship between Servetus and Calvin, and Calvin's demand that Servetus be arrested by French episcopal authorities, see Frans Pieter van Stam, *The Servetus Case: An Appeal for a New Assessment* (Droz, 2017).
21. Francisco de Enzinas, *Verdadera historia de la muerte del santo varón Juan Díaz, por Claude de Senarclens*, ed. Ignacio García Pinilla (Universidad de Castilla-La Mancha, 2008); Ignacio García Pinilla, "Juan Díaz, conquense: humanista, mártir y tópico literario," in José María Maestre Maestre, Luis Charlo Brea, and Joaquín Pascual Barea, eds., *Humanismo y pervivencia del mundo clásico: Homenaje al profesor Luis Gil* Vol. 1 (Universidad de Cádiz, 1997), 1495–1506.
22. Carlos Carnicer García and Javier Marcos Rivas, *Espías de Felipe II: Los servicios secretos del Imperio español* (La Esfera de los libros, 2005).
23. For new work on Casiodoro as a Hebraist, see Arturo Eduardo Terrazas Calderón, *Casiodoro de la Reina, hebraísta del siglo XVI: Red de conversos y la traducción de la Biblia*, doctoral dissertation, Universitat de Barcelona, 2022.
24. Werner Thomas, *La represión del protestantismo en España, 1517–1648* (Leuven University Press, 2001) 189–209.
25. Robert C. Spach, "Juan Gil and Sixteenth-Century Spanish Protestantism," *The Sixteenth Century Journal* 26 (1995): 863–72.
26. Tomás López Muñoz, *La Reforma en la Sevilla del siglo XVI*, Vol. 1 (Editorial MAD, 2011), 263–77.
27. A. Gordon Kinder, "Juan Pérez de Pineda (Pierius): A Spanish Calvinist Minister of the Gospel in Sixteenth-Century Geneva," *Bulletin of Hispanic Studies* 53 (1976): 99–112.
28. Michel Boeglin, "Religiosidad femenina y herejía: monjas y beatas 'luteranas' ante la Inquisición de Sevilla en tiempos del Emperador," *Scripta: revista internacional de literatura i cultura medieval i moderna* 8 (2016): 164–78. Frances Luttikhuizen, *Underground Protestantism in Sixteenth Century Spain: A Much-Ignored Side of Spanish History* (Vandenhoeck and Ruprecht GmbH and Co, 2017), 137–57, 229–60.
29. Lu Ann Homza, ed. and trans., *The Spanish Inquisition, 1478–1614: An Anthology of Sources* (Hackett, 2006), 189–90.

30. National Historical Archive [AHN], Inquisition [Inq], Book 249, ff. 124r–128v.
31. Miguel Jiménez Monteserin, *La Inquisición española. Documentos básicos* (Universitat de València, 2021), 261.
32. For English-language translations of some of the surviving evidence, see Homza, *The Spanish Inquisition*, 176–94.
33. See the introductory study of Marcos J. Herráiz Pareja, Ignacio J. García Pinilla, and Jonathan L. Nelson, eds., *Reginaldus Gonsalvius Montanus: Inquisitionis Hispanicae artes. The Arts of the Spanish Inquisition: A Critical Edition of the Sanctae inquisitionis Hispanicae artes aliquot (1567) with a Modern English Translation* (Brill, 2018).
34. For popular awareness among Toledo's residents of Carranza's arrest, see Gillian Ahlgren, ed. and trans., *The Inquisition of Francisca: A Sixteenth-Century Visionary on Trial* (The University of Chicago Press, 2005).
35. Homza, *The Spanish Inquisition*, 194–211.
36. See the historiographical synthesis by Michel Boeglin, "The Reception of the Protestant Reformation in the Iberian Peninsula," in Henry A. Jeffries and Richard Rex, eds., *Reformations Compared: Religious Transformations Across Early Modern Europe* (Cambridge University Press, 2024), 242–65.
37. José Ignacio Tellechea Idígoras, "El protestantismo castellano (1558–1559): Un *topos* (M. Bataillon) convertido en *tópico* historiográfico," in Manuel Revuelta Sañudo y Ciriaco Morón Arroyo, eds., *El erasmismo en España* (Sociedad Menéndez Pelayo, 1986), 305–21.
38. Carlos Gilly, "El influjo de Sebstien Castellion sobre los heterodoxos españoles del siglo XVI," in Michel Boeglin, Ignasi Fernández Terricabras, and David Kahn, eds., *Reforma y disidencia religiosa: la recepción de las doctrinas reforadas en la Península Ibérica en el siglo XVI* (Casa de Velázquez, 2018) 305–49.
39. Manuel Ardit Lucas and Miguel Almenara, "Nuevas perspectivas sobre los movimientos protestantes valencianos en el siglo XVI," *Estudis: Revista de historia moderna* 23 (1997), 75–100; Christine Wagner, "Los luteranos ante la Inquisición de Toledo en el siglo XVI," *Hispania Sacra* 46 (1994), 473–507; A. Gordon Kinder, "A Hitherto Unknown Group of Protestants in Sixteenth-Century Aragon," *Cuadernos de Historia Jerónimo Zurita* 51–52 (1985): 131–60; Michel Boeglin, "Aspectos de la Reforma en Aragón a finales del reinado del Emperador: el proceso del rector Miguel Monterde," *Manuscrits: Revista d'història moderna* 30 (2012): 139–59.
40. Thomas, *La represión*, 257.
41. E. William Monter, *Frontiers of Heresy: The Spanish Inquisition from the Basque Lands to Sicily* (Cambridge University Press, 1990).
42. Xavier Espluga, "Pere Galès: un protestante de Ulldecona profesor en Ginebra," in Michel Boeglin, Ignasi Fernández Terricabras, and David Kahn, eds., *Reforma y disidencia religiosa: La recepción de las*

doctrinas reformadas en la península ibérica en el siglo XVI, (Casa de Velázquez, 2018), 291–304.
43. Thomas, *La represión*, 320–4.

Suggestions for Further Reading

Boeglin, Michel, Ignasi Fernández Terricabras, and David Kahn. (coords.). *Reforma y disidencia religiosa: la recepción de las doctrinas reforadas en la Península Ibérica en el siglo XVI*. Casa de Velázquez, 2018.

Boeglin, Michel. "The Reception of the Protestant Reformation in the Iberian Peninsula." In Richard Rex and Henry Jeffries, eds., *Reformations Compared: Religious Transformation from across Early Modern Europe*. Cambridge University Press, 2024.

Contreras, Jaime. "The Impact of Protestantism in Spain, 1520–1600." In Stephen Haliczer, ed., *Inquisition and Society in Early Modern Europe*. Croom Helm, 1987.

Herráiz Pareja, Marcos J., Ignacio J. García Pinilla, and Jonathan L. Nelson, eds. *Reginaldus Gonsalvius Montanus: Inquisitionis Hispanicae artes. The Arts of the Spanish Inquisition: A Critical Edition of the Sanctae inquisitionis Hispanicae artes aliquot (1567) with a Modern English Translation*. Brill, 2018.

Kamen, Henry. "Spain." In Robert Scribner, Roy Porter, and Mikuláš Teich, eds., *The Reformation in National Context*. Cambridge University Press, 1994.

Kinder, A. Gordon. *Casiodoro de Reina: Spanish Reformer of the Sixteenth Century*. Tamesis, 1975.

Longhurst, John E., "Luther in Spain: 1520–1540." *Proceedings of the American Philosophical Society* 103 (1959): 66–93.

Monter, E. William. *Frontiers of Heresy: The Spanish Inquisition from the Basque Lands to Sicily*. Cambridge University Press, 1990.

Redondo, Augustin. "Luther et l'Espagne de 1520 a 1536." *Mélanges de la Casa de Velázquez* 1 (1965): 109–65.

Thomas, Werner. *La represión del protestantismo en España, 1517–1648*. Leuven University Press, 2001.

Bibliography

Avilés Fernández, Miguel. "El Santo Oficio en la primera etapa carolina." In Joaquín Pérez Villanueva and Bartolomé Escandell Bonet, eds., *Historia de la Inquisición en España y América* Vol. 1, 443–73. Biblioteca de Autores Cristianos/Centro de Estudios Inquisitoriales, 1984.

Alcalá, Ángel. "El control inquisitorial de intelectuales en el Siglo de Oro: De Nebrija al Índice de Sotomayor de 1640." In Joaquín Pérez Villanueva and Bartolomé Escandell Bonet. eds., *Historia de la Inquisición en España y América* Vol. 3, 829–956. Biblioteca de Autores Cristianos/Centros de Estudios Inquisitoriales, 2000.

Ardit Lucas, Manuel, and Miguel Almenara. "Nuevas perspectivas sobre los movimientos protestantes valencianos en el siglo XVI." *Estudis: Revista de historia moderna* 23 (1997): 75–100.

Bataillon, Marcel. *Erasmo y España*. Fondo de Cultura Económica, 1956.

Boeglin, Michel. "Aspectos de la reforma en Aragón a finales del reinado del Emperador: el proceso del rector Miguel Monterde." *Manuscrits: Revista de'història moderna* 30 (2012): 139–59.

"Religiosidad femenina y herejía: monjas y beatas 'luteranas' ante la Inquisición de Sevilla en tiempos del Emperador." *Scripta: revista internacional de literatura i cultura medieval i moderna* 8 (2016): 164–78.

"The Reception of the Protestant Reformation in the Iberian Peninsula." In Henry A. Jeffries and Richard Rex, eds., *Reformations Compared: Religious Transformations Across Early Modern Europe*. Cambridge University Press, 2024.

Carnicer García, Carlos, and Javier Marcos Rivas. *Espías de Felipe II: Los servicios secretos del Imperio español*. La Esfera de los libros, 2005.

Contreras, Jaime. "The Impact of Protestantism in Spain, 1520–1600." In Stephen Haliczer, ed., *Inquisition and Society in Early Modern Europe*, 47–63. Croom-Helm, 1987.

Enzinas, Francisco de. In Ignacio García Pinilla, ed., *Verdadera historia de la muerte del santo varón Juan Díaz, por Claude de Senarclens*. Universidad de Castilla-La Mancha, 2008.

Espluga, Xavier. "Pere Galès: un protestante de Ulldecona profesor en Ginebra." In Michel Boeglin, Ignasi Fernández Terricabras, and David Kahn, eds., *Reforma y disidencia religiosa: La recepción de las doctrinas reformadas en la península ibérica en el siglo xvi*, 291–304. Casa de Velázquez, 2018.

Firpo, Massimo. *Entre alumbrados y "espirituales": Estudios sobre Juan de Valdés y el valdesianismo en la crisis religiosa de '500 italiano*. Fundación Universitaria Española, 2000.

García Pinilla, Ignacio J. "Juan Díaz, conquense: Humanista, mártir y tópico literario." In José María Maestre, Luis Charlo Brea, and Joaquín Pascual Barea, eds., *Humanismo y pervivencia del mundo clásico: Homenaje al profesor Luis Gil* Vol. 1, 1496–1506. Universidad de Cádiz, 1997.

"*Aperiat oculos Hispania*: Los disidentes españoles exiliados del siglo XVI como activistas." In Francisco José Aranda Pérez and José Damião Rodrigues, eds., *De Re Publica Hispaniae: A Vindication of Political Culture in the Iberian Kingdoms in Early Modernity*. Silex, 2008.

Gilly, Carlos. "Juan de Valdés, traductor y adaptador de escritos de Lutero en su *Diálogo de doctrina christiana*." In Luis López Molina, ed., *Miscelánea de estudios hispánicos: homenaje de los hispanistas de Suiza a Ramón Sugranyes de Franch*. Abadía de Montserrat, 1982.

"El influjo de Sebstien Castellion sobre los heterodoxos españoles del siglo XVI." In Michel Boeglin, Ignasi Fernández Terricabras, and David Kahn, eds., *Reforma y disidencia religiosa: la recepción de las doctrinas reforadas en la Península Ibérica en el siglo XVI*. Casa de Velázquez, 2018.

Herráiz Pareja, Marcos J., Ignacio J. García Pinilla, and Jonathan L. Nelson, eds. *Reginaldus Gonsalvius Montanus: Inquisitionis Hispanicae artes. The Arts of the Spanish Inquisition: A Critical Edition of the Sanctae inquisitionis Hispanicae artes aliquot (1567) with a Modern English Translation*. Brill, 2018.

Homza, Lu Ann, ed. and trans. *The Spanish Inquisition, 1478–1614: An Anthology of Sources*. Hackett, 2006.

Kamen, Henry. "Spain." In Rob Scribner, Roy Porter, and Mikuláš Teich, eds., *The Reformation in National Context*, 202–14. Cambridge University Press, 1994.

Kinder, A. Gordon. "Juan Pérez de Pineda (Pierius): A Spanish Calvinist Minister of the Gospel in Sixteenth-Century Geneva." *Bulletin of Hispanic Studies* 53 (1976): 99–112.

"A Hitherto Unknown Group of Protestants in Sixteenth-Century Aragon." *Cuadernos de Historia Jerónimo Zurita* 51–2 (1985): 131–60.

Longhurst, John E. "Luther in Spain: 1520–1540." *Proceedings of the American Philosophical Society* 103 (1959): 66–93.

Luther's Ghost in Spain (1517–1546). Coronado Press, 1969.

López Muñoz, Tomás. *La Reforma en la Sevilla del siglo XVI*. 2 vols. Editorial MAD, 2011.

Luttikhuizen, Frances. *Underground Protestantism in Sixteenth Century Spain: A Much-Ignored Side of Spanish History*. Vandenhoeck and Ruprecht GmbH and Co, 2017.

Martínez Millán, José. "Corrientes espirituales y facciones políticas en el servicio del emperador Carlos V." In W. Blockmans and N. Mout, eds., *The World of Emperor Charles V*, 97–126. Royal Netherlands Academy, 2005.

Monter, E. William. *Frontiers of Heresy: The Spanish Inquisition from the Basque Lands to Sicily*. Cambridge University Press, 1990.

Ortega-Costa, Milagros. *El proceso de la Inquisición contra María de Cazalla*. Fundación Universitaria Española, 1978.

Pastore, Stefania. *Una herejía española: Conversos, alumbrados e Inquisición (1449–1559)*. Marcial Pons, 2010.

Redondo, Agustín. "Luther et l'Espagne de 1520 a 1536." *Mélanges de la Casa de Velázquez* 1 (1965): 109–65.

Spach, R. C. "Juan Gil and Sixteenth-Century Spanish Protestantism." *Sixteenth Century Journal* 26 (1995): 863–72.

Tellechea Idígoras, José Ignacio. "Los españoles en Lovaina, 1551–1558." *Revista española de Teología* 23 (1963): 21–45.

——— "El protestantismo castellano (1558–1559). Un *topos* (M. Bataillon) convertido en *tópico* historiográfico." In Manuel Revuelta Sañudo and Ciriaco Morón Arroyo, eds., *El erasmismo en España*, 305–21. Sociedad Menéndez Pelayo, 1986.

Thomas, Werner. *La represión del protestantismo en España, 1517–1648*. Leuven University Press, 2001.

van Stam, Frans Pieter. *The Servetus Case: An Appeal for a New Assessment*. Droz, 2017.

Wagner, Christine. "Los luteranos ante la Inquisición de Toledo en el siglo XVI." *Hispania Sacra* 46 (1994): 473–507.

9

Old Christians

In 1640, Juan de Llanos, a petty criminal imprisoned in Madrid's royal court, found himself the subject of an inquisitorial trial. Not only did Juan not uncover his head when the priest raised the Host during Mass, but his words so shocked jail authorities and other inmates that they brought them to the attention of the Holy Office. Juan would routinely swear by God, the Virgin Mary, Christ and a variety of saints. More seriously, he denied that swearing by the life of Christ was a sin, since God did not have a son. Even further, he expressed that it was better to believe in and follow Muhammad than God because at least the former could free the Moors from prison whereas the latter was not able to do so for Christians.

In a Spain that, after much tribulation, had decided to extirpate any traces of Islam among Muslims who had been forcibly converted to Christianity, one could imagine these expressions could lead to serious charges of heresy. But for Juan de Llanos this was not the case. Even though the theological consultants had found his expressions deeply troubling and the prosecutor, Paravicino y Vicente, had even accused him of idolatry given his expressed desire to follow Muhammad, most the inquisitors stuck to simple charges of blasphemy. As such, delving into Llanos's intent and potential for conscious heresy was not necessarily required; his expressions were merely considered an emotional outburst. Only Inquisitor Martín Real voted for torture to uncover intent, but he was rebuffed by the Suprema. The final result? Llanos was to abjure *de levi*, appear in public with the gag reserved for blasphemers, and receive one hundred lashes.¹ Within the juridical categorization of inquisitorial crimes, these penalties were considered minor: Abjuration *de levi* implied only a slight suspicion of heresy and did not include confiscation of goods, and Llanos would not be subject to the legal category of relapse – which meant automatic relaxation to the secular arm if convicted upon facing the Holy Office at a later date.

It likely made quite a difference that Llanos's trial took place well after the expulsion of the Moriscos in 1609. Although as late as the 1620s, the tribunal of Toledo saw significant activity against Moriscos (mostly in cases of slaves accused of Islamic heresy), no cases were tried in the 1630s or 1640s. By the mid-seventeenth century, Islamic heresy was not a preoccupation: At that time, the only inquisition cases tangentially related to Islam involved granting passports to freed Muslim slaves who wished to return to their homelands.² That Juan de Llanos was an Old Christian – that is, a Christian without any trace of Jewish or Muslim ancestry – was even more crucial in tilting the case in his favor. In the Introduction to this volume, Lu Ann Homza has outlined the emergence of this peculiar identity category that tended to essentialize religious difference in the fifteenth century. Not only did the distinction between Old and New Christian play a crucial role in the persecution of religious minorities, but these identity categories would also affect the outcomes of cases.

Thus, Moriscos and conversos could expect even otherwise minor cases of blasphemy, bigamy, or propositions to snowball into serious charges of Islamic heresy or crypto-judaizing. But Old Christians such as Juan de Llanos did not necessarily suffer intense interrogations over intent, the ignominy and terror of torture, or the more serious penalties that Moriscos and conversos did.³ Cases of major heresy did exist against Old Christians; they certainly could be relaxed to the secular arm. Still, the role of ancestry and ethnicity in shaping trial outcomes highlights the specific problems and approaches the Inquisition had with the majority of the Spanish Christian populace. Indeed, Old Christians would find themselves the object of a campaign of control and discipline, especially in the wake of the Counter-Reformation and its focus on standardizing Christian behavior. In the late sixteenth and seventeenth centuries, being considered an Old Christian constituted an important source of social status. Not only did it speak to the honor of an individual and their family, but it could also play a role in economic and social endeavors.

Consequently, when nun María de Chaves, who had engaged in a dispute with Inquisitor Bracamonte from Llerena, complained that he had publicly branded her ancestors as heretics, it was her identity as an Old Christian that had been impinged. "The lord inquisitor said that his predecessors had burned her ancestors at the stake, when in fact they were all Old Christians of pure blood," complained Chaves.[4] Not only had she lost reputation before her peers, but even her continuing membership in the convent was threatened by such spurious allegations. Like many institutions at the time – particularly ecclesiastical ones, colleges, and guilds – the nunnery required the blood purity of its members. Proof of ancestors' uninterrupted Christian identity and lack of Jewish or Muslim ancestry reflected the legal crystallization of genealogical discourses that differentiated between Old and New Christians. Laws about purity of blood had existed in the early fifteenth century, but they became both more popular and more controversial over time. In 1449, a rebellion in Toledo sought to exclude conversos from positions of municipal authority; in 1547, Cardinal Juan Martínez Silíceo, archbishop of Toledo, passed similarly restrictive regulations for his cathedral's governing body.[5]

In some ways, the purity of blood statues, in seeking to make effective a racializing and genealogical vision of religious difference, reflected both the importance of Old Christian identity and its fragility. On the one hand, the myriad disputes, litigation and corruption that accompanied the granting of blood purity certificates by the Inquisition reflects how much it mattered to families and individuals. On the other hand, blood purity itself, and thereby the category of Old Christian was not as clear-cut as imagined. Not only were statutes never applied consistently across space and time, but they were fungible enough to even allow Black slaves and freedmen in the Americas to claim the mantle of Old Christian and seek various opportunities. Given the difficulty in truly distinguishing Old and New Christian – for many of the latter could pass as the former – Old Christian as an identity marker remained elusive and transmutable.[6] It is not surprising that even a well esteemed inquisitor such as Baltasar de Oyanguren from Toledo sighed, "how long will this thing about being Old Christians last?"[7]

If Old Christians did end up under the purview of the Spanish Inquisition, it was less because of a concerted focus on them *as a group* than a general interest in heresies beyond crypto-judaizing and Islam, as well as an increasing attempt, in the wake of the Protestant Reformation, to discipline and effectively catechize Spain's Catholic population. Upon its founding in 1478, the Spanish Inquisition had a broad jurisdiction over heresy, but its first decades of activity were almost wholly focused on crypto-judaizing. However, as the organizational and legislative structure of the Holy Office solidified, as new processes such as district visitations were put in place and, as tribunals and the Suprema extended inquisitorial jurisdiction to both matters normally reserved for episcopal courts and mixed jurisdiction crimes, prosecutions for other infractions grew.[8] Despite the incompleteness of records before the middle of the sixteenth century, statistical studies have demonstrated a marked increase in prosecution of crimes for which Old Christians would have been liable. Whether we think of bigamy, sorcery, scandalous propositions, blasphemy, or sexual crimes, the jurisdictional tentacles of the Holy Office meant that local populations as a whole – and, therefore, Old Christians – could now be subject to the inquisitorial gaze. Moreover, between 1550 and 1700, the broader impetus of Catholic reform made such a focus the preeminent area of interest for the Holy Office, even with periodic upticks in the prosecutions of Moriscos and conversos.[9] In short, the Inquisition eventually became a tool of control aimed squarely at the Old Christian populace.[10]

When scholars speak of the Inquisition becoming an institution basically devoted to the control of the Old Christian population, they do so because of the avalanche of inquisition cases that can be categorized roughly as speech-related. These cases included a wide-ranging array of offenses: Blasphemy injurious to religion, scandalous speech, words uttered contrary to dogma, explicitly heretical utterances and even sacrilege, which usually included both speech and gestural acts. Although the exact chronology and scale of this phenomenon varied among tribunals, most studies have amply demonstrated the extent to which these types of crimes eventually came to dwarf those against new converts. Thus, in Toledo – one of the most important tribunals in Spain – speech crimes made up 35 percent of all cases and was the largest category, as opposed to crypto-Judaism, which accounted for 25 percent of trials. In Seville, the share of speech cases reached its maximum of over 25 percent between 1560 and 1599, while remaining quite high at just over 20 percent through 1640. It was largely these types of cases that ensured that during that period 44 percent of defendants were of Old Christian stock. In fact, across all tribunals, such offenses reflected one of the most important categories of prosecution from the mid-sixteenth century through 1700.[11] What accounted for this phenomenon?

Speech acts were never considered a single crime to be prosecuted but rather included, in a haphazard fashion, a variety of activities that eventually came under the purview of the Holy Office. Chief among them was the crime of blasphemy. Running all the way from swearing by divine figures to insulting them scandalously, blasphemy was an amorphous crime that, given its commonality in daily life and particularly in times of emotional stress, came to be punished by both ecclesiastical and secular courts. Thanks to the development of canon law and scholastic approaches to the question, medieval inquisitors had also laid claim to it. Specifically, the great Nicolau Eymeric, in his fourteenth-century inquisition manual that would become widespread through an important sixteenth-century commentary by Franciso Peña, argued that some types of blasphemy fell under the purview of the Holy Office. In particular, whereas the simple blasphemy of irreflexive injurious exclamations made under emotional stress might well be left to the secular authorities, expressions that in their content not only insulted the faith but questioned its dogmas – even if implicitly – might be said to reflect a heterodox intent. As such, this type of blasphemy, deemed heretical, could be pursued by inquisitors.[12]

Although cases of blasphemy in the Spanish Inquisition were relatively few in the first few years of inquisitorial activity, they slowly increased and became a source of contention. Indeed, local tribunals seemed to have already been stretching the limits of their jurisdiction in pursuing blasphemy for the many complaints of municipalities and national parliaments led the inquisitor-general to set parameters for this practice in the 1500 constitutions. Thereafter, tribunals were supposed to leave simple blasphemy to secular courts while focusing on heretical blasphemy. That said, the border between the two was anything but clear and canonists, theologians, and inquisitorial authorities continued to debate when a mere insult professed in the throes of anger should become the object of heretical suspicion. At the heart of the matter were disagreements regarding the connection between language – even if spontaneous and emotional – and belief. Whereas to some, such irreflexive expressions revealed the soul – potentially heterodox – of individuals, to others, such unfortunate utterances were mere cultural atavisms that did not imply heresy. Altogether, however, the lack of definitional certainty on the matter, the tendency of local tribunals to claim jurisdiction over any crimes that were deemed close to heresy, and the inability of the Suprema to effectively police such overreach (despite ongoing provisions on the matter), meant that simple as well as heretical blasphemy came under the purview of inquisitorial authorities.[13]

Aside from blasphemy itself, other prosecutable speech acts also accounted for the large number of cases tried. Although the term "propositions" was used as an umbrella category in the nineteenth-century archival organization of inquisition cases, the word also referred to a specific speech-crime that could be adjacent to and sometimes coexist with blasphemy. In particular, although blasphemy at its core constituted an insult injurious to the faith, propositions in inquisitorial jurisprudence required the uttered statement to be contrary to dogma. Such statements did not need to include blasphemous insults and could vary in gravity and theme: Most cases involved denial of the sacraments, the salvific role of the church, the existence of hell, or the power of God and the saints.[14] Finally, it should be noted that the much rarer crime of sacrilege was closely related to blasphemy, though it did not need to include actual speech acts. Here one may find what jurists considered to be grievous insults to the faith through the destruction or disrespect of objects – such as devotional images, the Cross, or the Eucharist, among others – that were crucial to church teaching. That they often were accompanied by verbal insults is reflected in many cases.

Most of this broad range of cases – blasphemy, statements contrary to dogma, sacrilege – tended to involve Old Christians and accounted for much of the persecutory pressure on Hispanic Catholic populations. Although the range of cases, typologies of crimes, and themes make it difficult to ascertain common trends, most of these offenses were penalized relatively lightly. Inquisitorial jurists generally considered such speech acts – if devoid of explicit heretical or idolatrous intent – as minor and part of the cultural apparatus of an uneducated population. The most common penance for such cases, therefore, were abjuration *de levi*, lashes, and temporary exile from the local area.[15] Granted, changing local contexts meant the chronology, themes, and victims prosecuted varied greatly. For example, in the Americas the phenomenon of Black slaves engaging in blasphemy in the throes of punishment from their masters was common. Some scholars have even seen such utterances as a particularly effective means of appealing to notions of martyrdom and even, through transfer to the Holy Office, publicizing and escaping a master's wrath and mistreatment.[16]

Likewise, in the last quarter of the sixteenth century, many Spanish tribunals became particularly invested in prosecuting the proposition that fornication was not a sin. Although sexual misbehavior outside marriage was not prosecuted by the Inquisition – instead, the offense belonged to the episcopal legal jurisdiction – in these cases, propositions about fornication reflected post-Tridentine efforts to effectively catechize and discipline the Christian population.[17] As such, both knowledge of doctrine and the contention of sexual sin went hand in hand in such campaigns. At first glance, fornication cases appear deceptively simple: Inquisitors prosecuted those who uttered that sex outside the bonds of marriage was not sinful. But in fact multiple issues and a broader educational context colored these cases.

On a purely doctrinal level, the Church had long considered fornication as a mortal sin. Yet, the Council of Trent's various canons on marriage, reaffirming its sacramental nature and condemning adultery and concubinage, had brought otherwise common sexual practices to the forefront as behaviors open to discipline and reform. Between roughly 1570 and 1630, therefore, two major campaigns of Tridentine moral reform went hand in hand in seeking such results: the curtailment and eventual ban of prostitution in Spain by 1623, and ongoing campaigns to reform young men's sexual excesses. Not surprisingly, when accused of uttering that fornication was not sinful, some of the most common arguments men put forth were typically old-fashioned and reflected in patristic and medieval sources: Sex with prostitutes was an acceptable outlet for male sexual desire for it prevented even worse sins and crimes.[18] But by the 1570s, in a Spain where major religious orders, such as the Jesuits, were actively campaigning against regulated legal prostitution with arguments that emphasized saving both female sex workers and their male clients from mortal sin, such arguments fell on deaf ears.[19]

Indeed, through the last quarter of the sixteenth century inquisitors participated in a concerted campaign to discipline sexuality through the prosecution of propositions on fornication. *Cartas acordadas* in 1573 and 1574 instructed local inquisitorial tribunals to act; inquisitors were to proceed "against those who hold this error as heretics, so that they will be punished and provide an example to others."[20] Significantly, medieval inquisitors had not prosecuted this crime; it was not mentioned in Eymeric's magisterial manual, or even Peña's 1578 commentary on Eymeric that reflected Spanish inquisitorial thinking at the time. Linking these statements to heresy and brandishing the exemplary nature of the punishments to be meted out, often in public *autos de fe*, signaled the serious intent of this concerted campaign to truly enforce post-Tridentine sexual and doctrinal standards on an either uneducated or uninterested population. Moreover, these juridical directives went hand in hand with orders to preachers to stress the issue in sermons.[21]

The results of the Spanish Inquisition's campaign against this offense were mixed, especially when it came to how it played out in local contexts. Certainly, proposition cases about fornication spiked in most tribunals through the 1590s. In some places, such as Seville, proposition/fornication trials made up almost three quarters of all proposition cases between 1560 and 1599 and a staggering one third of all cases.[22] In Granada, the pressure to prosecute was so intense that in a single decade, 1580–90, such trials accounted for more than half (148) the proposition/fornication cases prosecuted throughout the sixteenth century (271). Most of those prosecuted were young men, though depending on the tribunal different spaces seem to have mattered more than others: thus, in Toledo, Valencia, and Granada we see a preponderance of cases from urban areas, whereas in Córdoba and Galicia rural ones predominate.[23]

As with other cases of propositions, penances tended to fall on the lighter side in comparison to more serious heresy. Writing in the mid-seventeenth century, Inquisitor Santos de San Pedro argued that if the defendant was of little mental capacity, rustic, and ignorant of doctrine, he would have his sentence read in the privacy of the hearing chamber, abjure *de levi*, and suffer a period of exile from the area. If, however, the culprit demonstrated signs of willful doctrinal error, he should suffer the shame of appearing in a public *auto de fe* and the pain of lashes in addition to the abjuration *de levi* and exile. In Granada, about half the cases seem to have fallen on the lighter side of San Pedro's scale.[24] Sevillian inquisitors, on the other hand, seemed to have taken a harsher view of this crime: Culprits were much more likely to receive the punishment of lashes in a public appearance.[25] Although by the early seventeenth century, the pressure on fornicators seems to have lessened as other crimes came to occupy inquisitorial tribunals, these trials reflected the disciplinary focus on matters of sexuality – much beyond what one imagines as a true heresy case – on the part of inquisitors.

Another category of inquisitorial focus was bigamy, which touched on both the sacrament of marriage and sexuality. Certainly, both state and church had shown considerable interest in the matter over time. Thus, secular laws, such as the medieval *Siete Partidas*, which focused on the criminal and civil liabilities incurred by bigamists, condemned them to exile. Likewise, as the sacramental nature of marriage became especially emphasized in the later medieval period, episcopal courts could also enjoy jurisdiction over the matter. Although the Inquisition did not focus on this offense in its early years, the Protestant Reformation and its attack on the sacrament of marriage also made bigamy a matter of concern: Did erroneous views, including potential heresy, play a role when partners contracted a second marriage though their first partners were still alive? At least in theory, therefore, inquisitorial activity in relation to bigamy was to focus on the matter of belief – the threat of potential heresy, and especially Lutheranism, an ever-present specter.

The Spanish Inquisition was not the only legal jurisdiction that could interest itself in bigamy cases, but in practice, it came to virtually monopolize their prosecution.²⁶ Certainly, the natural tendency of the Holy Office was to extend its jurisdiction to any and all crimes that at least implied heresy, as we saw with blasphemy. Marrying twice, even if not necessarily as part of disbelief in the sacrament of marriage, uneasily approached heresy. Was not behavior the best barometer for the travails of the souls? Knowing what the church taught about this sacrament, did not a bigamous marriage reveal an inner rot that stank of heresy? Still, not everybody was convinced, and secular institutions, such as the 1512 Cortes of Monzón, clamored against what it saw as unjustified jurisdictional overreach: Members there argued that inquisitors should restrict themselves to bigamy cases that evinced explicit attacks on the sacrament of marriage. Trent and its aftermath, however, left inquisitors victorious in terms of their jurisdiction on the matter. Practically minded bureaucratic reforms that improved parish registers and made control over marriage and the investigation of any wrongdoings more viable helped the Spanish Inquisition dominate the prosecution of this offense.²⁷

Provocatively, however, inquisitorial tribunals very rarely prosecuted bigamy as a truly heretical matter, with a focus on the suspect's beliefs around the sacramental nature of marriage. In practice, bigamy cases were treated as matters of fraud, with the energy of inquisitorial courts resting on proving whether a second marriage had taken place or not. Penalties for bigamy varied as jurisprudence considered them arbitrary; inquisitors needed to use their discretion in sentencing according to the severity of the crime. Men often were condemned to galley service and women to exile, both usually with public lashes and abjuration *de levi*. This contrasted with other European inquisitorial jurisdictions, which considered bigamy as strongly indicative of heresy. Although such cases did happen in Spanish territories, they tended to go hand in hand with aggravated circumstances such as recidivism, or the suspects having lived in Protestant or Muslim realms.²⁸

Perhaps the most obvious and direct involvement of inquisitorial tribunals in policing sexuality entailed the prosecution of sodomy and bestiality in the tribunals of the Crown of Aragon. Sodomy had emerged by the thirteenth century as a particular preoccupation in both canon and secular law. Although in the former, concerns about untoward sexuality in monastic communities had led to provisions detailing the defrocking of culprits, it fell to secular courts across Europe to prosecute it. Known as the crime against nature, akin in severity to heresy and treason, sodomy and bestiality came to be heavily penalized.[29] Already Alfonso X's *Fuero Real* and *Siete Partidas* called for the execution of culprits in the thirteenth century, while the 1497 provisions by King Ferdinand and Queen Isabella further sensationalized the punishment of this crime by adding burning at the stake as an exemplary measure. But, at its heart, sodomy remained a crime punishable in secular courts and to which inquisitors had no claim: Indeed, attempts to prosecute sodomy had been initially rebuffed by the Suprema. The exception that would change the rule came about in 1524 when the Suprema, in its support of the Zaragoza tribunal's attempt to bring a political enemy to court, obtained a papal dispensation that allowed for the prosecution of sodomy in the Crown of Aragon.[30]

Issued by Pope Clement VII, the brief was distinct in inquisitorial jurisprudence because it tied the prosecution of sodomy in Aragonese inquisition tribunals to local secular laws. Indeed, under such circumstances, sodomy was being prosecuted exceptionally: not as heresy but as a regular crime. This meant that normal inquisitorial procedure went out the window. For example, unlike in heresy cases where defendants never knew the identity of witnesses testifying against them, in sodomy cases a *careación* or faceoff was essential: It both satisfied testimonial requirements in local law and allowed defendants to face their accusers in court. Presumably, depending upon the way this confrontation took place, inquisitors could derive a sense of guilt or innocence.[31] Likewise, in comparison to fornication cases where belief was the central question, sodomy trials focused on the specific sexual act and here secular law dictated the evidentiary threshold. Thus, in 1497 the Catholic monarchs had already mandated that consummated sodomy need not be proven for a conviction, with only proximate acts sufficing. By 1598, Philip II reduced the number of witnesses required to prove sodomy to only three adults or four, if one of the partners was included.[32] Because such sexual acts often happened away from prying eyes, the reduction in the number of witnesses made it easier to convict.

Although the 1524 papal dispensation was not necessarily taken up as an immediate impetus for the broad prosecution of sodomy, by the 1570s tribunals in the crown of Aragon started devoting more resources to this crime. Led by Zaragoza, both in terms of the intensity of prosecution and the harshness of penalties, inquisitions in the Crown of Aragon, including the tribunals of Valencia and Barcelona, filled their dockets with sodomy and bestiality cases. Although the sources are incomplete, the evidence suggests that the Aragonese inquisition tribunals carried out perhaps more than 600 sodomy trials between the late sixteenth century and 1700. In sodomy proper, most cases involved men; only a few featured heterosexual sodomy. Likewise, penalties based on secular law were much harsher than those of other crimes we have examined: 12 percent of all men tried for sodomy were burned at the stake; in cases of bestiality, this number rose to 23 percent.[33]

Although this trend would change after the first quarter of the seventeenth century – when the Suprema turned from a policy of making exemplars of sodomites to limiting the publicity of such crimes – sodomy prosecutions were exemplary for their indiscriminate harshness. Even famous noblemen, such as the last master of the Order of Montesa, Pedro Galcerán de Borja, were prosecuted, and clerics made common appearances in *autos de fe* where they were defrocked and later burned at the stake. Likewise, throughout the period Old Christians made up a great majority of defendants. While it is true that many Moriscos, particularly in Valencia, found themselves prosecuted for sodomy until their expulsion in 1609, the number of cases against them were disproportionately low for their population density in the region. On the other hand, Old Christians – in particular foreigners, especially Frenchmen in cases of bestiality and Italians in cases of sodomy – were overrepresented.[34]

Although inquisitorial jurisdiction over sodomy was exclusive to Aragon, other tribunals also looked askew at non-normative expressions of sexuality and gender. For example, in 1635 the Llerena tribunal carefully investigated the case of Juan Díaz Donoso, known in the town of Zafra as the "priestess." A cleric, Díaz Donoso claimed to be a hermaphrodite and apparently had slept with various young men. Although he was never brought to trial and documentation on the resulting investigation is missing, Spanish inquisitors would have had difficulty fitting their legal categories to marginal and non-normative expressions of gender and sexuality.[35]

Perhaps the most well-known case of this ilk involved the trial of Eleno de Cespedes in Toledo. A former slave who had been briefly married as a young woman, Eleno was living as a male surgeon by 1587 when he attempted to celebrate a wedding with his sweetheart. Faced with Eleno's claims that he had, at one point, spontaneously grown a penis and was, thus, entitled to live his life as a man and marry, inquisitors found it difficult to fit the case within accepted categories of jurisprudence. Medical examinations conducted in the inquisition's secret prisons revealed Eleno to have no traces of male genitalia: He claimed it had fallen off following an infection. Those examinations in turn contradicted ocular testimony as well as medical and episcopal certificates that had pronounced him a man, a discrepancy that raised all kinds of problems. Was this a case of sodomy, making inquisitorial involvement impossible given the lack of jurisdiction outside Aragon? Or, rather, did it involve trickery on the part of Eleno and even disrespect for the sacrament of marriage, therefore raising the specter of heresy? Could even the magical arts have been involved, for how could Eleno otherwise have so convinced friends, neighbors, and especially renowned physicians that he had a penis? Ultimately, inquisitors found Eleno guilty of sorcery and disrespect for the sacrament of marriage and condemned him to serve as a nurse at a local hospital. Paradoxically, Eleno's surgical background and rumors of his ability – perhaps magical – to manipulate the body in such a manner as to shift gender expression, meant local patients flocked to the hospital to be treated by him.[36]

The specter of magical intervention in Eleno's case points to another area of inquisitorial focus against the Old Christian population: magic and witchcraft. As fully discussed in much scholarship on Spain and elsewhere, the emergence of witchcraft by the late fifteenth century as an object of concern among demonologists and legal experts led to wide-ranging persecutions – often of women – that still shock in their harshness. That said, demonologists and theorists of magic distinguished between witchcraft and sorcery. The former included all the hallmarks that have become fodder for modern sensationalism. Witches made explicit pacts with the devil; they flew to venerate him in nocturnal ceremonies called sabbats; there, they engaged in rituals that inverted Christian dogma, and had sex with the devil and with each other, irrespective of biological sex. Witches practiced harmful magic under the devil's supervision: They murdered infants and adults, and engaged in the poisoning and ruin of agriculture and farm animals.

Sorcery, on the other hand, reflected an implicit pact with the devil in the superstitious belief by the practitioner about the efficacy of his or her spells. Common to such practices were love magic and healing, often employing Christian prayers and materials in sacrilegious ways or, at least, toward ends not sanctioned by Christianity. Alleged witches and sorcerers were categorized as heretics if they were baptized Christians because they were abandoning their baptismal vows to worship the enemy of God. While the Spanish Inquisition was interested in both witchcraft and sorcery throughout Spain, location mattered, just as it did with sodomy. Witchcraft seems to have been a relatively minor rural phenomenon, particularly in mountainous areas along the Pyrenees. Sorcery, on the other hand, was commonly practiced throughout urban areas.[37]

While witch hunts and their concomitant terrors were sporadically common elsewhere in Europe – especially parts of the Holy Roman Empire and in Scotland – the Spanish Inquisition's record on witchcraft prosecution was more ambiguous. In general, Spanish Inquisition tribunals were not allowed to confiscate the property of convicted witches, though some inquisitors tried and succeeded in doing so. The fact that inquisitors could not usually benefit financially from prosecuting suspected witches suggests a reason for their lack of interest. At the same time, witchcraft – with its demonic pacts and harmful magic – belonged to three legal jurisdictions in Catholic Spain and Italy. Bishops and inquisitors were interested in the salvation of accused witches' souls, while the secular justice system wanted to prosecute witches for harm done. There could thus be a tremendous degree of jurisdictional competition as inquisitors, bishops, and secular judges tried to be the first to put suspected witches on trial. It was not unusual for the Spanish Inquisition to become involved in episcopal- or secular-driven trials and to take over the cases, though its intervention was not inevitable.

In terms of instructions about suspected witches, even the Suprema mandated caution. In 1526, Inquisitor-General Alonso Manrique called an assembly of theological and legal experts to Granada to consider what could and should be done about witch suspects in Spain's northern

Kingdom of Navarre, who were currently on trial in the secular legal jurisdiction. The delegates in Granada split their opinions on some crucial issues. Some believed witches flew only in their imaginations and were deluded; others were convinced the flight was real. Some wanted the witches punished severely even if they were hallucinating or mentally ill; others advocated leniency in such circumstances. Some argued that witches could be convicted through their own confessions, while others recommended the matter be remitted to "senior jurists,"; still others interpreted the validity of the confession in terms of what it did or did not address.[38] Economically, theologically, and legally, Spanish inquisitors had reasons to be wary about prosecuting witch suspects, and the frequency and extent of their witchcraft trials throughout the sixteenth century generally reflected restraint.

Still, Spain ended up witnessing one of the most infamous witch hunts in European history. Beginning in December 1608 and extending through at least 1612, mountain villages in Navarre experienced a tsunami of witchcraft accusations that ended up involving thousands of people, mostly women and children. The three inquisitors who oversaw Navarre sentenced thirty-one witches in November 1610 to various penalties, including exile; eleven of the thirty-one were burned at the stake in person or in effigy; all the convicted witches had their property confiscated. Yet when significant improprieties and malfeasance in the Logroño tribunal were shared with the Suprema, the situation reversed itself. In 1614, the witches' convictions were overturned, testimonies implicating witchcraft were suppressed. and new regulations were issued that strengthened protections for those accused of this crime.[39]

Ultimately, for all our modern fascination with witchcraft, it was the more prosaic crime of sorcery that inquisition tribunals prosecuted more commonly. Most defendants were of Old Christian stock, although this category included a variety of populations, including racialized minorities in the Americas. As a practice, sorcery was widespread throughout the Hispanic world and, though frowned upon by authorities, provided a variety of services, such love magic, both as a formal paid enterprise and a household activity. Often relying on food, incantations mixed with prayers, and bodily fluids, this largely female activity crossed social and racial barriers so that we find everyone from the urban poor to the well-to-do caught in inquisitorial nets. Likewise, magical healing constituted a central aspect of sorcery that was practiced openly: In a plural medical marketplace, the option to seek the services of a magical healer was as legitimate as engaging physicians, barbers, quacks, and so forth.[40]

Notwithstanding the variability of magic in such a widespread marketplace, inquisition tribunals tended to punish such transgressions relatively lightly. In Toledo, for example, where sorcery accounted for almost 5 percent of all cases, with a marked spike in the first half of the seventeenth century, the overwhelming majority of the condemned were women who tended to receive lashes and temporary exile from their community as penalties. Similar trends – a majority of women being condemned to lashes and exile – can be found elsewhere in Spain and the Americas. At the heart of the matter, inquisitors treated sorcery – especially if practical, benign and informal – as superstitious behavior. Seen as a cultural reflection of an uneducated and largely female constituency, inquisitors dismissed sorcery as a relatively minor offense not worthy of the more serious considerations revolving around true heresy. Indeed, the control of sorcery reflected a broader attempt to inculcate a better understanding of the faith and a rejection of superstitious behavior.[41]

Ultimately, whether we think of the broad range of prosecutions over magic, speech crimes in their many facets, or various sex-related offences, an inquisitorial focus on these issues ensured contact with the great variety of peoples who could be deemed Old Christian. Often cutting across gender, racial, and class divides, these trials reflected a broad impetus toward Christian discipline that only grew stronger with Tridentine efforts and the Counter-Reformation. As such, the Inquisition's relationship with the broad Old Christian population across Spain and the Americas emerged as central for long-term processes of control and discipline. In effect, inquisitorial attention to a range of more prosaic crimes beyond crypto-judaizing rendered the Holy Office a constant presence in the lives of Old Christians. If, as some have argued, the Inquisition spread a mantle of fear across Hispanic populations, it was likely its focus on this broader range of more ordinary offenses that ensured its continuous presence in people's minds.

Notes

1. Archivo Histórico Nacional [AHN], Inquisición, Legajo 39, no. 45.
2. Archivo Histórico Nacional, *Catálogo de las causas*.
3. Iván Jurado Revaliente, *Cultura oral en la edad moderna* (Instituto Fernando el Católico, 2013), 4; Martí Gelabertó Vilagran, "Mentes sacrílegas, palabras impías: Ateísmo y blasfemia en Cataluña, siglos XVI-XVIII," *Revista de ciencias de las religiones* 19 (2014): 113.
4. "... como dicho señor inquisidor lo dijo de los ascendientes de esta declarante que los habían quemado sus antecesores siendo todos cristianos viejos y de limpia sangre." AHN, Inquisición, Legajo 1993, no. 5.
5. On blood purity, Albert A. Sicroff, *Les controverses des status de "pureté de sang" en Espagne du XVe au XVIIe siècle* (Didier, 1960); Juan Hernández Franco, *Sangre limpia, sangre española* (Cátedra, 2011), chapter 1.
6. For slaves and blood purity, Chloe Ireton, "'They are Blacks of the Caste of Black Christians': Old Christian Black Blood in the Sixteenth and Early Seventeenth Century Iberian Atlantic," *Hispanic American Historical Review* 97 (2017): 579–612. On the implementation of blood purity statues, Linda Martz, "Pure Blood Statutes in Sixteenth-Century Toledo: Implementation as Opposed to Adoption," *Sefarad* 54 (1994): 83–107; Christina H. Lee, *The Anxiety of Sameness in Early Modern Spain* (Manchester University Press, 2016).
7. "hasta cuando ha de durar esto de ser Christianos viejos." AHN, Inquisición, 2013, no. 2, image 298.
8. Leandro Martínez Peñas, "La reordenación jurídica de la Inquisición del año 1500: las instrucciones de Diego de Deza," *Isidorianum* 31 (2022): 75–100.
9. Michel Boeglin, *Inquisición y contrarreforma: el tribunal del Santo Oficio de Sevilla (1560–1700)* (Ediciones Espuela de Plata, 2007); Sara T. Nalle, "Inquisitors, Priests, and the People during the Catholic Reformation in Spain," *The Sixteenth Century Journal* 18 (1987): 557–87.
10. Jean-Pierre Dedieu, "Les causes de la foi de l'Inquisition de Tolède (1483–1820): Essai statistique," *Mélanges de la Casa de Velázquez* 14 (1978): 143–71; Dedieu, "Les quatre temps de l'Inquisition," in Bartolomé Bennassar, ed., *L'Inquisition espagnole XVe–XIXe siècles* (Hachette, 1979).
11. Dedieu, "Les quatre temps de l'Inquisition." Michel Boeglin, "Disciplina religiosa y asentamiento de la doctrina: el delito de proposiciones ante la Inquisición sevillana (1560–1700)," *Historia. Instituciones. Documentos* 2017, doi.org/10.12795/hid.2003.i30.04.
12. Gelabertó Vilagran, "Inquisición y blasfemias"; Maureen Flynn, "Blasphemy and the Play of Anger in Sixteenth Century Spain," *Past & Present* 149 (1995): 29–56.
13. Flynn, "Blasphemy and the Play of Anger"; Gelabertó Vilagran, "Inquisición y blasfemias."

14. Boeglin, "Disciplina religiosa."
15. Enrique Gacto Fernández, "Las circunstancias atenuantes de la responsabilidad criminal en la doctrina jurídica de la Inquisición," *Estudios penales y criminológicos* 15 (1991): 33; Gelabertó Vilagran, "Inquisición y blasfemias," 656.
16. Javier Villa-Flores, "To Lose One's Soul: Blasphemy and Slavery in New Spain, 1596–1669," *Hispanic American Historical Review* 82 (2002): 435–68.
17. Boeglin, "Disciplina religiosa."
18. Edward Behrend-Martínez, "Taming Don Juan: Limiting Masculine Sexuality in Counter-Reformation Spain," *Gender and History* 24 (2012): 333–52; José María García Fuentes, "Inquisición y sexualidad en el reino de Granada en el siglo XVI," *Chronica Nova* 13 (1982): 207–29.
19. Andrés Moreno Mengíbar and Francisco Vázquez García, "Poderes y prostitución en España: el caso de Sevilla," *Criticón* 69 (1997): 33–49.
20. "... contra los que tuvieren este error como con herejes para que a ellos sea castigo y a otros ejemplo." Boeglin, "Disciplina religiosa," 127.
21. Boeglin, "Disciplina religiosa," 127.
22. Boeglin, "Disciplina religiosa," 125–6.
23. García Fuentes, "Inquisición y sexualidad," 209; Jean-Pierre Dedieu, "Le modèle sexual: le défense du mariage chrétien," in Bartolomé Bennassar, ed., *L'Inquisition espagnole, XVe–XIXe siècle* (Hachette, 1979).
24. García Fuentes, "Inquisición y sexualidad," 211.
25. Boeglin, "Disciplina religiosa," 127.
26. José Martínez Millán, "La Inquisición contra la bigamia: en defensa del orden social," *Edad de Oro* 38 (2019): 173–95.
27. Enrique Gacto Fernández, "El delito de bigamia y la inquisición española," *Anuario de historia del derecho español* 57 (1987): 465–92.
28. Gacto Fernández, "El delito de bigamia."
29. John Boswell, *Christianity, Social Tolerance and Homosexuality: Gay People in Western Europe from the Beginning of the Christian Era to the Fourteenth Century* (The University of Chicago Press, 1981); Mark D. Jordan, *The Invention of Sodomy in Christian Theology* (The University of Chicago Press, 1998).
30. E. William Monter, *Frontiers of Heresy: The Spanish Inquisition from the Basque Lands to Sicily* (Cambridge University Press, 2009), 276–8.
31. Monter, *Frontier of Heresy*, 279–80; Cristian Berco, *Sexual Hierarchies, Public Status: Men, Sodomy and Society in Spain's Golden Age* (University of Toronto Press, 1997), 101–6.
32. Berco, *Sexual Hierarchies*, 92.
33. Berco, *Sexual Hierarchies*, 76; Monter, *Frontiers of Heresy*, 288.
34. Berco *Sexual Hierarchies*, chapter 6; Monter, *Frontiers of Heresy*, 290–5.

35. For the Díaz Donoso case, François Soyer, *Ambiguous Gender in Early Modern Spain and Portugal: Inquisitors, Doctors and the Transgression of Gender Norms* (Brill, 2012), 67–93.
36. Israel Burshatin, "Written on the Body: Slave or Hermaphrodite in Sixteenth-Century Spain," in Josiah Blackmore and Gregory S. Hutcheson, eds., *Queer Iberia: Sexualities, Cultures, and Crossings from the Middle Ages to the Renaissance* (Duke University Press, 1999): 420–56; Soyer, *Ambiguous Gender*, 50–67.
37. Julio Caro Baroja, *Las brujas y su mundo* (Alianza Editorial, 2015); Joseph Pérez, *Historia de la brujería en España* (Espasa, 2010).
38. Lu Ann Homza, ed. and trans., *The Spanish Inquisition, 1478–1614: An Anthology of Sources* (Hackett, 2006), document 13.
39. Gustav Henningsen, *The Witches' Advocate: Basque Witchcraft and the Spanish Inquisition (1609–1614)* (University of Nevada Press, 1980); Lu Ann Homza, *Village Infernos and Witches' Advocates: Witch Hunting in Navarre, 1608–1614* (Pennsylvania State University Press, 2022).
40. María Tausiet, *Urban Magic in Early Modern Spain: Abracadabra Omnipotens* (Palgrave Macmillan, 2014); Juan Blázquez Miguel, "Brujas e inquisidores en la América colonial (1569–1820)," *Espacio, tiempo y forma. Serie IV, Historia moderna* 7 (1994); 71–98; Amos Megged, "Magic, Popular Medicine and Gender in Seventeenth-Century Mexico: The Case of Isabel de Montoya," *Social History* 19 (1994): 189–207.
41. R Morales Estévez, "El algoritmo de la hechicería: Análisis cuantitativo y cualitativo del archivo inquisitorial Toledano," *Edad de Oro* 39 (2020): 43–56.

Suggestions for Further Reading

Dediu, Jean-Pierre. "Les quatre temps de l'Inquisition." In Bartolomé Bennassar, ed.,*L'Inquisition espagnole XVe- XIXe siècles*. Hachette, 1979.

García-Arenal, Mercedes. "Creating Conversos: Genealogy and Identity as Historiographical Problems (After a Recent Book by Ángel Alcalá)." *Bulletin for Spanish and Portuguese Historical Studies* 38, no. 1 (2013): 1–19.

Hernández Franco, Juan. *Sangre limpia, sangre española*. Cátedra, 2011.

Homza, Lu Ann. *Village Infernos and Witches' Advocates: Witch-Hunting in Navarre, 1608–1614*. Pennsylvania State University Press, 2022.

Ireton, Chloe. "'They Are Blacks of the Caste of Black Christians': Old Christian Black Blood in the Sixteenth- and Early Seventeenth-Century Iberian Atlantic." *Hispanic American Historical Review* 97 (2017): 579–612.

Lee, Christina H. *The Anxiety of Sameness in Early Modern Spain*. Manchester University Press, 2016.

Martz, Linda. "Pure Blood Statutes in Sixteenth Century Toledo: Implementation as Opposed to Adoption." *Sefarad* 54 (1994): 83–107.

Nalle, Sara T. "Inquisitors, Priests, and the People during the Catholic Reformation in Spain." *The Sixteenth Century Journal* 18 (1987): 557–87.

Sicroff, Albert A. *Les controverses des status de "pureté de sang" en Espagne du XVe au XVIIe siècle*. Didier, 1960.

Bibliography

Behrend-Martínez, Edward. "Taming Don Juan: Limiting Masculine Sexuality in Counter-Reformation Spain." *Gender & History* 24 (2012): 333–52.

Berco, Cristian. *Sexual Hierarchies, Public Status: Men, Sodomy, and Society in Spain's Golden Age*. University of Toronto Press, 2007.

Bethencourt, Francisco. *Racisms: From the Crusades to the Twentieth Century*. Princeton University Press, 2014.

Blázquez Miguel, Juan. "Brujas e inquisidores en la América colonial (1569–1820)." *Espacio, tiempo y forma. Serie IV, Historia moderna* 7 (1994): 71–98.

Boeglin, Michel. *Inquisición y Contrarreforma: El Tribunal del Santo Oficio de Sevilla (1560–1700)*. Ediciones Espuela de Plata, 2007.

Boswell, John. *Christianity, Social Tolerance and Homosexuality: Gay People in Western Europe from the Beginning of the Christian Era to the Fourteenth Century*. The University of Chicago Press, 1981.

Braude, Benjamin. "The Sons of Noah and the Construction of Ethnic and Geographical Identities in the Medieval and Early Modern Periods." *The William & Mary Quarterly* 54 (1997): 103–42.

Burshatin, Israel. "Written on the Body: Slave or Hermaphrodite in Sixteenth Century Spain." In Josiah Blackmore and Gregory S. Hutcheson, eds., *Queer Iberia: Sexualities, Cultures, and Crossings from the Middle Ages to the Renaissance*. Duke University Press, 1999.

Caro Baroja, Julio. *Las brujas y su mundo*. Alianza Editorial, 2015.

Dedieu, Jean-Pierre. "Le modèle sexual: la défense du mariage chrétien." In Bartolomé Bennassar, ed. *L'Inquisition espagnole, XV'-XIX' siècle*. Paris, 1979.

"Les quatre temps de l'Inquisition." In Bartolomé Bennassar, ed. *L'Inquisition espagnole, XV'-XIX' siècle*. Paris, 1979.

Flynn, Maureen. "Blasphemy and the Play of Anger in Sixteenth-Century Spain." *Past & Present* 149 (1995): 29–56.

Gacto Fernández, Enrique. "El delito de bigamia y la Inquisición española." *Anuario de historia del derecho español* 57 (1987): 465–92.

"Las circunstancias atenuantes de la responsabilidad criminal en la doctrina jurídica de la Inquisición." *Estudios penales y criminológicos* 15 (1991): 7–78.

García-Arenal, Mercedes. "Creating Conversos: Genealogy and Identity as Historiographical Problems (After a Recent Book by Ángel Alcalá)." *Bulletin for Spanish and Portuguese Historical Studies* 38, no. 1 (2013): 1–19.

García Fuentes, José María. "Inquisición y sexualidad en el reino de Granada en el siglo xvi." *Chronica Nova* 13 (1982): 207–29.

Gelabertó Vilagran, Martí. "Inquisición y blasfemias en la Cataluña de los siglos XVI y XVII." *Pedralbes: Revista d'Històra Moderna* 28 (2008): 651–76.

"Mentes sacrílegas, palabras impías. Ateísmo y blasfemia en Cataluña, siglos XVI-XVIII." *Revista de ciencias de las religiones* 19 (2014): 93–125.

Hernández Franco, Juan. *Sangre limpia, sangre española*. Cátedra, 2011.

Homza, Lu Ann, ed. and trans. *The Spanish Inquisition, 1478–1614: An Anthology of Sources*. Hackett, 2006.

Village Infernos and Witches' Advocates: Witch-Hunting in Navarre, 1608–1614. Pennsylvania State University Press, 2022.

Ireton, Chloe. "'They Are Blacks of the Caste of Black Christians': Old Christian Black Blood in the Sixteenth-and Early Seventeenth-Century Iberian Atlantic." *Hispanic American Historical Review* 97 (2017): 579–612.

Jordan, Mark D. *The Invention of Sodomy in Christian Theology*. The University of Chicago Press, 1998.

Jurado Revaliente, Iván. *Cultura oral en la edad moderna*. Instituto Fernando el Católico, 2013.

Lee, Christina H. *The Anxiety of Sameness in Early Modern Spain*. Manchester University Press, 2016.

Martínez-Dávila, Roger Louis. *Creating Conversos: The Carvajal–Santa María Family in Early Modern Spain*. University of Notre Dame Press, 2018.

Martínez Millán, José. "La Inquisición contra la bigamia: en defensa del orden social." *Edad de Oro* 38 (2019): 173–95.

Martínez Peñas, Leandro. "La reordenación jurídica de la Inquisición del año 1500: Las instrucciones de Diego de Deza." *Isidorianum* 31 (2022): 75–100.

Martz, Linda. "Pure Blood Statutes in Sixteenth Century Toledo: Implementation as Opposed to Adoption." *Sefarad* 54 (1994): 83–107.

Megged, Amos. "Magic, Popular Medicine and Gender in Seventeenth-Century Mexico: The Case of Isabel de Montoya." *Social History* 19 (1994): 189–207.

Monter, E. William. *Frontiers of Heresy: The Spanish Inquisition from the Basque Lands to Sicily*. Cambridge University Press, 2009.

Morales Estévez, R. "El algoritmo de la hechicería: Análisis cuantitativo y cualitativo del archivo inquisitorial toledano." *Edad de Oro* 39 (2020): 43–56.

Moreno Mengíbar, Andrés, and Francisco Vázquez García. "Poderes y prostitución en España: el caso de Sevilla." *Criticón* 69 (1997): 33–49.

Nalle, Sara T. "Inquisitors, Priests, and the People during the Catholic Reformation in Spain." *The Sixteenth Century Journal* 18 (1987): 557–87.

Netanyahu, Benzion. *The Origins of the Inquisition in Fifteenth-century Spain*. Random House, 1995.

Nirenberg, David. "Mass Conversion and Genealogical Mentalities: Jews and Christians in Fifteenth-Century Spain." *Past & Present* 174 (2002): 3–41.

Pérez, Joseph. *Historia de la brujería en España*. Espasa, 2010.

Sánchez Ortega, María Helena. "Sorcery and Eroticism in Love Magic." In Mary Elizabeth Perry and Anne J. Cruz, eds., *Cultural Encounters: The Impact of the Inquisition in Spain and the New World*. University of California Press 1991.

Sicroff, Albert A. *Les controverses des status de "pureté de sang" en Espagne du XVe au XVIIe siècle*. Didier, 1960.

Soyer, François. *Ambiguous Gender in Early Modern Spain and Portugal: Inquisitors, Doctors and the Transgression of Gender Norms*. Brill, 2012.

Tausiet, María. *Urban Magic in Early Modern Spain: Abracadabra Omnipotens*. Palgrave Macmillan, 2014.

Villa-Flores, Javier. "To Lose One's Soul: Blasphemy and Slavery in New Spain, 1596–1669." *Hispanic American Historical Review* 82 (2002): 435–68.

10

Texts

One of the most enduring visual representations of inquisitorial censorship, Pedro Berruguete's altarpiece painting *Santo Domingo y los albigenses* ("*Saint Dominic and the Albigensians*"), depicts a miraculous intervention that floats a volume of St. Dominic's writing above the fire that consumes Cathar texts. This work's association with the Spanish Inquisition is not a conflation by the popular imagination; this artwork was significant to this Inquisition. The panel hung in the Real Monasterio de Santo Tomás, the seat of Ávila's inquisitorial tribunal, where the first inquisitor-general, Tomás de Torquemada, supervised the production of the iconography for this Dominican monastery's church.[1]

When the Spanish Inquisition was established, the handwritten texts depicted in Berruguete's art – another version of the same scene shows the texts' handwritten leaves – were still the predominant means of textual circulation. In its early actions against texts, the Spanish Inquisition used a *modus operandi* similar to the one depicted in Berruguete's images: Religious texts in Hebrew were burned, as were books written in Arabic. One historian relates that the Inquisition routinely classified all Arabic-language texts as Qur'āns and burned them.[2]

But the spread of printing fundamentally changed the nature of textual transmission. The Spanish monarchy's institutions, including the Inquisition, had to react to this new technology. Based on the listings in the *Indices of Prohibited Books*, which beginning in 1584 also included texts to be expurgated, the Spanish Inquisition seems to be a formidable source of ideological control. However, the Inquisition's implementation of strictures regarding texts was flawed; personnel and authority were limited. Despite the Inquisition's efforts, prohibited texts were imported into the Spanish empire. Moreover, these proscriptions did not apply equally to all residents of Spain's territories. Some readers were licensed to consume prohibited texts. Evidence strongly suggests that some banned texts escaped the libraries of those authorized to own them to circulate among the general reading public.

Pre-Publication Censorship and the Inquisition

During the initial decades of the Spanish Inquisition's existence, there was no system in place to authorize the publication of texts. In 1502, the authority to license books printed in or imported into Castile was granted to the presidents of two high courts of appeal as well as bishops in five towns, not to the Inquisition. Admittedly, between 1520 and 1550, the Inquisition did license a few imprints. In 1558, regulations for pre-publication approvals became more stringent in the crown of Castile. (The crowns of Aragon and Navarre only respectively adopted this process in the early and late eighteenth century.) The Council of Castile designated reviewers who evaluated the text and, if they decided that the work could be printed, wrote endorsements that were included in the imprint. When inquisitorial functionaries issued these approvals, they listed their positions in the Inquisition, as Juan Ponce de León did in his *aprobación* to Luis Vélez de Guevara's novel *El diablo cojuelo*.[3]

Such individual actions belie the great Henry Charles Lea's assertion that the Inquisition astutely distanced itself from the licensing process to safeguard its "reputation for infallibility" if approved publications were later found to contain questionable content. The Inquisition's documents suggest a more mundane motive: the institution did not want to overstep its jurisdictional authority and encroach on that of other royal bureaucracies. As time passed, some suggested that the Inquisition should play a larger role in the pre-publication textual approval process. For example, when working on the 1612 Index of Prohibited Books, Diego Álvarez wrote that he wished that the Inquisition were charged with pre-publication textual approvals.[4]

The Inquisition and Textual Control

By 1540, the Inquisition commissioned bookstore visitors (*visitadores* in the Inquisition's terminology) to inspect bookstores in Madrid and Salamanca and thereafter in Alcalá de Henares to limit access to suspicious ideas. But correspondence from inquisitorial functionaries indicates that they lacked the resources necessary to carry out these tasks. In 1560, Master Vanegas wrote to seek redress for his work in inspecting books. In 1620, Juan de Miranda asked for a respite from his unrelenting workload and for more authority to better inspect bookstores in Madrid. In 1646 and 1647, Ponce de León requested help in expurgating books as he supervised the capital's bookstores. In 1652, the capital's bookstore visitors, Jerónimo Pardo and Juan Bautista Dávila, separately informed the Suprema that they needed more authority to curtail the circulation of prohibited and unexpurgated texts. These textual control responsibilities were incorporated into the existing bureaucracy. Some *visitadores* also were *calificadores*: Initially, such experts in theology or canon law evaluated testimonies from inquisitorial cases for unorthodox ideas. Their responsibilities expanded to include the assessment of circulating texts. Since the number of *calificadores* in each tribunal was limited to eight in the early seventeenth century, tribunals could not add additional *calificadores* as textual control responsibilities grew.[5]

Although inquisitorial functionaries sometimes discovered unknown texts at the border or at points of sale, the body generally did not search for texts to ban. Many works prohibited in Spain already were prohibited elsewhere. Beyond existing lists of prohibited works, the Inquisition asked the public to denounce suspicious texts. And the public did so. When an unknown text was denounced to the Inquisition, the Inquisition assigned *calificadores* to assess it. Occasionally, the Inquisition had to first locate a copy of a denounced work in order to have it evaluated, as happened with a prayer about our Lady of the Immaculate Conception in 1652. Other volumes needed no additional evaluation. When naval lieutenant Lorenzo Goycochea denounced a superior officer on the frigate *Santísima Trinidad* to the Inquisition in Cádiz in 1778, Goycochea alleged that Captain Francisco Javier Muñoz y Gossens possessed banned books in French by Voltaire and Rousseau that had never been inspected in customs.[6]

In addition to evaluating texts that came to its attention, the Inquisition was charged with preventing suspicious material from entering the Spanish empire. Although diplomatic agreements could exempt some vessels and certain individuals from inspection, in one expert's assessment, the inspection process at Spanish ports was "quite rigorous at least until the 1650s"; because this scholar's research focuses on scientific works, his assertion may be less applicable to other genres.[7] Still, many scientific and medical books were easy to target for additional scrutiny because they frequently contained diagrams and tables. Even an inquisitorial employee unfamiliar with the language in which the text was written would recognize these representations of data.[8] Such volumes may have been more thoroughly evaluated than other texts.

If the inspection of all types of printed matter was meticulous until circa 1650, the decline was rapid in Valencia. In 1651, Joseph Vicente del Olmo asserted that *calificadores* in that city either did not have sufficient knowledge of book prohibitions or they relied on lists provided by importers and neglected to check cargo for hidden texts.[9] Olmo admitted that prohibited material found its way into Spain and to booksellers. Despite Spanish interest in preventing the importation of radical texts from France, in 1792 an inquisitorial functionary working on the French border wrote to Madrid that he was the only staff member who knew French. Although the Inquisition discovered books concealed in trunks of used clothing and wig bags, customs officials were generally loath to open sealed containers during border inspection or to allow the Inquisition to do so. In 1793, the same functionary reported that customs officials removed him from inspecting goods, except for books.[10]

Spain was especially concerned about printed matter in the Americas where the importation of fiction, such as chivalric literature, was prohibited. Books traveling from Spain to the Americas were inspected in Spain and upon arrival. In 1569, when the Inquisition was authorized in the Americas, stopping the circulation of banned texts was part of its mission. These concerns never abated; commercial interests wanted to exploit the book market. In 1651, as peace between Spain and the Netherlands gave Dutch ships access to Hispanic ports, Juan Bautista Dávila reported that his information indicated these Dutch vessels would import prohibited volumes to the Americas. Dávila also was concerned that Samuel Arcerio, a Dutch bookseller resident in Madrid, had travelled to Cádiz to smuggle Dutch books into the Americas.[11] (Since there are two bookstore visitors with the surname Dávila, I use the given names Juan Bautista in the first mention of him in a paragraph and Dávila in subsequent ones. I refer to Antonio Dávila with his full name.)

Before delving further into the Inquisition's approach to textual censorship, we need to clarify what the institution considered to be a text. Although our twenty-first-century notion of textuality centers on the mechanically (or digitally) printed word, early modern Spain's conceptualization was broader. First, it included manuscripts, i.e. handwritten texts. As one scholar notes, because handwritten texts usually were discretely shared among acquaintances, this was the preferred format for the circulation of sensitive matters. Nonetheless, some handwritten texts were prohibited in indices. Second, textuality also encompassed oral production. The Inquisition assessed declaimed texts that were brought to its attention, including prayers and poems sung in the streets by visually challenged people in 1650, which were rife with false miracles and questionable doctrine; an "absurd *romance*" (a verse form with octosyllabic verses) sung by them in 1802, and sermons and various theological conclusions that were to be orally debated for lay audiences. In one such case in 1679, the Inquisition decided that one of the conclusions that the Jesuit *colegio* in Salamanca planned to defend was not outside of the norm.[12]

Finally, on occasion, the Inquisition also evaluated images, such as the prints of the seven deadly sins that were prohibited in 1660. In 1803, so too was the "magical lantern of love," a fan that, when backlit, revealed images of couples in various sexual positions. Although policing sensual images was not a significant focus of the Inquisition's efforts, one scholar has demonstrated that from 1814 to 1820, the Madrid tribunal doggedly attempted to suppress carnal imagery, thus contradicting the impression that the Inquisition languished in its final decades.[13]

Prohibitory and Expurgatory Indices

As printing became more commonplace, various institutions began to compile indices of banned texts. The Spanish Inquisition's first Index in

1551 merely appended some books in Spanish to the University of Louvain's Index. Readers who owned prohibited works were to turn them in to the Inquisition. In the following year, the Inquisition directed that only books by authors classified as heretical should be publicly burned. Prohibited works by Catholic authors were to be confiscated and stored in the inquisitorial tribunals.[14]

Following its first Index, from 1552 to 1554 the Inquisition censured and amended biblical translations and commentaries printed in Protestant hotspots, culminating in the emendation of sixty-five imprints of the Bible. After practicing Protestants were uncovered in Spain in 1557–8, the Inquisition reacted with a new Index. One historian calculates that almost two thirds of the texts prohibited in 1559 were Latin works published outside of Spain, but this Index also banned prominent texts written in Spanish, including a number of Spanish-language editions of Erasmus. (In 1612, his entire *œuvre* was banned in Spanish.) Most importantly, entire genres of religious works in Spanish that the laity used for private piety, including all translations of the Bible into vernacular languages, were prohibited. Popular printed spiritual books, such as Luis de Granada's *Libro de la oración*, were proscribed along with devotional manuscripts in Spanish, including Ignatius of Loyola's *Ejercicios espirituales*, which in 1559 had not yet been printed in Spanish.[15]

The goal of these broad prohibitions was to restrict access to spiritual materials to those who were educated enough to read Latin. Rather than read on their own and run the risk of committing religious errors, the less educated should depend on the clergy for spiritual advice. Since few women knew Latin, women interested in religious topics were particularly affected by these prohibitions. To fill the void left by the devotional texts proscribed in 1559, future saint Teresa de Jesús began writing spiritual texts in Spanish for her fellow nuns.[16]

The number of prohibited literary works in Spanish increased in 1559, including the poetry collection *Cancionero general* and the anonymous picaresque novel *Lazarillo de Tormes*. Although literature written in Spanish was relatively lightly affected until the eighteenth-century indices, scientific works were seriously affected in the seventeenth. Scholar Pardo Tomás determines that the largest numbers of scientific authors were prohibited in the indices between 1612 and 1640, seminal years for the publication of new scientific discoveries, followed by indices issued between 1584 and 1612.[17]

In 1584, the Spanish Inquisition published its first expurgatory Index. (This Index's prohibitions were published in 1583.) After Benito Arias Montano helped to compile the 1571 Antwerp Index, he brought the innovation of expurgation to Spain. In lieu of banning an entire text, expurgation removed problematic passages; however, this process introduced a new category of textual prohibition, withdrawal from circulation pending expurgation. Once the Inquisition issued expurgations, versions that made the requisite changes, whether via new editions or via obscuring the relevant passages in older ones, could licitly circulate. However, a temporary withdrawal could become a de facto permanent ban if the necessary expurgations were never issued. For example, Antonio de Torquemada's *Jardín de flores curiosas* was recalled pending expurgations in the 1632 Index, which it was still awaiting in 1873. Scholars have interpreted such oversights as a sign of the "inertia" and "complicated bureaucracy" of the Inquisition's censorial apparatus.[18]

Additional indices followed in 1612, 1632, and 1640, with supplements in 1614 and 1628. Although some studies refer to a 1667 Index, this is a reprinting of the 1640 Index, usually accompanied by the 1664 Roman Index. It seems clear that the sixty-seven-year gap between the Indices of 1640 and 1707 was a symptom of "lethargy" in the Inquisition's censorship practices. This institutional lassitude did not pass unnoticed by its functionaries, who struggled to learn about textual prohibitions made after 1640. During these years, the clerics who inspected bookstores in Madrid on behalf of the Inquisition consistently protested that neither they nor booksellers were informed of books that were prohibited by edicts. In 1645, Ponce de León complained about this point, as did Juan Bautista Dávila in 1653. In the latter case, the notation "You are to give him notice of the books that are being prohibited" conceded the veracity of this complaint. But in 1655, Dávila again made the same request. In 1661, Dávila and his fellow visitor Antonio Dávila jointly wrote to again ask to be informed about prohibitions by edict. They also warned that if they were unable to stop the circulation of prohibited printed matter, it was because of the lack of resources that they already had detailed in previous correspondence.[19]

The situation in Madrid reveals a systemic problem. If the Inquisition's *visitadores* in the capital were not informed of textual prohibitions and lacked sufficient support, those working in tribunals farther afield likely received even less. In point of fact, inquisitorial officials in Mexico repeatedly complained that they did not have sufficient copies of the indices.[20]

In the eighteenth and nineteenth centuries, indices were published in 1707, 1747, and 1790, with supplements in 1739 and 1805. In the later eighteenth century, indices and edicts banned specific French works that formed the ideological basis for the French Revolution and seditious texts in general. Once the Inquisition no longer played a role in censorship in Spain, Spanish bishops republished the Inquisition's prohibitions in 1844, a supplement in 1848 and, in 1873, prohibitions by the Inquisition along with episcopal prohibitions through 1872.[21]

Unfortunately for the study of the Inquisition's approach to textual censorship, the detailed criteria used to censor texts have not survived. Moreover, as one scholar has observed, censorship reports tend to be so highly idiosyncratic that it is difficult to extrapolate general operating principles from them.[22] We are therefore largely left with the listings of prohibited and expurgated texts in the indices. While the motives for the prohibition or expurgation of some texts are readily apparent, such is not always the case.

It seems possible that one could debate "almost any" topic in Latin without intervention by the Inquisition. For Spanish authors writing in Latin, this assertion can be broadened beyond the genre of the academic debate. (Jesús Martínez de Bujanda counts "some sixty" Latin texts by Spanish authors that were censured in Indices.)[23] But there is one important caveat. Tensions, either between individuals or religious orders, led to the prohibition of works by Spanish authors.

Even the process of compiling indices could be extremely contentious; the Roman Inquisition and the Congregation of the Index in Rome feuded, as did those working on indices in Spain. An important disagreement among Spanish clerics concerned the importance of the Vulgate Bible (the translation into Latin) versus biblical texts in their original languages. For example, when León de Castro, a University of Salamanca professor who staunchly defended the Vulgate, objected to the Antwerp Polyglot Bible prepared by Arias Montano, Juan de

Mariana assessed it. After Mariana did not concur with Castro's criticism of this Bible, other clerics took retribution by expurgating passages from Mariana's *Tractatus septem* in the 1612 Index, including his comment about the chilling effect that the Inquisition's prosecution of Luis de León had on Spanish intellectuals. Further expurgations were later made to other works by Mariana. One of Arias Montano's biblical commentaries also suffered expurgation in 1612; others were added in subsequent indices.[24] Such intellectual antipathy could become more vehement when mixed with anti-Semitism, as occurred with Castro's denunciation of *converso* colleagues at the University of Salamanca, including Luis de León, who was imprisoned by the Inquisition for nearly five years.[25]

Beyond scholarly circles or Latin texts, animus between Inquisitor-General Fernando de Valdés (along with Melchor Cano) and Archbishop Bartolomé de Carranza of Toledo resulted in Carranza's house arrest for sixteen years in Spain and Rome and the prohibition of his commentary on the catechism. Inquisitorial censor Juan de Pineda's enmities with Luis de Góngora and Francisco de Quevedo resulted in limits on the circulation of their works. Admittedly, Quevedo feuded with many and his political connections also brought negative attention to his texts, making the analysis of the censorship of his work "perhaps the most complicated" case of all, in one scholar's estimation. Ensuring that a rival's work appeared on an Index was an expedient way of dimming a reputation. In 1622, Alonso Maldonado, whom the Inquisition forced to abandon his planned public defense of his dating of Jesus's death to April 3, described this action as "a smear on my person and that of my habit [religious order]."[26]

Establishing such dates often employed sources considered controversial by the Inquisition, including Arabic astronomical observations. Any relationship between astronomical data, astrology, and human behavior or "fortune" was forbidden by rule 9 of the 1583 Index. In fact, any scientific observation, astronomical or otherwise, that could impinge on human free will resulted in the expurgation of such ideas, including content from medical works such as Juan Huarte de San Juan's *Examen de ingenios para las ciencias*. Huarte's book was one of seven medical works by Spanish authors that were expurgated between 1584 and 1707. Works by non-Catholic authors whose entire *œuvre* was banned constituted "more than 75 percent" of the 759 scientific texts prohibited between 1559 and 1707. When scientific works were to be expurgated, the texts did not always return to circulation. One historian has counted 122 scientific works in the 1632 Index that were prohibited pending expurgation that were never expurgated and therefore could not licitly circulate.[27]

The treatment of heliocentrism in Spain's indices is puzzling. As one scholar of the indices explains, Nicolaus Copernicus's *De revolutionibus orbium coelestium* was never banned. Although Copernicus's name was included in the list of prohibited authors at the beginning of the 1632 Index, his book was not banned in it. Surprisingly, this omission was not subsequently corrected.[28]

When historical and political works were prohibited or expurgated, they generally ran counter to the goals of the Spanish crown. In the case of Antonio Pérez, Philip II's secretary, scholarship concurs that the Inquisition's prosecution of Pérez was motivated by political intrigue. Pérez's proscribed *Relaciones*, which recounted his misadventures, nonetheless were found on the bookshelves of courtly notables, including Lorenzo Ramírez de Prado and Gregorio and Juan Antonio Mayans, who typically had licenses to read prohibited books.[29]

Spanish royal councils were so intent on supporting their monarch's legal positions that they defied book prohibitions from Rome. The treatment of Galileo Galilei's writing involved such political considerations. Scholars have theorized that Galilei's *Dialogo sopra i due massimi sistemi del mondo* was never banned in any Spanish Index because political circumstances favored the continued circulation of another work, *Notitiae Sicilensium ecclesiarum*, which was banned in the same Roman decree. The *Notitiae* defended the Spanish sovereign's legal right to intervene in ecclesiastical disputes in Sicily; endorsing the opposing view, the pope prohibited the *Notitae*. In order to allow an opinion favorable to the Spanish monarch to circulate, the Inquisition ignored the Roman decree. Moreover, the Inquisition was not the only Spanish royal council that chose not to promulgate a Roman prohibition when it suited Spanish interests. In 1647, a writ from the Council of Castile, in consultation with the Council of State, suspended Rome's prohibition pending expurgation of Juan de Solórzano Pereira's jurisprudence concerning Spain's American colonies because the Spanish crown affirmed the volume's assertions about the monarch's privileges to appoint bishops in the Americas.[30]

Fictional satires of the Catholic clergy typically were prohibited, as were the two parts of the *Historia del famoso predicador fray Gerundio de Campazas, alias Zotes*, pseudonymously published by José Francisco de Isla, in 1760 and 1776, and *Lazarillo de Tormes* in 1559. The expurgations made by Juan López de Velasco in the 1573 edition known as the *Lazarillo castigado* eliminated the Mercedarian friar's sexual exploits and the indulgence seller's deceptive sale tactics in their entirety. However, the gluttonous priest who underfeeds Lazarillo and the rumored affair between the Archpriest of San Salvador and Lazarillo's wife were not excised. Critiques of the clergy also survive in other genres, as in portions of Juan de Mal Lara's *Filosofía vulgar*. One expert has postulated that the cleric who issued the *Filosofía vulgar*'s pre-publication approval neglected to read the entire work. Such lack of attention is striking since the author, Mal Lara, had been detained by the Inquisition in 1561 because of his suspected authorship of anonymous anti-clerical poems.[31]

Sometimes the material that the Inquisition chose to expurgate is puzzling. According to the 1632 Index, Juan Pérez de Montalbán's short story "La mayor confusión" required expurgation. While the novella's incestuous plot line is left intact, Don Félix's discussions with religious authorities about what he should do once he learns that he is both the father and half-brother of his wife were expurgated.[32]

Beginning in the latter eighteenth century, indices became concerned with propriety, which led to expurgations of long-circulating works of fiction. Fernando de Rojas's text known as *La Celestina*, initially expurgated in the seventeenth century, was eventually prohibited in 1793. Liberal ideas and anti-clericalism, including critiques of the Inquisition, such as Leandro Fernández de Moratín's prohibited pseudonymous commentary on the 1610 *auto de fe* in Logroño, also were targeted.[33]

Catholic authors did not always accept any Inquisition's evaluations of their work, whether positive or negative. When the Roman Congregation of the Index considered censoring Juan Bautista Poza's treatise on Marian theology, *Elucidarium Deiparae*, Poza criticized the censorship system and proposed reforms. In 1628, after Luis de San

Alberto learned that his book *Escrutinio del corazón humano* had been withdrawn from circulation until it could be expurgated, he wrote to the Spanish Inquisition to request that he be allowed to consult with his text's censors so that he could remediate any inadvertent errors in it. San Alberto asserted that the Inquisition "owe[d]" him "this mercy" for his "zeal" in the service of the institution. A notation from the Suprema indicates that "there is no place for what he asks." Diego Niseno requested that the Spanish Inquisition expurgate a passage from his *Asuntos predicables* ..., even though the Inquisition's assessment had suggested adding an explanatory marginal note. The Index noted that the expurgation was the author's preference.[34]

Enforcement

The degree to which the Spanish populace supported the Inquisition lies outside of the scope of this chapter; we can say that people denounced suspicious books. But when the censorial actions of the Inquisition negatively affected people's interests, whether economic or intellectual, there was some resistance.

The Inquisition required booksellers to submit yearly inventory lists, but tensions arose between the Inquisition and booksellers in Madrid, who attempted to provide as little detail about their books as possible. In 1652, Madrid bookseller Lorenzo Sánchez appeared before Suprema member Tomás Rodríguez de Monroy because Sánchez's inventory was fifty days late and incomplete. When questioned about the prohibited books and others requiring expurgation in his shop, Sánchez offered a blasé response: "in such a large bookstore, it is no wonder that there may be some books in need of expurgation because the memory is fragile and one cannot have the entire expurgatory Index in one's head."[35]

The confiscation of prohibited texts represented an economic loss for book owners, as did expurgation. Initially, inquisitorial functionaries were expected to expurgate books, but the 1614 appendix specified that others could expurgate texts and bring them to the Inquisition for verification via a signature. In Mexico, several booksellers obtained licenses from the Inquisition to expurgate their stores and a university professor was granted expurgatory authority for his own library and those of his relatives.[36]

Imprints also demonstrate imperfect or untimely expurgations. One 1571 exemplar of Arias Montano's *Commentaria in duodecim prophetas*, which was to be expurgated according to the 1612 Index, was not expurgated until 1754, and the censor neglected to cross out the entirety of one passage. Another copy of the same edition was expurgated according to the 1612 Index in the 1620s. (The final digit is difficult to read in the digital version.) Additional undated notations affirm expurgations according to the 1640 and 1707 indices. A 1583 edition bears an undated annotation that it was expurgated according to the 1707 Index.[37]

In other works, passages that should be expurgated are marked, not rendered unreadable. Markings like this – and unexpurgated or prohibited books that circulated in Spain – likely are related to the fact that some readers could obtain licenses to consume prohibited books. Popes issued these licenses and starting in 1549, the Spanish Inquisition began to issue its own licenses so that select readers could consume prohibited texts for professional reasons, including theologians who countered non-Catholic ideas. Whereas most readers were granted licenses to consume specific texts for limited periods of time, less restrictive licenses were granted to affiliates of the Inquisition, other ecclesiastical officials, and important nobles. Although Inquisitor-General Antonio Zapata decided to suspend such licenses, his successor Antonio de Sotomayor resumed the practice. In the eighteenth century, some texts were prohibited even for readers with licenses. However, library inventories demonstrate that people nonetheless owned them, even when unrelated to professional needs. For example, the Mayans family's library includes a French novel and a book of satirical engravings, both prohibited even for license holders.[38]

When license holders died, the Inquisition was supposed to inspect their libraries before their sale to prevent prohibited texts from reaching the public at large. Heirs, however, were not eager to have valuable texts confiscated or expurgated.

In Madrid, unauthorized sales of private libraries were particularly problematic because so many court functionaries held licenses for prohibited books. In 1646, Ponce de León informed the Suprema that he would not accept bookseller Pedro Laso's list of volumes from the library purchased from Gonzalo de Córdoba's estate until Laso surrendered the prohibited and expurgatable works. (Without this assent from the Inquisition, Laso could not legally sell the books.) In 1650, Juan Bautista Dávila observed that a lawyer at court, Juan Calderón, had amassed a large book collection. In Dávila's assessment, Calderón, a "learned man, well born and pious, lets himself get carried away by curiosity, using extraordinary books, and even they whisper prohibited ones." Dávila wondered whether Calderón should be required to submit the same yearly list of his holdings that booksellers did. By 1653, Calderón had died and in April of that year, Dávila reported that Calderón's library had been sold for the third time to the bookseller Pedro García and that plans were afoot to quickly sell it due to "the sweet treat of exquisite and unseen books." The Inquisition intervened, and in the summer of 1653, Dávila related that he was comparing the list of Calderón's more than 1,000 volumes with the Index. In September of 1661 (after waiting eight years), the bookseller García conducted an unauthorized auction of Calderón's books. This sale was denounced by a purchaser who was surprised that the volume he bought had not been inspected by the Inquisition. When Antonio Dávila attempted to confiscate some prohibited books from the auction, Pedro Calvo, who married Calderón's widow, "violently" stopped Antonio Dávila's coach and threatened to cut the legs of the mules if the volumes were not returned to him. Calvo then snatched the books.[39]

While heated confrontation with an inquisitorial functionary in the street was unusual, the unauthorized sale of private libraries was less so. Following this 1661 incident, Antonio Dávila continued to investigate the sale of book collections without the requisite inquisitorial inspection in Madrid. Bookseller Juan Bautista Tavano testified under oath about private libraries that had been appraised by book professionals in the city as a first step to their sale. He himself admitted to conducting six of these valuations.[40]

A decade earlier, the Inquisition attempted to intervene in the sale of the library of the deceased royal chronicler José Antonio Salas, whose library contained some 250 books that were either prohibited or supposed to be expurgated. Despite orders to not sell the collection, the heirs sold half of the library's 2,424 volumes to various men at court. In 1653, a relative of Salas's widow, Pedro de la Escalera, a member of the Order of Calatrava, assured the Inquisition that what remained would be sold to "people of good conscience." In subsequent correspondence with Juan Bautista Dávila, Escalera noted that Gaspar Ibáñez, the nephew of the Inquisition's *comisario general*, had purchased some of the volumes in the initial round of sales.[41] Even the family of an inquisitorial official could not resist such texts.

Outside of seventeenth-century Madrid, others also chafed against the confiscation of prohibited books by the Inquisition upon the death of the reader licensed to consume them. In 1801, Teresa Vives de Cañamás, acting for her children, the grandchildren of Gregorio Mayans, argued that the Inquisition's confiscation of prohibited books from Gregorio and Juan Antonio Mayans' library would economically harm her children. She asked to be allowed to sell the volumes to the Calced Augustinian community in Valencia, which was licensed to have prohibited texts. The Inquisition's file does not contain a definitive resolution of this matter. While the Valencia tribunal ordered the confiscation of the books, its members suspected that Inquisitor-General Diego de Arce would allow their sale.[42]

Another episode offers insight into the process for granting licenses to read prohibited books. In an interview with the Inquisition, the Carmelite priest Francisco de Jesús y Jordá recalled that some years earlier the marchioness de Valle, Magdalena de Guzmán, wanted a license to keep a psalter in Spanish with "notes full of superstitions at the beginning of each psalm." The noble woman insisted so strenuously that she receive a license to read her psalter that the inquisitor-general acquiesced, blacked out the suspicious portions of the text, and returned it to her.[43]

The issue of Guzmán's psalter was uncovered in 1622 as the Inquisition investigated rumors about a vernacular language Bible in Madrid. In the case of this psalter, a subsequent interview revealed that the marchioness's legatee, her niece Ana de Mendoza, sent the volume away after hearing that women were not allowed to possess such texts. The recipient of the psalter, Andrés González, was a member of the Order of Minor Clerics: He testified that he had kept the book in his cell for some eight days, intending to bring it to the Inquisition. Other interviews uncovered several vernacular bibles in the possession of clerics with licenses to read them. But one person, Claudio Capillón, a servant in Jerónimo Courbes's bookstore, apparently brought a vernacular Bible to bookseller Juan de Morata's home. Since Capillón absented himself during the investigation, it seems likely that he was not authorized to own this prohibited Bible. (Capillón is rendered as Capallón in some documents.)[44]

Although the Inquisition prioritized the proscription of spiritual literature in the vernacular, it did not secure this Bible, nor another prohibited vernacular religious text. Beginning in February of 1651, Juan Bautista Dávila reported rumors to the Suprema that some booksellers had sold prohibited books, including a Qur'ān in French. In August of 1651, Dávila revealed that bookseller Baltasar Velero confessed to the sale of a vernacular-language Qur'ān. Dávila complained that since Velero was not punished for selling this volume, this incident offered "a perverse example for the rest who know about it." And the purchaser retained the copy of the Qur'ān.[45]

The expurgation of texts, the production of corrected editions, and efforts to confiscate prohibited works: Through these actions, the Spanish Inquisition sought to provide the Spanish reading public with doctrinally sound texts. However, this effort created opportunities for book professionals in other countries. Some historians have observed that Dutch printers earned the reputation for using other countries' listings of prohibited books as guides for future print runs, and that French printers did likewise. Analyses of errata and watermarks in paper prove that editions of José Francisco de Isla's prohibited novel ... *Fray Gerundio de Campazas* ... were printed in France.[46]

After reading these anecdotes, it would be easy to assume that readers could consume the texts that they wanted. For well-placed royal or ecclesiastical bureaucrats or nobles, this likely was close to reality. Yet the consequences could be serious if a reader without a license to read prohibited books was found in possession of them. The 1583 Index threatened excommunication to anyone holding banned books. During inquisitorial hearings, inquisitors frequently asked defendants if they could read and write. Some defendants who answered in the affirmative, such as Juan de Ceballos and the Franciscan friar Francisco de Torrijos, then were asked if they owned any prohibited books. In this legal context, those who had proscribed texts likely would be treated with more suspicion. For residents of the Americas, the consequences of sanction by the Inquisition could be particularly serious: They would face removal.[47]

Conclusion

Returning to this chapter's initial image of an inquisitorial book burning, a 1761 publication demonstrates the degree to which this act had become associated with the Inquisition. At the behest of the royal council, royal secretary José Antonio de Yarza explained that the Blessed Juan de Palafox y Mendoza's correspondence with Andrés de Rada had been burned outside Madrid's royal jail in 1759 because the volumes lacked the necessary printing licenses. There was no concern with their content.[48] As the monarchy lobbied for Palafox's canonization, Palafox's detractors no doubt were primed to interpret this book burning as an effort to impugn him. For the smear to be so credible that Yarza contradicted it in print, book burning had to have become synonymous with the Inquisition in the minds of Madrid's populace.

We can assess the impact of the Inquisition's censorship apparatus on particular texts. Some scholars point to the fact that some prohibited books have hardly any surviving exemplars, including Bartolomé de Torres Naharro's *Propalladia*, and note that some expurgated editions, such as the 1573 expurgated *Cancionero general*, proved so unpalatable to readers that the texts stopped circulating. The Inquisition's attention disrupted the circulation of *La Celestina*: It was not printed in Spain between 1633 and 1821. In one expert's analysis, inventories from 1634 of confiscated books in inquisitorial tribunals demonstrate that significant numbers of confiscated scientific works were not in fact prohibited. While some of these texts examined topics that were banned by the Inquisition's general rules, and some permitted texts likely were confused for prohibited titles by the same authors, there is no explanation as to why a number of medical, mathematical, geographical, and other scientific works were confiscated. Thus the Inquisition's impact on science extends beyond prohibited or expurgated titles.[49]

Furthermore, not all the Inquisition's effects are demonstrable through documentation. Authors who declined to circulate texts because of fear of inquisitorial recriminations generally did not document this fact. It is logical to assume that some authors in Spain made this choice, because those in similar situations did so. As experts note, René Descartes decided not to circulate his *Traité du monde ...*, and sixteenth-century Roman clerics did not print their texts after they observed others' negative experiences with censorship. Still, other scholars remain skeptical about this sort of "hidden damage" to Spanish letters.[50]

Beyond potential authorial self-censorship, scholarly opinion is divided about the overall effect of the Inquisition on Hispanic intellectual expression. Rather than the indices themselves, one historian believes that "systems of control" and "*formative* restrictions" constrained the intellectual climate. Another maintains that the Inquisition's strictures caused the decline of Spanish education and letters. In contrast, one Spanish scholar from the nineteenth century affirmed that Spanish literature flourished under the Inquisition; another from the twentieth century asserts that the linguistic innovation that characterizes seventeenth-century literature in Spanish developed because of the Inquisition's attention. Finally, one historian of science believes the Inquisition's censorship of scientific works in the lead-up to the Scientific Revolution stunted scientific research.[51]

Not all opinions about the impact of inquisitorial censorship are neutral assessments of the historical situation. During Francisco Franco's dictatorship, Antonio Sierra Corella praised the Inquisition's "high degree of surveillance of all intellectual activity" and thereby implicitly justified censorship.[52] As we have seen, the degree to which residents in Spain were affected by the Inquisition's textual regulations depended on their status, whether they were authors whose works were censured because of disputes, or well-positioned people with access to prohibited texts. In the final analysis, the diversity of opinions about the effects of the Inquisition's censorship signals a fruitful topic for further investigation.

Notes

1. Museo del Prado's text for Pedro Berruguete, *Santo Domingo y los albigenses,* www.museodelprado.es/en/the-collection/art-work/saint-dominic-and-the-albigensians/8159c487-73ed-48ba-be82-591b40b843ba.; Sonia Caballero Escamilla, "El convento de Santo Tomás de Ávila: Santo Tomás de Aquino, Santo Domingo de Guzmán y San Pedro Mártir, adalides de la propaganda inquisitorial," in Luis Ribot, Julio Valdeón, and Elena Maza, eds., *Isabel la católica y su época: Actas del Congreso Internacional Valladolid-Barcelona-Granada, 15 a 20 de noviembre de 2004,*

2 vols (Instituto Universitario de Historia Simancas, Universidad de Valladolid, 2007), 2: 1289–99. University of Kansas general research fund allocations 2166082 and 2301038 funded this archival research.
2. Berruguete, *La prueba del fuego*, www.museodelprado.es/coleccion/ obra-de-arte/la-prueba-del-fuego-santo-domingo-y-los-albigenses/ceda4 e10-2009-4cd2-bf94-ff2b75cf5c1d; Henry Kamen, *The Spanish Inquisition: A Historical Revision*, 4th edition (Yale University Press, 2014), 128–9, 162.
3. Kamen, *The Spanish Inquisition*, 118–19; María Marsá, *La imprenta en los siglos de oro (1520–1700)* (Laberinto, 2001), 24–7; see Adolfo Bonilla y San Martín's edition of *El diablo cojuelo*, 3v for the *aprobación*, archive.org/ details/eldiablocojuel00vluoft/page/2/mode/2up.
4. Henry Charles Lea, *A History of the Inquisition of Spain*, 4 volumes (Macmillan, 1906–7) 3:483; Archivo Histórico Nacional [AHN], Inquisición [Inq], Libro 1231, fols. 63v, 62v; Biblioteca Nacional de España [BNE], mss. 18.731/43 fols. 3–4, cited in Jesús Martínez de Bujanda, *El Índice de libros prohibidos y expurgados de la Inquisición española (1551–1819)* (Biblioteca de Autores Cristianos, 2016), 246.
5. AHN Inq. Libro [Lib]1279, fols. 172, 177 (1540); AHN Inq. Legajo [Leg] 4442, Number [Num] 25 (1560); AHN Inq. Leg. 4470 Num. 31 (1620, 1652); AHN Inq. Leg. 4470 Num. 30 (1646, 1647); Martínez de Bujanda, *Índice*, 239.
6. Kamen, *The Spanish Inquisition*, 131; AHN Inq. Leg. 4452 Num. 16 (Immaculate Conception); Antonio García-Molina Riquelme, "El navío Santísima Trinidad y la santa Inquisición," *Revista de historia naval* 31 (2013), 55–6.
7. All unattributed translations are mine.
8. José Pardo Tomás, *Ciencia y censura: La Inquisición española y los libros científicos en los siglos XVI y XVII* (CSIC, 1991), 32–3; see, for example, Galileo Galilei, *Dialogo di Galileo Galilei Linceo matematico sopraordinario dello stvdio di Pisa*, Fioreza, Gio Batista Landini, 1632, 4, catalog.lindahall.org/discovery/delivery/01LINDAHALL_INST:LHL/ 1291736690005961
9. I maintain original forms of names when I cannot determine whether to give a modern equivalent in Castilian or another peninsular language and in author's names in rare books.
10. AHN lnq. Leg. 4470 Num. 31 (1651); for a partial transcription of this document see Patricia W. Manning, *Voicing Dissent in Seventeenth-Century Spain: Inquisition, Social Criticism and Theology in the Case of El Criticón* (Brill, 2009), 69–70; AHN Inq. Leg. 4470 Num. 1 (1792, 1793).
11. Idalia García, "Los temibles ojos, oídos y brazos de la Inquisición: notas sobre la censura de libros en Nueva España entre los siglos XVII y XVIII," *Colonial Latin American Review* 28 (2019), 263; Pedro Vicente Sosa Llanos, "Persecución inquisitorial de los libros prohibidos en la Venezuela

colonial," *Revista de Historia de América* 139 (2008), 43; AHN Inq. Leg. 4470 Num. 31 (1651).
12. Fernando Bouza, *Corre manuscrito: Una historia cultural del siglo de oro* (Marcial Pons, 2001), 21, 63, 66–7; AHN Inq. Leg. 4470 Num. 31 (1650); AHN Inq. Leg. 4459 Num. 12 (1802); Martínez de Bujanda, *Índices*, 249; AHN Inq. Leg. 4480 Num. 8 (1679).
13. AHN Inq. Leg. 4470 Num. 10 (1660); AHN Inq. Leg. 4459 Num. 14 (1803); François Soyer, "The Inquisition and the Repression of Erotic and Pornographic Imagery in Early Nineteenth-Century Madrid," *History* 103 (2018), 62–4, 71–5.
14. Kamen, *The Spanish Inquisition*, 124; Jesús Martínez de Bujanda, "Índices de libros prohibidos del siglo XVI," in Joaquín Pérez Villanueva and Bartolomé Escandell Bonet, eds., *Historia de la Inquisición en España y América* Vol. 3 (Biblioteca de Autores Cristianos, Centro de Estudios Inquisitoriales, 2000), 787.
15. Kamen, *The Spanish Inquisition*, 124–8.
16. Kamen, *The Spanish Inquisition*, 128; Gillian T. W. Ahlgren, *Teresa of Ávila and the Politics of Sanctity* (Cornell University Press, 1996), 20, 23.
17. Kamen, *The Spanish Inquisition*, 126; Pardo Tomás, *Ciencia*, 104–5.
18. Kamen, *The Spanish Inquisition*, 129; see María José Vega, "Reading under Surveillance: Arias Montano and the Invention of the Expurgatory Index," in Rodrigo Cacho Casal and Caroline Egan, eds., *The Routledge Hispanic Studies Companion to Early Modern Spanish Literature and Culture* (Routledge, 2022), 107–23; for more about the Antwerp Index, Antonio Márquez, *Literatura e Inquisición en España (1478–1834)* (Taurus, 1980), 169–70, 183.
19. Martínez de Bujanda, *Índice*, xvi–xviii; Pardo Tomás, *Ciencia*, 104; AHN Inq. Leg. 4470 nums. 30 (1645), 31 (1653, 1655, 1661).
20. Archivo General de la Nación de México [AGN], Indiferente virreinal, caja 5486, exp. 10, AHN Lib. 1053, AGN Inq. 763, exp. 2 cited in García, "Temibles," 265, 275.
21. Martínez de Bujanda, *Índice*, xvii, xix, 198, 208, 233.
22. Ángel Alcalá, *Literatura y ciencia ante la Inquisición española* (Laberinto, 2001), 15.
23. Márquez, *Literatura*, 178; Martínez de Bujanda, *Índice*, 248.
24. Alcalá, *Literatura*, 70–2; see Kimberly Lynn, "Spanish Inquisitors, Print, and the Problem of Publication," in Kimberly Lynn and Erin Kathleen Rowe, eds., *The Early Modern Hispanic World: Transnational and Interdisciplinary Approaches* (Cambridge University Press, 2017) 242 for examples of feuds; Martínez de Bujanda, "Índices," 3:814; Martínez de Bujanda, *Índices*, 298, 771–2; Ángel Alcalá, "El control inquisitorial de intelectuales en el siglo de oro. De Nebrija al 'Índice' de Sotomayor de 1640," *Historia de la Inquisición*, 3:926–8.
25. Kamen, *The Spanish Inquisition*, 140–2.

26. Kamen, *The Spanish Inquisition*, 127, 208-11; Alcalá, *Literatura*, 117-21, 130-4; Márquez, *Literatura*, 161; AHN Inq. Leg. 4467 Num. 22 (1622).
27. See Martínez de Bujanda, "Índices," 3:817-19 for these rules; Alcalá, *Literatura*, 160, 168, 173; Pardo Tomás, *Ciencia*, 211-13, 106, 121.
28. Martínez de Bujanda, *Índice*, 125-6.
29. Márquez, *Literatura*, 98; Alcalá, *Literatura*, 138; AHN Inq. Leg. 4470 Num. 11 (Ramírez de Prado); Antonio Astorgano Abajo, "La venta de los libros prohibidos de la biblioteca mayansiana (1801)," in Antonio Mestre Sanchis, ed., *Actas del congreso internacional sobre Gregorio Mayans. Valencia-Oliva, 6 al 8 de mayo de 1999* (Ayuntamiento de Oliva, 1999), 650.
30. Pardo Tomás, *Ciencia*, 186-9; Martínez de Bujanda, *Índice* lists the texts prohibited by the Spanish Inquisition; Fermín de los Reyes Gómez, ed., "Cédula," *El libro en España y América: Legislación y censura (siglos XV-XVIII)*, 2 volumes (Arco, 2000) 2:875-6.
31. *Vida del Lazarillo de Tormes castigado, o Lazarillo de la Inquisición*, ed. Gonzalo Santonja (España Nuevo Milenio, 2000), 43-52, 68-71; Otis H. Green, *Spain and the Western Tradition: The Castilian Mind in Literature from El Cid to Calderón*, 4 volumes (The University of Wisconsin Press, 1963-6) 4:160-1.
32. *Novvs index librorvm prohibitorvm et expvrgatorvm*, Sevilla, Francisco de Lyra, 1632, 705, archive.org/details/A295133/page/n5/mode/2up.
33. Alcalá, *Literatura*, 179-83, 97-9, 185-9, 140.
34. See Manuel Peña Díaz, *Escribir y prohibir. Inquisición y censura en los siglos de oro* (Cátedra, 2015) 62-72 for details about Poza; AHN Inq. Leg. 4467 Num. 5 (1628); AHN Inq. Leg. 4444 Num. 20 (Niseno).
35. AHN Inq. Leg. 4470 Num. 31.
36. Martínez de Bujanda, *Índice*, 100; see Elspeth Healey, "Banned Books Week: Redacted for the Inquisition," *Inside Spencer: The KSRL Blog*, blogs.lib.ku.edu/spencer/tag/inquisition/ for a Dante volume with signatures confirming expurgations; AGN Inq. 438 Exp. 30, 825. Exp. 3, Indiferente Virreinal, Caja 5271, Exp. 44 cited in García, "Temibles," 266, 271, 275, 276.
37. Benedicti Ariæ Montani, *Commentaria in dvodecim prophetas*, Antwerpiæ, Christophori Plantini, 1571, handwritten annotation, 173-4 (BNE R/39.124); handwritten annotations in Arias Montano, *Commentaria in dvodecim prophetas*, Antwerpiæ, Christophori Plantini, 1571 (BNE 7/13.226), bdh-rd.bne.es/viewer.vm?id=0000230521&page=; handwritten annotation in Arias Montano, *Commentaria in dvodecim prophetas*, Antwerpiæ, Christophori Plantini, 1583 (BNE 2/37.123), bdh-rd.bne.es/viewer.vm?id=0000263798&page=1.
38. See Vega, "Reading," 109 for an example of a marked passage; Pardo Tomás, *Ciencia*, 41, 306-7, 42; Astorgano Abajo, "Venta," 649, 650-1.
39. AHN Inq. Leg. 4470 Num. 30 (1646); AHN Inq. Leg. 4470 Num. 31 (1650, 1653, 1661).

40. AHN Inq. Leg. 4470 Num. 31.
41. AHN Inq. Leg. 4470 Num. 3.
42. Astorgano Abajo, "Venta," 626–7, 631, 640–1.
43. AHN Inq. Leg. 4470 Num. 2; see Sergio Fernández López, "Algo más sobre la supuesta biblia de Alba: El hebraísta Pedro de Palencia interrogado por la Inquisición," *Etiópicas*, 4 (2008): 162–4 for a transcription of Jordá's interview.
44. AHN Inq. Leg. 4470 Num. 2.
45. AHN Inq. Leg. 4470 Num. 31.
46. Henri-Jean Martin, *The French Book: Religion, Absolutism, and Readership, 1585–1715*, trans. Paul and Nadine Saenger (The Johns Hopkins University Press, 1996), 67; José Jurado, "Ediciones tempranas de *Fray Gerundio de Campazas*," *Bulletin Hispanique* 87 (1985): 139–40, 145, 147n34, 152–4.
47. Martínez de Bujanda, "Índices," 3:816–17; AHN Inq. Leg. 33 Num. 35 fol. 14r. (Ceballos), Leg. 234 Num. 5 fol. 118v (Torrijos); Leyes de Indias 10, tít. 19, libro 1 cited in José Toribio Medina, *Ensayos* (Editorial del Pacífico, 1952), 132.
48. Joseph Antonio de Yarza, "D[on] Joseph Antonio de Yarza, Secretario del Rey nuestro Señor, su Escrivano de Camara mas antiguo, y de Govierno del Consejo, certifico, que los Señores de èl se diò y proveyò el Auto del tenor siguiente," [Madrid], Antonio Sanz, [1761?], [1], [2], bibliotecadigital.jcyl.es/es/consulta/registro.do?id=4005.
49. Rodríguez-Moñino, *Poesía*, 78 cited in Márquez, *Literatura*, 173; Martínez de Bujanda, *Índice*, 121; Pardo Tomás, *Ciencia*, 322–6, 346.
50. Martínez de Bujanda, *Índice*, 252–3; Fragnito, "Central," 48–9 cited in Lynn, *Spanish*, 242; Kamen, *The Spanish Inquisition*, 152.
51. Kamen, *The Spanish Inquisition*, 133; Lea, *Spanish Inquisition*, 4:528; Marcelino Menéndez Pelayo, *Historia de los heterodoxos españoles*, 2nd edition, ed. Enrique Sánchez Reyes, 8 volumes (CSIC, 1965) 4:438–40; Ciriaco Morón Arroyo, "La Inquisición y la posibilidad de la gran literatura barroca española," in Ángel Alcalá, ed., *Inquisición española y mentalidad inquisitorial* (Ariel, 1984), 317–18; Pardo Tomás, *Ciencia*, 346–7.
52. Antonio Sierra Corella, *La censura de libros y papeles en España y los Índices y catálogos españoles de los prohibidos y expurgados* (Cuerpo Facultativo de Archiveros, Bibliotecarios y Arqueólogos, 1947), 9.

Suggestions for Further Reading

Homza, Lu Ann, ed. and trans. *The Spanish Inquisition, 1478–1614: An Anthology of Sources*. Hackett, 2006.
Vega Ramos, María José, ed. *Malos libros. La censura en la España moderna*. Biblioteca Nacional de España, 2023.
Vílchez Díaz, Alfredo, *Autores anónimos españoles en los Índices inquisitoriales*. Universidad Complutense, 1986.

Bibliography

Ahlgren, Gillian T. W. *Teresa of Ávila and the Politics of Sanctity.* Cornell University Press, 1996.

Alcalá, Ángel. "El control inquisitorial de intelectuales en el siglo de oro. De Nebrija al 'Índice' de Sotomayor de 1640." In Joaquín Pérez Villanueva and Bartolomé Escandell Bonet, eds., *Historia de la Inquisición en España y América* Vol. 3. Biblioteca de Autores Cristianos/Centro de Estudios Inquisitoriales, 2000.

Literatura y ciencia ante la Inquisición española. Laberinto, 2001.

Astorgano Abajo, Antonio. "La venta de los libros prohibidos de la biblioteca mayansiana (1801)." In Antonio Mestre Sanchis, ed., *Actas del congreso internacional sobre Gregorio Mayans: Valencia-Oliva, 6 al 8 de mayo de 1999.* Ayuntamiento de Oliva, 1999.

Bouza, Fernando. *Corre manuscrito: Una historia cultural del siglo de oro.* Marcial Pons, 2001.

Caballero Escamilla, Sonia. "El convento de Santo Tomás de Ávila: Santo Tomás de Aquino, Santo Domingo de Guzmán y San Pedro Mártir, adalides de la propaganda inquisitorial." In Luis Ribot, Julio Valdeón, Elena Maza, eds., *Isabel la católica y su época: Actas del Congreso Internacional Valladolid-Barcelona-Granada, 15 a 20 de noviembre de 2004.* 2 volumes. Instituto Universitario de Historia Simancas & Universidad de Valladolid, 2007.

García, Idalia. "Los temibles ojos, oídos y brazos de la Inquisición: Notas sobre la censura de libros en Nueva España entre los siglos XVII y XVIII." *Colonial Latin American Review,* 28 (2019): 258–80.

García-Molina Riquelme, Antonio. "El navío Santísima Trinidad y la santa Inquisición." *Revista de historia naval* 31 (2013), 55–67.

Green, Otis H. *Spain and the Western Tradition: The Castilian Mind in Literature from El Cid to Calderón.* 4 volumes. The University of Wisconsin Press, 1963–6.

Jurado, José. "Ediciones tempranas de *Fray Gerundio de Campazas.*" *Bulletin Hispanique* 87 (1985): 137–65.

Kamen, Henry. *The Spanish Inquisition: A Historical Revision.* 4th edition. Yale University Press, 2014.

Lea, Henry Charles. *A History of the Inquisition of Spain.* 4 volumes. Macmillan, 1906–7.

Lynn, Kimberly. "Spanish Inquisitors, Print, and the Problem of Publication." In Kimberly Lynn and Erin Kathleen Rowe, eds., *The Early Modern Hispanic World: Transnational and Interdisciplinary Approaches.* Cambridge University Press, 2017.

Manning, Patricia W. *Voicing Dissent in Seventeenth-Century Spain: Inquisition, Social Criticism and Theology in the Case of El Criticón.* Brill, 2009.

Márquez, Antonio. *Literatura e Inquisición en España (1478-1834)*. Taurus, 1980.

Martin, Henri-Jean. *The French Book: Religion, Absolutism, and Readership, 1585-1715*. Trans. Paul and Nadine Saenger. The Johns Hopkins University Press, 1996.

Martínez de Bujanda, Jesús. "Índices de libros prohibidos del siglo XVI." In Joaquín Pérez Villanueva and Bartolomé Escandell Bonet, eds., *Historia de la Inquisición en España y América* Vol. 3. Biblioteca de Autores Cristianos/Centro de Estudios Inquisitoriales, 2000.

—. *El Índice de libros prohibidos y expurgados de la Inquisición española (1551-1819)*. Biblioteca de Autores Cristianos, 2016.

Menéndez Pelayo, Marcelino. *Historia de los heterodoxos españoles*. Ed. Enrique Sánchez Reyes. 2nd edition. Volume 4. CSIC, 2008.

Morón Arroyo, Ciriaco. "La Inquisición y la posibilidad de la gran literatura barroca española." In Ángel Alcalá., ed., *Inquisición española y mentalidad inquisitorial*. Ariel, 1984.

Pardo Tomás, José. *Ciencia y censura: La Inquisición española y los libros científicos en los siglos XVI y XVII*. CSIC, 1991.

Peña Díaz, Manuel. *Escribir y prohibir: Inquisición y censura en los siglos de oro*. Cátedra, 2015.

Reyes Gómez, Fermín de los. "*Cédula,*" *El libro en España y América: Legislación y censura (siglos XV-XVIII)*. 2 volumes. Editorial Arco, 2000.

Sierra Corella, Antonio. *La censura de libros y papeles en España y los Índices y catálogos españoles de los prohibidos y expurgados*. Cuerpo Facultativo de Archiveros, Bibliotecarios y Arqueólogos, 1947.

Sosa Llanos, Pedro Vicente. "Persecución inquisitorial de los libros prohibidos en la Venezuela colonial." *Revista de Historia de América* 139 (2008): 39-60.

Vega, María José. "Reading under Surveillance: Arias Montano and the Invention of the Expurgatory Index." In Rodrigo Cacho Casal and Caroline Egan, eds., *The Routledge Hispanic Studies Companion to Early Modern Spanish Literature and Culture*. Routledge, 2022.

Vida del Lazarillo de Tormes castigadoo Lazarillo de la Inquisición. Ed. Gonzalo Santonja. Nuevo Milenio, 2000.

Part III

Geographical Reach

MARINA TORRES ARCE
TRANSLATED BY LU ANN HOMZA

11

Sicily

Sicily was a complex environment for an inquisition.[1] A large island in the central Mediterranean, and a kingdom incorporated into the Crown of Aragon since the end of the thirteenth century, it had powerful barons and an important network of cities that answered to royal or seignorial dominion. King Ferdinand II of Aragon established an inquisition tribunal there – "of the Spanish sort" – in 1487. Yet the Inquisition in Sicily did not begin to function in a consistent way until 1500, when its tribunal was installed in Palermo, seat of the viceregal court and of the main courts of the kingdom.[2] Its location was not entirely stable, because Palermo and Messina had disputed which should be Sicily's capital for centuries. In 1503, King Ferdinand ordered that there should be a place in Messina to host the inquisitorial tribunal when it moved to that city, and yet the tribunal was not transferred. In 1591, King Philip II granted Messina the right to be the official seat of the viceregal court for eighteen months, and an inquisitor moved there as well.

Nevertheless, from 1500 until 1600, the inquisitors, their officers, and their trial defendants generally occupied different buildings across the urban space of Palermo, in a journey that reflected the difficult process of inserting the Inquisition into both the juridical-institutional framework of the kingdom and its social fabric. Finally, in 1600, the court was installed in the imposing palace of the Chiaramonte family, known as Steri and located in Piazza Marina in Palermo.[3] It remained there until 1782 when it was abolished by Domenico Caracciolo, viceroy of Ferdinand I of the Two Sicilies.

The inquisitors' activity in Sicily resulted in more than 6,000 sentences, though undoubtedly many more people were the object of their attention. In conformity with its mission in other territories of the Spanish crown, the tribunal's objective in Sicily was to uncover heresy and apostasy in order to protect the integrity of Catholicism, preserve religious unity, and thereby ensure procure social cohesion and peace. As was the case in other locations, Sicily's inquisitors targeted first and foremost conversos who allegedly continued to practice Judaism. However, their geographical location gave them special concerns. Sicily was a territory through which people passed; it was a space for the circulation of individuals, goods, and ideas. As a result, the island's inquisition tribunal had a particular responsibility as the last bastion of Catholicism in the Mediterranean.

The Royal General Council of the Inquisition, called the Suprema, was well aware of the multiple threats that Sicily might pose, as were Spanish monarchs. The inquisitors there reported:

> this kingdom is located in the middle of the Mediterranean Sea, having on the East the provinces of Greece, which are schismatic . . . On the south side it has Africa, whose natives, besides being Muslims, abound in all kinds of superstitions . . . To the north, it has the Kingdom of Naples and with the other kingdoms contiguous to it which have no inquisition, such as Venice, Germany and Romania, where so many synagogues are founded and where so many heretics congregate on account of commerce and easy communication with this kingdom . . . . Furthermore, this kingdom of Sicily is very suitable for trade because of its abundance of silk, wheat, wine and oil, and because it is, as we have said, in the middle of the sea near the three parts of the world, Asia, Africa and Europe. If there was no Inquisition in it, and its ministers were not supported with respect and veneration, it is very certain that Christianity would lose this kingdom . . .[4]

According to Sicily's inquisitors, the kingdom faced dangers not only from the outside but from within as well, given that residents there were fond of novelty. In this land of frontiers and restless people, the tribunal was defined as "a very strong wall that defends [the kingdom] from the invasion of heretics and keeps it under the obedience of the Church and Your Majesty."[5]

As a result of these multiple responsibilities, Sicily's inquisitors attempted to control the movement of people, ideas, and foreign merchandise. They or their agents visited ships in the ports; they watched over the Jewish, Greek, Albanian, and other foreign communities that lived there. But their tribunal was also supposed to ensure that the beliefs, practices, and behavior of all the Christians in the kingdom were in line with Catholic orthodoxy and morality. This would theoretically guarantee not only religious cohesion but also the tranquility of the inhabitants and thus the "conservation of the kingdom" in the Spanish monarchy. As was the case in other locations, this last major commitment involved the Sicilian tribunal in efforts at social control in spheres that were wholly political.

In the early modern period, Spain had a composite or polycentric monarchy: Its kingdoms preserved their own laws, privileges, and institutions. Sicily was no exception, but as was the case in other Spanish territories, the Inquisition had a superior and universal jurisdiction. It was the only Spanish institution with the capacity to act independently and intervene in domains where other jurisdictions and other authorities, including the royal one, found limitations. This ability to supersede had two conflicting effects: Early on, it provoked criticism and opposition in the kingdom, but it also strengthened the relevance of the Inquisition for the Spanish religious and imperial project in Sicily. Ultimately, the theoretical and legal autonomy of Sicily's inquisitors justified kings and popes granting them greater preeminence than other officers and authorities. The inquisitors there also were granted more extensive privileges and immunities than their counterparts in other territories.

None of these circumstances, however, meant that the Spanish Inquisition in Sicily functioned easily. Rather, its tribunal was in continuous conflict with other courts, institutions, and powers of the kingdom over its autonomy and preeminence. Sicily's inquisitors were affected by the political, social, and economic characteristics of the island: The configuration of their tribunal, their activities, and their institutional trajectory had to take into account the local environment. The history of the Sicilian Inquisition shows the institution's ability to adapt to particular social and institutional contexts and to changing political situations. But it also reveals dissidence and resistance to the model of confessional society that the inquisitorial institution represented and promoted. How all this came about is the subject of this chapter.

The Inquisition *al modo di Spagna* in the Kingdom of Sicily

In January of 1698 the inquisitors of Palermo received word from Madrid about their new work calendar (Figure 11.1). The amended layout was a response to concerns expressed by the inquisitor-general and the Suprema over the absenteeism, abuses, and enormous delays in the resolution of trials that were afflicting the tribunal in Palermo.[6] This was not the first time that the hours and days of work in Palermo had been regulated, nor were the problems to which the leadership alluded at all new.

While the tribunal was supposed to function correctly – to work for "service of God and the King, to the good of the Holy Office, to its greater credit, authority and esteem, to public peace and tranquility and to the administration of justice" – the reality was different.[7] Instead, irregularities in trial procedures in the causes of faith, in the titles for court personnel, and in economic management were the order of the day. There were denunciations and complaints about the number and competence of officers and district servants, as well as the abusive application of the inquisitorial legal jurisdiction. All these problems gave rise to criticism and tensions around the tribunal in Palermo. The inquisition leadership in Madrid attempted to supervise and regulate their far-flung employees, whether by means of instructions, decrees, or, extraordinarily, inspections.

The inquisition tribunal usually could count on having the following personnel. The inquisitors numbered two or three. They were assisted by a prosecutor, a bailiff to make arrests, and five notaries, four *del secreto*, who took down witness testimony, and one who recorded the sequestration of property. There was also an official to receive the sequestered property, with his assistant and an accountant. There was a warden for the tribunal's secret prison, a messenger, and one or two porters; they were accompanied by lawyers who took care of the tribunal's treasury. Finally, the Palermo tribunal had a tax lawyer, a master notary and a receiver for the "civil and criminal court outside the principle of secrecy and legal matters," up to four lawyers for the defendants, a doctor, a surgeon, an apothecary, a barber, and two chaplains.

From 1500 to 1713, practically all the inquisitors of Palermo were jurists of Castilian or Aragonese origin, as were almost always the

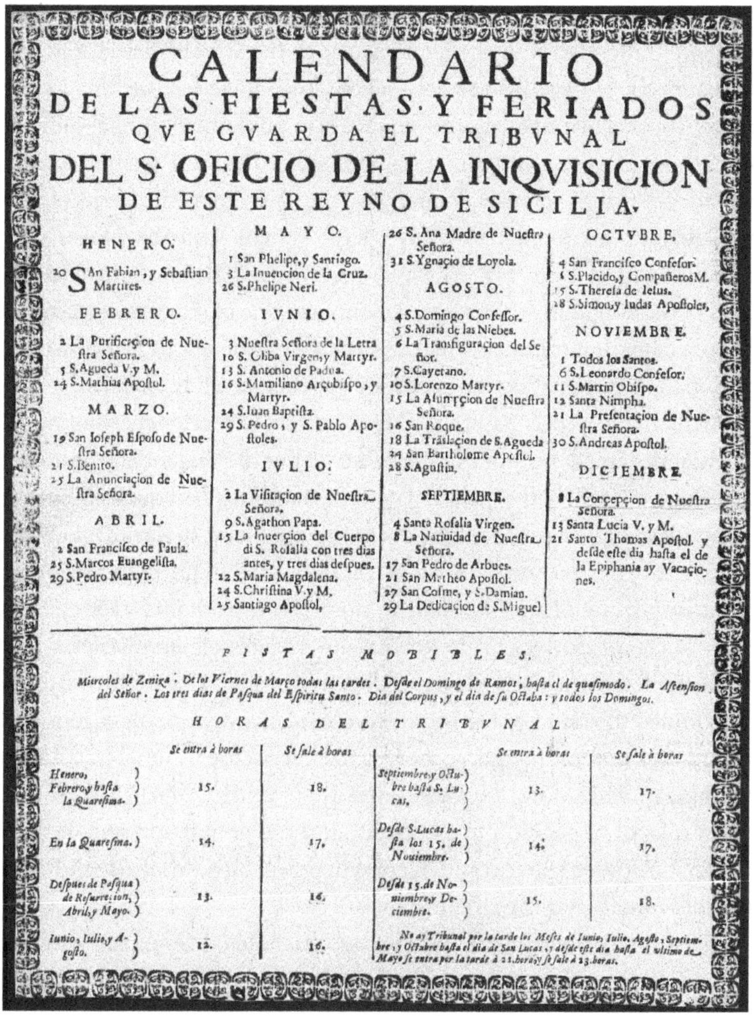

CALENDARIO
DE LAS FIESTAS Y FERIADOS
QVE GVARDA EL TRIBVNAL
DEL S. OFICIO DE LA INQVISICION
DE ESTE REYNO DE SICILIA.

HENERO.

20 SAn Fabian, y Sebaſtian Martires.

FEBRERO.

2 La Purificaçion de Nueſtra Señora.
5 S.Agueda V.y M.
24 S.Mathias Apoſtol.

MARZO.

19 San Ioſeph Eſpoſo de Nueſtra Señora.
21 S.Benito.
25 La Anunciaçion de Nueſtra Señora.

ABRIL.

2 San Franciſco de Paula.
25 S.Marcos Euangeliſta.
29 S.Pedro Martyr.

MAYO.

1 San Phelipe, y Santiago.
3 La Inuencion de la Cruz.
26 S.Phelipe Neri.

IVNIO.

3 Nueſtra Señora de la Letra
10 S. Oliba Virgen, y Martyr.
13 S. Antonio de Padua.
16 S.Mamiliano Arçobiſpo, y Martyr.
24 S.Iuan Baptiſta.
29 S. Pedro, y S. Pablo Apoſtoles.

IVLIO.

2 La Viſitaçion de Nueſtra Señora.
9 S.Agathon Papa.
15 La Inuerçion del Cuerpo di S. Roſalia con tres dias antes, y tres dias deſpues.
22 S.Maria Magdalena.
24 S.Chriſtina V.y M.
25 Santiago Apoſtol.
26 S. Ana Madre de Nueſtra Señora.
31 S.Ygnaçio de Loyola.

AGOSTO.

4 S.Domingo Confeſſor.
5 S.Maria de las Niebes.
6 La Transfiguraçion del Señor.
7 S.Cayetano.
10 S.Lorenzo Martyr.
15 La Aſumpçion de Nueſtra Señora.
16 San Roque.
18 La Träslaçion de S.Agueda
24 San Bartholome Apoſtol.
28 S.Aguſtin.

SEPTIEMBRE.

4 Santa Roſalia Virgen.
8 La Natiuidad de Nueſtra Señora.
17 San Pedro de Arbues.
21 San Matheo Apoſtol.
27 San Coſme, y S.Damian.
29 La Dedicaçion de S.Miguel

OCTVBRE.

4 San Franciſco Confeſor.
5 S.Placido, y CompañerosM.
15 S.Thereſa de Ieſus.
28 S.Simon, y Iudas Apoſtoles.

NOVIEMBRE.

1 Todos los Santos.
6 S.Leonardo Confeſor.
11 S.Martin Obiſpo.
12 Santa Nimpha.
21 La Preſentaçion de Nueſtra Señora.
30 S.Andreas Apoſtol.

DICIEMBRE.

8 La Conçepçion de Nueſtra Señora.
13 Santa Lucia V. y M.
21 Santo Thomas Apoſtol. y deſde eſte dia haſta el de la Epiphania ay Vacaçiones.

FISTAS MOBIBLES.

Miercoles de Zeniza. De los Viernes de Março todas las tardes. Deſde el Domingo de Ramos, haſta el de quaſimodo. La Aſcenſion del Señor. Los tres dias de Paſqua del Eſpiritu Santo. Dia del Corpus, y el dia de ſu Octaba: y todos los Domingos.

HORAS DEL TRIBVNAL

	Se entra à horas	*Se ſale à horas*		*Se entra à horas*	*Se ſale à horas*
Henero, Febrero, y haſta la Quareſima.	15.	18.	*Septiembre, y Octubre haſta S. Lucas.*	13.	17.
En la Quareſma.	14.	17.	*Deſde S.Lucas haſta los 15. de Nouiembre.*	14.	17.
Deſpues de Paſqua de Reſurreçion, Abril, y Mayo.	13.	16.	*Deſde 15. de Noviembre, y Deciembre.*	15.	18.
Iunio, Iulio, y Agoſto.	12.	16.			

No ay Tribunal por la tarde los Meſes de Iunio, Iulio, Agoſto, Septiembre, y Octubre haſta el dia de San Lucas, y deſde eſte dia haſta el ultimo de Mayo ſe entra por la tarde à 21.horas, y ſe ſale à 23.horas.

Figure 11.1 Calendar of the court of Sicily between 1623 and 1698. Source: AHN, Madrid, Inq, Leg. 2298, Palermo 28/8/1698.[8]

notaries *del secreto*. The Inquisition preferred to staff its court in Sicily with Spanish men or men from families of Spanish origin, although it was not uncommon for them to become naturalized as Sicilians through marriage or prolonged stays in the kingdom.

The Spanish origin of inquisitors and officials was considered a guarantee of independence in the kingdom and loyalty to the monarchy.

But at the same time it was a problem. Judges and officials often arrived without knowledge of the Italian language or the Sicilian dialect, and had no connections in Sicilian society, all of which impeded the functioning of the court. Their Spanish provenance also posed institutional difficulties. As was the case with other autonomous Aragonese territories integrated into the Spanish monarchy, the fact that the inquisitorial jurisdiction was foreign to Sicily's legal system, and the judges who administered it were not Sicilians, contravened the custom and the laws of the kingdom. That contravention was one of the main arguments for opposing the tribunal, which could be considered an instrument of domination imposed on the kingdom by the Spanish monarchy.[9]

Sicilians, as well as naturalized foreigners and foreigners residing on the island, gained positions in the tribunal, but they essentially occupied positions related to the treasury or other, minor posts such as porter, messenger, defendant's lawyer, doctor or chaplain. It was through the titles of district servants – such as captains or bailiffs, commissioners (*comisarios*), familiars (*familiares*), notaries, consultants over charges or verdicts, or porters in the towns and villages of the district – that Sicilians became tied en masse to the Inquisition. The profile of those who joined the ranks of the Inquisition in Sicily was heterogeneous and varied over time, although, according to experts, the tribunal was always strongly rooted among the middle and upper ranks of the urban groups. The ranks of opposition to the court, and the population sectors with which it disputed spheres and degrees of power also varied according to the individuals and the circumstances.

The urban governments and the parliament led the opposition to the Spanish Inquisition as soon as it was installed. (The parliament was the assembly that guarded the privileges of the kingdom, in which three branches were represented: the military, composed of nobles with fiefs; cities answerable to the crown; and ecclesiastics.) They presented denunciations to the Suprema as well as petitions to the king: Their first goal was to reverse the installation of the tribunal; over time, their ambition was to annul its judicial procedure and to stop its actions that were abusive and outside the proper spheres of the faith.

Even at the start of the sixteenth century, in a context of significant political instability in the Castilian–Aragonese crown, strong tensions were unleashed in Sicily that greatly affected its young Inquisition. In

Palermo, riots broke out in 1511, 1516, and 1517 against the inquisitors, who were singled out for proceeding in an irregular and extremely harsh manner against the converso community, and for protecting their servants who committed robberies and other violent acts. Between 1516 and 1519, inquisition activity by Palermo's tribunal was practically suspended. Nevertheless, neither popular violence nor protests and petitions succeeded in getting the Spanish Inquisition to stop operating in Sicily – unlike in the Kingdom of Naples, where the royal project to impose the Inquisition was stopped on several occasions by a cohesive front of social opposition. From 1518 onward, Charles I resolutely pushed for the tribunal in Palermo to recommence operations; with papal support, he reinforced its autonomy and authority in the kingdom.[10]

The visit of Charles – now Holy Roman Emperor Charles V – to Sicily in September 1535 offered an opportunity for the opposition to be heard. At the end of that year, Charles suspended the Sicilian tribunal's jurisdiction in civil and criminal matters by royal decree, for five years, as had been requested by the parliament and supported by a one-time donation of 250,000 ducats. Historians can frame Charles's decision as part of a general reform for Sicilian courts as a whole but they also can explain it via the international context and the king's imperial objectives, which were to reform the church, overcome disagreements with Protestants, and reestablish a *communitas christiana,* headed by the emperor himself to confront the Muslim enemy.[11]

For the Inquisition in Sicily, not being able to prosecute civil and criminal cases – a prohibition that was renewed for five more years in 1540 – was a hard blow. From the inquisitors' point of view, "the temporal jurisdiction ... gives vigor and strength to the spiritual": to be without the former meant that the "spiritual jurisdiction in cases of the faith was suspended and as if dead."[12] In spite of that negative outlook, during those years the court of Palermo did not cease its action in matters of faith or stop celebrating public *autos de fe.*[13] What happened in this regard with the Sicilian Inquisition was not extraordinary. A bit later, inquisition tribunals in Castile and Aragon also had suspensions and limitations of inquisitorial privilege and underwent a profound reform. The courts and their districts were reorganized, their sources of income were stabilized, and the conditions of access for inquisitors and their employees were formalized, including the requirement of purity of blood (*limpieza de sangre*) from Jewish or Muslim ancestry.

In 1543, the crown restored to Sicily's tribunal its temporal privileges and reaffirmed its jurisdictional autonomy in the kingdom. Behind this decision lay royal concern over the discovery of Lutherans on the island as well as the fear of revolts in the kingdom.[14] Upon its restoration, the Inquisition achieved a "sudden popularity" among the Sicilians.[15] Up to that time, the inquisitorial ranks had been nourished essentially by the urban middle class: notaries, merchants, artisans, and ecclesiastics. Once the institutional position of the Inquisition in the kingdom was reconfirmed, the nobility and the urban oligarchies became more interested in inquisitorial titles, especially those of the familiars.

The interest of the Sicilian elites in holding inquisitorial titles and positions was not so much related to their religious zeal or their identification with purity of blood and honor, but rather with inquisitorial jurisdiction. In 1543, the now-reinstated, jurisdictional privilege meant that only inquisitors could try and sentence their own employees for any and all crimes and offenses. Moreover, that monopoly on jurisdiction could extend to relatives and properties, servants, and even slaves of inquisitorial employees. Enjoying such a right was a magnificent protection against a secular justice system that at the time was determined to control the excesses of feudalism as well as economically dominant groups on the island.

As it allied itself with local elites, the Inquisition in Sicily was able not only to extend control over territory but also to penetrate the socioeconomic, political, and institutional spheres that the elites controlled. The civic identity of the Inquisition was strengthened through the intensification of its public presence – with the celebration of *autos de fe*, the printing and dissemination of edicts of faith, and participation in urban ceremonies – as well as through the formation of religious confraternities linked to its servants, values, and activities.[16] The broadening of the Inquisition's social base of support was key to its consolidation in the kingdom, but in having to protect its dependents' interests, it intensified its civil and criminal litigation. At times, in fact, the Palermo tribunal was accused of being more intent on resolving its employees' legal woes than in finding and prosecuting heretics.

In any case, after the middle of the sixteenth century, the Inquisition was presented as the centerpiece of the royal religious project in Sicily, while it claimed to represent and mediate royal grace and patronage in Sicilian society. Scholars believe that two great power blocks then competed for hegemony in the kingdom. One was led by the Inquisition, which included the nobles and merchant elites. The other was led by the royal viceroy, who was supposed to be the *alter ego* of the Spanish king and head of his government; remarkably, in Sicily that royally endorsed supervision extended to the Catholic Church, thanks to a special and spurious papal concession (the *Legazia apostólica*) as well as to the judges of the kingdom's high courts and urban officers in royal cities.[17]

The conflicts among the Inquisition, viceroy, and magistrates of the kingdom essentially revolved around the damage caused by the inquisitorial jurisdiction to royal justice, but they were also staged on the symbolic level, in terms of reputation and representation.[18] As for clashes involving ecclesiastical authorities, those issues revolved around which legal system – inquisitorial or episcopal – should hear cases of potential heresy such as bigamy, blasphemy, sorcery, witchcraft, and the clerical solicitation of sexual favors from their penitents. Problems also arose when inquisitors wanted to act as sole judges in cases that affected ecclesiastics – who, along with their families and associates, served the tribunal. The inquisitors' claims in these regards were viewed as "detrimental to the jurisdiction of the prelates of that kingdom," and they also impinged upon the royal viceroy's supervision of the Sicilian Catholic Church.[19]

The viceroy, Catholic Church, and royal and inquisitorial courts were the institutional pillars of royal rule in Sicily. They were supposed to collaborate, and they did so, especially during political upheaval. At least from the mid-sixteenth century, the inquisitors, supported by their extensive networks of dependents, played a significant role as political mediators at times of crisis in the kingdom. They did so in 1560 in the riot that broke out in Palermo led by the notary Tarsino Cataldo; a century later, in 1647, ties between the tribunal and the middle classes and guilds of Palermo were decisive in restoring order.[20] Yet even as Sicily's inquisitors defined themselves as faithful and committed servants of the king, they nevertheless tenaciously resisted admitting the superiority of another authority. Conflict between institutions and corporations over legal jurisdiction was part of the functioning of the Spanish government. Behind it moved personal circumstances and interests, interwoven in networks of kinship, friendship, and patronage that connected local dynamics with those of the royal court as well as Rome.

In the last decades of the sixteenth century, and continuing into the seventeenth, formal concords, negotiated between royal and inquisitorial authorities, were supposed to repair matters in Sicily. In 1580, the first such pact allowed the Inquisition to preserve its full authority, privileges, and independence in the kingdom, circumstances that were nuanced and limited in successive royal dispositions. In the pact of 1597, the public preeminence of the viceregal authority was explicitly sanctioned, while the scope of the Inquisition's legal jurisdiction was diminished in favor of secular justice. Following previous viceregal mandates, nobles and barons who were lords of vassals were excluded from inquisitorial jurisdiction for civil and criminal offenses.

Yet despite pacts, decrees, and instructions, the inquisitors in Palermo continued to manage their court with great autonomy.[21] In fact, in 1635, a third deal had to be promulgated that again tried to limit the inquisitors' handling of civil and criminal cases. The inquisitors continued to present themselves as faithful servants and royal advisors in Sicily; they did not renounce their jurisdictional independence or recognize their subordination to the viceroy. In fact, conflicts of competence, privilege, and courtesy did not diminish; on the contrary, in the first decades of the sixteenth century and in the 1660s, the relationships among inquisitors, viceroys, and magistrates in Sicily reached very high levels of tension and friction.

These struggles were, as always, expressions of the political-institutional dialectic of the kingdom, but they also had a strong personal and factional component, closely connected to local and supra-local dynamics. Manuel Monje, inquisitor in Sicily from 1658 to 1664, clearly revealed such contexts when he explained that his complicated situation in the tribunal was due to his enmity with the other two inquisitors, who loathed the close relationship that Monje had with the viceroy. Monje went on to note that the deaths of prominent royal counselors in Madrid had left the viceroy in an even worse position.[22] Monje's own professional trajectory also depended upon patronage contacts. When his good friend, Viceroy Fernando de Ayala, left Sicily in 1663, Monje was sent to visit the court of Sardinia, which looked like a step backward in his career. However, when Ayala joined the royal councils of state and war in 1667, Monje returned to Sicily as a judge in the royal court. With his friends' support, Monje ultimately moved to Madrid in 1672 and became the representative for Sicily on the royal council of Italy.

Trajectories like Monje's were not so unusual. Inquisitors in Palermo in the sixteenth and seventeenth centuries not infrequently held the position of royal judge or consultant to the viceroy; they could be promoted to a bishopric or archbishopric, or rise to the royal councils of the monarchy. Obviously not all of them had such successful destinies. When Manuel Monje arrived in Sicily in 1658, some of his predecessors had died by nefarious means. Juan López de Cisneros had been murdered; Pablo Escobar Barata had died of poisoning.

According to experts, beginning in the middle of the 1600s, the Spanish monarchy began to value more deeply the Inquisition in Sicily: the context for that rise in appreciation lay in the Messina War (1674–6), as well as the uncertainty surrounding the succession to King Charles II. In moments of serious political instability and challenges on the island, its viceroys assiduously turned to inquisitors and their employees to carry out advisory and information tasks, or occupy administration and government positions that needed to be filled by "loyal Spaniards." In such moments, the Inquisition always cooperated with the government, seeking to monitor the "moods" of the populace, and to control behavior, speech, or writings that could threaten the established order.

In the second half of the seventeenth century, the inquisitorial court's involvement in state affairs was intense. In the Steri palace, the Inquisition's headquarters, cells had been built by Philip II that were destined, if necessary, to hold prisoners of state; numerous people accused of crimes of "felony and riot" were held there, with inquisitors often participating in their apprehension. As of the 1680s, despite the explicit prohibition of the Suprema, the Inquisition's jails for penanced defendants were used, by viceregal order, for inmates sentenced by the ecclesiastical jurisdiction overseen by the viceroy.[23] Inquisitors justified these alliances as demonstrating their essential role in preserving the kingdom. The Suprema in Madrid was not pleased with what it deemed the excessive and public partnership of its judges with the viceroys in matters of government. From the leadership's perspective, such collaboration harmed the reputation and the fulfillment of the proper functions of an inquisition tribunal. Tribunals were supposed to represent "the apostolic see [of Rome], from which [the Inquisition] emanates and in whose name it exercises its jurisdiction, and its true purpose is to authorize, assist, and strengthen the apostolic [power], not to diminish its authority and prerogatives."[24] From the middle of the seventeenth century, the apostolic character of the Spanish Inquisition was a central argument in defense of its independence and the superiority of its authority.

In 1696, a conference in Madrid denounced inquisitors in Sicily for having no respect for either royal orders or pacts. In 1699, an inspection of the Palermo tribunal occurred after inquisitors there intervened in dismantling a popular anti-Spanish plot.[25] The inquisitors defended themselves: Mandates and norms might exist, but they and their inquisitorial superiors always would be confronted with "disappointment in the practical act of experience." The way they managed their tribunal and supervised its employees was not irregular or novel; rather, they were acting in accordance with custom, according to the characteristics of the island, the Kingdom of Sicily, and its population.[26] There was nothing seriously awry with their way of proceeding: After all, their tribunal had always been able to fulfill its role as a protective wall for Catholic orthodoxy and a guarantor of Sicilian loyalty to the king.

Prisoners, Jails, and Sentences of the Palermo Inquisition Tribunal

Remarkably, the walls of the inquisition jails in the Steri palace have preserved testimonies – in the form of graffiti, drawings, and writings – of some of the people held there.[27] By the time the prisoners began to occupy this prison complex at the beginning of the seventeenth century, the Palermo tribunal had passed the phase of its most energetic repression. Likewise, by that time the tribunal had largely altered the orientation of its action as protector of religious unity on the island, moving from the persecution of conversos, Moriscos, and followers of the Protestant Reformation to the control and discipline of Catholics, in accordance with religious orthodoxy and the Tridentine decrees.

According to one expert, out of all the inquisitorial courts in the Kingdom of Aragon, Sicily's had the greatest number of defendants relaxed to the secular arm between 1511 and 1530.[28] In that period, baptized Christians accused of judaizing were the greatest objects of the repression that began in 1487, when the first edict of faith was published in Sicily and the first *auto de fe* was held in Palermo. The decree of expulsion promulgated by Isabella and Ferdinand for the Jews of their kingdoms was also published in Sicily in June 1492, whereupon a significant proportion of the 6,300 Jewish families that lived in the island's Jewish quarters fled. Specialists have calculated that approximately 2,000 people stayed and converted, a number that coincides with the quantity of inquisition trials conducted for judaizing between 1500 and 1550, in which approximately 450 individuals were relaxed in person or in effigy. After the middle of the sixteenth century, conversos practically disappeared from the lists of those prosecuted by the Palermo tribunal.[29]

The *auto de fe* held in Palermo on May 30, 1542, marked a turning point. While seventeen Christians were reconciled for judaizing – along with one more for following Islam – two defendants were sentenced for Lutheranism, one of whom was from Messina and was the first Protestant relaxed to the secular arm in Sicily. The discovery of individuals on the island who were following Luther prompted the tribunal to reset its operations. Henceforth, Palermo's inquisitors actively prosecuted any of the Sicilians' practices or beliefs that could be connected to the Reformation in some way. They also attempted to curb the dissemination of Protestantism by controlling the circulation of people, speeches, and books.

The inquisitors' efforts to squelch the Reformation affected about five hundred people. Half were Sicilians; many were priests, monks, or friars, and those prosecuted also included knights and urban artisans. At the end of the sixteenth century, inquisitors focused above all on natives of other Italian territories as well as the German, English, French, and Dutch individuals who passed through the island or resided there. Some of these foreigners intended to spread Protestantism on the island, but most were there because of commercial, maritime, or military activities in the Mediterranean. As was always the case for inquisition tribunals, Palermo's prosecutions of non-natives were conditioned to some extent by international agreements between the Spanish monarchy and other countries.

Inquisitors in Sicily prosecuted non-Catholic foreigners who were denounced for behaving scandalously. Nevertheless, they dealt above all with foreign individuals who presented themselves spontaneously in the tribunal to request absolution and convert to Catholicism. Among them were Lutherans, Anglicans or Calvinists who had been baptized and instructed in Catholicism at some point in their lives; they had moved, sometimes on more than one occasion, from one confession to another, although they always made it clear that, in their inner self, they only recognized the Catholic religion as the true way to salvation. In this way, they avoided a possible accusation of apostasy, but not all of them succeeded. In the first half of the seventeenth century, six foreigners were relaxed to the secular arm for being followers of the Reformation.

Yet other targeted groups were tied to Islam, whose presence on the island could be closely connected with proximity to Barbary and the western border of the Ottoman empire, or with the traffic of goods and the movement of people – many in the context of the slave market – across the Mediterranean. From the start, the Palermo tribunal tried to identify and punish baptized Christians who continued to follow Islam, but this activity gained momentum from the mid-sixteenth century onward. Those converts were often North Africans – some coming from the Iberian peninsula – as well as slaves: Having converted from Islam to Catholicism, they had secretly maintained their first faith. After 1609, when Spain formally expelled its Morisco population, Sicilian inquisitors also had to find and expel those who landed there.

One particular problem encountered by the inquisitors arose with the so-called renegades (*renegados*). These were Christians who had either voluntarily joined or been captured by Muslim pirates or corsairs: They had converted to Islam in the process but upon returning to Christian lands such as Sicily had to prove that they had only converted to save their lives. If inquisitors judged them to be sincere, they could avoid prosecution for apostasy. Many renegades presented themselves voluntarily to Palermo's inquisitors with narratives of forced conversion to Islam and the desire to be once again a Catholic; the inquisitors' attitude toward them was, in general, benevolent. At the same time, the inquisitors were not compassionate if they saw signs of relapse into Islam or stubbornness in heretical beliefs. Such defendants could be excommunicated or relaxed to the secular arm, though sentences to row in the royal galleys were much more common.

There was also a community of Greek and Albanian Orthodox Christians in Sicily, established since the mid-fifteenth century under royal protection, which by the beginning of the seventeenth century numbered around 20,000 individuals. The Inquisition kept an eye on this group but did not consider them de facto heretics; instead, its actions toward them focused on immoral statements and behavior that could imply heresy, such as controversial propositions, blasphemy, or sorcery. This group also had some renegades – individuals who voluntarily converted to Islam or were forced to do so, and they also appeared before the inquisitorial tribunal of Sicily; many were reconciled and reincorporated into Catholicism, while others faced charges of apostasy as crypto-Muslims.[30]

While many prisoners told Palermo's inquisitors that Catholicism was the true religion and the path to salvation, recent studies have also revealed other prisoners' convictions that each one could save himself according to his own faith. More rarely, inquisition defendants argued that no religion could save them. Early modern Sicily was home to many nationalities and ethnicities; it was a liminal space that witnessed an endless convergence of different people and creeds. Inquisition trials held there reveal cross-confessional contamination, syncretism, ancestral beliefs about divine powers and a magical world, and independent interpretations of sacred texts. All these possibilities strained the Catholic confessional model promoted by the Spanish Inquisition.[31] A significant proportion of the practices, beliefs, and public manifestations uncovered by the inquisitors challenged the authority of the Catholic Church and its dogmas, precepts, and moral norms.

Just as Palermo's inquisitors reduced their prosecutions of Protestants after the 1540s, so they saw fewer cases against crypto-Muslims and renegades from the 1640s. Nevertheless, the tribunal did not forsake its role as a protective wall for Catholicism in the Mediterranean. In 1695, inquisitors in Sicily warned:

> Cases of faith in the kingdom of Sicily are many and very serious. Even if there are no trials of Jews (sic), there are plenty of others over any number of transgressions, especially sorcery, necromancy, idolatry and blasphemy, and there usually are some causes of dogmatizing heretics as well, because the kingdom has a lot of trade, and it is where many nations from the north and Levant meet.[32]

By 1705, the tribunal was facing cases such as those of a Roman man who spontaneously presented himself before an inquisition commissioner in Messina after having been in "the land of the Moors," as well as that of a London "Calvinist" who spontaneously went to the inquisitors to be reconciled and instructed in Catholicism. In August 1710, Marco Antonio Gato, a Venetian soldier, appeared in one of the last inquisitorial sentencings in Palermo. After Gato was captured by the Turks, he not only "lived like them" but married two Turkish women. Although he denied having sincerely forsaken Catholicism, he was prosecuted for apostasy. Gato was sentenced to wear the *sambenito* and to abjure a vehement suspicion of heresy; he was absolved with a caution but nevertheless sentenced to six months of confinement in the penitential prisons to be instructed in the Catholic faith. At the end of that time, he was supposed to be banished from the kingdom for eight years.

In the last decades of its existence, the Inquisition in Sicily also pursued followers of Miguel de Molinos (d. 1696), who was born in Aragon, educated by members of the Society of Jesus, and sent to Rome in 1663 to monitor a case of beatification pending before the papacy. He developed a reputation in Rome as a spiritual director and in 1675, he published *The Spiritual Guide*, a handbook for spiritual contemplation. The spirituality Molinos promoted was known as Quietism. His book was highly successful and was translated into multiple European languages; it was published in Sicily in 1681 under the auspices of the archbishop of Palermo, Jaime de Palafox. Nevertheless, after Molinos was arrested for heresy by the Roman Inquisition in 1685, *The Spiritual Guide* was denounced and banned by the Spanish Inquisition. Inquisition efforts in Sicily uncovered a significant number of individuals who appeared to be following Molinos's counsel: They pursued passive prayer, contemplation, and spiritual abandonment to the love of God in convents and parishes throughout the island.[33] Most were friars, nuns, and tertiaries of mendicant orders, such as the Discalced Augustinians or the Capuchins. In some cases, the priests and friars prosecuted for Quietism were also accused of soliciting sex from their female penitents. Solicitation in general was widely prosecuted by the Spanish Inquisition from the end of the sixteenth century, as part of the active vigilance it developed after the Council of Trent over the behavior of ecclesiastics. Where this heresy was concerned, the inquisitors of Palermo entered into fierce disputes with the bishops over jurisdiction; the same conflicts occurred over which court should handle other offenses, such as bigamy.

When Spanish inquisitors left Sicily in 1713, after the kingdom passed into the hands of Vittorio Amedeo of Savoy in compliance with the treaties of Utrecht, there were still some cases pending in the secret chambers of the tribunal. Among them were those of Sister Gertrude Maria Cordovana, a tertiary of St. Benedict, a native of Caltanissetta, and then about forty-five years old, and that of Friar Romualdo, a Discalced Augustinian layman, also a native of Caltanissetta and about fifty years old. Both had been arrested in 1699 as followers of Miguel de Molinos; both were tried and sentenced on two occasions in 1703. They ended up being categorized as impenitent and stubborn; they were relaxed to the secular arm, although their sentences were not carried out until 1724, when the Palermo tribunal, like Sicily itself, was under the control of Holy Roman Emperor Charles VI.[34]

In conclusion, the investigations and prosecutions carried out by the Inquisition in Sicily essentially targeted ecclesiastics and people from the middling socioeconomic sectors of urban communities, with the latter including artisans and members of the liberal professions. Inquisitorial attention also fell upon farmers, urban workers, and sometimes slaves. More men were tried than women, with women being accused mainly of crypto-Judaism, crypto-Islam, and Quietism. In the crimes of superstition, although there was a balance between investigations of men and women, men appeared more frequently in trials related to magic, while women were more frequently prosecuted for witchcraft and superstitious cures.[35] One expert has highlighted "the boldness, imagination, and inventiveness" of the men and some women who were tried for blasphemy and scandalous propositions in Sicily.[36] Inquisition proceedings testify to the harsh and traumatic experiences of the people whom the Inquisition sought to discipline and silence. Yet the extant records also offer evidence of personal conviction, variegated forms of religiosity, and diverse ways of thinking about divinity and salvation on the part of the women and men who, more or less consciously, challenged the order promoted and protected by the Spanish Inquisition.

The history of the Sicilian Inquisition shows the institution's ability to adapt to different social and political contexts. While sharing the same fundamental goals and being subject to overarching control from the Suprema and inquisitor-general in Madrid, the Sicilian tribunal was profoundly shaped by the island's distinctive geopolitical location and the kingdom's complex power structures, its particular social fabric, and changing local and supra-local political dynamics. The Inquisition in Sicily was a court whose purpose was to maintain Catholic orthodoxy on an island that became a strategically important "bastion of Catholicism" in the Mediterranean. Therefore, its focus shifted from internal threats to external ones; its inquisitors were always particularly preoccupied with preventing the infiltration of heresy from outside. The Inquisition in Sicily was supposed to play a role in preserving the kingdom for the Spanish monarchy, but its attempts to exercise its superior and universal jurisdiction in Sicily often provoked resistance. The institution was embedded within, and constantly negotiating with, Sicilian society. It faced persistent challenges to its authority from local powers, and the shifting attitudes of various social groups (urban middle and popular groups, nobility) towards the Inquisition over time. Its history underscores the fluidity of social alliances and the absence of a unified Sicilian response to the institution.

Notes

1. Research carried out at the Universidad de Cantabria under the grant PID2021–124823NB–C22, funded by MICN/AEI/10.13039/501100011033/ and ERDF, "A Way of Making Europe."

2. Valeria La Motta, *Contra Haereticos: L'Inquisizione spagnola in Sicilia* (Istituto Poligrafico europeo, 2019), 128–130.
3. Marina Torres Arce, "Un palacio para la Inquisición de Palermo: espacios urbanos, conflictividad y relaciones de poder," *Investigaciones Históricas, Época Moderna y Contemporánea* 38 (2018): 11–48.
4. National Historical Archive of Madrid [AHN], Inquisition [Inq], Leg. 1571, exp. 3.
5. Vittorio Sciuti Russi, "La Inquisición española en Sicilia," *Studia Historica. Historia Moderna*, 26 (2004): 81.
6. Biblioteca Nacional de España [BNE], manuscript [ms] 2827, Madrid 22/2/1698.
7. AHN, Madrid, Inq, Leg. 1755, exp. 2.
8. AHN, Madrid, Inq, Leg. 2298, Palermo 28/8/1698.
9. Fernando Ciaramitaro, *Santo Oficio imperial: Dinámicas globales y el caso siciliano* (Gedisa-Universidad Autónoma de la Ciudad de México, 2022).
10. La Motta, *Contra Haereticos*, 135–55.
11. Francesco Renda, *L'Inquisizione in Sicilia: I fatti, le persone* (Sellerio, 1997), 64.
12. AHN, Madrid, Inq, Leg. 2302, Palermo 15/12/1735.
13. Maria Sofia Messana, *Inquisitori, negromanti e streghe nella Sicilia moderna (1500–1782)* (Sellerio, 2007), 596.
14. Renda, *L'Inquisizione*, 71–83.
15. Manuel Rivero Rodríguez, "La Inquisición española en Sicilia (siglo XVI a XVIII)," in Joaquín Pérez Villanueva and Bartolomé Escandell, eds., *Historia de la Inquisición en España y América* Vol. 3 (Biblioteca de Autores Cristianos/Centro de Estudios Inquisitoriales, 2000), 1061.
16. Messana, *Inquisitori*, 43–7.
17. Rivero Rodríguez, "La Inquisición española," 1063-84; Sciuti Russi, "La Inquisición española," 82–7.
18. Torres, "Un palacio," 21–48.
19. BNE, ms 2827, Madrid 7/10/1661.
20. Rivero, "La Inquisición, 1183–96.
21. Ciaramitaro, *Santo Oficio*, 186–99.
22. AHN, Inq, Leg. 1751, exp. 2, Palermo 29/3/1663.
23. Marina Torres Arce, "La Inquisición y la última conjura antiespañola del siglo XVII en Sicilia," in José Martínez Millán, Manuel Rivero Rodríguez, and Carlos Álvarez Nogal, eds., *Centros de poder italianos en la Monarquía Hispánica (siglos XV-XVIII)* Vol. 2 (Ediciones Polifemo, 2010), 878–9.
24. AHN, Madrid, Inq, Lib. 303, Madrid 26/5/1671.
25. Torres, "La Inquisición," 837–92.
26. AHN, Inq, Leg. 2300, Palermo 7/29/1700
27. Giovanna Fiume, *Del Santo Uffizio in Sicilia e delle sue carceri* (Viella, 2021); Mercedes García-Arenal, "A Polyphony of Voices: Trials and Graffiti

of the Prisons of the Inquisition in Palermo," *Quaderni storici* 157 (2018): 37–68.
28. E. William Monter, *Frontiers of Heresy. The Spanish Inquisition from the Basque Lands to Sicily* (Cambridge University Press, 1990), 21.
29. La Motta, *Contra*, 99–104; Ciaramitaro, *Santo Oficio*, 163–8.
30. Fiume, *Del Santo*, 145–61.
31. Fiume, *Del Santo*, 183–9, 323–41.
32. AHN, Madrid, Inq, Leg. 2298, 30/5/1695.
33. AHN, Madrid, Inq, Leg. 2302, *Relación de personas penitenciadas en los tres autos particulares celebrados en las salas del tribunal a puertas abiertas en 1, 9 de agosto y 6 de septiembre de 1710*.
34. Vittore Sciuti-Russi and Marina Torres Arce have worked on the final stage of the Inquisition in Sicily in recent years: Ciaramitaro, *Santo Oficio Imperial*, 158–9.
35. Fiume, *Del Santo*, 109–11.
36. Monter, *Frontiers*, 166, 170.

Suggestions for Further Reading

Ciaramitaro, Fernando. *Santo Oficio imperial: Dinámicas globales y el caso siciliano*. Gedisa-Universidad Autónoma de la Ciudad de México, 2022.
Fiume, Giovanna. *Del Santo Uffizio in Sicilia e delle sue carceri*. Viella, 2021.
La Motta, Valeria. *Contra Haereticos: L'Inquisizione spagnola in Sicilia*. Istituto Poligrafico Europeo, 2019.
Messana, Maria Sofia. *Inquisitori, negromanti e streghe nella Sicilia moderna (1500–1782)*. Sellerio, 2007.
Monter, E. William. *Frontiers of Heresy: The Spanish Inquisition from the Basque Lands to Sicily*. Cambridge University Press, 1990.
Renda, Francesco. *L'Inquisizione in Sicilia: I fatti, le persone*. Sellerio, 1997.
Rivero Rodríguez, Manuel. "La Inquisición española en Sicilia (siglo XVI a XVIII)." In Joaquín Pérez Villanueva and Bartolomé Escandell Bonet, eds., *Historia de la Inquisición en España y América* Vol. 3. Biblioteca de Autores Cristianos/Centro de Estudios Inquisitoriales, 2000.
Sciuti-Russi, Vittorio. "La Inquisición española en Sicilia." *Studia Historica. Historia Moderna* 26 (2004): 75–99.
Torres Arce, Marina. "La Inquisición y la última conjura antiespañola del siglo XVII en Sicilia." In José Martínez Millán, Manuel Rivero Rodríguez, and Carlos Álvarez Nogal, eds., *Centros de poder italianos en la Monarquía Hispánica (siglos XV-XVIII)* Vol. 2. Ediciones Polifemo, 2010.

"Un palacio para la Inquisicón de Palermo: espacios urbanos, conflictidad, y relaciones de poder." *Investigaciones Históricas. Época Moderna Y Contemporánea* 38 (2018): 11–48.

Bibliography

Ciaramitaro, Fernando. *Santo Oficio imperial: Dinámicas globales y el caso siciliano*. Gedisa-Universidad Autónoma de la Ciudad de México, 2022.

Fiume, Giovanna. *Del Santo Uffizio in Sicilia e delle sue carceri*. Viella, 2021.

García-Arenal, Mercedes. "A Polyphony of Voices: Trials and Graffiti of the Prisons of the Inquisition in Palermo." *Quaderni storici* 157 (2018): 37–68.

La Motta, Valeria. *Contra Haereticos: L'Inquisizione spagnola in Sicilia*. Istituto Poligrafico Europeo, 2019.

Messana, Maria Sofia. *Inquisitori, negromanti e streghe nella Sicilia moderna (1500–1782)*. Sellerio, 2007.

Monter, E. William. *Frontiers of Heresy: The Spanish Inquisition from the Basque Lands to Sicily*. Cambridge University Press, 1990.

Renda, Francesco. *L'Inquisizione in Sicilia: I fatti, le persone*. Sellerio, 1997.

Rivero Rodríguez, Manuel. "La Inquisición española en Sicilia (siglo XVI a XVIII)." In Joaquín Pérez Villanueva and Bartolomé Escandell, eds., *Historia de la Inquisición en España y América* Vol. 3. Biblioteca de Autores Cristianos/Centro de Estudios Inquisitoriales, 2000.

Sciuti-Russi, Vittorio. "La Inquisición española en Sicilia." *Studia Historica: Historia Moderna* 26 (2004): 75–99.

Torres Arce, Marina. "La Inquisición y la última conjura antiespañola del siglo XVII en Sicilia." In José Martínez Millán, Manuel Rivero Rodríguez, and Carlos Álvarez Nogal, eds., *Centros de poder italianos en la Monarquía Hispánica (siglos XV-XVIII)*. Ediciones Polifemo, 2010.

"Un palacio para la Inquisicón de Palermo: espacios urbanos, conflictidad, y relaciones de poder." *Investigaciones Históricas. Época Moderna Y Contemporánea* 38 (2018): 11–48.

12

Mexico

Introduction: The Social and Historical Context of Spain's Presence in America

Spain's conquest of the Americas was a complex, controversial, and lengthy process that lasted from the late fifteenth to the early nineteenth century.[1] The historical and social contexts for this process are fundamental elements for fully understanding the forces that came together to shape American societies at the time of the Spaniards' arrival and well afterward. In 1492, Queen Isabella of Castile financed Columbus's first voyage, which led to an encounter between two worlds, Europe and America. Men such as Hernán Cortés and Francisco Pizarro subsequently led expeditions that resulted in the establishment of viceroyalties, captaincy generals, and colonies throughout what came to be known as Latin America.

There were three principal reasons for Spain's early voyages to America: the search for new commercial routes to Asia, so as to avoid the Portuguese; the desire to obtain wealth; and the expansion of the Kingdom of Castile.[2] The encounter between such different civilizations was both abrupt and unequal. Spain was intent upon imposing European practices on Indigenous cultures; Spain's actions led to brutal and insidious forms of control and repression. Furthermore, in no way was the Spanish "conquest" carried out by Spaniards alone in a straightforward or complete way. In what we now call Mexico, Cortés and his supporters were helped tremendously by Indigenous animosities toward the Mexica; after they destroyed Tenochtitlan, they had not conquered Mexico but merely torn apart the Mexica empire. Furthermore, Spain's alleged conquest was not over for decades. In 1542, when Spaniards founded a new colonial capital in the Yucatan called Mérida, they might have told the Spanish monarchy that their "conquest" was complete, but in fact they controlled only a tiny portion of that peninsula and would have to fight one band of Mayans after another for years.[3]

Still, Spaniards did create and impose the *encomienda* system on Indigenous peoples, which allowed them to exploit those populations' land and labor widely. The colonial economy created by Spain was based on the extraction of natural resources, which in turn depended upon labor that was utterly dependent upon the *encomienda* system and, later, the importation of slaves from Africa. A new social structure, the so-called *casta* system, emerged as a result, leading to racial stratification that endures to this day. Then there was the question of religious conversion, a process in which the Spanish Catholic Church played a fundamental role.[4] Surviving documentation of Catholic missionary activity illustrates the breadth and depth of evangelization campaigns carried out by various Catholic religious orders. Over time, such campaigns led to social, economic, and cultural transformations for the native population.[5]

Of course, Indigenous peoples did not necessarily accept all these transformations, and there were rebellions, including the 1540–2 Mixtón War and the great Pueblo Revolt of 1680, not to mention the movements of the late eighteenth and early nineteenth centuries that resulted in independence.[6] In short, the historical and social contexts for Spain's colonization of America were complex and multifaceted, and the same holds for the effects of their presence, which can be seen today throughout Latin America in aspects such as language, culture, customs, and social structures. In what follows I focus on one region in particular, New Spain, and explore a key institution of Spanish political and religious control there in the early modern period: the Spanish Inquisition.[7]

Establishment of the Inquisition in New Spain

Significantly, inquisitorial activities in New Spain were not originally carried out by Spanish inquisitors, nor were Spanish Inquisition tribunals immediately imposed upon American territory, a detail that speaks to the incomplete character of the conquest as well as the very large geographical area covered by New Spain. The colony encompassed the unknown lands north of Mexico, reached as far south as Nicaragua, included Cuba to the east, and incorporated the Philippines across the Pacific. This territory amounted to more than 1,158,306 square miles and included almost half a million inhabitants, excluding Indigenous peoples.[8] Given its extent, it is not surprising that the Spanish monarchy and the Spanish Inquisition leadership were hesitant at first to pin down a location for a tribunal. Furthermore, there were geographical challenges in New Spain, with mountain ranges, wide rivers, lagunas, and swamps often impeding travel and access.[9] Small, scattered settlements repeatedly fell victim to epidemics; inhabitants were diverse, including nomads in the north, hunters and gatherers in the south, European immigrants, and eventually African slaves.

Instead of using Spanish inquisitors, in the first phase from 1522 to 1536 inquisitions into heresy in New Spain were carried out by the provincials or leaders of monastic orders such as the Dominicans and Franciscans. On May 10, 1522, Pope Adrian gave mendicant friars in the Americas the ability to act as inquisitors, and to "exercise almost all episcopal authority" if they found themselves unable to reach a diocesan bishop within two days.[10] Consequently, the first inquisitor in New Spain was a Franciscan, Martín de Valencia, who arrived in 1524 with a group of Franciscan missionaries later dubbed the twelve apostles. Only fragments of inquisition records survive from Valencia's tenure.[11] In 1526, Fray Tomás Ortiz arrived in America with an appointment as inquisitorial commissioner signed by the Audiencia de Santo Domingo.[12] In 1527, Ortiz handed the job over to a Dominican, Domingo de Betanzos, who presided over nineteen trials for blasphemy against Spanish colonists and initiated a campaign against witchcraft in New Spain. Betanzos was followed by yet another Dominican, Vicente de Santa María, who oversaw the New World's first *auto de fe* in 1528: Hernando Alonso and Gonzalo de Morales, baptized Catholics and allegedly brothers, were sentenced to death for practicing Judaism. (Alonso had been a ship's carpenter in 1521 for Hernan Cortés.)[13] Modern investigations demonstrate that Dominican monastic inquisitions conducted fifty-five trials between 1526 and 1536.[14]

Basque Franciscan Fray Juan de Zumárraga was named the first bishop of New Spain, and on arrival in Mexico City in 1534 he signed his first verdict against heresy. In 1535, he was appointed apostolic inquisitor for New Spain and its bishopric; in 1536 he established the Holy Office in the episcopal palace, where it remained until 1571. By virtue of his episcopacy and his commission, Zumárraga attempted to create a monopoly on cases of heresy and to oversee them all, with his targets comprising Indigenous peoples, Spanish colonists, and individuals of mixed ethnic background. Nevertheless, monastic inquisitions continued to exist in outlying provinces of New Spain, with horrific use of torture against Indigenous suspects in Teitipac in 1560, and again in Yucatán in 1562; in the latter instance, many Maya committed suicide.[15]

Significantly, Zumárraga himself was hardly benevolent. He conducted 156 trials from 1536 to 1546, including one in 1539 against the cacique of Texcoco, Don Carlos Ometochtzin, whom he sentenced to be burned at the stake, and whose trial record is extant.[16] Zumárraga was ultimately reprimanded for his severity by Spanish king and Holy Roman Emperor Charles V, and was forced to give up his title of apostolic inquisitor in 1546. He was replaced as archbishop by Tello de Sandoval, who then was replaced by Fray Alonso de Montúfar in 1556. During Archbishop Montúfar's tenure, the fight against Lutheranism intensified thanks to his vicar, Dr. Luis de Anguis, who was also a spy for King Philip II. The Lutherans in question tended to be English and French pirates. During the 1550s, the episcopal inquisitions overseen by New Spain's archbishops and bishops conducted more than 100 trials in the dioceses of Mexico, Oaxaca, Guadalajara, Yucatan, and Guatemala.[17]

Friars, bishops, and archbishops in New Spain were trained to be pastoral forces for conversion. They were not lawyers; they were hardly educated in inquisitorial procedure and their trials for heresy lacked central oversight. Remarkably, it was Spanish colonists who asked King Philip II to establish a permanent tribunal of the Spanish Inquisition, and he did so via a royal decree of January 25, 1569. By 1570, Spanish inquisitors were operating in Mexico City; on August 16, 1570, another royal decree removed New Spain's Indigenous populations from inquisitorial jurisdiction. Instead, the Indigenous henceforth would be corrected for errors in the faith by the episcopal courts. The first defendants before the newly installed inquisition tribunal in Mexico City were two musicians who had refused to play at the opening ceremonies unless they were paid in advance.

The Supreme Council of the Inquisition in Spain, known as the Suprema, was relatively uninterested in its new tribunal in New Spain. There were very few personnel there – just two inquisitors, a prosecutor, a notary, and a prison warden. In comparison, Toledo, which covered far less territory, had four inquisitors, one prosecutor, four notaries, and many staff members.[18] Inquisitors willing to make the voyage to America were either young men wanting adventure or older men who had not risen through the ranks and hoped the new destination might provide them with an opportunity.[19]

Ultimately, the establishment of the Spanish Inquisition in New Spain was driven by religious, political, and social factors. Its goal was to preserve Catholic unity in the face of Protestantism, to eradicate the dangers of heresy, and to maintain social order and political control through censorship of the publication and diffusion of books that did not align with the norms of faraway Spain.[20] After 1570, the inquisition tribunal in Mexico City would watch Spaniards, Mestizos, Creoles, and Africans for signs of heresy.

Inquisitorial Procedure in New Spain

New Spain's inquisition tribunal in Mexico City imported its procedures from Spain. In the Old World, papal inquisitorial procedure, based on canon and Roman law, had been solidified between the late twelfth century and the mid-fourteenth century. As a result, inquisitors, named by medieval popes, were endowed with effective and explicit legal procedures. In the late fifteenth century, after pressure from King Ferdinand II of Aragon, Pope Innocent VIII appointed Tomás de Torquemada as inquisitor-general of Catalonia and of the city and bishopric of Barcelona. He was responsible for the establishment of inquisitorial tribunals on the Iberian peninsula and for the institution's first formal *Instructions*, issued in Seville in 1484 and 1485, in Valladolid in 1488, and in Ávila in 1498. By the middle of the 1480s, the Inquisition's power was absolute throughout the kingdom, with close cooperation between its officials and civil authorities, especially during the preparatory phase of trials as set forth in inquisitors' manuals.[21]

Compendiums of inquisitorial instructions rekindled hatred of any sign of heresy, driving harassment and persecution of anyone whose behavior did not conform to the ecclesiastical and theological standards of the time. Manuals for inquisitors laid out the attitude to be adopted toward anyone denounced before the Inquisition, how interrogations should be carried out, when and how torture should be inflicted, the scale for punishments, when and where *autos de fe* should be held, what sort of hierarchy should be observed in those public ceremonies, and so on. Such manuals amount to a horror museum that is hard to read on account of their cruelty, intolerance and depravity.[22] Out of all the manuals, the one used the most in New Spain was the *Directorium inquisitorum* of Nicolas Eymeric, written around 1378, and translated and expanded by Francisco Peña 200 years later.[23] The first inquisition trials in New Spain revealed the limitations and dangers of a model imported from Spain, but little by little the realities of the Viceroyalty encouraged a rebalancing and adaptation.[24] Adjustments were made over time.[25] Still, every inquisition trial had to adhere to a concrete procedure.

Accusation, Arrest, and Jail

When a well-regarded person denounced someone before New Spain's inquisitorial tribunal, the accusation was recorded by a notary. When the inquisitors decided they had sufficient proof – a conclusion that depended upon their discretion – they asked an inquisitorial bailiff to arrest the suspect, who might have no idea why he or she was being taken in. Ultimately, proof in the Spanish Inquisition, no matter where the trial was taking place, had to rest on two eyewitnesses to the same event or a confession. The identity of witnesses for the prosecution was never supposed to be disclosed to the defendant, a principle that could encourage anonymous denunciations or ones grounded in hatred, though a defendant could attempt to guess a witness's identity and recuse her for capital enmity. Witnesses for and against the defendant were supposed to ratify their statements before the latter could be used in court. Inquisitorial questioning of witnesses in New Spain followed the guidelines laid out in Eymeric's manual as revised by Francisco Peña, which was viewed as an authoritative source.[26]

Depending on the gravity of the accusation – and especially if the suspected heresy turned on belief rather than action – a list of propositions was drawn up for theologians to assess. These theologians were selected by the individual inquisition tribunal and tended to perform this function over time; they helped the inquisitors decide whether the propositions were serious enough to warrant a trial. The theological assessment was called *calificación*, with the experts called *calificadores*. Many cases ended with this phase rather than moving on to a prosecution.[27] In this regard, members of New Spain's inquisitorial tribunal followed the example of their colleagues in Spain, who also used *calificadores* for the same purpose.[28]

Next, precautionary measures related to time and conditions were taken. These could be modified. The accused party was ordered to appear; if she were accused of heresy she was confined in the Inquisition's so-called "secret jails" – though everyone knew they existed. There, the accused should have been isolated, with men held separately from women. Prisoners had to pay for their own food, drink, medicine, and hygiene as well as the guards' wages. These expenses were covered by the court seizing or sequestering the accused's belongings, which would be inventoried and whose safekeeping would be placed under a secretary for sequestration: Those belongings were supposed to pay for the prisoner's needs while in jail.[29] In New Spain, however, this process did not always occur: In the trial of Rafael Enríquez, for example, her entry into the jail was not registered and she was able to keep gold, silver, jewelry, clothing, and valuable objects.[30]

Inquisitors tried to force the accused to confess so that the sentence was not based solely on witness statements, but on the accused's words. Inquisition manuals made it clear that confession was "the queen of proofs" (*regina probationum*). To that end, over time the interrogations of a particular suspect would grow longer and increasingly complex. Inquisitors would try to elicit endless details about the accused, her family background, if she knew the reasons for her confinement, what possible crimes she might have committed against the church, and so on. The same questions were asked again and again in the hope of uncovering some contradiction or gap in the defendant's statements. These interrogations were spaced over months in order to create uncertainty and confusion for the accused, which could then be used to elicit a confession. Although the inquisitor theoretically had to visit prisoners twice a month to encourage them to confess, laziness and inertia tended to take over, and there were cases in which years went by without a visit. Such was the case of Catalina de Campos, whom inquisitors discovered dead and half eaten by rats in her cell when they went to see her.[31] Of course, her case begs the question of whether the warden and quartermaster also failed to see and perhaps even to feed her.

Finally, once seized and jailed, the defendant was supposed to receive up to three admonitions, or formal warnings, from the inquisitors as additional spurs to confess. This was a crucial moment marking the formalization of the accusation and the start of the final phase of proceedings. At this point, with the arraignment, the charges were made explicit and the defendant could understand what she faced and prepare for the next, decisive phase.

The Accusatory Phase

In an inquisition trial, the accusatory phase was a decisive stage for the exposition of charges relating to a crime against the Catholic faith. This stage began with an accusation or denunciation, which could be made by anyone anonymously so long as there was corroborating evidence for the charge. (Defendants could also accuse themselves and confess during an earlier interrogation.) Next came the preliminary investigation, when evidence was collected and the credibility of the incriminations was assessed: Here, the tribunal could amass depositions, records, and any other facts that would back up or refute the denunciation. Third in order would be a list of the prosecution's questions for the defendant: Not surprisingly, each inquisition defendant could be subjected to different queries depending upon the allegations as well as the inquisitor's discretion and judgment. Torture could also be formally authorized in order to secure answers.[32] The fourth step was the formal presentation of the charges: If the proofs were sufficiently consistent and acceptable to back up the denunciation, the inquisitor would explain the indictment to the defendant. The defendant did have the right to defend herself; she was assigned a defense attorney who prepared a list of questions for her witnesses, with the aim of explaining her version of events and disarming the prosecution. Finally, the inquisitor evaluated all the evidence that arose from these measures and decided whether there was a basis to continue with a formal trial. The underlying objective was always to discover the truth and save the defendant's soul.

The Evidentiary Phase

After all these steps, a phase began in which both sides offered proof, with the inquisitor taking an active role in the investigation of deeds and the collection of truthful evidence. Every witness for each side had to swear an oath to tell the truth; all their words were supposed to be written down verbatim by a notary *del secreto* ("of the secret"), who was authorized by the inquisitors to record such sensitive information. The tribunal's prosecutor offered his witnesses first: He questioned them secretly, in a location other than the courtroom. Prosecution witnesses were always asked if they were motivated by hostility or ill will toward the accused, and their responses went into the record. Statements by the prosecution witnesses were transcribed and given to the defense, although details that could identify them were omitted.

The defense attorney then presented his own witnesses to speak on behalf of the accused, as guarantors of her innocence. He would create a different list of questions for the accused's witnesses from the one deployed by the prosecutor. Typically, many of the defense attorney's queries were designed to reveal or imply the defendant's orthodox beliefs and behaviors, such as whether the defendant attended Mass on a regular basis and owned a crucifix. Other defense questions might be intended to expose anyone in the community who wished to harm the defendant: If those enemies had testified for the prosecution, and if their hostility was sufficiently demonstrated, their depositions could be stricken from the record and not serve as proof. Ultimately, the defense attorney's greatest aspiration was to be so convincing that the prosecution's case fell apart.

Sentencing

Once all the trial depositions and interrogations were compiled, the inquisitors sent them to an advisory board (*junta*) of consultants (*consultadores*) to discuss the verdict. The consultants included the inquisitors, a representative from the relevant bishop or archbishop, and other learned men. Each member voted; a unanimous verdict was required for the death penalty. Once defense and prosecution had filed their closing arguments and the board voted, the defendant was asked to abjure a light (*de levi*) suspicion of heresy if the prosecution case was considered weak, or a vehement (*de vehementi*) suspicion of heresy if the prosecution was considered solid. After the abjuration had occurred, the inquisitors read the defendant the final sentence, which included the penalties. If the defendant was sentenced to death at the stake, the inquisitors announced that she would be "relaxed to the secular arm," which meant that civil authorities were charged with executing her. (Inquisitors were not allowed to shed blood.) The coordination here between church and state exemplifies a situation in which "the church used the secular branch (of government), and political power in turn committed itself to carry out strictly religious ends."[33]

Death was not a frequent punishment in inquisition trials, but rather the exception. Still, inquisition trials in both New Spain and Spain could last a very long time, as could the pre-trial proceedings. If a defendant was held in a tribunal's secret jail until the verdict was issued, and all the measures spelled out in the inquisition manuals were, in fact, followed, years might pass. Given that conditions in those jails were potentially harmful and even dangerous, a defendant could die there. In the early years of their tribunal, inquisitors in New Spain commented on the unhealthiness of their prisons, which were located in the basements of the tribunal's palace. The walls of the cells were made of adobe, and the dirt floors could become soaked with water. Prisoners suffered accordingly. Historian John F. Chuchiak IV has noted that the adobe walls facilitated communications between the inquisition cells, and yet few defendants managed to flee.[34] When they did so, they escaped to a new place where they were not known, or where they could take on a new identity.

Nevertheless, even if the defendant died, could not be found for an arrest, or ran away, the trial went on. If the missing defendant had been sentenced to death, she was burned in effigy as a symbol of her identity. It was very rare that cases ended with a live defendant tied to a post being set alight; instead, if the defendant showed the slightest sign of repentance a quicker death by strangulation might be the outcome, before the dead body was thrown into the flames.

Carrying out a death sentence in the Spanish Inquisition usually occurred two or three days after the verdict was announced. This gave the convicted time to confess and save her soul. In New Spain, the burning occurred near a river or by the sea. Once the flames had devoured the body, the ashes were thrown into the water where they would dissolve, making it impossible for the guilty to be reincarnated on the day of the Last Judgment.

Types of Crimes: Blasphemy, Sex Crimes, Heresy, Magic, Idolatry

Most inquisition defendants in New Spain were Spanish-born.[35] During the sixteenth century, the most common offenses pursued by New Spain's inquisitors were blasphemy, followed by a variety of sex crimes, such as bigamy, polygamy, and the clergy's solicitation of sexual favors; next came heresy, magic, and idolatry. In all these prosecutions, immoral behavior was viewed by New Spain's tribunal as evidence of improper religious belief. Blasphemy tended to coincide with anger, such as losing at cards or being pressured over a debt. It was prosecuted because it was irreverent, an attack on religion, and indicative of a heretical outlook, especially if the curses were uttered by Black slaves and people of mixed racial background.

Prosecutions for solicitation pertained to Catholic clergy who propositioned their female penitents during confession. Bigamy and polygamy were crimes associated with Spaniards' arrival in the New World.[36] Some immigrants quickly forgot about their wives in Spain and remarried. Others took advantage of their mobility, whether geographical or social, to marry multiple times. Spanish men might arrive on American shores with Spanish wives but soon abandon them in preference for Indigenous women. The Inquisition could do nothing about so-called "venal" love affairs, in which men and women lived together without the Catholic Church's consecration of the union.

Heresy was what planted the seed for the eventual formal establishment of the Spanish Inquisition in Mexico City in 1571, though without a doubt, suspected heretics there did were not considered so important or face the repercussions that they faced in Spain. True heresy cases – over religious beliefs that contradicted or dismissed Catholicism – were few and far between in New Spain; historian Solange Alberro has calculated that there were only 400 such trials over the duration of New Spain's inquisition tribunal.[37] In those instances, most defendants were Portuguese conversos who saw the Americas as a place to make a quick fortune while being able to safely practice Judaism. In the late sixteenth century, however, and later in the 1640s with the arrival of Inquisitor Juan Sáenz de Mañozca, they were fiercely prosecuted and practically extinguished.[38] One of the best-known cases was that of the Carvajal family. The patriarch of the family, Don Luis, was denounced along with family members for practicing Judaism. Don Luis was sentenced to banishment but died in prison before he could leave. His relatives were sentenced to death in 1596.[39]

We must take into account, then, that the number of serious heretics in New Spain was fairly small. Heresy among the Indigenous populations was none of the Spanish Inquisition's concern, since that offense belonged to the episcopal court system. The inquisition tribunal in Mexico City did not forcefully seek out heretics unless it needed money to cover its expenses, at which point it would launch a campaign against Portuguese conversos, since they held great wealth. The expansion of the Spanish empire into the Americas created a favorable atmosphere for heretical groups to emigrate from Iberia, something that the Spanish church and state did their utmost to minimize.

As for magic, this charge did not trigger many inquisition trials in New Spain.[40] On the contrary, it was considered more of a custom than a crime, a practice that had permeated all social levels and was engaged in by practically everyone to attain luck, make money, attract a loved one, or recover from a disease. For that reason, when a denunciation of magic arrived at the tribunal in New Spain, the inquisitors tended to archive it in order not to give it fuel or stir up the emotions of a population that seemingly without tension combined the new mechanistic thinking and an ancestral way of life, where magic, witchcraft, and even a touch of demonology all played a role.

The Inquisition in New Spain functioned to detect and eradicate any threat to Catholic orthodoxy, which Spanish monarchs were bound to uphold. At the same time, the Inquisition's overarching religious objective was to reconcile penitent heretics to the Catholic Church and restore the possibility of their salvation after death. Ultimately, the Catholic Church and the Inquisition in New Spain became fundamental tools for maintaining the social structure there.

Ideological and Social Control: Censorship

The Inquisition in New Spain was an instrument of power, a force of political and ultimately social consolidation. Its crucial function turned on its affirmation and strengthening of royal power over New Spain's population, because Spanish kings demanded that population's obedience and complete loyalty. This strategy had another objective, as well: to mitigate any potential problems that could arise from Indigenous insurrection.[41]

One of the tools in the hands of the inquisitors in New Spain was cultural control via book censorship. Censorship was an effective means for supervising and regulating ideological expression; it theoretically allowed inquisitors to decide who could say what to whom. Following the lines of practice in Spain, censorship had a significant impact on literature and art, setting limits on permissible themes for exploration and distribution.[42] Inquisition censors – also called *calificadores* – were ecclesiastical examiners and experts in theology charged with evaluating and approving books before publication. They reviewed the content of texts, searching for any sort of material that could be considered heretical, blasphemous, immoral, or contrary to Catholic doctrine.

These censors were appointed by the Inquisition, and they played a crucial role in controlling literary production. Their primary aim, and the reason they existed, was to prevent the diffusion of any idea that could be considered harmful for Catholic orthodoxy or social stability. Many writers and artists censored themselves: They feared their books would not sell, they would lose the support of their patrons and social status, or they could be insulted, wronged, or despised by members of their social milieu. Caution was their byword, yet at the same time, they became skilled at skirting offense by using indirect or allegorical expressions, whereby they succeeded in spreading certain ideas or criticisms under a smokescreen of orthodoxy. One well-known example is Sor Juana Inés de la Cruz, who practiced these techniques with such success that even today some of her writings are difficult to decode.[43]

In New Spain, the Inquisition developed a censorship system to flag any appearance of variation from established Catholic dogma. This ideological control encompassed a wide range of texts, including scientific, literary, and religious works, and especially biblical translations. The intention was to preserve the fundamental pillars of Catholicism and loyalty to the Spanish monarchy in an American context. Restrictions fell upon pre-scientific texts such as those by Galileo, religious books such as the Qu'rān, authors such as Luther and Calvin, and then in the eighteenth century, French Enlightenment ideas expressed by authors such as Voltaire and Rousseau.[44]

The *Index librorum prohibitorum* went into effect nearly as soon as the Inquisition was formally established in New Spain in 1571. It was a list of publications considered heretical, obscene, or licentious, whose reading was considered harmful to society. There were two levels of prohibition: An entire work could be prohibited, or certain parts had to be revised or crossed out.[45] Published indices were never issued in such quantities that everyone could own one. Instead, the content of an index was spread through inquisitorial edicts hung in public places, in order to give the widest possible dissemination as to which new publications were being prohibited. Such edicts contained the name of the author, the title of the work being banned or redacted, the language in which it was written, where it was published and by which press, and the reasons for its being prohibited – and therefore subject to confiscation.

Inquisitors were especially interested in the Bible, given that not everyone knew how to read in Latin and thus turned to translations in the vernacular, which could open a space for heretical or reformist ideas. They also prohibited literary works such as *La Celestina* and the second part of *Lazarillo de Tormes*, and censored treatises by popular spiritual authors such as Fray Luis de León and Fray Luis de Granada. Cervantes's *Don Quixote* was regarded with great distrust and New Spain's intellectual elite did not read it. Still, the greater the censorship, the more imaginative the responses for evading it.

Booksellers generally collaborated with the Inquisition, seeing that if they did not, they might lose all their books or even their property if they were caught selling a volume on the index.[46] If someone was discovered to possess a book on the index, two things could happen: Either the book was simply taken away, or the individual was taken to the secret prisons of the Inquisition and a trial began on charges of spreading heretical ideas contrary to the Catholic faith. The latter occurred to the chief architect of the Mexico City cathedral, Melchor Pérez de Soto. Arrested in December 1654, he was imprisoned for owning prohibited books. After months of solitary confinement, he was given a cellmate who then killed him. Because Pérez de Soto's property was sequestered and inventoried upon his arrest, historians know that he possessed 1,592 books in his library.[47]

Yet despite the censorship and control, the era saw a wave of works in print, many closely linked to the evangelization efforts of Franciscans, Dominicans, Augustinians, and Jesuits in the Americas. Chronicles, sermons, and religious manuals guided missionaries in their work to convert Indigenous peoples to Christianity.[48] Among these treatises were *Historia de los indios de la nueva España*, by Fray Toribio de Benavente, known as "Motolinía," *Confesionario en lengua mexicana y castellana*, by Fray Juan Bautista, *Confesionario mayor y menor en lengua mexicana*, by Fray Bartolomé de Alva, *Confessionario breve en lengua castellana y mexicana*, by Fray Alonso de Molina, and *Manual de sacerdotes*, by Juan Palafox y Mendoza.[49]

Final Considerations

The first years of the Inquisition in New Spain set the course for this ecclesiastical tribunal in its new territories. It was a crucial period for defining the reach, procedure, and impact of the tribunal not only at the start but in the centuries that followed. Though its structure was similar to the Inquisition in Spain, it had to deal with widely scattered territories and the sociocultural differences of a New World population.

The Inquisition in New Spain did not have absolute power; its powers were more limited than is frequently thought. One reason was that Spanish inquisitors sometimes took posts in America simply because they sought wealth and prestige, as well as the possibility that an inquisitorial post in New Spain might enable them to rise in the ranks at home. Many were mediocre at their jobs – inexperienced, lazy, or incompetent. Soon after taking possession of their posts, they often fell victim to inquisitorial inertia; uninterested in their work and paying little attention to the inhabitants of their jails, they did as little as possible and hoped that time would fly by until they could return home with honor and assume the posts they thought they deserved in Spain. As a result, the Suprema in Madrid viewed its tribunal in New Spain with considerable distrust.

Another reason for the Inquisition's lack of power in New Spain was the relatively small number of people it prosecuted for serious heresy. Between 1571 and 1700, surviving inquisition prosecutions in New Spain amount to only 1,913, compared to 38,249 in Spain.[50] The Holy Office in New Spain knew its limits. At the same time, its officials also recognized the role their institution played within the Spanish monarchy. It was an exceptional and privileged instrument whose largest aim, like those of the viceroy and the bishops, was to control society.

The Inquisition was one of the first modern machines of repression, controlling hearts and minds through fear of torture, the devil, and burning at the stake. By propagating fear of the devil and heretics, the Inquisition in New Spain hoped to establish submission to state and church. Inquisitors framed their institution as a necessary instrument to achieve unity between God and new systems of obedience forged by men and imposed upon the world. In the process, the Inquisition provoked distrust and resistance among the local population, which finally led to its abolition in 1820.[51]

Notes

1. This chapter is part of the scientific production generated by the research group "Magical Mentalities and Anti-Superstition Discourse (Sixteenth, Seventeenth, and Eighteenth Centuries)," Universidad Autónoma de Madrid (Spain).
2. Solange Alberro, *Inquisición y sociedad en México, 1571–1700* (Fondo de Cultura Económica, 2004), 7–29.
3. Matthew Restall, *Seven Myths of the Spanish Conquest* (Oxford University Press, 2008), 69–70; Camilla Townsend, *Fifth Sun: A New History of the Aztecs* (Oxford University Press, 2018).

4. Robert Ricard, *La 'Conquête spirituelle' du Mexique: Essai sur l'apostolat et les méthodes missionnaires des Ordres mendiants en Nouvelle-Espagne de 1523–24 à 1572* (Institut d'Ethnologie, 1933).
5. Sonia Corcuera de Mancera, *El fraile, el indio y el pulque: Evangelización y embriaguez en la Nueva España (1523–1548)* (Fondo de Cultura Económica, 2010).
6. Alberto Carrillo Cázares, *El debate sobre la guerra chichímeca* (Colegio de Michoacán, 2000).
7. Abelardo Levaggi, *La Inquisición en Hispanoamérica* (Ediciones Ciudad Argentina, 1997); María Águeda Méndez, *Secretos de Oficio: Avatares de la Inquisición Novohispana* (El Colegio de México/Universidad Nacional Autónoma de México, 2001); Sonia Corcuera de Mancera, *Del amor al temor: Borrachez, catequesis y control en la Nueva España (1555–1771)* (Fondo de Cultura Económica, 2012).
8. Chuchiak, *The Inquisition*, 22; Solange Alberro, *La actividad del Santo Oficio de la Inquisición en Nueva España, 1571–1700* (Instituto Nacional de Antropología e Historia, 1981), 23–6.
9. Miguel Rodrigues Lourenço, "La periferia del poniente: Filipinas en el distrito de la Inquisición de México," in Fernando Ciaramitaro and Miguel Rodríguez Lourenço, eds., *Historia imperial del Santo Oficio (siglos XV-XIX)* (Bonilla Distribución y Edicion, Universidad Autónomia de la Ciudad de México, 2022), 583–630.
10. Richard E. Greenleaf, *The Mexican Inquisition of the Sixteenth Century* (University of New Mexico Press, 1969); Fernando Ciaramitaro and Miguel Rodríguez Lourenço, eds., *Historia imperial del Santo Oficio (siglos XV-XIX)* (Bonilla Distribución y Edición, Universidad Autónoma de la Ciudad de México, Cátedra de Estudios Sefarditas Alberto Venveniste, 2022).
11. José Luis Soberanes Fernández, "La Inquisición en México durante el siglo XVI," *Revista de la Inquisición* 7 (1998): 284; Chuchiak, *The Inquisition*, 9, n. 40.
12. The first Spanish judicial institution in America was the Real Audiencia de Santo Domingo, also known as the Audiencia y Cancillería Real. It was established in 1511, but as a result of disagreements between Governor Diego Colón and the crown, it began operations only in 1526.
13. Seymour B. Liebman, "The Jews of Colonial Mexico," *Hispanic American Historical Review* 43 (1965): 95–6.
14. Chuchiak, *The Inquisition*, 9.
15. Chuchiak, *The Inquisition*, 10.
16. Patricia Lopes Don, "The 1539 Inquisition and Trial of Don Carlos of Texcoco in Early Mexico," *Hispanic American Historical Review* 88 (2008): 573–606.
17. Chuchiak, 10–11, 360n. 47; Greenleaf, *The Mexican Inquisition*, 130–2; Jorge Traslosheros, *Iglesia, justicia y sociedad en la Nueva España: La*

Audiencia del Arzobispado de México, 1526–1668 (Editorial Porrúa y Universidad Iberoamericana, 1994).
18. Francisco Tomás y Valiente, *Gobierno e instituciones en la España del Antiguo Régimen* (Alianza Editorial, 1982); Miroslav Hroch and Anna Skybová, *Ecclesia Militans: The Inquisition* (Dorset Press, 1990); Fernando Ciaramitaro, "El Santo Oficio en el imperio español: Interpretaciones, temáticas, metodología y geografía," in Ciaramitaro and Rodríguez, eds., *Historia imperial*, 23–87.
19. Luis René Guerrero Galván, *De acciones y transgresiones: Los comisarios del Santo Oficio y la aplicación de la justicia inquisitorial en Zacatecas, siglo XVIII* (Universidad Autónoma de Zacatecas, 2010).
20. Luis René Guerrero Galván, "El Santo Oficio en Nueva España: Una revisión estructural," in Ciaramitaro and Rodríguez, eds., *Historia imperial*, 527–46.
21. Jean Plaidy, *The Rise of the Spanish Inquisition* (The Citadel Press, 1967).
22. María Jesús Zamora Calvo, *Artes maleficorum. Brujería, magia y demonología en el Siglo de Oro* (Calambur, 2016), 199–202.
23. Nicolas Eymeric, *Directorivm inqvisitorvm* (Aedibus Populi Roman, 1585).
24. Arthur Stanley Turberville, *The Spanish Inquisition* (Oxford University Press, 1949); Henry Kamen, *The Spanish Inquisition: A Historical Revision* (Weidenfeld & Nicolson, 1997); Bruno Aguilera Barchet, "El procedimiento de la Inquisición española," in Joaquín Pérez Villanueva and Bartolomé Escandell, eds., *Historia de la Inquisición en España y América* Vol. 1 (Biblioteca de Autores Cristianos/Centro de Estudios Inquisitoriales, 1984).
25. Arthur Stanley Turberville, *The Spanish Inquisition* (Oxford University Press, 1949); Kamen, *The Spanish Inquisition*; Aguilera Barchet, "El procedimiento de la Inquisición española;" Alberro, *Inquisición y sociedad*, 21.
26. Chuchiak, *The Inquisition*, 32–3; Martin A. Nesvig, *Ideology and Inquisition: The World of the Censors in Early Mexico* (Yale University Press, 2009), 35–44.
27. Lea, *A History of the Inquisition*, Vol. 2.
28. "Cada uno se llama por su profesión: el teólogo para calificar y el letrado para la consulta y votar"; Archivo Histórico Nacional (Madrid) [AHN] Inquisición, Libro 1305, fol. 58; see also Roberto López Vela, "El calificador en el procedimiento y la organización del Santo Oficio: Inquisición y órdenes religiosas en el siglo XVII," in Escudero López, ed., *Perfiles jurídicos*, 345–70.
29. José Martínez Millán, *La hacienda de la Inquisición* (Consejo Superior de Investigaciones Científicas, 1984); Solange Alberro, "Indices económicos e inquisición en la Nueva España, siglos XVI y XVII," *Cahiers des Amériques Latines* 9–10 (1974), 247–64.

30. Archivo General de la Nación (Mexico City), Inquisición, vol. 402, exp. 1, fols. 95–6, proceso contra Rafaela Enríquez (1642).
31. AHN Inq. leg. 1737, no. 12, cargo no. 23, visita de Medina Rico.
32. Inquisition torture in New Spain was not as intense or as coercive as it was in Spain.
33. Francisco Tomás y Valiente, *El derecho penal de la monarquía absoluta (siglos XVI-XVII-XVIII)* (Editorial Tecnos, 1969), 221–2.
34. Chuchiak, *The Inquisition*, 122–3.
35. Alberro, *La actividad del Santo Oficio*, 93–4.
36. Luis René Guerrero Galván, *Procesos inquisitoriales por el pecado de solicitación en Zacatecas (siglo XVIII)* (Tribunal Superior de la Justicia del Estado de Zacatecas, 2003).
37. Alberro, *Inquisición y sociedad*, 172.
38. Eva Alexandra Uchamany, *La vida entre el judaismo y el cristianismo en la Nueva España, 1580–1606* (Archivo General de la Nación-Fondo de Cultura Económica, 1994).
39. Miriam Bodian, *Dying in the Law of Moses: Crypto-Jewish Martyrdom in the Iberian World* (Indiana University Press, 2007).
40. Graciela Rodríguez Castañon, *Transgresión mágica e Inquisición novohispana en Zacatecas* (Universidad Autónoma de Zacatecas, 2014).
41. Cristina Gómez Álvarez and Guillermo Tovar de Tersa, *Censura y revolución: Libros prohibidos por la Inquisición en México (1790–1819)* (Trama Editorial, 2009); Carlos Alberto González Sánchez and Enriqueta Vila Vilar, eds., *Grafías del imaginario: Representaciones culturales en España y América (siglos XVI-XVIII)* (Fondo de Cultura Económica, 2003).
42. María José Vega, *Disenso y censura en el siglo XVI* (Seminario de Estudios Medievales y Renacentistas, 2012); María José Vega, Mathilde Albisson, and José Luis Gonzalo, *Malos libros: La censura en la España moderna* (Biblioteca National de España, 2023).
43. The Catholic monarchs in 1502 signed an edict, or *pragmática*, in this regard, which can be seen as marking the beginning of the era of censorship aimed at protecting Catholic orthodoxy from destabilizing ideas. Any printed work had to obtain a licence from civil or ecclesiastical authorities. It was also illegal to obtain books from abroad without prior approval from Church authorities.
44. César Manrique Figueroa, "Libros, lectores y bibliotecas del México colonial," *Iberoamericana Global* 1 (2008): 190–200; Manuel Suárez Rivera, *La alhaja más preciosa: Historia de la biblioteca de la Real Universidad de México* (Universidad Nacional Autónoma de México, 2022); Manuel Suárez Rivera, *Dinastía de tinta y papel: Los Zúñiga Ontiveros en la*

cultura novohispana (1756–1825) (Universidad Nacional Autónoma de México, 2019).
45. Manrique Figueroa, "Libros, lectores."
46. Suárez Rivera, *Dinastía de tinta*.
47. The John Carter Brown Library at Brown University curated an exhibit in 2011 entitled, "Melchor Pérez de Soto: A Book Collector Faces the Inquisition." Pérez de Soto's collection has been called one of the finest private printed book collections of the seventeenth century.
48. Claudia Ferreira Ascencio, *Cuando el cura llama a la puerta: orden sacramental y sociedad. Los padrones de confesión del Sagrario de México (1670–1825)* (El Colegio de México, 2014).
49. Fray Toribio de Benavente, "Motolinia," *Historia de los Indios de Nueva España* (Real Academia Española, 2014), www.fundacionaquae.org/wp-content/uploads/2017/07/Historia-de-los-Indios.pdf; Fray Juan Bautista, *Confesionario en lengua mexicana y castellana* (Melchor Ocharte, 1599); Bartolomé de Alva, *Confesionario mayor y menor en lengua mexicana* (Francisco Salbago, 1934); Alonso de Molina, *Confesionario breve en lengua castellana y mexicana* (Antonio de Espinosa, 1565); Juan Palafox y Mendoza, *Manual de sacerdotes*.
50. Chuckiak, *The Inquisition*, 7.
51. Gabriel Torres Puga, *Los últimos años de la Inquisición en la Nueva España* (Consejo Nacional para la Cultura y las Artes, 2014).

Suggestions for Further Reading

Alberro, Solange. *Inquisición y sociedad en México 1571–1700*. Fondo de Cultura Económica, 2004.

Chuchiak IV, John F. *The Inquisition in New Spain, 1536–1820: A Documentary History*. The Johns Hopkins University Press, 2012.

Ciaramitaro, Fernando and Miguel Rodriguez Lourenço, eds. *Historia imperial del Santo Oficio (siglos XV–XIX)*. Bonilla Distribución y Edición, Universidad Autónoma de la Ciudad de México, Cátedra de Estudios Sefarditas Alberto Venveniste, 2022.

Corcuera de Mancera, Sonia. *De pícaros y malqueridos: Huellas de su paso por la Inquisición de Zumárraga (1539–1547)*. Universidad Nacional Autónoma de México/Instituto Tecnológico Autónomo de México/Fondo de Cultura Económica, 2009.

Greenleaf, Richard E. *La Inquisición en Nueva España: Siglo XVI*. Fondo de Cultura Económica, 2012.

Méndez, María Águeda. *Secretos del Oficio: Avatares de la Inquisición Novohispana*. El Colegio de México/Universidad Nacional Autónoma de México, 2001.

Bibliography

Águeda Méndez, María. *Secretos de Oficio: Avatares de la Inquisición Novohispana*. El Colegio de México/Universidad Nacional Autónoma de México, 2001.

Aguilera Barchet, Bruno. "El procedimiento de la Inquisición española." In Joaquín Pérez Villanueva and Bartolomé Escandell, eds., *Historia de la Inquisición en España y América* Vol. 1. Biblioteca de Autores Cristianos/Centro de Estudios Inquisitoriales, 1984.

Alberro, Solange. "Indices económicos e inquisición en la Nueva España, siglos XVI y XVII." *Cahiers des Amériques Latines* 9-10 (1974): 247-64.

La actividad del Santo Oficio de la Inquisición en Nueva España, 1571-1700. Instituto Nacional de Antropología e Historia, 1981.

Inquisición y sociedad en México, 1571-1700. Fondo de Cultura Económica, 2004.

Carrillo Cázares, Alberto. *El debate sobre la guerra chichimeca*. Colegio de Michoacán, 2000.

Chuchiak IV, John F. *The Inquisition in New Spain, 1536-1820: A Documentary History*. The Johns Hopkins University Press, 2012.

Ciaramitaro, Fernando. "El Santo Oficio en el imperio español: Interpretaciones, temáticas, metodología y geografía." In Fernando Ciaramitaro and Miguel Rodríguez Lourenço, eds., *Historia imperial del Santo Oficio (siglos XV-XIX)*. Universidad Autónoma de la Ciudad de México, Cátedra de Estudios Sefarditas Alberto Venveniste, 2022.

Ciaramitaro, Fernando and Miguel Rodríguez Lourenço, eds. *Historia imperial del Santo Oficio (siglos XV-XIX)*. Bonilla Distribución y Edición, Universidad Autónoma de la Ciudad de México, Cátedra de Estudios Sefarditas Alberto Venveniste, 2022.

Corcuera de Mancera, Sonia. *El fraile, el indio y el pulque: Evangelización y embriaguez en la Nueva España (1523-1548)*. Fondo de Cultura Económica, 2010.

Del amor al temor: Borrachez, catequesis y control en la Nueva España (1555-1771). Fondo de Cultura Económica, 2012.

Ferreira Ascencio, Claudia. *Cuando el cura llama a la puerta: orden sacramental y sociedad. Los padrones de confesión del Sagrario de México (1670-1825)*. El Colegio de México, 2014.

Gómez Álvarez, Cristina and Guillermo Tovar de Tersa. *Censura y revolución: Libros prohibidos por la Inquisición en México (1790-1819)*. Trama Editorial, 2009.

González Sánchez, Carlos Alberto, and Enriqueta Vila Vilar, eds. *Grafías del imaginario: Representaciones culturales en España y América (siglos XVI-XVIII)*. Fondo de Cultura Económica, 2003.

Greenleaf, Richard E. *The Mexican Inquisition of the Sixteenth Century*. University of New Mexico Press, 1969.
Guerrero Galván, Luis René. *Procesos inquisitoriales por el pecado de solicitación en Zacatecas (siglo XVIII)*. Tribunal Superior de la Justicia del Estado de Zacatecas, 2003.
De acciones y transgresiones: Los comisarios del Santo Oficio y la aplicación de la justicia inquisitorial en Zacatecas, siglo XVIII. Universidad Autónoma de Zacatecas, 2010.
Hroch, Miroslav, and Anna Skybová. *Ecclesia Militans: The Inquisition*. Dorset Press, 1990.
Kamen, Henry. *The Spanish Inquisition: A Historical Revision*. Weidenfeld & Nicolson, 1997.
Levaggi, Abelardo. *La Inquisición en Hispanoamérica*. Ediciones Ciudad Argentina, 1997.
Liebman, Seymour B. "The Jews of Colonial Mexico." *Hispanic American Historical Review* 43 (1965): 95–108.
López Vela, Roberto. "El calificador en el procedimiento y la organización del Santo Oficio: Inquisición y órdenes religiosas en el siglo XVII." In José Antonio Escudero López, ed., *Perfiles jurídicos de la inquisición española*. Universidad Complutense de Madrid, Instituto Histórico de la Inquisición, 1986.
Manrique Figueroa, César. "Libros, lectores y bibliotecas del México colonial." *Iberoamericana Global* 1 (2008): 190–200.
Martínez Millán, José. *La hacienda de la Inquisición*. Consejo Superior de Investigaciones Científicas, 1984.
Plaidy, Jean. *The Rise of the Spanish Inquisition*. The Citadel Press, 1967.
Restall, Matthew. *Seven Myths of the Spanish Conquest*. Oxford University Press, 2008.
Ricard, Robert. *La "Conquête spirituelle" du Mexique: Essai sur l'apostolat et les méthodes missionnaires des Ordres mendiants en Nouvelle-Espagne de 1523-24 à 1572*. Institut d'Ethnologie, 1933.
Rodrigues Lourenço, Miguel. "La periferia del poniente: Filipinas en el distrito de la Inquisición de México." In Fernando Ciaramitaro and Miguel Rodríguez Lourenço, eds., *Historia imperial del Santo Oficio (siglos XV-XIX)*. Universidad Autónomia de la Ciudad de México, 2022.
Rodríguez Castañon, Graciela. *Transgresión mágica e Inquisición novohispana en Zacatecas*. Universidad Autónoma de Zacatecas, 2014.
Soberanes Fernández, José Luis. "La Inquisición en México durante el siglo XVI." *Revista de la Inquisición* 7 (1998): 283–95.
Suárez Rivera, Manuel. *Dinastía de tinta y papel: Los Zúñiga Ontiveros en la cultura novohispana (1756-1825)*. Universidad Nacional Autónoma de México, 2019.

La alhaja más preciosa: Historia de la biblioteca de la Real Universidad de México. Universidad Nacional Autónoma de México, 2022.

Tomás y Valiente, Francisco. *Gobierno e instituciones en la España del Antiguo Régimen*. Alianza Editorial, 1982.

Torres Puga, Gabriel. *Los últimos años de la Inquisición en la Nueva España*. Consejo Nacional para la Cultura y las Artes, 2014.

Townsend, Camilla. *Fifth Sun: A New History of the Aztecs*. Oxford University Press, 2018.

Traslosheros, Jorge. *Iglesia, justicia y sociedad en la Nueva España: La Audiencia del Arzobispado de México, 1526-1668*. Editorial Porrúa/Universidad Iberoamericana, 1994.

Turberville, Arthur Stanley. *The Spanish Inquisition*. Oxford University Press, 1949.

Uchamany, Eva Alexandra. *La vida entre el judaismo y el cristianismo en la Nueva España, 1580-1606*. Archivo General de la Nación-Fondo de Cultura Económica, 1994.

Vega, María José. *Disenso y censura en el siglo XVI*. Seminario de Estudios Medievales y Renacentistas, 2012.

Vega Ramos, María José, Mathilde Albisson, and José Luis Gonzalo Sánchez. *Malos libros: La censura en la España moderna*. Biblioteca National de España, 2023.

Zamora Calvo, María Jesús. *Artes maleficorum: Brujería, magia y demonología en el Siglo de Oro*. Calambur, 2016.

13

Peru

Introduction

This chapter covers the Lima tribunal of the Holy Office of the Spanish Inquisition from 1570 until 1820, with an emphasis on its inquisitors' activities in the seventeenth century. Inquisition records from Lima are scattered across different archives; the surviving sources are highly incomplete, which probably explains why this tribunal has received less attention in modern scholarship. This chapter examines tribunal jurisdiction in terms of both geography and the peoples it supervised, with the latter including Europeans, Africans, and Indigenous peoples. It considers the lives and careers of prominent inquisitors, and the variety of alleged offenders as defined by the Holy Office. It presents different phases of tribunal activity, provides examples of the offenses that Lima's inquisitors targeted in each phase, and delves into trials of faith for the heresy of crypto-Judaism, the so-called "Great Complicity" of 1635–9. My examination of the Great Complicity covers the development of the trials, the alleged religious activities of the Portuguese New Christians who were accused, the strategies developed by incarcerated prisoners during their trials of faith, and the overall impact of these trials in the history of Lima's Inquisition.

The Creation of the Tribunal

In accordance with instructions issued by King Philip II, in 1570 the Holy Office of the Inquisition established two tribunals in the Spanish colonies: one located in the city of Mexico that covered the Viceroyalty of New Spain, and the other in the city of Lima, covering the Viceroyalty of Peru. Even though for bureaucratic purposes the Spanish colonies belonged to the Kingdom of Castile, when these two tribunals of the Inquisition were created, they were placed under the Inquisition Secretariat of Aragon. As in the Iberian peninsula, these new tribunals in Mexico and Peru operated as guardians of the Christian Faith; they had to identify, locate, and bring to trial perpetrators of different heretical offenses.[1]

Each tribunal was responsible for the territory of the respective Viceroyalty. Until 1776, the Spanish colonies were organized into two viceroyalties that covered vast amounts of land. The Tribunal of the Inquisition of New Spain in the city of Mexico was in charge of what today is Mexico, most of Central America (except Panama), the islands of the Spanish Caribbean, part of Venezuela, and the Philippine Islands in the Pacific. In addition, portions of what today is the southwest of the United States, together with the states of California, Florida, and Louisiana, were at some point part of New Spain, and therefore under the jurisdiction of the Mexican tribunal. The Viceroyalty of Peru stretched over an enormous surface that today is occupied by the following countries: Peru, Bolivia, Ecuador, Colombia, part of Venezuela, Panama, Chile, Argentina, Uruguay, and Paraguay. Following the same logic, the Lima tribunal of the Inquisition was responsible for watching over those lands.

For inquisitorial purposes the jurisdictions of the tribunals located in the cities of Lima and Mexico were too large and thus unmanageable. Throughout the seventeenth century and even as late as the eighteenth, inquisitors from Lima argued that at least a third tribunal but preferably also a fourth one was needed: They justified their request through a combination of geographic coverage and the constant arrival of suspicious people to the colonies. They suggested as possible locations the cities of La Plata (in what today is Bolivia), Santa Fé de Bogotá (Colombia), San Miguel de Tucumán, and Córdoba del Tucumán (both of which are today in Argentina). After several petitions and suggestions, in 1610 a third tribunal of the Inquisition was established in the city of Cartagena of the Indies (Colombia). The jurisdiction of the third tribunal was created by carving out territories from the other two, reducing the expected coverage of each tribunal and therefore making the load more manageable. Still, the officers of the Lima tribunal were responsible for a very large area. Even though the Lima inquisitors were instructed to visit the entire territory included under their jurisdiction, either personally or by sending delegates, they never completed this task. They did establish a network that included *comisarios* and other personnel, who resided in the most important towns and cities under their jurisdiction. That staff assisted Lima's tribunal by sending information, such as denunciations and witness statements, as well as detaining suspects for trial. In total, though, the Lima tribunal of the Inquisition had approximately 250 functionaries for the entire Viceroyalty, and only twelve familiars – men in charge of collecting and providing information for the inquisitors – for the city itself.[2]

From the Inquisition's inauguration to abolition, around forty inquisitors were appointed to as Lima's inquisitors. The men first named to the position were Serván de Cerezuela and Andrés de Bustamante. In 1570, they traveled from Spain to the Viceroyalty of Peru together with Viceroy Francisco de Toledo, who began his tenure in that same year. When Andrés de Bustamante died in Panama, he was replaced by Antonio Gutiérrez de Ulloa. Typically, the Lima tribunal had two inquisitors at a time, but occasionally three and eventually four, according to the number of cases. An increase of inquisitors occurred, for example, during the 1630s when Lima had four inquisitors: Andrés Juan Gaitán, Juan de Mañozca y Zamora, Juan Gutiérrez Flores, and Antonio de Castro y del Castillo. Toward the end of the tribunal's existence, the last two inquisitors were José Ruiz Sobrino and Pedro de Zalduegui.

Like those in the Iberian peninsula, inquisitors in Lima had to have a university degree and a specialization in ecclesiastical or canon law. Before entering the Inquisition, they had usually followed a professional trajectory in law or in higher education. They might also have occupied posts in other parts of the royal bureaucracy or moved in that direction after serving on the tribunal. If they were not ordained as priests when they were appointed to the post of inquisitor, they were allowed about six months to secure their ordination. In their inquisitorial careers, their most common path was to enter the tribunal as a prosecutor and then slowly move upward. After learning how the tribunal operated, they were eventually appointed as junior (or second) inquisitor and finally, as senior (or principal) inquisitor. These promotions could happen in a single local tribunal, or across different tribunals on both sides of the Atlantic. For many, the post of Lima inquisitor was the pinnacle and final post of their careers.

An exception to the trend mentioned above, however, is the life and career of Juan de Mañozca y Zamora. Mañozca y Zamora was a man who in different capacities held posts in all three colonial tribunals; like other inquisitors, he had close relatives appointed to the Spanish Inquisition in different places. Born in Spain, he was a student in Mexico City when his maternal uncle was a staff member of the Mexican tribunal. At a young age, he was appointed inquisitor of Cartagena of the Indies in 1609 and was in charge of inaugurating this tribunal. Later, he was appointed inquisitor of Lima in 1624 and remained in that post until the 1630s, alternating with other roles in the Spanish colonial bureaucracy. In Lima, Mañozca y Zamora acted as senior inquisitor even though his peer at the time, Andrés Juan Gaitán, had been inquisitor in Lima before him. (Gaitán was also older than Mañozca y Zamora, which highlights the latter's dominance and ambition.) From Lima, Mañozca y Zamora became a member of the Suprema in Madrid in 1639. Before his death in 1650, Juan de Mañozca y Zamora was the archbishop of Mexico, while his cousin Juan Sáenz de Mañozca y Murillo acted as inquisitor of the Mexican tribunal.[3]

Obviously, every person appointed to or hired by an inquisition tribunal had to be a good Christian Catholic. In addition, they had to provide evidence of blood purity (*limpieza de sangre*) that demonstrated their Old Christian ancestry. A person who represented the Spanish Inquisition could not have ancestors connected to either Jews or Muslims. These requirements applied to inquisitors as well as to other personnel involved in tribunal activities, no matter the location of the tribunal and no matter their position in the inquisitorial bureaucracy. In Lima, during the last two decades of the sixteenth century, there were discussions about whether the ancestry of tribunal familiars (men with an honorary position, usually in charge of providing information) had been properly vetted. This referred to both the men holding the appointments and their wives, who were suspected of being Moriscas, that is, Christians of Muslim descent. These discussions indicate both the presence of Moriscos and Moriscas in the Spanish colonial world, though they were theoretically prohibited from emigrating, as well as the colonial tribunals' need to supply their posts with available people in the Spanish colonies.[4]

Fortunately for inquisitors and staff, when the Lima tribunal was formally approved in 1570, an existing building, located near the church and convent of La Merced, was available to be remodeled and to serve as the primary location for inquisition activities. All inquisition tribunals required a specially organized compound to function, with three discrete areas: the courtroom, secret prisons, and a chapel. When conducting trials, inquisitors needed space for hearings and interrogations, torture chambers, and, equally importantly, the storage of records. They had to be sure that information related to trials and property confiscations could be accessed as needed. They needed secret cells to hold prisoners on trial. They also required rooms that could serve as residences for the inquisitors as well as additional personnel such as cooks, prison stewards, prison guards, and the like. For other personnel involved in the inquisition activities, there was no need to reside in the tribunal compound; examples would be the *calificadores* who determined if a specific statement had heretical content, the *comisarios* who heard and sent on confessions or denunciations, and the familiars who acted as intelligence agents.

The spatial organization of the tribunal was directly connected to the peculiarities of conducting an inquisition trial. The entire procedure was supposed to be confidential; prisoners were supposed to be isolated in secret cells for the duration of their trials. Furthermore, inquisitors had to be on call in case a prisoner decided to confess at any moment of the day or night; thus we can see why secret cells and inquisitors' lodgings were in the same compound. Prisoners and inquisitors met in the hearing rooms, in formal encounters that were scheduled. Still, it was preferable to have both residing in the same compound to avoid the need to transfer prisoners on the streets, or have inquisitors arriving from the outside on certain days of the week or late at night. The same need for secrecy helps to explain why torture chambers were in the compound as well: The room dedicated to torture held the instruments, and could be used when the tribunal issued a specific torture order during a trial.

No matter their location in the Spanish empire, no one beyond inquisitors and their staff theoretically knew the contours or outcomes of trials until a sentence was applied in a formal act of sentencing called an *auto de fe* or "act of faith." *Autos de fe* could be public or private, at the inquisitors' discretion and depending on how many sentences they were handing down. A public *auto de fe* required a great deal of planning and a large number of verdicts in order to be worthwhile as an educational spectacle.

While their initial compound near La Merced allowed the Lima inquisitors to start operations, they quickly found that the building was not big enough to fully accommodate their activities. According to historian José Toribio Medina, the building could only house one inquisitor, and even that space had to be curtailed to allow room for the torture chamber.[5] The location was also considered inconvenient because it was too centrally located: Bystanders could see prisoners brought in and out of the tribunal, which compromised procedural secrecy. The preferred setting for an inquisition tribunal was outside the central area of a city. Close to fifteen years after its inauguration, in 1584, the Lima Inquisition inherited money left by a bishop. The tribunal used the money to relocate to an area that was slightly distant from the city downtown so it could operate in a compound that fully satisfied the needs of the institution. The Lima Inquisition functioned in its new setting from the mid-1580s until 1820, even though in 1609, 1655, and 1746 the building suffered the impact of earthquakes and needed repairs. Interestingly, at the time of Peru's 1821 Declaration of Independence, the same building was used for the Republican Congress; toward the end of the nineteenth century, it was put to use as a penitentiary.[6] Now there is a museum in Lima called the *Museo del Congreso y de la Inquisición*, located in the facilities that the Lima tribunal used from the mid-1580s until it was abolished in 1820.

Following the Inquisition's general instructions, Lima's inquisitors had to locate and prosecute people who committed offenses such as clerical solicitation, blasphemy, and sorcery.[7] They also were supposed to prosecute baptized Christians who allegedly practiced Judaism, Islam, or Protestantism, who were formally categorized as heretics. Given the range of offenses that Lima's inquisitors were supposed to notice – which were the same throughout the Spanish empire – we can see the Lima tribunal pursuing religious orthodoxy and social control, while also exhibiting religious devotion and royal allegiance to the Catholic values of Spanish kings.

Furthermore, the instructions given to Lima's first inquisitors established that they were to observe the behavior of newcomers in the colonies, meaning people from Europe and Africa who arrived in the Peruvian Viceroyalty through the port of El Callao (located on the Pacific Ocean coast, close to Lima), through the Panama Isthmus, or through other regions in South America such as the port of Buenos Aires or the Portuguese colony of Brazil. Whether these newcomers arrived in the Spanish colonies voluntarily and legally, with documentation issued in Seville authorizing their migrations, or illegally without documentation, or as slaves in a forced migration, upon entering the Viceroyalty of Peru they were all under the eyes of the tribunal.

Of course, the logical question is who watched the Christian population before the creation of the Lima tribunal in 1570? Prior to that date, bishops vetted Catholic religious orthodoxy in their dioceses, including the behavior of Indigenous peoples. However, in 1570 the crown decided that since Native Americans had not been exposed to Christianity before 1492, they would not be placed under inquisitorial jurisdiction. Instead, the crown created different tribunals, called Tribunals of Extirpation of Idolatries, to look after the Indigenous population. If we combine jurisdiction, geography, and populations, it becomes clear that inquisition tribunals in the Spanish colonies were primarily concerned with residents of urban centers and port cities. In contrast, in the Iberian peninsula the Spanish Inquisition held jurisdiction over the entire population no matter their race or location: It was concerned with the entire territory, though its dominion did not always correspond to effective and competent oversight.[8]

Tribunals of Extirpation of Idolatries had similarities with and differences to those of the Inquisition. Both operated following general guidelines that repressed offenses to the Christian faith, both left written records that have been extensively studied by scholars, and both celebrated public ceremonies while handing out sentences in the same central plaza in Lima. However, the Extirpation was an ad hoc tribunal that functioned when it was deemed necessary, whereas the Inquisition functioned steadily in the Spanish colonies from 1570 until the period of Independence in the early 1800s. While the Lima tribunal cannot be described as a wealthy institution, it had its own facilities and budget, whereas the Extirpation tribunals had to justify the launching of each campaign. Furthermore, even though Extirpation campaigns also culminated in public ceremonies of punishment, wherein Indigenous peoples were punished for idolatries, the Indigenous were not relaxed to the secular arm and executed like heretics. Extirpation campaigns disinterred ancestors, and burned mummies and sacred objects, but did not burn people at the stake. Finally, the Extirpation of Idolatries had a more obvious pastoral mission.[9]

Although colonial tribunals of the Inquisition acted with more autonomy because of their physical distance from the Suprema in Madrid, when conducting trials or any other procedure the Lima tribunal had to follow guidelines stipulated for tribunals in general under the Spanish crown. They had to report twice a year sending summaries of trials of faith, called in Spanish *relaciones de causas*, to the Suprema. In cases of split votes or before relaxing someone to the secular arm, Lima inquisitors were instructed to request the opinion of the Suprema, which had to have substantially delayed the outcome.

Local inquisition tribunals cooperated with each other in the colonies. After the unification of the Spanish and Portuguese crowns, from 1580 to 1640 this cooperation included the three tribunals of the Portuguese Inquisition. Portugal did not establish inquisition tribunals in Brazil: instead, Brazil was under the jurisdiction of the Lisbon tribunal and periodically received personnel to conduct visitations and collect information. If someone was imprisoned on suspicion of heresy, the prisoner was sent from Brazil to Lisbon for trial. If tribunals in the Spanish colonies needed Portuguese help, exchanges of information were conducted through the respective Supremas of Madrid and Lisbon.[10] Examples of such transatlantic and transnational cooperation occurred in the seventeenth century, when Lima's inquisitors reached out to the tribunals of Coimbra and Évora for information about Portuguese New Christians. These New Christians were on trial in Lima for judaizing; inquisitors there suspected that the defendants might have been tried previously by inquisitors in Portugal.[11] Trials, trial summaries, descriptions of *autos de fe*, itemized lists of property confiscations, communication between Lima and the Suprema in

Madrid or in Lisbon, correspondence between local tribunals at either side of the Atlantic: these are the extremely valuable and extant primary sources that allow scholars to study the activities of the Lima inquisition. Such sources are preserved in archives located in Madrid, Spain; in Lima, Peru; and in Santiago, Chile.

Tribunal Activities

As part of the larger institution, Lima's inquisition tribunal conducted trials for heresy as well offenses such as blasphemy, bigamy, sorcery, pacts with the devil, solicitation, and other offenses to Catholicism. Intermittently, the tribunal also paid attention to book censorship.[12] The intensity of tribunal activities varied throughout these 250 years, which allows scholars to ask about trends in prosecutions over time. Historian Teodoro Hampe Martínez has found that between 1570 and 1820, the Lima tribunal celebrated close to forty public sentencings of groups of heretics, called *autos de fe*, with the first official inquisitorial one occurring in 1573.[13] *Autos de fe* in the Viceroyalty of Peru, carried out by bishops, occurred before 1573, the earliest when a man accused of Lutheranism was relaxed to the secular arm in 1548, as well as other *autos* in 1560 and 1565. Experts note that forty-eight people died at the stake because of inquisitorial sentencing in Lima. If we collate a total of forty-eight deaths with 1,447 inquisition sentences and 250 years of activity, the execution rate in Lima rate appears low.[14] Significantly, despite long-standing myths about the Spanish Inquisition, scholars have concluded that Spanish inquisitors everywhere only sentenced close to 2 percent of defendants to death at the stake, though we should note that the earliest records of inquisition trials and sentences in Spain have mostly disappeared.[15] Thus while we can call the Spanish Inquisition brutal in terms of its procedures and sentences, we also must acknowledge that such viciousness appears to have been the exception and not the norm.

In terms of change over time, modern scholars explain that the activities of the Lima tribunal can be divided into three phases, the first from 1570 to 1635, the second from 1636 to 1699, and the third from 1700 to 1818. During the first phase, the Lima tribunal was dedicated to several tasks. After settling down in their own facilities, the tribunal faced significant financial struggles. Inquisition tribunals received a royal allowance, a clear indication that secular authorities were also contributing to the battle against heresy. This allowance was not granted automatically: Instead, it had to be requested periodically and justified. Moreover, the amount was adjusted over time according to fluctuating circumstances in the finances of both the Inquisition and the crown. The allowance had to be supplemented with income generated by tribunal activities such as fines and property confiscations, or through gifts of individual donors. If tribunal activities generated a substantial income, secular authorities questioned the need for the allowance. In such a case, a local tribunal was expected to send funds to the Suprema in Madrid and eventually to the crown. During its foundational period of 1570–1635, the Lima tribunal experienced serious financial worries. At different moments, the tribunal reported delays in salary payments for tribunal members, difficulties in coming up with money to repair the compound facilities after an earthquake, and postponements in the celebration of public *autos de fe* when funds could not be found to construct the main stage.

Still, a lack of funds did not equal a lack of activity. During the first phase, the tribunal was busy: It was mainly concerned with visionaries, heretical propositions, blasphemy, and bigamy. The surviving trial records of Fr. Pedro del Toro, Fr. Francisco de La Cruz, and Doña María Pizarro illustrate that the three were connected through accusations that combined heretical propositions, visions, and the presence of pacts with the devil. María Pizarro, tried from 1572 to 1573, admitted to having visions, but said she was unsure as to whether saints or demons appeared in them, an ambiguity that challenged the inquisitors when it came to classifying her offenses. While imprisoned, Pizarro became ill with high fevers and changed her confession several times, which confused Lima's inquisitors even more. She died in 1573 before the tribunal issued a sentence; she was buried in La Merced, which was a sign that the inquisitors were not sure of her guilt. She did not receive a final sentence until 1595, when the Suprema in Madrid approved the Lima tribunal's recommendation to suspend her trial and to notify her relatives of the outcome.

After 1580, Lima's inquisitors paid more attention to the presence of New Christian merchants from Portugal who were seen as potential crypto-Jews, and whose entry into the Viceroyalty increased due to

Portugal's unification with Spain. Their presence became even more visible after the general pardon of 1604, in which Pope Clement VIII instructed that New Christian prisoners with pending inquisition cases had to be freed, unless a sentence was issued within a year in Europe, or within two years in overseas territories.[16] During the 1620s a Portuguese man named Garci Méndez de Dueñas told inquisitors in Lima about his covert Jewish religious practices, as well as his participation in transatlantic commercial networks. In his confession, Méndez de Dueñas provided information about connections with Iberian crypto-Jews living in France, including his wife and daughter, who resided there to avoid the Inquisition. The networks mentioned by Méndez de Dueñas connected Spain, Portugal, and Lima with France, Guinea, Hispaniola, Cartagena, and Nicaragua. Méndez de Dueñas committed suicide in 1624, before his final sentencing; in Lima's 1625 *auto de fe*, his bones were released to the secular arm to be burned.

Clerics who committed the sin of solicitation were also a concern for Lima inquisitors in the initial decades, as were Protestants and the question of forbidden books entering the Peruvian Viceroyalty. Given that Lima's inquisitors were concerned to establish their authority, it is not surprising that they also prosecuted individuals who obstructed tribunal activities, committed perjury, or publicly confronted the tribunal and its personnel. With the available sources, scholars have established that from 1570 to 1635, the Lima Inquisition issued a total of 790 sentences, which exceeded the number of sentences imposed in the following two phases.

A turn toward focusing on the persecution of alleged crypto-Jews marks the end of the first phase in 1635 and the beginning of the second one, which lasted from 1636 to 1699. The Lima tribunal had gathered information about important crypto-Jewish networks since at least the 1620s – see the coverage of Méndez de Dueñas above – but it was in 1634 that the inquisitors surged into action, assessing the evidence and launching a series of imprisonments in the following year. By 1636, they were conducting close to 100 trials that they labeled in their records as *la Complicidad Grande* or *la Gran Complicidad* (the Great Complicity).[17] The tribunal identified a network of New Christian merchants who were either Portuguese or of Portuguese descent, and who resided in Lima or its surroundings. The suspects' commercial activities covered a wide spectrum, from petty merchants who sat outside with a box of relatively inexpensive items for sale, to large-scale agents who participated in the Atlantic slave trade and deposited proceeds in the most important financial institutions in Lima.

The members of the Great Complicity were accused of crypto-Jewish heresy, albeit to different degrees. On one side of the spectrum was the charge of occasionally fasting; preserving kosher dietary rules, such as avoiding the consumption of pork, and respecting the Saturday Sabbath by lighting candles on Friday night and avoiding work on Saturdays. For the Inquisition, these behaviors revealed the rejection of Christ, an adherence to the Law of Moses, and thus a heretical attempt to preserve a hidden Jewish identity. Let us recall that since 1492, the presence of Jews was not theoretically allowed in any Spanish territory, whether peninsular or colonial.

On the other side of the spectrum, not only were the crypto-Jewish defendants heretics because they were baptized Christians who continued to practice Judaism, but they also were suspected of a conspiracy with a chief enemy of the Spanish crown, namely the Dutch. From 1580 to 1640, the territories of Spain and Portugal were unified under a Spanish monarch. In 1624, the Dutch attempted an invasion in the port of El Callao in Lima, but failed; between 1630 and 1654, however, Dutch incursions via the Atlantic succeeded in Brazil. Given the unification of the monarchy in the Iberian peninsula, enemy attacks on Portuguese territory had direct repercussions for Spain. In 1635, inquisitors as well as secular authorities in Lima and Madrid were concerned about the possibility of another Dutch attempt to invade Lima.

From the perspective of Spanish kings and state and ecclesiastical authorities, heretics were associated with civil rebellion. Their suspicion that Portuguese crypto-Jews could be conspiring with the Dutch amplified their concerns, not least because Dutch stances on religious toleration might appeal to Portuguese conversos. Worldwide, the early modern Dutch did not implement policies enforcing conversion to Christianity. They had no interest in creating institutions in charge of investigating and prosecuting Christian heretics. On the contrary, the Dutch allowed the open practice of Judaism in the Netherlands, which turned Amsterdam into a magnet for the migration of Iberian conversos and crypto-Jews who wanted to return to Judaism. In the area under their control in Brazil, the Dutch abolished the Inquisition and allowed the open practice of Judaism. The first synagogue in the Americas was inaugurated in Recife, Brazil, during the 1630s, although it only existed while the Dutch controlled the area. Even though finding hard evidence of a crypto-Jewish/Dutch conspiracy was a difficult task for Lima's inquisitors, in 1635 they assumed that Portuguese New Christians had reasons to support a Dutch invasion of Spanish or Portuguese territories.

From 1636 to 1639, the Lima tribunal conducted close to 100 prosecutions, concentrating predominantly on crypto-Jews. This level of inquisitorial activity was quite unusual in Lima and was unsustainable in terms of the Inquisition's infrastructure. Lima's inquisition tribunal had sixteen secret cells, but with close to a hundred prisoners on trial, the tribunal needed to place more than one prisoner in a cell. Later, the tribunal rented neighboring houses to expand its facilities, but the rooms in those buildings had to be adapted to serve as secret holding places. Though the inquisitors tried, the improvised cells did not provide the levels of isolation and secrecy expected during a trial. As the inquisitors detailed in correspondence sent to the Suprema in Madrid as well as other archival materials, their prisoners communicated with one another from the improvised secret cells, supported each other when the application of torture was imminent, bribed prison personnel to obtain additional information, plotted to modify the content of their confessions, and conspired to denounce Old Christians as New Christians and potential crypto-Jews. The collective strategies deployed by these prisoners confounded the Lima tribunal and delayed the sentences.[18]

On January 23, 1639, most of the prisoners related to the Great Complicity received their sentences in an *auto de fe* celebrated in Lima's central plaza, although some cases took longer to resolve. Eleven accused men died after being relaxed to the secular arm. Whether they were executed or reconciled to the Church and forced to wear a *sambenito*, the alleged crypto-Jews received the most severe punishments in 1639, though they were not the only ones sentenced. For example, two men and a woman were punished with exile from the city for breaking secrecy; a bigamist received 100 lashes and was sent to the galleys. Women found guilty of sorcery received a combination of punishments – abjuration, lashes, and exile.[19] Two years later, in 1641, Lima's inquisitors found what they believed to be another judaizing/Dutch conspiracy in Cuzco and sentenced fourteen people for heresy. Over the next twenty years, however, the tribunal's activities were considerably less intense. In 1664, Lima's tribunal celebrated another public *auto de fe*, but inquisitors were turning their attention toward issues of social control, looking into bigamy, sorcery, and superstition, and occasionally investigating foreigners who were suspected of Protestantism.

The prisoners of the Great Complicity were overwhelmingly men, with only three women. The gender balance is different when it comes to cases of sorcery. Out of sixty individuals charged with sorcery in the second half of the seventeenth century, forty-nine were female. Most of these women belonged to the lower socioeconomic levels in the city, although there is no clear category of race or ethnic affiliation among sorcerers. In the description of their practices there was also a combination of European, African, and Indigenous traditions.[20]

As for numbers, in its second phase the Lima tribunal issued the lowest number of sentences, a total of 297 – fewer than half the number of sentences issued in the first phase (790) and fewer again than sentences issued in the third one (390). Still, the trials of the Great Complicity conducted during the second phase had a long-term impact upon the tribunal because they drastically improved its finances. Most trials for crypto-Jewish heresy from 1636 to 1639 included property confiscations, whether or not the individual sentences entailed reconciliation or relaxation to the secular arm. Some of the alleged heretics prosecuted during the Great Complicity were very wealthy merchants. Among them, Manuel Bautista Pérez and Sebastián Duarte, brothers in law and commercial partners, deserve special mention. Their combined wealth was probably equivalent to $33 million dollars in current monetary values, and it represented half of what the Lima Inquisition confiscated during the trials.

The confiscations related to the Great Complicity did not go directly into the inquisitors' pockets. They paid for expenses incurred during the trials, including renting additional space for secret cells, as well as the celebration of the 1639 *auto de fe*. The Lima tribunal also absorbed any financial obligations the prisoners had before their trials and paid pending debts. The task of processing and organizing the confiscations occupied the tribunal until 1650, which is probably why historians have found that in the twenty years following the 1639 *auto de fe*, there was a decrease in tribunal activity. After obligations were discharged, what remained for the Lima tribunal was close to 30 percent of the goods and income confiscated during the Great Complicity persecution. That sum was enough to initiate a period of prosperity that lasted until the eighteenth century.[21]

During the third phase (1700–1818) Lima's inquisitors paid attention to offenses such as bigamy, superstition, and blasphemy. Most of the tribunal's trials occurred between 1700 and 1745. Officials noticed the behavior of the clergy and put them on trial for solicitation; they worried about the arrival and confiscation of prohibited books. Protestants, who were also foreigners in Spanish lands, were the heretics who appeared more often in front of the tribunal during this phase. Between 1705 and 1713, military conflicts with England and with the Netherlands turned the attention of the Inquisition toward people from those territories. Most of these trials were initiated by the very same foreigners, who spontaneously appeared in front of the Lima tribunal and confessed to being Protestants. In keeping within inquisitorial guidelines, Lima reconciled them to the Church with lighter penances that included abjuration, reclusion, and exile. The Treaty of Utrecht, signed in 1713, provided a broad agreement that diminished inquisitorial attention to Protestants in the Spanish colonies. The pace of activities of the Lima tribunal drastically declined after 1745, mainly due to lack of personnel and, once again, problems with money.

This chapter has investigated the main characteristics of the Lima tribunal of the Inquisition with an eye to royal guidelines, activities, and finances. It also has explored the variety of offenses and provided examples of the most relevant trials of faith conducted by the Lima tribunal between 1570 and 1820.

Given its vast geography, inquisitors attached to the Lima tribunal never completed an inspection of their entire jurisdiction, which could create the impression that the tribunal was a dormant and inactive office. However, since in the Spanish colonies only Europeans and Africans were under the tribunal's supervision, and Indigenous Americans were not, the location of an inquisition tribunal in a port city such as Lima made sense because it was where potential prisoners of the tribunal tended to reside.

Lima's inquisitors conducted trials over some 250 years. The surviving evidence indicates that they issued a total of 1,447 sentences, with forty-eight defendants relaxed to the secular arm. The Lima tribunal was interested in the same range of offenses covered by its counterparts in Spain. Tribunal members were concerned about the presence of hidden Jews, Muslims, and Protestants in the Peruvian Viceroyalty and worried about the effects they might have. They also were preoccupied with minor offenders such as visionaries, sorcerers, and bigamists. Among the trials of faith conducted in Lima, those that took place between 1635 and 1639 for the heresy of crypto-Judaism, known as the Great Complicity, marked a peak of the Inquisition's activities there, with a combination of long trials, severe sentences, and a crucial improvement of tribunal finances thanks to property confiscations.

Notes

1. Henry Charles Lea, *The Inquisition in the Spanish Dependencies* (The Macmillan Company, 1908); José Toribio Medina, *Historia del Tribunal de la Inquisición de Lima, 1569–1820* Vol. 2, 2nd edition (Fondo Histórico y Bibliográfico J. T. Medina, 1956). There is a vast amount of scholarship on the Lima Inquisition. For reasons of space the citations are limited to a few authors.
2. Toribio Medina, *Historia del Tribunal*; Bartolomé Escandell Bonet, "Las adecuaciones estructurales: Establecimiento de la Inquisición en Indias," in Joaquín Pérez Villanueva and Bartolomé Escandell Bonet, eds., *Historia de la Inquisición en España y América* Vol. 1 (Biblioteca de Autores Cristianos/ Centro de Estudios Inquisitoriales, 1984).
3. Kimberly Lynn, *Between Court and Confessional: The Politics of Spanish Inquisitors* (Cambridge University Press, 2013).
4. Karoline Cook, *Forbidden Passages: Muslims and Moriscos in Colonial Spanish America* (University of Pennsylvania Press, 2016).
5. Medina, *Historia del Tribunal*.
6. Manuel Atanasio Fuentes, *Lima: Apuntes históricos, descriptivos, estadísticos y de costumbres* (Librería Escolar e Imprenta E. Moreno, 1925 [1867]).
7. For solicitation, see Chapter 4 of this *Cambridge Companion*.
8. As an example of the Logroño tribunal's inability to control events in Navarre, Lu Ann Homza, *Village Infernos and Witches' Advocates: Witch*

Hunting in Navarre, 1608–1614 (Pennsylvania State University Press, 2022).
9. Kenneth Mills, *Idolatry and Its Enemies: Colonial Andean Religion and Extirpation, 1640–1750* (Princeton University Press, 1997).
10. François Soyer, "The Extradition Treaties of the Spanish and Portuguese Inquisitions (1500–1700)," in *Estudios de Historia de España* 10 (2008): 201–38.
11. Nathan Wachtel, *The Faith of Remembrance: Marrano Labyrinths*, trans. Nikki Halpern (University of Pennsylvania Press, 2013); Ana E. Schaposchnik, *The Lima Inquisition: The Plight of Crypto-Jews in Seventeenth Century Peru* (University of Wisconsin Press, 2015).
12. Pedro Guibovich Pérez, *Censura, libros e Inquisición en el Perú colonial, 1570–1754* (Consejo Superior de Investigaciones Científicas, Escuela de Estudios Hispano-Americanos, Universidad de Sevilla, Diputación de Sevilla, 2003).
13. Teodoro Hampe Martínez, "Recent Works on the Inquisition and Peruvian Colonial Society, 1570–1820," *Latin American Research Review* 31 (1996): 43–65.
14. Paulino Castañeda Delgado and Pilar Hernández Aparicio, *La Inquisición de Lima, Tomo 1 (1570–1635)* (Deimos, 1989); *La Inquisición de Lima, Tomo 2 (1635–1696)* (Deimos, 1995); René Millar Carvacho, *La Inquisición de Lima, Tomo 3 (1697–1820)* (Deimos, 1998).
15. Jaime Contreras and Gustav Henningsen, "Forty-Four Thousand Cases of the Spanish Inquisition (1540–1570): Analysis of a Historical Data Bank," in Gustav Henningsen and John Tedeschi, eds., *The Inquisition in Early Modern Europe* (Northern Illinois University Press, 1986); Jaime Contreras, "Estructura de la actividad procesal del Santo Oficio," in Joaquín Pérez Villanueva and Bartolomé Escandell Bonet, eds., *Historia de la Inquisición en España y América* Vol. 2 (Biblioteca de Autores Españoles/Centro de Estudios Inquisitoriales, 1993).
16. Claude Stuczynski, "New Christian Political Leadership in Times of Crisis: The Pardon Negotiations of 1605," in Moises Orfali, ed., *Leadership in Times of Crisis* (Bar-Ilan University Press, 2007).
17. Schaposchnik, *The Lima Inquisition*.
18. Ana E. Schaposchnik, "The Dungeons of the Lima Inquisition: Corruption, Survival, and Secret Codes in Colonial Peru," *Colonial Latin American Review* 29, no. 3 (2020).
19. Ana E. Schaposchnik, "Exemplary Punishment in Colonial Lima: The 1639 Auto de Fe," in Martina Will de Chaparro and Miruna Achim, eds., *Death and Dying in Colonial Spanish America* (The University of Arizona Press, 2011).
20. María Emma Mannarelli, "Inquisición y mujeres: Las hechiceras en el Perú durante el siglo XVII," *Revista Andina* 3 (1985): 141–55.

21. Lea, *The Inquisition in the Spanish Dependencies*; Castañeda Delgado and Hernández Aparicio, *Inquisición de Lima, Tomo 2*; René Millar Carvacho, *Inquisición y sociedad en el Virreinato peruano* (Ediciones Universidad Católica de Chile, 1998); Matthew Warshawsky, "Manuel Bautista Pérez and the *Complicidad Grande* in Colonial Peru: Inquisitorial Hysteria or Crypto-Jewish Heresy?," *Journal of Spanish, Portuguese, and Italian Crypto-Jews* 2 (2010): 132–50.

Suggestions for Further Reading

Bodian, Miriam. *Dying in the Law of Moses: Crypo-Jewish Martyrom in the Iberian World*. Indiana University Press, 2007.
Guibovich Pérez, Pedro. *The Inquisition and Book Censorship in the Peruvian Viceroyalty, 1570–1813*. Congreso del Perú, 2000.
Lea, Henry Charles. *The Inquisition in the Spanish Dependencies*. The Macmillan Company, 1908.
Mannarelli, María Emma. *Hechiceras, beatas y expósitas: Mujeres y poder inquisitorial en Lima*. Congreso del Perú, 1998.
Millar Carvacho, René. *Inquisición y sociedad en el Virreinato Peruano: Estudios sobre el Tribunal de la Inquisición de Lima*. Ediciones de la Universidad Católica de Chile, 1998.
Schaposchnik, Ana E. *The Lima Inquisition: The Plight of Crypto-Jews in Seventeenth Century Peru*. University of Wisconsin Press, 2015.
Silverblatt, Irene. *Modern Inquisitions: Peru and the Colonial Origins of the Civilized World*. Duke University Press, 2004.
Studnicki-Gizbert, Daviken. *A Nation Upon the Ocean Sea: Portugal's Atlantic Diaspora and the Crisis of the Spanish Empire, 1492–1640*. Oxford University Press, 2007.
Suárez, Margarita. *Desafíos transatlánticos: Mercaderes, banqueros, y el estado en el Perú Virreinal, 1600–1700*. Pontificia Universidad Católica del Perú, Instituto Riva Agüero, Fondo de Cultura Económica, Instituto Francés de Estudios Andinos, 2001.
Wachtel, Nathan. *The Faith of Remembrance: Marrano Labyrinths*. Trans. by Nikki Halpern. University of Pennsylvania Press, 2013.

Bibliography

Castañeda Delgado, Paulino, and Pilar Hernández Aparicio. *La Inquisición de Lima, Tomo 1 (1570–1635)*. Deimos, 1989.
La Inquisición de Lima, Tomo 2 (1635–1696). Deimos, 1995.
Contreras, Jaime. "Estructura de la actividad procesal del Santo Oficio." In Joaquín Pérez Villanueva and Bartolomé Escandell Bonet, eds., *Historia*

de la Inquisición en España y América. Vol. 2. Biblioteca de Autores Españoles & Centro de Estudios Inquisitoriales, 1993.

Contreras, Jaime, and Gustav Henningsen. "Forty-Four Thousand Cases of the Spanish Inquisition (1540–1570): Analysis of a Historical Data Bank." In Gustav Henningsen and John Tedeschi, eds., *The Inquisition in Early Modern Europe.* Northern Illinois University Press, 1986.

Cook, Karoline. *Forbidden Passages: Muslims and Moriscos in Colonial Spanish America.* University of Pennsylvania Press, 2016.

Domínguez Ortiz, Antonio. *Los Judeoconversos en España y en América.* Istmo, 1971.

Escandell Bonet, Bartolomé. "Las adecuaciones estructurales: establecimiento de la Inquisición en Indias." In Joaquín Pérez Villanueva and Bartolomé Escandell Bonet, eds., *Historia de la Inquisición en España y América* Vol. 1. Biblioteca de Autores Cristianos/Centro de Estudios Inquisitoriales, 1984.

Fuentes, Manuel Atanasio. *Lima: Apuntes históricos, descriptivos, estadísticos y de costumbres.* Librería Escolar e Imprenta E. Moreno, 1925 [1867].

Guibovich Pérez, Pedro. *Censura, libros e Inquisición en el Perú colonial, 1570–1754.* Consejo Superior de Investigaciones Científicas, Escuela de Estudios Hispano-Americanos, Universidad de Sevilla, Diputación de Sevilla, 2003.

Hampe Martínez, Teodoro. "Recent Works on the Inquisition and Peruvian Colonial Society, 1570–1820." *Latin American Research Review* 31, no. 2 (1996): 43–65.

Homza, Lu Ann. *Village Infernos and Witches' Advocates: Witch Hunting in Navarre, 1608–1614.* Pennsylvania State University Press, 2022.

Israel, Jonathan. *Empires and Entrepots: The Dutch, the Spanish Monarchy and the Jews, 1585–1713.* The Hambledon Press, 1990.

Lea, Henry Charles. *The Inquisition in the Spanish Dependencies.* The Macmillan Company, 1908.

Lynn, Kimberly. *Between Court and Confessional: The Politics of Spanish Inquisitors.* Cambridge University Press, 2013.

Mannarelli, María Emma. "Inquisición y mujeres: Las hechiceras en el Perú durante el siglo XVII." *Revista Andina* 3 (1985): 141–55.

Medina, José Toribio. *Historia del Tribunal de la Inquisición de Lima, 1569–1820.* 2nd ed. Vol. 2. Fondo Histórico y Bibliográfico J. T. Medina, 1956.

Millar Carvacho, René. *Inquisición y sociedad en el Virreinato peruano.* Ediciones Universidad Católica de Chile, 1998.

La Inquisición de Lima, Tomo 3 (1697–1820). Deimos, 1998.

Mills, Kenneth. *Idolatry and Its Enemies: Colonial Andean Religion and Extirpation, 1640–1750.* Princeton University Press, 1997.

Schaposchnik, Ana. "Exemplary Punishment in Colonial Lima: The 1639 Auto de Fe." In Martina Will de Chaparro and Miruna Achim, eds., *Death and Dying in Colonial Spanish America*. The University of Arizona Press, 2011.

The Lima Inquisition: The Plight of Crypto-Jews in Seventeenth Century Peru. University of Wisconsin Press, 2015.

"The Dungeons of the Lima Inquisition: Corruption, Survival, and Secret Codes in Colonial Peru." *Colonial Latin American Review* 29, no. 3 (2020): 398–413.

Silverblatt, Irene. "The Black Legend and Global Conspiracies: Spain, the Inquisition, and the Emerging Modern World." In Margaret Greer, Walter Mignolo, and Maureen Quilligan, eds., *Rereading the Black Legend: The Discourses of Religious and Racial Difference in the Renaissance Empires*. The University of Chicago Press, 2007.

Soyer, François. "The Extradition Treaties of the Spanish and Portuguese Inquisitions (1500–1700)." *Estudios de Historia de España* 10 (2008): 201–38.

Stuczynski, Claude. "New Christian Political Leadership in Times of Crisis: The Pardon Negotiations of 1605." In Moises Orfali, ed., *Leadership in Times of Crisis*. Bar-Ilan University Press, 2007.

Studnicki-Gizbert, Daviken. *A Nation Upon the Ocean Sea: Portugal's Atlantic Diaspora and the Crisis of the Spanish Empire, 1492–1640*. Oxford University Press, 2007.

Wachtel, Nathan. *The Faith of Remembrance: Marrano Labyrinths*. Trans. Nikki Halpern. University of Pennsylvania Press, 2013.

Warshawsky, Matthew. "Manuel Bautista Pérez and the *Complicidad Grande* in Colonial Peru: Inquisitorial Hysteria or Crypto-Jewish Heresy?" *Journal of Spanish, Portuguese, and Italian Crypto-Jews* 2 (2010): 132–50.

ANA MARÍA DÍAZ BURGOS

14

Cartagena de Indias

After traveling for about three months from Spain, inquisitors Don Juan de Mañozca and Don Pedro Matheo de Salcedo arrived in Cartagena de Indias on September 21, 1610. On royal orders, the governor of Cartagena, Diego de Velasco, had prepared their welcome to the port city with fanfare. Once music and fireworks had been exhausted, a multitude escorted Mañozca and Matheo de Salcedo to their provisional house. As they probably expected, however, not everyone embraced their presence with such enthusiasm. Archbishop Juan de Ladrada showed his discontent from the beginning, forseeing the jurisdictional conflicts that might divide the city and the government's support. Ladrada would be proven correct. Tensions arose soon after and escalated throughout the seventeenth century. Such conflicts would come to characterize inquisitorial interactions with religious and public authorities throughout the duration of the tribunal in Cartagena (1610–1821).

In 1610, Mañozca and Salcedo inaugurated the Holy Office of the Inquisition's third outpost in the Spanish Americas, forty years after the establishment of Lima's and Mexico City's tribunals in 1571. Colonial governors and inquisitors had petitioned several times for metropolitan approval to launch a Caribbean tribunal to strengthen Spanish control and surveillance across the region. Cartagena was chosen mainly because of its economic and strategic relevance, despite not being considered a political center like Santo Domingo or Santa Fe due to its lack of an *audiencia*, a university and an archbishop.[1] Its jurisdiction would consist of the New Kingdom of Granada, Santo Domingo's dependent provinces, and the Barlovento islands. The port-city's location as a key node in the circulation and flow of peoples, commodities, and ideas across the Atlantic, however, made it a strategic geopolitical position from which inquisitors could closely monitor threats and offenses (Figure 14.1).

In the larger scheme of things, if a hierarchy of inquisition tribunals in Spanish America were established, Cartagena's would place after Mexico and Lima's in terms of the number of cases and the distribution of prosecutions. Whereas, in the period between 1570 and 1700, Mexico's tribunal saw 1,933 trials and Lima's 1,176 cases, Cartagena's dealt only with 731 cases between 1610 and 1700, out of which five defendants were burned at the stake.[2]

This chapter presents an overview of the crimes, victims, and power dynamics that characterized Cartagena's Inquisition. I pay special attention to the extent to which the pageantry exhibited in public celebrations, the secrecy involved in the inner workings of the tribunal, and local and metropolitan politics shaped institutional and personal rivalries and alliances in the region and influenced inquisitorial decisions. First, I will delineate how the Inquisition's rule took root in the city and discuss some of the main prosecutions during the tribunal's first three decades.[3] Then I will address the travels of inquisitors Don Martín del Real (1643–1645) and Don Pedro de Medina Rico (1647–1650), who were visiting inspectors (*visitadores*), as a turning point in the tribunal's trajectory. These visiting inspectors' reports record local inquisitors' institutional and personal alliances and disputes and the many ways in which these permeated decisions made inside and outside the courtroom. The conflicts ultimately undermined the image of the tribunal in the second half of the seventeenth century, when the institution devolved into infighting and scandals, leaving the defense of inquisitorial law on the sidelines. Finally, I will focus on the opacity of the institution's role in eighteenth-century Cartagena and address the circumstances that led to its disappearance in 1821.

Before investigating the tribunal's presence in the port city, though, it is important to bear in mind that in contrast to other inquisitorial repositories from the Americas, Cartagena's archival records were damaged by adverse weather conditions, termites (*comejenes*), and the destruction of the city in 1697 by French corsair Baron de Pointis. As a result, few trials

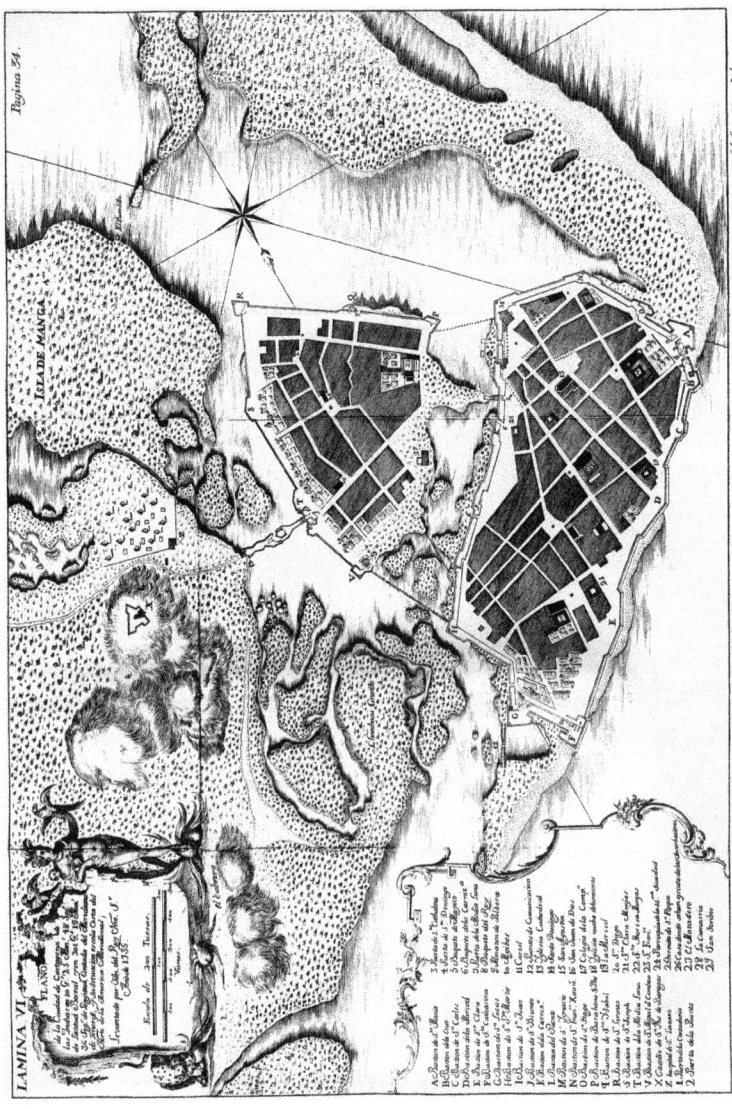

Figure 14.1 Plan of Cartagena de las Indias. Source: Jorge Juan y Antonio de Ulloa, Relación histórica del viage a la América meridional (1748).

(*procesos de fe*) have survived in their entirety, and whatever information remains about the people prosecuted has been preserved through the case summaries (*relaciones de causa*) that inquisitors periodically sent to the Supreme Council of the Inquisition in Madrid, the Suprema. These summaries present quick profiles of defendants; they briefly list the main accusations against them, make a few references to the witnesses, and give the sentences. Additionally, information related to inquisitorial procedures, inquisitors, and trials can be found in the epistolary communication between local and metropolitan authorities of the city. Today, this documentation is housed in the National Historical Archive (*Archivo Histórico Nacional*) in Madrid, Spain, with additional materials in the Colombian Institute of Anthropology and History (*Instituto Colombiano de Antropología e Historia*), and the Luis Ángel Arango Library, both located in Bogotá, Colombia, as well as the University of Cartagena.

Upon their arrival in 1610, inquisitors Mañozca and Salcedo made every effort to display their authority, even if their personalities were radically different.[4] Not only were they publicly present at local secular and religious festivities but they also occupied three main houses (*casonas*) in the Notaries' Public Portal (*Portal de los Escribanos*). In fact, a few days after their arrival, they gathered the population in the cathedral and read an edict of grace, a document that listed the heresies and crimes prosecuted by the Inquisition. The edict condemned practices that must have sounded foreign to Cartagena, such as the proscription of the "law of Moses, the sects of Mohammed, of Luther, and of *alumbrados*."[5] Yet, it also denounced heresies that resonated more with the locals' daily lives and practices, as reflected in the first prosecutions for witchcraft, sorcery, blasphemy, and bigamy. Through the edict, the inquisitors gave the local population six days to voluntarily denounce anyone, including themselves, for having committed offenses against the edict.[6] On the seventh day, the inquisitors would start their inquiries and begin their prosecutions.

While the inquisitors were adjusting to their new context, they asked the metropolitan authorities to speed up their support to build the Inquisition's prisons; the first thirteen cells were constructed by 1612. Soon enough, just like their counterparts in Mexico City and Lima, the newly arrived inquisitors came to realize the discrepancies in matters of faith between letter and practice, and between peninsular and American circumstances. Like all inquisitors elsewhere, Mañozca and Salcedo had to keep in mind where, exactly, they were doing their jobs. They used their discretion as they realized Cartagena called for a different set of strategies to keep the jurisdiction's inhabitants under control.

Along with the public pomp of the new institution, Mañozca and Salcedo imposed a regime of fear and secrecy to underscore the tribunal's power in Cartagena. The first trials culminated in the celebration of a grandiloquent *auto de fe* in 1614. In Spain, public *autos* aimed to closely represent the imagined theatrics of the Day of Judgment.[7] In Spanish American territories, they did so as well, but with the additional purpose of displaying and legitimizing imperial control.[8] The spectacle required defendants to wear penitential garments that symbolized the gravity of their offenses against Catholic orthodoxy and the shame they had to endure to repent and be reincorporated to the Church.

In the inaugural *auto*, inquisitors Mañozca and Salcedo publicly read twenty sentences out of the thirty-six defendants prosecuted during the first four years of the tribunal (1610–14). The remaining sixteen were presented for sentencing at different times in the inquisitorial courtroom (*sala de audiencia*). During these years, inquisitors had predominantly prosecuted sorcery and word crimes (*delitos de palabra*), which included *blasfemia* or blasphemy, understood as offenses against the Christian God and Catholic faith, as well as *reniego*, which was renunciation of the same God and faith. The inquisitors prosecuted "mistaken propositions" (*proposiciones*), by which they referred to publicly stated misinterpretations of Catholic orthodoxy.[9] These crimes implied heresy. Their authors were Spanish American and European people, free and enslaved, from across the social spectrum. Although sorcery and word crimes were considered minor offenses in the Iberian peninsula, their prevalence in the everyday life of Cartagena, across race and socioeconomic status, concerned the new inquisitors.

In the first *auto*, six women and a man were prosecuted for sorcery. Out of these, the case of Doña Lorenzana de Acereto stands out. It is one of the few trials that has been preserved – because it was originally misplaced.[10] Doña Lorenzana, a twenty-seven-year-old Creole (*criolla*), wife of the city's royal scribe, and mother of four children, was prosecuted for sorcery and superstition.[11] In her practices, Doña Lorenzana collaborated with her elite Creole peers as well as Afro-descendant and

Indigenous women and men, free and enslaved. After ten months in the inquisitorial prisons, Doña Lorenzana was sentenced to a spiritual penance, an onerous fine, and banishment from the city for two years. Immediately, though, her husband successfully appealed the sentence to recover the family's honor and the hefty fees paid to the Inquisition. Her case shows the practices and beliefs that women such as Doña Lorenzana used to solve a variety of conflicts related to love, health, and wealth before the tribunal's establishment in the city and how they clashed with and redefined the metropolitan patterns of virtue and deviance. Additionally, her prosecution was part of a personal quarrel between Mañozca and Sargent Francisco de Santander, Doña Lorenzana's lover, which was one of the multiple conflicts Mañozca had in the city.

Between 1610 and 1640, there were twenty-nine cases for blasphemy, eighteen for renunciation, and twenty-two for mistaken propositions.[12] In the case of *blasfemia*, most blasphemers were resident European artisans, sailors, or priests, or men who held military or public posts. According to their confessions, their imprecations arose in settings of male sociability or resulted from dire circumstances such as desperation, economic problems, rivalries, questions of honor, and so on. Defendants expressed their remorse and emphasized that they did not mean to question the principles of Catholic orthodoxy, which they diligently followed.[13] Depending upon their social status, their sentences involved lashes, pecuniary fees, and banishment, as well as being sent to the galleys, hospitals, or convents.

In turn, most cases of renunciation involved enslaved women and men who blasphemed when slave owners were punishing them for having run away or allegedly disobeying their orders. While blasphemers' sinful behavior had to be denounced to the Inquisition, these renunciation trials also revealed the slaveholders' abuses, which could, if extreme cruelty was proven, potentially result in a reassignment of the household. In their defense, those accused of renunciation normally expressed regret and explained that they were "out of themselves" when they uttered the offensive words: They had done so because they were suffering extreme duress and they expressed their fear of losing their souls.[14] With these arguments, enslaved subjects emphasized their Christian piety and, at the same time, exposed slaveholders' violence.[15]

Both these rhetorical tactics foregrounded blasphemy as a strategic tool to interrupt the otherwise habitual practices of forced labor exploitation and enslavement. However, these interruptions did not always result in a permanent solution or guarantee a positive outcome for the defendant. Although inquisitors continued prosecuting the various sorts of blasphemy as well as mistaken propositions throughout the seventeenth century, the number of cases sharply declined after the decade of 1630, when inquisitorial interest turned to practices of witchcraft and crypto-Judaism. By the late seventeenth century, Cartagena's tribunal ceased prosecuting enslaved people for blasphemy throughout its jurisdiction.[16]

Cartagena's inquisitors became even busier after their first *auto de fe* in 1614. In subsequent years, Mañozca and Salcedo prosecuted more defendants – fifty – and for different forms of heresy. Now, suspects were charged not only with blasphemy but also with Protestantism, bigamy, crypto-Judaism, and solicitation, among other offenses. Yet there were no *autos de fe*: instead, the inquisitors either read their sentences in the cathedral, or in the tribunal's courtroom. The lack of public *autos de fe* in the years between 1614 and 1622 indicates both the inquisitors' relentless work and the limitations of their budget and personnel.

Cartagena's place in the world altered after Portugal was annexed to the Spanish crown in 1580. The city underwent significant demographic, economic, commercial, and institutional changes, and the creation of an inquisition tribunal added another layer of complexity. As Cartagena's role in transatlantic commerce, contraband, and the slave trade became more prominent in the first half of the seventeenth century, it experienced a dramatic increase in its Portuguese, African, and Afro-descendant populations.[17] Demographic, economic, and social diversity raised concerns about unorthodox practices, heretical conspiracies, and social uprisings; secular and inquisitorial authorities intensified their mechanisms of surveillance. Salcedo passed away in 1621. Mañozca, who had been accused of corruption and abuse of power in Madrid, returned unscathed to Cartagena after his legal battles and staged a second public *auto* in 1622, which singled out African and Afro-descendant enslaved people in prosecutions for witchcraft.

Although the tribunal received more than 100 denunciations about practices of witchcraft, involving the destruction of crops, inexplicable infant deaths, obstructions of gold mining, and rumors of a rebellion, Mañozca only prosecuted six individuals for this particular heresy. Four were African enslaved (*bozales*) women and a man from the mining region of Zaragoza, located about 450 kilometers southwest of Cartagena in what is today Antioquia, Colombia. Two more were Afro-descendant women from the wider Caribbean, one from Santo Domingo and one from Cuba.[18] Their sentences involved prison, yet due to the tribunal's spatial and budgetary limitations, the women condemned to perpetual imprisonment were placed to work at the convent of San Francisco instead. In addition, two individuals were prosecuted for sorcery, two for bigamy, and one for abuse of inquisitorial power. Additionally, an English man, Adam Edon, was tried as a Protestant heretic and was relaxed to the secular arm, meaning that he was turned over to secular authorities to die at the stake.[19] After this *auto*, Mañozca was promoted, and sent to Lima as senior inquisitor in 1623. Don Agustín de Ugarte Saravia replaced him.[20]

Following his predecessors, Inquisitor Ugarte celebrated his first *auto* with great pomp in the city's main square or *plaza mayor* in 1626. As usual, the celebration of the *auto* coincided with the arrival of the Spanish galleon in Cartagena, so that prominent Spanish guests could attend and later report back to metropolitan authorities. This *auto* featured the sentences of twenty-two people. Nine were prosecuted for sorcery and eight for crypto-Judaism. One charged with crypto-Judaism appeared in effigy, as he had died in the inquisitorial prisons; another, Juan Vicente, was relaxed to the secular authorities.[21] Additionally, there were two people prosecuted for blasphemy, one for bigamy, one for Protestantism, and one for being a married priest. A couple of months later, a former attorney of the Inquisition (*fiscal*), Don Domingo Vélez de Asas y Argos, was promoted to inquisitor and joined Ugarte in office. Together they reported to the Suprema on cases that were still open in 1627, and then celebrated a public *auto* in 1628, sentencing twelve people in the cathedral in 1628. A year later, Ugarte left for Chiapas, in New Spain, and Don Martín de Cortázar y Ascárate assumed his duties as the second inquisitor in Cartagena.

The racialized scrutiny and local rivalries Mañozca had inaugurated after 1610 reached their peak between 1632 and 1636, during the tenure of inquisitors Vélez de Asas y Argos and Cortázar y Ascárate. They considered Tolú, a coastal city near Cartagena, as a hotbed of witchcraft; they were extremely concerned with the alleged presence of crypto-Jewish practices among baptized Christians; finally, they viewed Governor Francisco de Murga and his allies as foes of their work.[22] Their inquiries on alleged witchcraft outbreaks in Tolú and Cartagena led to the celebration of an *auto* in the cathedral in 1633. Twenty-one women out of the twenty-five defendants were prosecuted for witchcraft: One was a Spanish woman, who was part of Tolú's elite, and the rest were Afro-descendant. In addition, there were two people prosecuted for blasphemy, one person for bigamy, and one woman for sorcery.

Most of the witch suspects declared that one of the two most powerful Afro-descendant women in Cartagena – either Paula de Eguiluz or Elena de Viloria, well-known for their healing skills and love magic practices – had persuaded them to be witches and participate in the nocturnal gatherings (*juntas*) each one of them celebrated.[23] While inquisitors Vélez de Asas y Argos and Cortázar y Ascárate referred to those gatherings as Sabbaths, Afro-descendant participants used them rather as spaces to freely discuss matters, whether quotidian or questions of freedom and subversion. Defendants declared having renounced God, the Virgin Mary, and all the saints, having danced, had sexual intercourse with the devil and other participants, and even having flown on certain occasions. Their testimonies fit the European standards of witchcraft and included local details in terms of resources and participants, all of which fueled inquisitors' preconceptions and fears. The initial sentences consisted of property confiscation, banishment, and lashes. Additionally, inquisitors determined that several defendants had to be relaxed to the secular arm, but when they submitted their sentence to the Suprema for its approval, the council objected and requested a different punishment.

One of the ringleaders named in Cartagena's 1633 witchcraft prosecutions, Paula de Eguiluz, was put on trial three times by Cartagena's inquisition tribunal between 1624 and 1638 for witchcraft, sorcery, and apostasy. The ample prosecution record of her three inquisitorial trials has survived the vicissitudes of time and can be consulted at the National Historical Archive in Madrid.[24] An Afro-descendant woman from Santo Domingo, Paula was born into slavery and freed by her slaveowner around 1630. After completing the sentence of her first trial in 1626 – for which she had been brought to Cartagena from Cuba under accusations of witchcraft – she established herself there. She quickly developed an intricate and expensive repertory of unorthodox rituals and practices to solve everyday matters in the city, which quickly made her a powerful economic and social player across the region.

In 1632, Paula was arrested once more on suspicion of relapsing into witchcraft. In her declarations, she denounced a wide network of people involved in her own practices, but also emphasized the wrong-doing of her rivals, including Elena de Viloria and Diego López, an Afro-descendant surgeon, whereby she effectively pulled the latter into the Inquisition's investigations; he was sentenced in the 1633 *auto de fe*.[25] In 1634, new incriminatory testimonies against Paula from a group of women, who were secluded in the secret prisons of the Inquisition while on trial for retracting their declarations of being witches months after being condemned for witchcraft in the same *auto de fe* as Paula, led to her third trial in 1635. Her accusers declared she had secretly communicated with other prisoners and coordinated what to confess in order to expedite their trials and obtain the inquisitors' mercy. Although she denied the accusations and emphasized her role as a healer in Cartagena, inquisitors sentenced her to be relaxed in 1638. Luckily, once again the Suprema intervened, and Paula continued living in Cartagena after the trial. Throughout her lengthy prosecution, both her testimonies and those by others show how she learned inquisitorial rhetoric about witchcraft, as well as the strategies she developed to incriminate other people and produce self-defense arguments to mitigate her sentences.[26]

Paula's exceptional healing skills as well as her cultural, economic, and inquisitorial knowledge were not isolated, especially during the 1630s. For instance, a small group of four women condemned in the 1633 witch trials – the Afro-descendant sisters Justa and Rufina, Juana Zamba, and Ana María – retracted their previous confessions months after their sentence, unleashing what inquisitors described as the witchcraft conspiracy (*conjuración de brujería*).[27] In 1634, part of the new testimonies accused Paula of persuading them to produce their original confessions of witchcraft. Their retractions threatened the Inquisition's legitimacy insofar as they undermined Vélez de Asas y Argos and Cortázar y Ascárate's ruling. As a result, the inquisitors opened new trials for these women in order to find the reasons behind their retractions and punish whoever was behind the conspiracy. In their inquiries, inquisitors found out that Governor Francisco de Murga and his collaborators bribed the one of the prison guard's enslaved men, who was in charge of watching the cells overlooking the street, to bypass the inquisitorial prisons' security. The enslaved man let Murga visit Justa and Rufina to dissuade them from contesting the veracity of their previous trials and ask their cellmates to do the same. In the end, inquisitors resorted to torture to get the defendants to retract their previous retractions and so reestablish the tribunal's authority before their peers, the Suprema, and the public arena.

Throughout this process, Diego López, Paula de Eguiluz's nemesis, who had been serving his sentence and was involved in the witchcraft conspiracy, played a crucial role in revealing internal and external communications within the inquisitorial prisons.[28] More importantly, though, during his own trial for witchcraft and with the aim of gaining inquisitors' benevolence, he also denounced crypto-Jewish practices in Cartagena. López described in detail the rituals in which several Portuguese men and women participated, including one of the city's surgeons, Blas de Paz Pinto, and prominent merchant Juan Rodríguez Mesa, both of whom were arrested in 1636. López had heard of the secret gatherings from his lover, an enslaved Afro-descendant woman who had worked at the house of a Portuguese-descendant woman accused of being a regular attendee at the secret synagogue.[29] López's depositions allowed for an expansion of inquisitors' inquiries into the Portuguese community in the region, and revealed the connections between these communities and the Afro-descendant populations of Cartagena.

In addition to Diego López's incriminatory testimonies about crypto-Judaism, inquisitors Vélez de Asas y Argos and Cortázar y Ascárate received information about crypto-Jewish communities in Cartagena from Lima in 1635. Lima's inquisitors uncovered regional crypto-Judaism networks by sharing the testimonies of a defendant with Vélez de Asas y Argos and Cortázar y Ascárate. He denounced a Portuguese man, Juan Rodríguez Mesa, and his friends of covertly practicing the Law of Moses in Cartagena.[30] Moreover, in 1636, there were also rumors of collaborations between Portuguese merchants established in Cartagena with a Dutch brotherhood (*Cofradía de Holanda*) and the Dutch West India Company (*Compañía de Holanda*), which intended to develop transatlantic religious and economic connections.[31] As a result, inquisitors launched a prosecution of crypto-Judaism under the name of "the Great Complicity" between the 1635 and 1639, borrowing the terminology from Lima and Mexico City's tribunals. Although the Cartagena prosecution was on a much smaller scale than the concurrent investigations against crypto-Jews carried out first in the Peruvian and New Spanish viceroyalties, it was no less damning.[32] Twenty people prosecuted for crypto-Judaism were sentenced in the *auto* of 1638, out of which nine people were convicted and eleven causes were suspended or absolved. In contrast, the two other tribunals, during their own "great complicity," carried out 272 cases combined.[33] In Cartagena, defendants were predominantly (un)licensed physicians, sailors, and a wide variety of merchants, from slave traders to shoemakers, who established their families mainly in the Caribbean, Antioquia, and Popayán.[34] When interrogated, they incriminated close and distant friends, relatives, and rivals, mostly under torture, and thereby exposed transoceanic networks. Contrary to the records in Lima and Mexico City's tribunals, in which multiple Portuguese and Portuguese-descendant women were prosecuted for crypto-Judaism due to their role in the household and in the instruction of Mosaic Law, in Cartagena, there were only three cases of crypto-Judaism whose main defendants were women.[35] Nonetheless, trials against crypto-Jewish men also documented the Portuguese female presence in Cartagena, showing the deep roots the Portuguese community had established across the region.

As these processes went on, politics made the tribunal's work even more complicated. Disputes between Inquisitor Vélez de Asas y Argos and Governor Francisco de Murga escalated. They accused each other of corruption and launched civil and inquisitorial investigations against each other. Eventually, the Suprema intervened, and summoned Vélez de Asas y Argos back to Spain. Add to that the fact that, in 1639, Inquisitor Cortázar y Ascárate fell ill and died. Although Vélez de Asas y Argos and Cortázar y Ascárate aimed to prevent former secretary Juan Ortiz and his family from ruling the tribunal, Cortázar y Ascárate's death left the office vacant in the midst of social turmoil and conflicts between members of the Inquisition and prelates from the city. In the end, Ortiz occupied the inquisitor's post in 1640 and named Juan de Uriarte, his son-in-law, secretary. This move furthered the perception of entrenched endogamic corruption in the tribunal and provoked discontent among local secular and religious authorities, who petitioned to have a metropolitan inspector (*visitador*) intervene.[36]

In response to the petitions, the Suprema appointed Don Martín del Real as visiting inspector, charged with evaluating and reporting on the tribunal's functioning. A new inquisitor, Don Juan Bautista Villadiego, a former relentless prosecutor of crypto-Judaism overseas, arrived in Cartagena in 1643. Months later, visiting inspector Del Real inaugurated his investigations with what many considered a heavy-handed approach. He conducted interviews and gathered information about the tribunal's prosecutor as well as the legal performance of the tribunal's members. Resistance followed, with the current inquisitors, Juan Ortiz and Bautista Villadiego, providing contradictory information. Del Real condemned Bautista Villadiego's behavior and denounced his connections and friendship with reconciled crypto-Jews, as well as his concupiscence and corruption. The visiting inspector's findings included a plethora of economic and procedural inconsistencies and compromised several people inside and outside the tribunal. His reports argued that these inconsistencies, along with the widespread culture of dishonesty and power struggles, impaired the inquisitorial mission in the region. As their quarrels worsened, metropolitan authorities removed Bautista Villadiego and sent Don Juan de Pereira Castro to replace him in 1644. In retaliation, disgraced inquisitor Bautista Villadiego excommunicated Del Real, and then began to run a parallel inquisition tribunal out of his own house. Still, like Mañozca at the beginning of the seventeenth century, Bautista Villadiego came out unscathed from the accusations. In 1646, he returned to Spain to become an inquisitor in Cuenca.

Far from appeasing institutional and local tensions, Del Real's presence produced more hostility and political conflict. As a result, the Suprema decided to cancel his visit and Del Real fled Cartagena in 1645, with the excuse of fearing for his life. Two years later, in 1647, Don Pedro de Medina Rico was sent to Cartagena to finish the investigation. Despite continued opposition, after three years, the new visitor concluded his report, amassing 115 charges against Inquisitor Pereira, with a similar quantity against the tribunal's notary. The two men, inquisitor and notary, died in 1650 and 1651, respectively, before facing their sentences.

As part of his duties, visiting inspector Medina Rico also served as inquisitor. He reviewed several cases he believed contained procedural flaws, including those of people accused of crypto-Judaism, such as Luis Franco and Luis Gómez Barreto, and witchcraft, such as Paula de Eguiluz, to name a few. Like his predecessor, Medina Rico questioned the tribunal's commitment to preserving the Catholic faith and social control in the region. His report also revealed the inquisitors' mismanagement of money and bureaucratic flaws in record-keeping, which related to the sequestration and confiscation of defendants' property, especially during the 1630s. Taken together, the visitations of Del Real and Medina Rico illustrate the complexity of social, political, and institutional turmoil that shaped Cartagena's history in the mid-seventeenth century, which affected the tribunal's credibility and operations until the turn of the century. It is not a surprise that after 1638, the number of prosecutions declined, reduced to a handful of defendants each year for crypto-Judaism, witchcraft, and blasphemy.

Between 1652 and 1683, Cartagena witnessed the arrivals and departures of six new inquisitors who continued to conflict with one another as well as other authorities in the city. Divisiveness could reach such a peak that ecclesiastical functions were paused (*cesatio a divinis*).[37] In other instances of turmoil within an inquisition tribunal, the Suprema could try to intervene: in the early seventeenth century, for instance, the council removed an inquisitor from the tribunal in Logroño, which oversaw Navarre, and posted him elsewhere. Distance made such direct and rapid intervention by the Suprema practically impossible for the tribunals in the Americas.

When Don Francisco Valera arrived in Cartagena from Lima in 1683, he found himself in the middle of a tremendous conflict between church and state. The bishop, Don Miguel Antonio de Benavides, did not wait long to argue publicly with Valera about the hierarchy of their legal jurisdictions, the episcopal versus the inquisitorial. The governor was even removed from office due to his inability to control the situation. The new governor, Don Juan Martínez Pando, placed soldiers to secure custody of the bishop's palace, which temporarily returned peace to the city.

Despite these ongoing disputes, Valera reviewed the trials of the four defendants he found in the inquisitorial prisons and celebrated an *auto* in August 1683. The defendants had been in the tribunal's prisons between five and twenty years: In another sign of the difficulties of distance, the prisoners had been relaxed to the secular arm, but their sentences had been pending since they needed the approval of the Suprema. Valera requested the Suprema to transfer the Inquisition's tribunal to Santa Fe (nowadays Bogotá), the capital of the New Kingdom of Granada. He prepared an elaborate petition full of the same complaints his predecessors had mentioned: Cartagena lacked enough competent personnel to support the tribunal's mission; the weather inhibited the preservation of documents and made life unbearable.[38] Despite the Suprema's agreement in 1688 to move the tribunal to Santa Fe, the tribunal lacked the economic means to transfer itself and remained in place.

From 1687 to 1695, the tenure of new inquisitor Don Gómez Suárez de Figueroa looks almost uneventful. He conducted several trials and celebrated private *autos* and small public *autos*, in which no more than ten people were sentenced at a time. His prosecutions focused on blasphemy, sortilege, solicitation, and heresy, but also noted more changes in the city's cultural and demographic makeup. There was an upsurge in women using coca in their practices; there was an increase in cases of heretical blasphemy, due to newcomers and visitors from the British and Dutch Caribbean. These changes went hand in hand with an increase in regional contraband, which along with institutional disputes with Santa Fe occasionally interfered in the tribunal's functioning.[39] As he was promoted to serve in Lima's tribunal, his successor Don Juan de Laiseca Alvarado arrived in Cartagena in 1695.

Inquisitor Don Juan de Laiseca Alvarado's time after 1695 was dominated by the experiences he endured when French corsair Baron de Pointis attacked Cartagena in 1697.[40] After the first cannonballs struck several buildings in the city, and Laiseca realized the lack of response from Governor Don Diego de los Ríos y Quesada, he broke ranks and left. In the company of some of the tribunal staff, he started toward Mompox, a port city on the River Magdalena, carrying with him some inquisitorial documents and funds, along with prisoners. During his journey, he celebrated a small *auto* in San Roque's chapel, located in the town of Majetes, before sending his ministers and the prisoners to Mompox and returning to Cartagena after hearing the looters had left. Upon his return he found the attackers had not only destroyed documents related to the tribunal's treasury and taken anything they deemed valuable but also mocked an *auto de fe* by taking on roles as inquisitors and defendants while laughing at the ceremony. Seeing the destruction of records, tribunal notary Don Felix Zambrano recommended making wooden boxes in which their secret archive could be transported in case of an emergency. His fears seemed reasonable, given the continuous threats against Caribbean ports at the turn of the century. The effects of the French attack from 1697 were still apparent in 1704.

Over the next decade, inquisitors continued prosecuting heresy, blasphemy, and solicitation, though at a slow pace. Their treasury declined. In 1717, Spanish king Philip V created the new Viceroyalty of New Granada, which was part of the Bourbon reform plan and favored Cartagena's position in Caribbean trade and defense. English admiral Edward Vernon attacked the city in 1741. Although Vernon did not manage to sack it, as Baron de Pointis had done four decades before, his cannon fire wrecked part of the inquisition tribunal. Though documents were saved, the tribunal was left in deplorable shape.[41] By then, the post of Cartagena inquisitor had become so infamously unappealing that most candidates rejected it.

Over the second part of the eighteenth century, Cartagena's inquisitors faced augmented challenges. As part of his reforms, King Charles III authorized foreign trade of essential products in the Americas: As a result, he opened the doors to Jewish and Protestant traders who laid down roots in Cartagena despite inquisitorial objections. With those traders, the circulation of prohibited books increased across New Granada, and the Inquisition focused on banning books and opposing Enlightenment ideas. Among the materials censured were books of hours, indecent images and paintings, the *Declaration of the Rights of Man*, copies of the epic poem *Gli animali parlanti* by Giambattista Casti, and many books related to political freedom and independence.

Napoleon's invasion of Spain (1808–14) led to a halt in inquisitorial investigations and trials. On November 11, 1811, the local population revolted against the Spanish authorities. They demanded the closure of the Inquisition and declared independence from the metropolis. Inquisitors transferred their archival record to the bishop, shifted their treasury to the royal treasury, as ordered by the city's new government, and found shelter in Santa Marta, which was still loyal to the Spanish monarchy. When King Ferdinand VII was restored to power in Spain in 1814, the Holy Office was reestablished. As part of a process of reconquest, the troops of Pablo Morillo had suppressed Cartagena's rebellion by the end of 1815, and inquisitors returned to the port city. Despite inquisitorial efforts to prosecute rebels and restore the status quo, they were not successful. Once the independence campaigns led by Simón Bolívar and his allies reached Cartagena in 1821, the tribunal closed its doors once and for all.

Although inquisitorial activity in Cartagena ceased in the early nineteenth century, the Palace of the Inquisition (*Palacio de la Inquisición*), the eighteenth-century building that hosted inquisitors, prisoners and documents, is today one of the main touristic attractions in the city. It not only stands out for its architectural appeal, but also hosts historical and artistic exhibitions, as it houses the Historical Museum of Cartagena (*Museo Histórico de Cartagena*). Despite undergoing multiple transformations after Bolivarian independence, its walls attest to Cartagena's geopolitical significance in early modern times. The strategic position of the port city led to the creation of a smaller tribunal in the Spanish Americas, compared to those in Mexico City and Lima, yet one that played a crucial role in controlling both official and unofficial trade in the wider Caribbean. In terms of scale, due to the human and natural causes that reduced its archival records, Cartagena's Inquisition offers a limited but salient perspective on jurisdictional conflicts, dynamics of power and fear, and individual agendas, all of which influenced the institution's operations and, more critically, the prosecution and sentencing of individuals and specific groups. Finally, the tribunal's distance from the metropolis also shaped the relationships inquisitors established with local authorities and elites, as well as the ways in which they carried out their duties, highlighting the contingent nature of Spanish American inquisitorial tribunals.

Notes

1. José Toribio Medina, *La Inquisición en Cartagena de Indias*, 2nd edition. 1899 (Carlos Valencia Editores, 1978), 38; Ricardo Escobar Quevedo, *Inquisición y judaizantes en América española* (Editorial Universidad del Rosario, 2008), 100–1.
2. Anna María Splendiani, ed. *Cincuenta años de inquisición en el Tribunal de Cartagena de Indias 1610-1660*. 4 Vols. (Centro Editorial Javeriano,1997), 1:119; Escobar Quevedo, *Inquisición y judaizantes*, 332.
3. For recent studies on the Tribunal of the Holy Office in Cartagena de Indias, see Jaime Borja, *Rostros y rastros del demonio en la Nueva Granada: Indios, negros, judíos, mujeres y otras huestes de satanás* (Ariel Historia, 1998); Diana Luz Ceballos Gómez, *"Quien tal haze que tal pague": sociedad y prácticas mágicas en el Nuevo Reino de Granada* (Ministerio de Cultura, 2002); Adriana Maya Restrepo, *Brujería y reconstrucción de identidades entre los africanos y sus descendientes en la Nueva Granada, siglo XVII* (Ministerio de Cultura, 2005); Escobar Quevedo, *Inquisición y judaizantes*; Nicole von Germeten, *Violent Delights, Violent Ends: Sex, Race and Honor in Colonial Cartagena de Indias* (University of New Mexico Press, 2013); Ana María Díaz Burgos, *Tráfico de saberes: Agencia femenina, hechicería e Inquisición en Cartagena de Indias (1610–1614)* (Iberoamericana-Vervuert, 2020).
4. Escobar Quevedo, *Inquisición y judaizantes*, 105–8; Kimberly Lynn, *Between Court and Confessional: The Politics of Spanish Inquisitors* (Cambridge University Press, 2013), 243–5.
5. Lynn, *Between Court and Confessional*, 248.
6. Splendiani, *Cincuenta años*, 1:110.
7. For a discussion on staging *autos de fe*, see Maureen Flynn, "Mimesis of the Last Judgment: The Spanish Auto de Fe," *The Sixteenth-Century Journal* 22 (1991): 281–97; Francisco Bethencourt, "The Auto-da-Fe: Ritual and Imagery," *Journal of the Warburg and Courtauld Institutes* 55 (1992): 155–68.
8. For a study of *autos de fe* in Spanish American tribunals, consult Alejandro Cañeque, "Theater of Power: Writing and Representing the Auto

de Fe in Colonial Mexico," *The Americas* 52 (1996): 321–43, and Diana Luz Ceballos Gómez, "Ante las llamas de la inquisición," in Jaime Borja and Juan Pablo Rodríguez, eds., *Historia de la vida privada en Colombia* Vol 1 (Bogotá: Taurus, 2011).

9. For a discussion on blasphemy in the context of Cartagena de Indias, see María Fernanda Cuevas Oviedo, *Castigo y resistencia de los esclavos y sus descendientes en la Nueva Granada durante el siglo XVII* (Centro de Estudios Socioculturales e Internacionales, Universidad de los Andes, 2007); Karla Escobar Hernández, "¿Del dicho al hecho hay mucho trecho? El delito de blasfemia en los tribunales de Cartagena y Lima 1570–1700," *Fronteras de la Historia* 14 (2009): 13–39; Andrés Vargas Valdés, *Errores, reniegos e irreverencia: Los delitos de palabra y su significado en el tribunal inquisitorial de Cartagena de Indias (1610-1660)* (Editorial de la Universidad del Rosario, 2017) and "Illicit Reassertions of the Faith: Blasphemy and the Early Cartagena Inquisition, 1612–1660" *Colonial Latin American Review* 29 (2020): 414–33.
10. Splendiani, *Cincuenta años*, 2:93.
11. Doña Lorenzana de Acereto's trial is in the Archivo Nacional Histórico in Madrid: AHN, Inquisición, 1620, Exp. 1.
12. Escobar Hernández, "¿Del dicho al hecho," 62.
13. Vargas Valdés, "Illicit reassertions," 419.
14. Javier Villa-Flores, *Dangerous Speech: A Social History of Blasphemy in Colonial Mexico.* (University of Arizona Press, 2006), 128.
15. Villa-Flores, *Dangerous Speech*, 129.
16. Escobar Hernández, "¿Del dicho al hecho," 6–7, 14; Kristen Block, *Ordinary Lives in the Early Caribbean: Religion, Colonial Competition, and the Politics of Profit* (University of Georgia Press, 2012), 59.
17. Lynn, *Between Court and Confessional*, 247.
18. Splendiani, Cincuenta años, 2:208–38; Lynn, *Between Court and Confessional*, 249; Darío Sánchez Mojica, "La bruja negra como alteridad abismal del poder esclavista: Cartagena de Indias 1618–1622," *Nómadas* 45 (Octubre 2016): 156–64.
19. Splendiani, *Cincuenta años*, 2:208–38; Escobar Quevedo, *Inquisición y judaizantes*, 109–10.
20. Lynn, *Between Court and Confessional*, 256–8.
21. Escobar Quevedo, *Inquisición y judaizantes*, 119–22.
22. Carlos Guilherme Rocha, "Entre Tratos e Desacatos: Fraudes, Denúncias e Comércio Ultramarino no Conflito entre o Governador Francisco de Murga e o Tribunal da Inquisição de Cartagena das Índias (1629–1636)," *Tempos Gerais- Revista de Ciências Sociais e Historia-UFSJ* 5 (2014): 135, 140–3.
23. For an analysis of Paula de Eguiluz's prosecution, see Luz Adriana Maya, "Paula de Eguiluz y el arte del bien querer. Apuntes para el estudio del

cimarronaje femenino en el caribe, siglo XVII," *Historia Crítica* 24 (2002): 101–18; Sara Vicuña Guengerich, "The Witchcraft Trials of Paula de Eguiluz, a Black Woman, in Cartagena de Indias 1620–1636," in Kathryn Joy McKnight and Leo J. Garofalo, eds., *Afro-Latino Voices. Narratives from the Early Modern Iber-Atlantic World, 1550–1812* (Hackett, 2009); von Germeten, *Violent Delights* and Nicole von Germeten, "Paula de Eguiluz. Seventeenth-Century Puerto Rico, Cuba and New Granada (Colombia)," in Erica Ball, Tatiana Seijas and Terri Snyder, eds., *As If She Were Free: A Collective Biography of Women and Emancipation in the Americas* (Cambridge University Press, 2020); Kathryn Joy McKnight, "Performing Double-Edged Stories: The Three Trials of Paula de Eguiluz," *Colonial Latin American Review* 25 (2016): 154–74; Ana María Silva Campo, "Fragile Fortunes: Afro-descendant Women, Witchcraft, and the Remaking of Urban Cartagena," *Colonial Latin American Review* 30 (2021): 197–213.
24. Paula de Eguiluz's three heresy prosecutions in 1624–6, 1632–3, and 1635–6 are located in the Archivo Histórico Nacional in Madrid: AHN, Inquisición, 1620, Exp. 10.
25. Vicuña Guengerich, "The Witchcraft Trials," 176; Germeten *Violent Delights* 114–22; McKnight, "Performing," 154–5; Silva Campo, "Fragile Fortunes," 199.
26. McKnight, "Performing," 156.
27. Ana María Díaz Burgos, "Tras la conjuración de brujería en Cartagena de Indias (1634–1636): Retractaciones, espacios carcelarios y tortura," *Edad de Oro* 38 (2019): 315.
28. Jonathan Schorsch, *Swimming the Christian Atlantic: Judeoconversos, Afroiberians and Amerindians in the Seventeenth Century*, 2 vols. (Brill, 2009), 1:129–34; Pablo Gómez, *The Experiential Caribbean: Creating Knowledge and Healing in the Early Modern Atlantic* (The University of North Carolina Press, 2017), 72–84.
29. Escobar Quevedo, *Inquisición y judaizantes*, 169–70; Schorsch, *Swimming*, 1:133–8; Gómez, *The Experiential Caribbean*, 72–8.
30. Medina, *La Inquisición*, 222.
31. Aliza Moreno-Goldschmidt, *Conversos de origen judío en la Cartagena colonial: Vida social, cultural y económica durante el siglo XVII* (Editorial Pontificia Universidad Javeriana, 2018), 275–9.
32. For recent studies on the Portuguese presence in the New Reign of Granada and their inquisitorial prosecution, consult Escobar Quevedo, *Inquisición*; María Cristina Navarrete, *La diáspora judeoconversa en Colombia siglos XVI y XVII: Incertidumbres de su arribo, establecimiento y persecución* (Universidad del Valle, 2010); Moreno-Goldschmidt, *Conversos*.
33. Escobar Quevedo, *Inquisición y judaizantes*, 167, 365–403.

34. Navarrete, *La diáspora*, 159–81; Linda A. Newson and Susie Minchin, *From Capture to Sale: The Portuguese Slave Trade to Spanish South America in the Early Seventeenth Century* (Brill, 2014), 244.
35. Fermina Álvarez Alonso, *La Inquisición de Cartagena de Indias durante el siglo XVII* (FUE, 1999), 118; Escobar Quevedo, *Inquisición y judaizantes*, 328.
36. Álvarez Alonso, *La Inquisición*, 85–112, and "Cartagena de Indias: el último tribunal americano de la Inquisición española," in Fernando Ciaramitaro and Miguel Rodrigues Lourenço, eds., *Historia imperial del Santo Oficio (siglos xv-xix)* (Bonilla Artigas/Universidad Autónoma de la Ciudad de México, 2022), 729, 731.
37. Medina, *La Inquisición*, 311–23; Nicole von Germeten "Archival Narratives of Clerical Sodomy and Suicide from Eighteenth-Century Cartagena," in Zeb Tortorici, ed., *Sexuality and the Unnatural in Colonial Latin America* (University of California Press, 2016), 26.
38. Escobar Quevedo, *Inquisición y judaizantes*, 150–1.
39. Francisco A. Eissa-Barroso, *The Spanish Monarchy and the Creation of the Viceroyalty of New Granada (1717–1739): The Politics of Early Bourbon Reform in Spain and Spanish America* (Brill, 2017), 60–1.
40. For studies exploring the French attack on Cartagena, consult Eissa-Barroso, *The Spanish Monarchy*, 60–7; Ana María Díaz Burgos, "Inquisitorial Mission or Colonial Protocol: Rethinking the Spanish Black Legend in the Long-Eighteenth-Century Cartagena de Indias," in Catherine M. Jaffe and Karen Stolley, eds., *The Black Legend of Spain and its Atlantic Empires in the Eighteenth Century. Constructing National Identities*, eds. (Liverpool University Press, 2024), 103–26.
41. Kris Lane, *Pillaging the Empire: Piracy in the Americas, 1500–1700* (Routledge, 1998), 96.

Suggestions for Further Reading

Borja Gómez, Jaime Humberto. *Rostros y rastros del demonio en la Nueva Granada: indios, negros, judíos, mujeres y otras huestes de Satanás*. Editorial Ariel, 1998.

Ceballos Gómez, Diana Luz *"Quien tal haze que tal pague": sociedad y prácticas mágicas en el Nuevo Reino de Granada*. Ministerio de Cultura, 2002.

Díaz Burgos, Ana María. *Tráfico de saberes: agencia femenina, hechicería e Inquisición en Cartagena de Indias (1610–1614)*. Iberoamericana/Vervuert, 2020.

Escobar Quevedo, Ricardo. *Inquisición y judaizantes en América española*. Editorial Universidad del Rosario, 2008.

Germeten, Nicole von. *Violent Delights, Violent Ends: Sex, Race, and Honor in Colonial Cartagena de Indias*. University of New Mexico Press, 2013.

Gómez, Pablo. *The Experiential Caribbean: Creating Knowledge and Healing in the Early Modern Atlantic*. The University of North Carolina Press, 2017.

Maya Restrepo, Luz Adriana. *Brujería y reconstrucción de identidades entre los africanos y sus descendientes en la Nueva Granada, siglo XVII*. Ministerio de Cultura, 2005.

McKnight, Kathryn Joy. "Performing Double-Edged Stories: The Three Trials of Paula de Eguiluz." *Colonial Latin American Review* 25 (2016): 154–74.

Silva Campo, Ana María. "Fragile Fortunes: Afro-descendant Women, Witchcraft, and the Remaking of Urban Cartagena." *Colonial Latin American Review* 30 (2021): 197–213.

Splendiani, Anna María. *Cincuenta años de inquisición en el tribunal de Cartagena de Indias 1610–1660*. Centro Editorial Javeriano, 1997.

Bibliography

AHN, Inquisición. 1620. *Exp. 1. Proceso de fe de Doña Lorenzana de Acereto, mujer de Andrés del Campo*.

AHN, Inquisición. 1620. *Exp. 10. Procesos de fe de Paula de Eguiluz*.

Álvarez Alonso, Fermina. *La Inquisición de Cartagena de Indias durante el siglo XVII*. Fundación Universitaria Española, 1999.

"Cartagena de Indias: el último tribunal americano de la Inquisición Española." In Fernando Ciaramitaro and Miguel Rodrigues Lourenço, eds., *Historia imperial del Santo Oficio (siglos xv-xix)*. Bonillo Artigas/Universidad Autónoma de la Ciudad de México, 2022.

Bethencourt, Francisco. "The Auto-da-Fe: Ritual and Imagery." *Journal of the Warburg and Courtauld Institutes* 55 (1992): 155–68.

Block, Kristen. *Ordinary Lives in the Early Caribbean: Religion, Colonial Competition, and the Politics of Profit*. University of Georgia Press, 2012.

Borja, Jaime. *Rostros y rastros del demonio en la Nueva Granada: Indios, negros, judíos, mujeres y otras huestes de satanás*. Ariel Historia, 1998.

Cañeque, Alejandro. "Theater of Power: Writing and Representing the Auto de fe in Colonial Mexico." *The Americas* 52 (1996): 321–43.

Ceballos Gómez, Diana Luz. *"Quien tal haze que tal pague": sociedad y prácticas mágicas en el Nuevo Reino de Granada*. Ministerio de Cultura, 2002.

"Ante las llamas de la inquisición." In Jaime Borja and Juan Pablo Rodríguez, eds., *Historia de la vida privada en Colombia* Vol 1. Taurus, 2011.

Cuevas Oviedo, María Fernanda. *Castigo y resistencia de los esclavos y sus descendientes en la Nueva Granada durante el siglo XVII*. Centro de

Estudios Socioculturales e Internacionales, Universidad de los Andes, 2007.
Díaz Burgos, Ana María. "Tras la conjuración de brujería en Cartagena de Indias (1634–1636): Retractaciones, espacios carcelarios y tortura." *Edad de Oro* 38 (2019): 315–28.
— *Tráfico de saberes: Agencia femenina, hechicería e Inquisición en Cartagena de Indias (1610–1614)*. Iberoamericana-Vervuert, 2020.
— "Inquisitorial Mission or Colonial Protocol: Rethinking the Spanish Black Legend in the Long-Eighteenth-Century Cartagena de Indias." In Catherine M. Jaffe and Karen Stolley, eds., *The Black Legend of Spain and its Atlantic Empires in the Eighteenth Century: Constructing National Identities*. Liverpool University Press, 2024.
Eissa-Barroso, Francisco A. *The Spanish Monarchy and the Creation of the Viceroyalty of New Granada (1717–1739): The Politics of Early Bourbon Reform in Spain and Spanish America*. Brill, 2017.
Escobar Hernández, Karla. *¿Del dicho al hecho hay mucho trecho? El delito de blasfemia en los tribunales de Cartagena y Lima 1570–1700*. Instituto Colombiano de Antropología e Historia, 2008.
Escobar Quevedo, Ricardo. *Inquisición y judaizantes en América española*. Editorial Universidad del Rosario, 2008.
Flynn, Maureen. "Mimesis of the Last Judgment: The Spanish Auto de Fe." *The Sixteenth-Century Journal* 22 (1991): 281–97.
Germeten, Nicole von. *Violent Delights, Violent Ends: Sex, Race and Honor in Colonial Cartagena de Indias*. University of New Mexico Press, 2013.
— "Archival Narratives of Clerical Sodomy and Suicide from Eighteenth-Century Cartagena." In Zeb Tortorici, ed., *Sexuality and the Unnatural in Colonial Latin America*. University of California Press, 2016.
— "Paula de Eguiluz: Seventeenth-Century Puerto Rico, Cuba and New Granada (Colombia)." In Erica Ball, Tatiana Seijas and Terri Snyder, eds., *As If She Were Free: A Collective Biography of Women and Emancipation in the Americas*. Cambridge University Press, 2020.
Gómez, Pablo. *The Experiential Caribbean: Creating Knowledge and Healing in the Early Modern Atlantic*. The University of North Carolina Press, 2017.
Lane, Kris. *Pillaging the Empire: Piracy in the Americas, 1500–1750*. Routledge, 1998.
Lynn, Kimberly. *Between Court and Confessional: The Politics of Spanish Inquisitors*. Cambridge University Press, 2013.
Maya Restrepo, Adriana. "Paula de Eguiluz y el arte del bien querer: Apuntes para el estudio del cimarronaje femenino en el caribe, siglo XVII." *Historia Crítica* 24 (2002): 101–24.
— *Brujería y reconstrucción de identidades entre los africanos y sus descendientes en la Nueva Granada, siglo XVII*. Ministerio de Cultura, 2005.

McKnight, Kathryn Joy. "Performing Double-Edged Stories: The Three Trials of Paula de Eguiluz." *Colonial Latin American Review* 25 (2016): 154–74.

Medina, José Toribio. *La Inquisición en Cartagena de Indias*. 2nd edition. Carlos Valencia Editores, 1978.

Moreno-Goldschmidt, Aliza. *Conversos de origen judío en la Cartagena colonial: Vida social, cultural y económica durante el siglo XVII*. Editorial Pontificia Universidad Javeriana, 2018.

Navarrete, María Cristina. *La diáspora judeoconversa en Colombia siglos XVI y XVII. Incertidumbres de su arribo, establecimiento y persecución*. Universidad del Valle, 2010.

Rocha, Carlos Guilherme. "Entre Tratos e Desacatos: Fraudes, Denúncias e Comércio Ultramarino no Conflito entre o Governador Francisco de Murga e o Tribunal da Inquisição de Cartagena das Índias (1629–1636)." *Tempos Gerais- Revista de Ciências Sociais e Historia-UFSJ* 5 (2014): 132–46.

Sánchez Mojica, Darío. "La bruja negra como alteridad abismal del poder esclavista: Cartagena de Indias 1618–1622." *Nómadas* 45 (2016): 153–67.

Schorsch, Jonathan. *Swimming the Christian Atlantic: Judeoconversos, Afroiberians and Amerindians in the Seventeenth Century*. 2 vols. Brill, 2009.

Silva Campo, Ana María. "Fragile Fortunes: Afro-descendant Women, Witchcraft, and the Remaking of Urban Cartagena." *Colonial Latin American Review* 30 (2021): 197–213.

Splendiani, Anna María, ed. *Cincuenta años de inquisición en el Tribunal de Cartagena de Indias 1610-1660*. 4 vols. Centro Editorial Javeriano,1997.

Vargas Valdés, Andrés. *Errores, reniegos e irreverencia. Los delitos de palabra y su significado en el tribunal inquisitorial de Cartagena de Indias (1610–1660)*. Editorial de la Universidad del Rosario, 2017.

"Illicit Reassertions of the Faith: Blasphemy and the Early Cartagena Inquisition, 1612–1660." *Colonial Latin American Review* 29 (2020): 414–33.

Vicuña Guengerich, Sara. "The Witchcraft Trials of Paula de Eguiluz, a Black Woman, in Cartagena de Indias 1620–1636." In Kathryn Joy McKnight and Leo J. Garofalo, eds., *Afro-Latino Voices. Narratives from the Early Modern Iber-Atlantic World, 1550–1812*. Hackett, 2009.

Villa-Flores, Javier. *Dangerous Speech: A Social History of Blasphemy in Colonial Mexico*. University of Arizona Press, 2006.

Index

abjuration, 36, 209, 214, 287
Abravanal, Isaac, 120
accusatory phase of inquisition cases, 285
Acereto, Lorenzana de, 325
Alba-Cobham Treaty, 199
Alhambra Decree, 7
alumbradismo
  agency of inquisitors and, 167
  beatas and nuns and, 167–8
  Catholic orthodoxy and, 169, 172, 177–8
  characteristics and emphases of, 172
  connections and, 173
  edicts and, 172–3, 175–80
  Eucharist and, 169, 175, 177
  evolution of and accompanying charges with, 46, 169–70
  global cases and recession of, 180
  groups and definitions of, 171, 173–4, 175
  heresy of, 164, 165, 166, 180–1
  influences on, 171
  lack of support from Rome for, 166
  Lutheranism and, 187
  male advocates and, 168
  malleability of charge of, 164
  persecutorial protagonists and, 173
  punishments for, 168
  "sect" status and, 165, 166, 175, 181
  sexual and rebellious implications of, 178
  Spaniards and, 168
  Valdés and, 186
Antwerp Polyglot Bible, 238
Aragon, 1, 5–6, 29, 144–5, 219–20, 257
Arbués de Epila, Pedro, 5
Arce, José de, 11
archives of the Inquisition
  alumbradismo and, 167
  Cartagena tribunal and, 322, 336, 337
  case summaries and, 130
  individual officials and, 50
  Lima tribunal and, 61, 301, 308
  medieval, 28–9
  Moriscos and, 157–9
  personal dynamics and, 62
  prisoner messages and, 53, 313
  "propositions" and, 214
  protection of, 34
  scholarly approaches to, 157–8
Arianism, 25
Artacho, Francisca de, 108–9
Artes de la Inquisición Española (Montano), 196

autobiographical consciousness. *See also discursos de la vida* (discourses of life)
   autobiographies by mandate and, 78
   confessors' manuals and, 83–5
   culture of, 75
   emergence of, 73
   inquisition cases and, 72
   Pérez de Ayala and, 82
   sacrament of penance and, 83–4
   Simancas and, 82
   texts and, 86
autos de fe
   alumbradismo and, 166, 168, 175, 180
   Cartagena tribunal and, 327–9, 336
   Flores and, 48
   Jewish practices and, 133
   Lima tribunal and, 309, 313, 314
   procedure of, 37, 306, 325
   Protestantism and, 195–6, 198–9
   sexual misconduct and, 216, 220
   Sicily and, 269
   signaling of seriousness and, 166, 175, 216
   social capital and, 54
   Spanish America and, 325
   Teruel and, 6

Barcelona tribunal, 99, 219
Bautista Villadiego, Juan, 333
Bear Bible, 197
beatas, 167–8, 174, 177, 180
Benedict XIII, pope, 2
Berruguete, Pedro, 231
bestiality, 219
bibles, 238, 245, 291
bigamy, 217–18, 288
Black Legend, 13–15, 17
Blanco, Alonso, 97
blasphemy
   Cartagena tribunal and, 326–7, 335
   enslaved people and, 214, 326–7
   jurisdictions and, 213–14
   Mexico City tribunal and, 288
   prevalence of, 209
   propositions versus, 214
   severity of, 35
bloody purity. *See limpieza de sangre* (blood purity)
Bonaparte, Napoleon, 9, 10, 337
book bans. *See under* prohibition of books
book burning, 187, 231, 235, 247
booksellers and prohibition of texts, 234–5, 237, 242, 243–6, 292
bookstore visitors, 233, 234, 237–8, *see also* Dávila, Juan Bautista, Dávila, Antonio
Bourbon monarchs, 8–9, 336
Brazil, 308, 312–13
Burckhardt, Jacob, 72, 84, 86
burning at the stake, 28, 36, 195, 218–20, 287–8, 309, *see also* punishment, death sentences

calificadores (censors), 51, 233–4, 284, 290
Calvinism, 36, 190, 197–8, 270, *see also* Protestantism, Lutheranism
canon law, 24, 213, 219
careers of inquisitors
   Cortés and, 59
   difficulty of tracing, 62
   Gutiérrez Flores and, 48
   inquisitors-general and Suprema and, 58
   Lima tribunal and, 303
   Peralta and, 59
   Reinoso and, 45–7
   Sáenz de Mañozca and, 47
   Sicily tribunal and, 266–7
   status and upward mobility in, 54, 57
   typical features of, 49–50

Carranza, Bartolomé de, 81, 197, 239
Cartagena de Indias, 327, 334, 335, 336–8
Cartagena tribunal
　archival records and, 322, 336, 337
　autos de fe and, 325–6, 327–8
　Baron de Pointis attack and, 336
　circulation of prohibited texts and, 336
　corruption and investigation of, 332–4, 335
　crypto-Judaism and, 331–2
　decline in activity of, 336
　divisiveness and, 334
　edict of grace and, 324
　Eguiluz case, 329–31
　establishment of, 302, 321–2
　heresies prosecuted by, 325–6, 327
　jurisdictional disputes and, 335
　legacy of, 337
　local context and, 322, 324–5, 327, 337
　Mañozca y Zamora and, 304
　relocation request and, 335
　witchcraft cases and, 328, 329–31
cartas acordadas, 216
Carvajal, Luis de, 47, 289
case summaries (*relaciones de causa*), 130, 198, 308, 322
casta system, 279
Castile
　Christian–Muslim relations and, 143–4, 154
　conversos and, 3, 7, 29
　power over, 123
　Spanish colonies in the Americas and, 278, 302
　textual control and, 232
　tribunals and, 5, 263
　unification of Spain and, 1, 8
Catholic orthodoxy. *See also individual heresies and targets of the Inquisition*
　alumbradismo and, 165, 177
　Cortes of Cádiz and, 10–11
　debates over, 25
　edicts of grace and, 178
　Erasmus and, 186
　Indigenous people and, 307
　Inquisition and assessment of boundaries of, 142
　Inquisition and preservation of, 13, 290
　origins of heresy and, 25
　trials of Old Christians and, 212
Cazalla, María de, 32, 34, 173, 189, 193
censors. *See calificadores* (censors)
censorship practices. *See also prohibition of books, indices of prohibited books, calificadores (censors)*
　Americas and, 234
　artwork and, 231
　book burning and, 231, 247
　bookstore visitors and, 233, 237–8
　concepts of textuality and, 235
　critiques of, 239, 241
　enforcement and, 234, 242–6
　expurgation and, 237, 238, 239, 241, 242–3, 291
　illicit trade and, 234, 246
　impact of, 237, 247–8
　Latin and, 238
　Lima tribunal and, 309
　Mexico City tribunal and, 282, 290–2
　oral production and, 235
　principles of, 238
　printing and, 231, 246
　Protestantism and, 190, 201
　punishment and, 246
　reform of Inquisition structure and, 190
　resistance to, 241–2
　self-censorship and, 248, 290

censorship practices (cont.)
  text approval and, 232–3
Cespedes, Eleno de, 221
Charles I, king of Spain, 144, 262–3,
  see also Charles V, Holy Roman
  Emperor
Charles II, king of Spain, 180
Charles III, king of Spain, 336
Charles IV, king of Spain, 9
Charles V, Holy Roman Emperor, 13,
  151, 153, 185–6, 191, 194, 263
  See also Charles I, king of Spain
Chaves, María de, 211
Cisneros, Francisco Jiménez de,
  171, 185
Clement V, pope, 26
Çolivera, Juan de, 6–7
comisarios (commissioners), 30, 52,
  60–1, see also tribunal personnel
compurgation, 32
confession. See sacrament of penance
confession in inquisition cases. See
  also *discursos de la vida*
  (discourses of life)
  confessors' manuals and, 83–6
  conversos and, 129
  edicts of faith and, 147
  medieval inquisition and, 27–8
  Moriscos and, 145
  procedure and, 31–2, 283, 284
  Roman law and, 23, 27
  sacrament of penance and, 83–6,
    87
  solicitation charges and, 102
  torture and, 33–4
  witchcraft and, 222, 330
confessors' manuals, 83–6
confiscation
  abjuration and, 209
  Alba-Cobham Treaty and, 199
  "Great Complicity" and, 314–15
  heresy and, 26, 37
  Moriscos and, 151–2, 156, 158

prohibited books and, 235, 242,
  243–4, 245, 246, 247
tribunal finances and, 151–2, 156,
  309, 316, 334
tribunal personnel and, 52
witchcraft and, 222–3
conquest and colonization of the
  Americas, 278–9
Constitution of 1812, 10–11, 12–13
conversion. *See* Moriscos, *see* forced
  conversion, *see* conversos
conversos. *See also* Judaizing, crypto-
  Judaism
  accusations against, 118,
    123–5, 128
  alumbradismo and, 171, 189
  background of, 3, 118
  Castro and, 238
  Catholic orthodoxy and, 121
  cultural practices and, 124–6,
    132, 137
  death sentences for, 130
  defense tactics of, 129–30
  "Great Complicity" and, 136, 301,
    311–14, 331
  identification of, 121
  inadvertent knowledge of Judaism
    and, 133
  inquisitorial attention to, 5, 118,
    136–7
  Mexico City tribunal and, 289
  migration and mobility of,
    120–1, 134
  need for inquisitors and, 29
  Old Christians and, 3–4
  as politically and religiously
    dangerous, 123
  Portuguese, 134–6
  Protestantism and, 189
  Seneor and, 117–18
  Sicily tribunal and, 258, 269
  of Sigüenza, 59
  testimonies of, 127–8, 129, 130

Tortosa disputation and, 2
  as "truly" Jewish or Christian, 3
  use as term, 119
Copernicus, Nicolaus, 240
Córdoba tribunal, 45, 46
Coreses, Miguel, 103, 106
Corpus Diacrónico del Español (CORDE), 74–5
Corpus iuris civilis (body of civil law), 24
Corro, Antonio del, 14, 196, 197
Cortázar y Ascárate, Martín de, 328–9, 332
Cortes of Cádiz, 9–11, 12
council of 1477, 4
Council of Castile, 232, 241
Council of Nicaea, 25
Council of Trent, 84–5, 86, 190, 201, 215
Cruz, Juana Inés de la (Sor Juana), 290
crypto-Judaism. *See also* Judaizing, Jewish communities in Spain, conversos
  Cartagena tribunal and, 328, 331–2, 334
  gender and, 273
  "Great Complicity" and, 331
  Inquisition focus on, 212–13
  Lima tribunal and, 311–14, 316
  Portuguese merchants and, 311
Cuenca tribunal, 56, 59–61

Dávila, Antonio, 237, 243–4
Dávila, Juan Bautista, 234, 237, 243, 246
de la Fuente, Alonso, 173–5
death sentences, 28, 36, 130–2, 195–6, 287–8, 309, *see also* punishment, burning at the stake, *autos de fe*
definitional power, 126–8, 137, 142
Del Real, Martín, 322, 333–4
denunciation, 102, 104, 145, 147, 283, 285, 289

Deza inquisitorial visitation, 46, 147
Díaz Donoso, Juan, 220
Directorium inquisitorum (Eymeric and Peña), 80, 213, 216, 283
Discovery and Plaine Declaration, A (Montanus), 14
discursos de la vida (discourses of life). *See also* autobiographical consciousness
  autobiographical consciousness and, 73
  bureaucratization of trials and, 132
  conversos and, 127–8
  declarant motivations and, 78
  emergence of, 74–5, 79–80
  mandate for, 79, 81, 82
  manuals and, 80–1, 85
  Moriscos and, 149
  sacrament of penance and, 86, 87
  structure and characteristics of, 75–8, 79, 86
Don Quixote (Cervantes), 291
Donatism, 25
Dutch Republic, 200, 246, 312–14, 331

Edict of Faith of 1487, 269
Edict of Faith of 1525, 172–3, 187
Edict of Faith of 1574, 175, 177
Edict of Grace of 1623, 176–80
edicts of faith (non-specific), 31, 102, 147, *See also* general edicts of faith
edicts of grace (non-specific), 31, 324
Egidio (Juan Gil), 192–3, 198
Eguiluz, Paula de, 329–31
encomienda system, 279
enforcement in censorship practices, 242–6, *See also* censorship practices, *calificadores* (censors)
enslaved people
  blasphemy cases and, 214, 288, 326–7

enslaved people (cont.)
  Moriscos and, 154, 210, 270
  Old Christian status and, 211
  Roman law and, 23
  social and labor systems in the Americas and, 279
  witchcraft cases and, 328
episcopal legal jurisdiction. *See also* jurisdictional concerns
  bigamy and, 217
  conflict with inquisition jurisdiction and, 26, 212, 265
  Indigenous people and, 281, 289
  mendicant friars in the Americas and, 280
  Protestantism and, 281
  sexual misbehavior and, 215
Erasmus, Desiderius, 171, 186–7, 188, 235
Erauso, Elena de, 106
Espinosa, Diego de, 151
espionage networks, 191–2
estupro cases, 104
Eucharist and *alumbradismo*, 169, 175, 177
evangelization in the Americas, 279
evidentiary phase of Inquisition cases. *See also* witnesses
  accusations and, 285
  alumbradismo and, 181
  auxiliary personnel and, 30
  justification for arrest and, 31
  Moriscos and, 145–7, 150
  procedure and, 286
  torture and, 33
expulsion of Jews, 7–8, 16, 120–1, 269
expulsion of Moriscos, 46, 148, 152, 155–6, 210
expurgation of texts, 237, 238, 239, 241, 242–3, 291, *see also* censorship practices

expurgatory indexes, 237, 242–3, *see also indices of prohibited books*
Eymeric, Nicolas, 80, 213, 216, 283

familiares (familiars), 30, 61–2, *see also* tribunal personnel
feigned sanctity, 182
Ferdinand II of Aragon
  ability to name inquisitors, 29
  Alhambra Decree and, 7
  context of Inquisition and, 123
  council of 1477 and, 4
  Guadalupe and, 117
  Laws of Valladolid and, 2
  motivations for Inquisition and, 7
  Muslims and, 143–4
  origins of Inquisition and, 4–5
  Sicily and, 257
  unification of Spain and, 1
Ferdinand VII, king of Spain, 9, 11–13
Fernández Portocarrero, Juan Dionisio, 97, 178–9
fiscales (prosecutors). *See also* tribunal personnel
  confessions and, 129, 303
  discursos de la vida and, 132
  inquisitorial careers and, 57
  Mexico City tribunal and, 282
  role of, 31, 51, 286
  Sicily tribunal and, 260
  social and educational profile of, 59
forced conversion, 2, 134, 143–4, 148–9, 270, *see also* Moriscos, conversos
fornication cases, 215–17
Frederick I, Holy Roman Emperor, 26
Frederick II, Holy Roman Emperor, 26
French Revolution, 8, 238
fueros, 5, 8

Galès, Pere, 199
Galilei, Galileo, 241

García de Trasmiera, Diego, 57
García, Pablo, 80, 85
garrucha (torture technique), 33
gender
  alumbradismo and, 167–8, 178
  crypto-Judaism and, 331
  "Great Complicity" and, 314
  Judaizing and, 124–5
  Moriscas and, 147
  non-normative sexuality and, 220–1
  Protestantism and, 193
  sexual misconduct cases and, 103–9
  sorcery and, 223–4, 314
  visionary mystics and, 125
General Edicts of Faith, 166, 175, 179
Germanías rebellion, 144
Gil, Juan (Dr. Egidio), 192
Gómez, Ana, 127
Góngora, Luis de, 45, 239
González de Mendoza, Pedro, 4
González, Juana, 127
González, María, 127–8
González, Marina, 34
Granada, 143, 153–5, 216, *see also* Moriscos
Granada tribunal, 155, 216
Granadan War, 143
grand inquisitor. *See* inquisitor-general
"Great Complicity" (*gran complicidad*), 136, 301, 311–14, 331
Gregory IX, pope, 26
Gregory XV, pope, 100
Guadalupe, Spain, 117–18, 130
Gutiérrez Flores, Juan, 48, 303

heresy. *See also individual heresy charges*, solicitation, Protestantism, Moriscos, Lutheranism, Judaizing, conversos, blasphemy, *alumbradismo*
  abjuration and, 209, 287
  administrative response to, 26–7
  bestiality and, 219
  bigamy and, 217–18, 288
  Cartagena tribunal and, 325
  categories of greater and lesser, 36
  conversos and, 3, 121
  debates of orthodoxy and, 25
  fornication and, 215–17
  intention and, 35
  Islamic, 142, 145, 150, 210
  medieval inquisition and, 27–8
  Mexico City tribunal and, 289
  Old Christians and, 212
  origins of, 24–5
  propositions and, 214, 215–17, 284, 325
  punishment for. *See* punishment
  resistance to inquisitors, 28
  sin and crime and, 86
  sodomy and, 218–20
  sorcery and magic and, 221–2, 223–4, 273, 289, 314, 325
  speech acts and, 212–14
  use as term, 24
  witchcraft and, 221–3, 328, 329–31
Herrera, Inés de, 125
History of the Inquisition in Spain, A (Lea), 14
Hoces, Alonso de, 176, 179
homicide by tribunal personnel, 98–9
hood (torture technique), 33

Ierategi, Andrés de, 106
iluso, 170
Index librorum prohibitorum. *See indices of prohibited books*
indices of prohibited books. *See also* prohibition of books, censorship practices
  compilation of, 238–40
  eighteenth- and nineteenth-century, 238

indices of prohibited books (cont.)
  Erasmus and, 188
  establishment of, 190, 235–6, 291
  expurgatory indices and, 237, 242
  limitations of, 231, 237
  manuscripts and, 235
  propriety and, 241
  Protestantism and, 201
  punishment and, 246
  scientific works and, 236–7, 241
  stifling of intellectual development and, 248
Indigenous people
  conquest and colonization of the Americas and, 278–9
  jurisdiction over, 168, 281, 289, 307–8
  Spanish bigamy and, 288
  Spanish mitigation of rebellion of, 290
individualism, 72, 73, 86, *see also* autobiographical consciousness
Innocent III, pope, 26
Innocent VIII, pope, 6
"inquisition" (term), 23
inquisition cases/trials. *See also individual targets of the Inquisition*, procedure and structure of the Inquisition, jurisdictional concerns
  Acereto and, 325
  admonitions and, 285
  autobiographical requirement and, 72
  bureaucratization and formalization of, 131–2
  Carranza and, 197
  case summaries and, 130
  categories of heresies and, 36
  Catholic orthodoxy and, 126
  changing context and evolution of, 129–30
  charges and, 31
  classification of individuals and, 126
  compurgation and suspense in, 32
  confessions and, 149, 284
  definitional power and, 126–7
  duration of, 56
  Egidio and, 192
  espionage networks and, 191–2
  Felipe and, 39–41
  French immigrants and, 198
  Galès and, 199
  "Great Complicity" and, 136
  historical claims and, 35
  institutional values and, 39–41
  intention and mistakes in, 35
  learned opposition to, 35
  Llanos and, 209–10
  missing defendants and, 287
  modes of resistance and defense in, 33–5
  motivations for, 123, 134
  Occassio and, 200
  pastoral goals of, 37
  Portuguese conversos and, 135–6
  prisoner communication and, 130
  property of defendants and, 37
  roles of inquisitors in, 50, 55
  Servetus case and, 191
  slavery and, 326–7
  terminology and, 119
  torture and, 33
  treaties with England and, 199–200
  tribunal personnel for, 51
  use of secular branches in, 287
  witnesses and, 32, 34
inquisitional treatises, 131
inquisitor-general. *See also individual inquisitors-general*
  backgrounds of, 58
  blasphemy cases and, 213
  book censorship and, 188
  Protestantism and, 189
  role of, 30, 52

Sicily tribunal and, 260
inquisitorial autobiographies. *See discursos de la vida* (discourses of life)
inquisitorial treatises, 80–1, 282–4, see also *Orden de Processar* (García), *Instructions* (Valdés), *Directorium inquisitorum* (Eymeric and Peña)
inquisitors. *See also* careers of inquisitors
  archives and, 28
  assassination of, 5
  authority of, 31
  background requirements and preparation of, 57
  Cartagena tribunal and, 322, 324
  clientage and patronage networks and, 49, 57
  confidentiality of scandals and, 100
  defiance toward, 6–7
  early naming of, 29–30
  individual pursuit of conversos by, 136
  influence of individuals and, 50
  leaders of monastic orders as, 280
  Lima tribunal and, 303–4
  Mañozca y Zamora and, 304
  medieval papal, 26–9
  monarchical authority and, 4
  New Spain and, 282, 292
  numbers and activities in tribunals, 55–7
  personal approaches to judicial work of, 59
  position privileges of, 96
  range of judgment of, 37
  reliance on witnesses, 39
  responses to *alumbradismo* by, 167
  scandal and, 96, 97–8
  self-mythologizing of, 57
  shedding of blood and, 287
  shifting role of, 30
  tribunals and, 5
institutional values of the Inquisition, 39–41
Institutiones Catholicae (Simancas), 82
Instructions (Valdés), 77, 79–81, 85, 186
Isabella I of Castile
  ability to name inquisitors, 29
  Alhambra Decree and, 7
  context of Inquisition and, 123
  council of 1477 and, 4
  Guadalupe and, 117
  motivations for Inquisition and, 8
  Muslims and, 143–4
  origins of Inquisition and, 4–5
  unification of Spain and, 1
Islamic religious practices, 145, 146, 148, *see also* Moriscos
ius commune (common system of legal thought), 24

Jacome, Juan, 106–7
Jewish communities in Spain. *See also* "Great Complicity" (*gran complicidad*), conversos
  assaults on, 1, 144
  conversos and, 3–4, 137
  expulsion of, 7–8, 16, 120–1
  forced conversion and, 2, 120
  Laws of Valladolid and, 2
  memory of observances and, 123
  mobility and migration of, 120–1, 134
  Sicily and, 269
  women's religious activities and, 124–5
Judaizing. *See also* crypto-Judaism, conversos
  accusations of, 3, 118, 123, 128
  bureaucratization of trials and, 132
  case summaries and, 130
  Christian interpretations of, 125

Judaizing (cont.)
  decline of trials for, 136
  identification and prosecution of, 121–2
  inadvertent teaching of, 133
  migration of Portuguese conversos and trials for, 135
  use as term, 119
  women's religious activity and, 124–5
jurisdictional concerns. *See also* episcopal legal jurisdiction
  bigamy and, 217–18
  Cartagena Tribunal and, 335
  global reach of Inquisition and, 135
  Roman law and, 24–5
  scandal and, 98
  Sicily tribunal and, 259, 261, 265–6
  Spanish America and, 307–8
  status of inquisitorial officials and, 54
  Suprema and, 41
  text licensing and, 232
  unique nature of Inquisition and, 259
  witchcraft and, 222–3

Laiseca Alvarado, Juan de, 335–6
Laws of Valladolid, 2
Lea, Henry Charles, 14, 232
León, Luis de, 84, 238
licenses to obtain prohibited books, 243–4, 245–6, 296, *see also* prohibition of books, censorship practices
Lima tribunal
  concerns with Dutch invasion, 312–13
  crypto-Jews and, 311–14
  employment requirements for, 304
  establishment of, 302
  facilities of, 305–6, 313
  finances of, 314
  first phase of, 309–11
  focuses of, 301, 306, 311, 316, 321
  inquisitors of, 303–4
  jurisdiction of, 302–3
  Mañozca y Zamora and, 304
  operation guidelines for, 308
  overview of activity of, 315–16
  overview of phases of, 309
  Portuguese Inquisition and, 308
  punishment and, 309
  relocation of, 306
  second phase of, 311–14
  suggestion for additional tribunals and, 302
  surveillance of newcomers by, 307
  third phase of, 315
limpieza de sangre (blood purity), 54, 61, 144, 158, 211–12, 263, 304
Llanos, Juan de, 209–11
Llerena tribunal, 174, 175, 220
Logroño tribunal, 37, 39, 62, 96–7, 99, 223
López de Cortegana, Diego, 57
López de Montoya, Juan, 174–5
López, Diego, 330, 331
Louis XVI, king of France, 8
Lucius III, pope, 26
luteranos. *See* Protestantism, *see* Lutheranism
Luther, Martin, 35, 36, 185, 201
Lutheranism. *See also* Protestantism
  alumbradismo and, 171, 173
  arrival in Spain of, 185, 187–8
  circulation of texts and, 187–8
  discovery of organization of, 193
  domestic and foreign practitioners of, 198
  inquisition cases and, 189–90
  Inquisition punishment of, 188
  Inquisition use of term, 201
  New Spain and, 281
  revitalization of Inquisition and, 185–6
  Sicily tribunal and, 269

Madrid tribunal, 235, *see also* Suprema (Supreme Council of the Inquisition)
magic, 221–2, 223–4, 273, 289, *see also* witchcraft, sorcery
Mallorca tribunal, 5, 48
Mañozca y Zamora, Juan de, 48, 136, 303–4
Mañozca, Juan de, 321–2, 324–6, 327–9
Manrique, Alonso de, 151, 188–9, 222
manuals. *See* inquisitorial treatises, *see* confessors' manuals
Maria Cristina, queen of Spain, 12
Mariana, Juan de, 238
Márquez, Antonio, 77
"Marrano" (term), 119–20, *see also* conversos
Matienzo, Juan Ortiz de, 97
medieval inquisition, 26–9, 31–2
Medina Rico, Pedro de, 322, 334
Méndez de Dueñas, Garci, 311
Messina, Sicily, 257
Mexico City tribunal
  activity of, 293, 321
  blasphemy and, 288
  censorship and, 290–2
  early operation of, 280
  establishment of, 279, 281–2, 302
  heresy and, 289
  Indigenous people and, 281
  issues with inquisitors and, 292
  jurisdiction of, 302
  local context of, 292
  Lutheranism and, 281
  magic and, 289
  print and, 292
  prisons and, 284, 287
  procedures in, 282–4
  religious objective of, 290
  sex crimes and, 288
  staffing of, 282
  torture and, 281, 296
  types of crime and, 288
  Zumárraga and, 281
Mier y Campillo, Francisco Javier, 12
Mireles, Domingo, 107–9
Molinos, Miguel de, 170, 180, 272–4
molinosismo. *See* Quietism
monastic inquisitions, 280–1
Monje, Manuel, 240–1
Montano, Arias, 237, 238, 243
Montano, Reginaldus Gonsalvius, 196
Monterde de Villanueva de la Huerva, Miguel, 198
Morillo y Morillo, Pablo, 12, 337
Morisco era of the Inquisition, 144, 152–5, 159
Moriscos
  community ties of, 147
  concordias and, 151
  confessions of, 149
  confiscation of property and, 151–2, 156, 158
  conspiracies and, 150
  Deza visitation and, 46, 147
  dissent and, 157
  evidence of Islamic heresy and, 146
  expulsion of, 46, 148, 152, 155–6, 210
  forced conversion and, 142, 143–4
  Germanías rebellion and, 144
  harsh treatment of, 150–1, 154–5
  inquisitional trials and, 142
  Islamic heresy and, 145
  jofores and, 149
  lack of unified identity of, 148
  Lima tribunal and, 304
  Morisco era of the Inquisition and, 144, 152–5, 159
  negotiations for protection and, 151–2
  Núñez Muley memorandum and, 154–5
  persecution rates and, 210

Moriscos (cont.)
  practice and ignorance of Catholic practices and, 146
  pre-conversion customs and, 145–7
  prosecution rates and, 152
  rebellion of, 152
  scrutiny of Granadan, 153–5
  Second War of the Alpujarras and, 37, 153, 154
  Sicily tribunal and, 269, 270
  situados and, 156
  sodomy cases and, 220
  sources and, 157–9
  status claims and, 158
  subjection of inquisitorial activity of, 150
  survival of knowledge of Islam and, 149
  taqiyya and, 148
  terminology for, 142, 144
Multorum querela (Clementine papal bull), 26
Munõz, Diego, 60
Murga, Francisco de, 329, 330, 332
Muslim communities in Spain. See also Moriscos
  fear of Morisco rebellions and, 152
  forced conversion of, 142
  Granada and, 123
  Islamic religious beliefs and, 145
  Laws of Valladolid and, 2
  practices of, 146
  relations on Iberian peninsula of, 143–4, 151–2

Navarre witchcraft cases, 223
Navarro, Martín, 6
New Christians, 118–20, 144, 210, 308, 310–13, See also Old Christians, Moriscos, "Great Complicity" (*gran complicidad*), conversos
New Granada, 12, 336–7
New Spain, 278–82, 290, 292–3, 302, see also Mexico City tribunal
notaries, 51, 96, 260, see also tribunal personnel
Núñez Muley, Francisco, 154–5
Núñez Tenorio, Francisco, 98
nuns, 101, 167, 236

oaths, 24, 27, 31, 32, 286
Occasso, Martin de, 200
Old Christians
  conversos and, 3–4, 118, 124–5, 133
  Inquisition control of, 212–13, 220, 224
  limpieza de sangre and, 211–12, 304
  magic and witchcraft and, 221–4
  Moriscos and, 157, 158
  New Christians vs., 210
  orthodoxy and, 126, 146
  religious requirements and, 146
  sodomy cases and, 220
  status and, 123, 144, 210–11
Old Instructions, 117, 131, see also inquisitional treatises
Omnis utriusque sexus, 83
Orden de Processar (García), 80, 85
order of 1502, 143–4
Ortiz, Juan, 332–3
Ottoman empire, 152, 155

Pacheco, Andrés, 176
Palace of the Inquisition (Cartagena de Indias), 337
Palermo, Sicily, 257, see also Sicily tribunal
Paul IV, pope, 194–5
Peace of Munster of 1648, 200
Pelagianism, 25
Peña, Francisco, 283
penances, 27, 37, 188, 315, see also Sacrament of Penance, punishment

Peninsular War (War of Independence), 9
people of African descent, 211, 214, 288, 329–31 *see also* enslaved people
Peralta y Robles, Alonso de, 59
Pereira Castro, Juan de, 333–4
Pérez de Ayala, Martín, 82–3
Pérez de Pineda, Juan, 192, 196
Pérez de Soto, Melchor, 292, 297
Pérez, Antonio, 240
Peruvian Inquisition. *See* Lima tribunal
Peter II of Aragon, 26
Philip II, king of Spain, 153, 191–2, 194–5, 197, 257
Philip III, king of Spain, 155
Philip V, king of Spain, 8, 336
Philippines, 167, 279, 302
picaresque novels, 78–9
Pius IV, pope, 100
Pius VII, pope, 11
Pizarro, María, 310
Pointis, baron de (Bernard Desjean), 336
Ponce de León, Juan, 232, 237, 243
Portocarrero, Pedro de, 97
Portugal, 134–5, 136 *see also* "Great Complicity" (*gran complicidad*)
Portuguese Inquisition, 134–5, 180, 308
Portuguese New Christians, 301, 310–13
potro (torture technique), 33
prisons. *See also* torture, punishment
  Cartagena tribunal and, 335
  communication of prisoners and, 15, 34, 130, 313, 330
  conditions in, 284, 287
  Lima tribunal and, 313
  Mexico City tribunal and, 284, 287
  scandal and, 99
  Sicily tribunal and, 267, 268
procedure and structure of the Inquisition, 23–4, 27, 31–2, 282–4, 285–6, *see also* witnesses, tribunals, tribunal personnel, torture, Suprema (Supreme Council of the Inquisition), punishment, inquisitors, inquisitorial treatises, inquisitor-general, inquisition cases/trials, evidentiary phase of inquisition cases, *autos de fe*
prohibition of books. *See also* indices of prohibited books, censorship practices, *calificadores* (censors)
  author refutations and, 241
  bans and, 188, 190, 234–5
  Cartagena tribunal and, 337
  censorship criteria and, 238
  control of language and, 236–7
  expurgation and, 237, 238, 239, 241, 242–3, 291
  feuds and, 239
  frustrations of bookstore visitors about, 237–8
  historical and political works and, 240
  in eighteenth and nineteenth centuries, 238
  Latin and, 238
  licenses to obtain texts and, 243–4, 245–6, 296
  literary works and, 236, 241, 291
  monarch favoritism and, 241
  punishment and, 246, 292
  scientific works and, 236, 239–40, 241, 248, 291
  specific topics and, 241
  The Spiritual Guide and, 272
  vernacular bibles and spiritual literature and, 84–5, 171, 190, 245–6
pronunciamientos, 12, 17

propositions (scandalous statements), 214, 215–17, 284, 325
prosecutors (*fiscales*). *See fiscales* (prosecutors)
prostitution, 100, 215
Protestantism. *See also* Lutheranism
  Alba-Cobham Treaty and, 199
  autos de fe and, 195–6
  Carranza trial and, 197
  case summaries and prevalence of, 198
  context of Inquisition armament against, 190
  critiques of Spanish treatment of, 196
  Dutch treaties with Spain protecting, 200
  early condemnations and lack of ties to, 188
  early Spanish responses to, 187
  English merchants and, 199–200
  evolving persecution of, 201
  indices of prohibited texts and, 236
  inquisition punishments for, 195
  Inquisition search for individual practitioners of, 199
  Inquisition use of "Lutheranism" for, 201
  Jeanne d'Albret and, 197
  later prevalence in Spain of, 198
  Lima tribunal and, 313, 315
  persecution beyond Spain of, 191
  persecution of Spaniards and, 192
  Philip II responses to, 194–5
  political and social alarm over, 197
  presence in inquisition cases of, 190
  prevalence in Spain and theology of, 193
  Reformation in Spain and, 201
  Servetus case and, 191
  Sicily tribunal and, 269–70
  Spanish espionage networks and, 191–2
  Suprema and, 188–9, 194–5
  tolerance toward French, 200
  true believers and diversity of, 197
  Valdés and, 186
pulley (torture technique), 33
punishment. *See also* torture, sentencing, prisons, confiscation, *see also autos de fe*
  abjuration and, 36, 209, 214, 287
  alumbradismo and, 168–9
  banishment and exile and, 26, 168, 199
  bigamy and, 218, 313
  blasphemy and, 326
  burning at the stake and, 28, 36, 195, 218–20, 287–8, 309
  Cartagena tribunal and, 326–7
  death sentences and, 28, 36, 130–2, 195–6, 287–8, 309
  extirpation campaigns and, 307
  galleys and, 102, 153, 218, 270
  "Great Complicity" and, 313–14
  lashes and, 10, 217, 218
  manuals and, 283
  Moriscos and, 153
  penances and, 27–8, 37, 188, 315
  proposition cases and, 217
  Protestantism and, 38, 188, 196, 198, 315
  public humiliation and, 37
  relaxation to the secular arm and, 36, 198, 273, 287, 316
  Roman law and, 23
  sambenitos and, 37
  seclusion and, 102
  sodomy and bestiality and, 218–20
  sorcery and, 224, 313
  speech acts and, 214
  witchcraft and, 223

questionnaires for tribunal
    visitations, 77, 97–8
Quevedo, Francisco de, 239
Quietism, 170, 180, 272–4

rack (torture technique), 33
Ramírez, Josepha, 107–9
Ramírez, Román, 147, 149
Real Audiencia de Santo
    Domingo, 294
redemption of captives, 117
Reformation, 166, 201, 217, 269–70,
    see also Protestantism
Reformed Franciscans, 171
Reina, Casiodoro de, 192, 196, 197
Reinoso, Alonso Jiménez de, 45–7
relaciones de causa. *See* case
    summaries (*relaciones de causa*)
relaxation to the secular arm, 36, 198,
    269–71, 273, 287, 316
renegados, 270–1
resistance to inquisitorial model,
    33–4, 35, 273, *see also*
    jurisdictional concerns
Ribadeneira, Felipe, 39–40
Roman Congregation of the Index,
    238, 241
Roman Inquisition, 190, 238
Roman law, 23–4, 27
Ruiz, Mari, 130

Sacrament of Penance, 83–6, 87,
    100–2, *see also* solicitation
Sáenz de Mañozca, Pedro, 47, 49,
    53, 289
Salcedo, Matheo de, 321–2,
    324–5, 327
sambenitos, 37
San Pedro, Santos de, 217
Santiago de Compostela tribunal, 97
Sanz de Taberna, Martín, 96
Sardinia tribunal, 5, 29
scandal

confidentiality and, 100
Coreses case and, 103, 106
early modern Europe and, 95
homicide and, 98
inquisitors and, 97–8
invocation of, 96
Jacome case and, 106–7
Mireles case and, 107–9
money and, 99
prisons and, 99
role of jurisdiction in sexual
    misconduct cases and, 103–6
sexual misconduct and, 98
solicitation and, 100–3
tribunals and, 96
Second War of the Alpujarras, 37,
    153, 154
"Sect of Alumbrados" (general edicts
    of faith), 175, 179
secular justice in western Europe,
    24–5, 222, 264, 266, *see also*
    jurisdictional concerns
self-censorship, 248, 290, *see also*
    censorship practices
Seneor, Abraham, 117–18, 137
Sentencia-Estatuto, 3
sentencing. *See also* punishment,
    death sentences, *autos de fe*
    confessions and, 284
    conversos and, 130
    discretion and, 218
    infamy (designation) and, 37
    inquisitional jurisdiction and, 264
    procedure and, 287–8
    Protestantism and, 195–6, 198
    range of, 28, 270, 326, 329
    solicitation cases and, 103
    Suprema and, 100
seroras, 105–6
Servetus, Miguel, 191
Seville tribunal, 4, 179, 193, 195, 212
sexual misconduct cases, 98, 103–9,
    220–1, 288–90, *see also*

solicitation, sodomy, scandal, propositions (scandalous statements), fornication cases, bigamy, bestiality
Sicily tribunal
  cases of faith and reconciliation and, 271–2
  Charles V reforms and, 263
  civic identity of, 264
  competition for hegemony and, 265
  context of, 258, 259, 274
  conversos and, 269
  establishment of, 257
  goals of, 258, 268
  Greek and Albanian Orthodox Christians and, 1
  inquisitor career trajectories and, 266–7
  inspection of, 268
  issues with, 260
  jurisdictional disputes and, 259, 263–4, 265–6
  Molinos and, 272–3
  Moriscos and, 269, 270
  opposition to, 262–3
  political instability and, 267
  prosecution of non-natives and, 269–70
  Protestantism and, 269–70
  renegados and, 270
  restoration and titles for elites in, 264
  secret chamber cases and, 273
  Sicily as liminal space and, 271
  staffing of, 260–2
  state affairs and, 267
  targets of, 273
Simancas, Diego de, 74, 81–2, *see also Instructions* (Valdés)
situados (tribute payments), 151–2, 156–7
Sixtus IV, pope, 1, 4, 5, 29

slavery, 152, 154, 326–7, *see also* enslaved people
sodomy, 218–20
solicitation
  character investigations of women and, 109
  Coreses case and, 103, 106
  Jacome case and, 106–7
  La Concepción case, 101
  Lima tribunal and, 311, 315
  Mireles case and, 107–9
  prosecution of, 102–4, 106, 272, 288
  Sacrament of Penance and, 100–2
Sor Juana (Juana Inés de la Cruz), 290
sorcery, 221–2, 223–4, 314, 325, *see also* witchcraft
Sotomayor, Antonio de, 52, 243
Spain
  Black Legend and, 13–15, 17
  Bourbon monarchs and, 8
  establishment of Inquisition in, 3–5, 7–8, 9, 12, 13, 15, 282
  French Revolution and, 8
  monarchical autonomy and, 29
  Napoleon and, 9–10
  Peninsular War and, 9
  restoration of Ferdinand VII and, 12–13
  unification of, 1
Spanish America, 12, 278–9, *see also individual Spanish American tribunals*
speech acts cases, 212–15, *see also* propositions (scandalous statements), *see also* blasphemy
Spiritual Guide, The (Molinos), 272
Steri palace (Sicily tribunal), 257, 267, 268
structure of the Inquisition. *See* procedure and structure of the Inquisition
Suárez de Figueroa, Gómez, 335

Suprema (Supreme Council of the Inquisition). *See also* inquisitor-general
alumbradismo and, 174–5, 178–80
Cartagena tribunal and, 332–4, 335
case summaries and, 130–2, 322
establishment of, 30
jurisdiction and, 41, 212, 213, 218, 267
Mexico City tribunal and, 282, 292
Occassio case and, 200
personnel of, 52, 58
prohibition of books and, 189
Protestantism and, 194
sodomy cases and, 218–20
struggle for control of, 188–9
treatment of Moriscos and, 150
Treaty of London and, 199
tribunal divisiveness and, 334
tribunal finances and, 309
tribunal scandals and, 97
witchcraft and, 222–3, 329
surveillance, 39, 155, 201, *see also* censorship practices

tachas, 32, 127, 132
taquiyya, 148
Teresa de Jesús, Saint (also known as Teresa of Ávila), 73, 74, 132, 236
Teruel, 6–7
textual control. *See* prohibition of books, *see* censorship practices
toca (torture technique), 33
Toledo tribunal, 99, 106, 167, 171–2, 210, 212, 282
Tolú witchcraft conspiracy, 329–31
Torquemada, Tomás de, 5–6, 30, 117, 231, 282
torture
    accusatory phase and, 285
    confessions and, 23

Europe secular court systems and, 33
facilities and, 305
frequency of, 130
inquisition trials and, 33, 127–8
medieval inquisition and, 27
Mexico City tribunal and, 281, 296
oversight and, 131, 283
Roman uses of, 23
techniques used, 33
testimonials and, 127
tribunal facilities and, 305
Treatise (García), 80
Treaty of London of 1604, 199
Treaty of Utrecht, 315
tribunal personnel. *See also* inquisitors, *fiscales* (prosecutors)
    appeal of inquisitorial careers and, 54
    bookstore visitors and, 233, 234, 237–8
    calificadores (censors) and, 51, 233–4, 284, 290
    comisarios (commissioners) and, 30, 52, 60–1
    conducting trials and, 51
    employment requirements for, 304
    familiares (familiars) and, 30, 61–2
    hierarchy and authority and, 51
    homicide and, 98
    household members and, 53
    imprisonment and, 52
    information exchanges and, 53
    inquisitors-general and, 52
    jurisdiction for, 54
    Lima tribunal and, 302
    limpieza de sangre and, 54
    notaries and, 51, 96, 260
    operations and, 52
    residence of, 305
    scandals and, 98, 100

tribunal personnel (cont.)
  social capital and, 54
  study of, 62
  Suprema, 52
tribunals. *See also individual tribunals*
  alumbradismo cases and, 167, 180
  case procedure and, 31–2
  consequences of Morisco expulsion for, 156
  development and reach of, 5, 29, 131, 135
  employment requirements for, 304
  facilities for, 305
  finances of, 151–2, 156, 309, 316, 334
  fornication cases and local context of, 216
  hierarchy and authority in, 51
  inquisitor approaches to judicial work and, 59
  internal conflict and, 50, 334
  Morisco property protections and, 151
  numbers and activities of inquisitors in, 55–7
  precedents for, 5–6
  prosecution of blasphemy and, 213
  questionnaires for visitations of, 97–8
  Reinoso visitations and, 46
  relationship with Portuguese Inquisition of, 308
  scandal and, 96–7
  situados and, 156
  sodomy cases and, 219–20
  staffing of, 30–1 *see also* tribunal personnel
  suggestions for additional Spanish American, 302
  textual control efforts and, 233
  witchcraft cases and, 222
Tribunals of Extirpation of Idolatries, 307–8
Twelve Years' Truce, 205

Ugarte Saravia, Agustín de, 328
United States Naval Academy, 103

Valdés, Fernando de, 72–3, 79–81, 85, 190, 195, 239
Valdés, Juan de, 186
Valencia Decree, 11
Valencia tribunal, 151, 152, 156, 245
Valera, Francisco, 335
Valladolid tribunal, 5, 56–7, 146, 151, 156, 193, 195
Vélez de Asas y Argos, Domingo, 328–9, 332
Vergara, Juan de, 34, 99
vernacular bibles and spiritual literature, 84–5, 171, 190, 236, 245–6, 291
Vernon, Edward, 336
Vida y Cosas Notables, La (Simancas), 82
Villanueva, Pedro de, 101
visitations. *See also calificadores* (censors), bookstore visitors
  bookstores and, 233, 237–8
  Deza and, 46, 149
  edicts of faith and, 147
  scandal and, 97–8, 322
  tribunals and, 45, 55, 322, 333–4
Vulgate Bible, 238

War of Independence. *See* Peninsular War (War of Independence)
wars of religion in France, 197
witchcraft, 221–3, 328, 329–31
witnesses
  accusations and, 31, 39
  alumbradismo and, 165, 172
  case procedure and, 31–5, 102, 219, 283

converso trials and, 132
evidentiary phase and, 286
intimidation and bribing of, 28
medieval inquisition and, 27
motivations of, 127

quantity of, 107
Roman law and, 23

Zaragoza tribunal, 99, 152, 156, 219
Zumárraga, Juan de, 281